Melissa Leapman

KNITTING MODULAR

Shawls, Wraps, and Stoles

Storey Publishing

To Nancy Baisch, CEO, with love

ACKNOWLEDGMENTS

I'm grateful to the following individuals for knitting the samples in this book:

Nancy Baisch, Adrienne Carmack, Danelle Howard, Kim Jensen, Cheryl Keeley, Joan Murphy, Candace Musmeci, Brooke Nico, Patty Olson, Sue Paules, Margarete Shaw, and Norma Jean Sternschein.

I am grateful to Cascade Yarns for providing every bit of the yarn used in the many shawl building samples. Hurrah for beautiful Cascade 220, an ever-present workhorse yarn in my design studio!

Once again, I've been lucky to surround myself with the best team in the business.

Thank you, Brooke Nico, Carol Sulcoski, and Patty Lyons for sharing your generous technical expertise (not to mention your unconditional love and laughter).

The mission of Storey Publishing is to serve our customers by publishing practical information that encourages personal independence in harmony with the environment.

Edited by Gwen Steege and Michal Lumsden
Art direction and book design by Jessica Armstrong
Text production by Liseann Karandisecky
Indexed by Nancy D. Wood
Cover and interior photography by © Melinda DiMauro, except knitting swatches by Mars Vilaubi and author photo by Marcus Tullis
Charts created by Melissa Leapman
Illustrations by Alison Kolesar

Storey Publishing
210 MASS MoCA Way
North Adams, MA 01247
storey.com

Printed in China by Shenzhen Reliance Printing Co., Ltd.
10 9 8 7 6 5 4 3 2 1

LIBRARY OF CONGRESS CATALOGING-IN-PUBLICATION DATA
Names: Leapman, Melissa, author.
Title: Knitting modular shawls, wraps, and stoles : an easy, innovative technique for creating custom designs, with 185 stitch patterns / by Melissa Leapman.
Description: North Adams, MA : Storey Publishing, [2018] | Includes index.
Identifiers: LCCN 2018030471 (print) | LCCN 2018033491 (ebook) | ISBN 9781612129976 (ebook) | ISBN 9781612129969 (hardcover : alk. paper)
Subjects: LCSH: Shawls. | Knitting—Technique.
Classification: LCC TS1781 (ebook) | LCC TS1781 .L34 2018 (print) | DDC 677/.028245—dc23
LC record available at https://lccn.loc.gov/2018030471

CONTENTS

PART 1

SHAPE
YOUR SHAWL!

Imagine hundreds — perhaps even thousands — of lovely shawl designs at your fingertips.

Shawls and stoles are the most versatile and eye-catching accessories you can knit. From a light and lacy splash of color to accent an outfit to a full worsted-weight cover-up to provide warmth and insulation from the elements, shawls are your go-to companions. Whether you are knitting for yourself or making a gift for a special (and lucky!) friend, a shawl will become a cherished addition to any wardrobe.

Each pattern in this book is based on a wedge shape, which starts at the top with just a few stitches to form a tab. Easy, decorative yarn-over increases worked at the sides of every wedge on right-side rows create a triangular shape. (Bonus: In most patterns, wrong-side rows are easy "rest rows." Just mindlessly knit or purl across!) This simple rate of increase makes it easy to fill the center of the shawl with beautiful stitch patterns and opens up opportunities to combine the wedges into many different and useful shawl silhouettes.

At first glance, the patterns in this collection will look different from the ones you're accustomed to seeing. In addition to offering concrete instructions for specific designs, I'm presenting recipes for creating custom, one-of-a-kind shawls. (The Gallery of Shawls on page 268 has 20 complete recipes for the finished shawls featured throughout this book. These recipes will help get you started creating your own unique shawl designs.) You can think of each stitch pattern as a building block to craft your own masterpiece. Once you understand the basic concept, you'll find it easy (and fun) to use. Just plug and play. The possibilities are nearly endless!

Modular Shawl Construction in 7 Easy Steps

Want a plain shawl with a knockout border? You can knit it. Prefer an allover lace pattern with a beaded border? No problem! You can choose a single pattern for the entire shawl or build a masterpiece by combining several patterns. Here's how to get started.

Most shawls in this book begin with a tab of just a few stitches (see page 10). It's an easy way to get a number of stitches on the needle, ready to work the first row, and it provides a smooth, seamless start. The type of edgings you use along the outer sides of the wedges will determine which tab you start with. Learn how easy a tab cast on is on pages 10–11. (If you decide to work from the center out to create a square design, you will use a Magic Loop cast on, page 278, instead of a tab.)

Strategically placed increases create the shape of each wedge. It's simple: Add one yarn-over increase on each side of the triangular wedge every other row.

When multiple wedges are combined in a design, single "spine" stitches or wider vertical insertions separate the different elements, and yarn-over increases are worked on the sides of each wedge. A spine stitch is a single stitch worked in smooth stockinette to set apart the patterned sections of a shawl; a vertical insertion is a decorative panel that serves to separate the wedges.

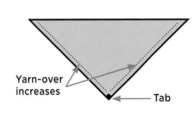

EXAMPLE OF A SINGLE WEDGE WITH TAB CAST ON and yarn-over increases at the beginning and end of every right-side row.

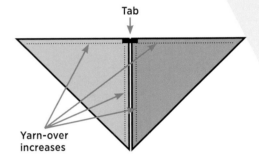

EXAMPLE OF A TWO-WEDGE SHAWL WITH A TAB CAST ON. Yarn-over increases at the beginning and end of every right-side row within each wedge create the final silhouette.

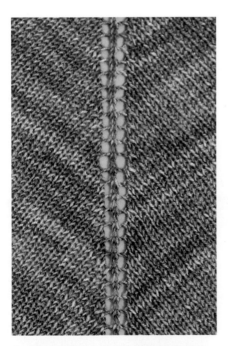

A spine stitch is a single stitch worked in smooth stockinette to set apart the patterned sections of a shawl. See page 6 for instructions.

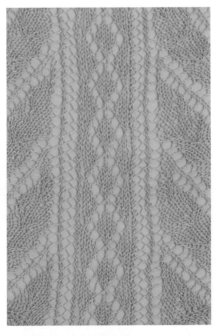

A vertical insertion is a decorative panel that serves to separate the wedges.

7 STEPS
to Shawl Success

1. Choose a SILHOUETTE.

2. Choose a STITCH PATTERN.

3. Choose a BACKGROUND TEXTURE.

4. Choose an EDGING.

5. Choose a CAST ON TAB.

6. Choose a BORDER.

7. Choose a BIND OFF.

2 WEDGES

The simplest construction design is to combine two mirror-image wedges to create a triangle.

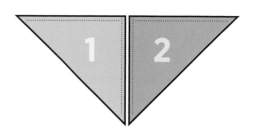

All at Once

Many knitters prefer to work the entire shawl all at once, regardless of how many wedges there are in the design. This keeps you from having to seam together individual wedges later. To join two or more wedges using a spine stitch, add 1 stockinette stitch (knit on right-side rows and purl on wrong-side rows) between each wedge in the shawl.

3 WEDGES

Three wedges combined in one piece will form a three-quarter square shawl, which will sit nicely on the shoulders.

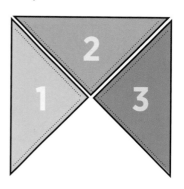

The same three wedges sewn together will create a fluid, flowing, trapezoidal shawl.

Seaming the Wedges Together

If you choose to work each wedge separately, use one of the following techniques to seam the wedges together:

- For stockinette side edges, use horizontal mattress stitch (see page 283).

- For garter and fagoted side edges, use invisible weaving (see page 283).

SHAWL #12

Three wedges sewn together as a trapezoid make a long and lovely wrap. See page 275 for instructions.

6

Four wedges connected by a spine stitch (see page 6) create a full-coverage shawl that will drape over the shoulders.

When worked in the round, four wedges will, of course, create a perfect square silhouette.

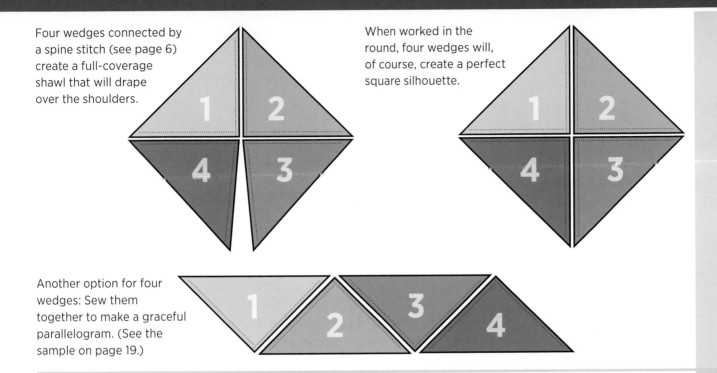

Another option for four wedges: Sew them together to make a graceful parallelogram. (See the sample on page 19.)

Six wedges, when aggressively blocked (see page 283), form a gorgeous cape-like silhouette that overlaps in the front.

For added fun and complexity, add vertical insertions, which create more design interest. You can place them in the center of a two-wedge shawl (instead of the usual spine stitch) or immediately next to the side edges for a design element down the front of a shawl. Two wedges and one vertical insertion make a trapezoidal shawl.

Two wedges with three vertical insertions form a triangular polygon. See Shawl #2 on pages 270–271.

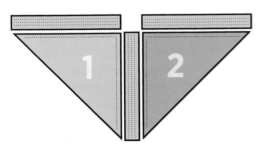

Three wedges and four vertical insertions combine to create a three-quarter square shawl.

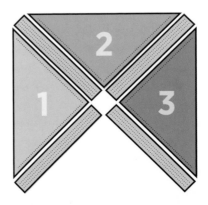

Here's the really fun part. Select the pattern (or two or more) that you want to use to fill your wedges (see pages 22–209). Be creative. Use your imagination. Use the gallery of shawl designs (page 268) to get started. These suggestions are just a tiny glimpse at the limitless universe of shawls that you can create. You are the designer!

Now, there is a tiny bit of math ahead — don't be afraid! In order to provide you with the most versatile set of options for designing your custom shawl, I have included stitch patterns with varying numbers of stitches. The number of stitches in each repeat (the stitch multiple) ranges from 2 to 16. Each wedge pattern includes 1 additional stitch in each row to center the pattern.

Mixing and Matching Patterns

One option is to fill your wedge with more than one stitch pattern, perhaps a main wedge pattern from pages 22–209, plus a lower border from pages 234–259.

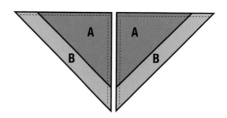

In this example, stitch pattern A is worked for two-thirds of the rows, and then pattern B is worked for the rest of the shawl.

Patterns with the same stitch multiple can be combined easily. Within the pattern charts, bold boxes show stitch and row repeats. Work to the end of the row repeat, then begin the new pattern, starting with the first of its repeat rows. For example, to add pattern 78 (page 130) in the middle of a wedge, begin with Row 11 rather than Row 1.

COMBINING STITCH MULTIPLES								
MULTIPLES	2-stitch	4-stitch	6-stitch	8-stitch	10-stitch	12-stitch	14-stitch	16-stitch
2-stitch	x	x	x	x	x	x	x	x
4-stitch	x	x		x		x		x
6-stitch	x		x			x		
8-stitch	x	x		x				x
10-stitch	x				x			
12-stitch	x	x	x			x		
14-stitch	x						x	
16-stitch	x	x		x				x

Accounting for Multiples

Before adding an additional pattern to your shawl, count the stitches in each wedge. Be sure you have a multiple of the stitch repeat **plus 1 extra stitch** in each wedge, not including spine or edging stitches. The 1 extra stitch balances the pattern so it appears centered on the wedge. Each row of each wedge has an odd number of stitches, starting with 1, and since the stitch repeats are all even numbers, there will always be one extra stitch on one side.

Patterns with different stitch multiples can be worked in sequence, *as long as* the final row of one design is divisible by the stitch multiple of the other. In other words, a 16-stitch multiple will meld perfectly with an 8- or a 4-stitch multiple. For example, if pattern A is a 16-stitch multiple, pattern B can be a 4-, an 8-, or a 16-stitch multiple.

If pattern A is a 4-stitch multiple, however, you will have to count your stitches to determine when you can switch to an 8- or a 16-stitch pattern. Let's say you end pattern A with 40 stitches on your needle. Because 8 goes into 40 evenly, you could then switch to a pattern with an 8-stitch multiple. But 16 does not go into 40 evenly, so you cannot switch to a 16-stitch multiple pattern.

In order to combine two stitch patterns with different multiples within a single wedge, the stitch multiples must be compatible. (In mathematical terms, they must be factors of each other.) So you don't have to stress about the math, refer to the tables above and on page 286 to see which stitch multiples will work with each other. (Note: It is possible to work out ways to combine "incompatible" stitch multiples, but that actually does require you to do some math. Grin.)

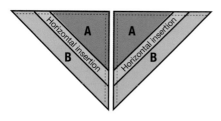

Add a horizontal insertion (or two) to separate the two primary stitch patterns and add even more interest to your shawl. (For an example, see Shawl #3 on pages 65 and 272.) Make sure the stitch multiples are compatible. Two-stitch repeats can be used in any shawl.

STEP THREE: *Choose a Background Texture*

Most of the shawls in this book can be knitted in smooth stockinette stitch or in textured garter stitch, depending on how the wrong-side rows are treated. Most charts show the stockinette option, with purl stitches on wrong-side rows, but these can be transformed into garter stitch by knitting stitches on the wrong side. Patterns where this approach is possible show both the "stockinette" and "garter" icons.

Each stitch pattern will look completely different based on whether you knit the wrong-side rows (garter stitch) or purl them (stockinette). This doubles the number of options you have for filling your wedges. Experiment with the different textures to see how the look of the stitch pattern changes. Be sure to check out other possible textures for simple wedges on pages 18–21.

The same stitch pattern knit in stockinette and garter stitch.

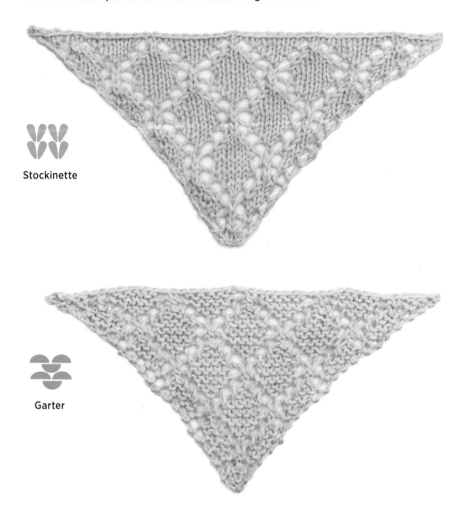

Stockinette

Garter

STEP FOUR: *Choose an Edging*

For most shawl silhouettes, you can use any of these edgings: textured garter stitch (a), unobtrusive stockinette (b), or delicate fagoting for a lacy look (c). All are interchangeable — knitter's choice! The edging you choose will determine which tab cast on you use. See pages 10–11 for instructions. These decorative stitches will be used *only* on the outside edges of your shawl's outermost wedges.

Note: If your shawl is knitted in the round, you will skip step 4.

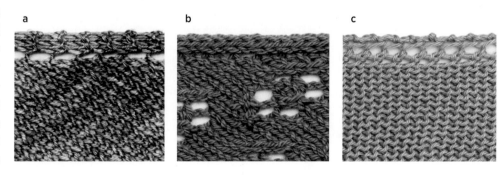

a   b   c

All of the shawl silhouettes except those knit in the round begin with a tab. There are three different tabs (garter, stockinette, and fagoted), and the one you use depends on the side edging you chose in step 4. Each tab starts with a provisional cast on (at right). The number of stitches in the initial cast on determines the width of the side edgings. (In this book, I have used 3-stitch side edgings, but you can be creative and use a wider edging if you choose.)

The following instructions are for a standard two-wedge triangular shawl with no vertical insertions. After beginning with the provisional cast on, continue using one of these tabs.

Provisional Cast On

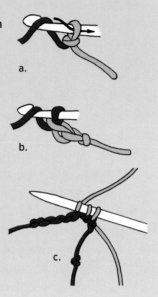

NOTE: Use a dark-colored yarn contrasting with your main shawl yarn to make it easier to pick up stitches later.

With an appropriately sized crochet hook, chain 7 with waste yarn (a and b).

Cut the yarn, and pull the end through the last chain you made to secure it. Since a crocheted chain unravels only in one direction, tie a loose knot on this tail to mark it as the end you'll use later to unravel the chain.

Turn the crocheted chain over. Use your main yarn and a knitting needle to pick up and knit 1 stitch through the back loop of each crocheted chain until you have cast on 3 stitches (c).

Garter Tab

After the Provisional Cast On (see above), knit 7 rows of garter stitch.

Rotate the piece 90°, and pick up and knit 3 stitches along the side edge, picking up 1 stitch for each garter ridge.

Rotate the piece 90° again. Unzip your provisional cast on, pick up the 3 live stitches along the provisional cast-on edge with your free needle, and knit them. (9 stitches) Turn.

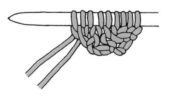

SETUP ROW: On the wrong side, knit the first 3 stitches, purl 3 stitches, then knit 3 stitches. (9 stitches)

NOTE: The first 3 and last 3 stitches of every row will be knit stitches and will serve as the side edges. The center stitch in the middle 3 stitches is the base of the spine connecting the two wedges. On wrong-side rows, kinit or purl these middle stitches according to the texture you chose in step 3.

Add Some Bling

Adding beads can give your custom shawl some extra pop. Several lower border patterns (pages 238, 242, and 248) already include beads, but you can add them to almost any design in this book. Try placing beads on a stockinette edging, a horizontal insertion, or anywhere else you wish to add a highlight.

Stockinette Tab

After the Provisional Cast On (see page 10), knit the right-side rows and purl the wrong-side rows for a total of 7 rows. Start and end with a knit row.

Rotate the piece 90°, and pick up and knit 3 stitches along the side edge, picking up 1 stitch for every other row; rotate the piece 90° again. Unzip your provisional cast on, pick up the 3 live stitches along the provisional cast-on edge with your free needle, and knit them. (9 stitches) Turn.

SETUP ROW: Purl across. (9 stitches) The first 3 and last 3 stitches of every row will be knitted on the right side and purled on the wrong side, creating the stockinette side edging. The center stitch in the middle 3 stitches is the base of the spine connecting the two wedges. On wrong-side rows, kinit or purl these middle stitches according to the texture you chose in step 3. (This 3-stitch stockinette edge will naturally roll, giving you the look of an i-cord edge with a lot less work.)

Fagoted Tab

After the Provisional Cast On (see page 10), knit 7 rows in the following pattern: K1, yarn over, k2tog.

Rotate the piece 90°, and pick up and knit 3 stitches along the side edge, picking up 1 stitch for each ridge; rotate the piece 90° again. Unzip your provisional cast on and pick up the 3 live stitches along the provisional cast-on edge with your free needle, k1, yarn over, k2tog, (9 stitches) Turn.

SETUP ROW: K1, yarn over, k2tog, p3, k1, yarn over, k2tog. (9 stitches)

The first 3 and last 3 stitches of every row will follow the instructions for the Fagoted Lace Pattern on page 17. The center stitch in the middle 3 stitches is the base of the spine connecting the two wedges. On wrong-side rows, kinit or purl these middle stitches according to the texture you chose in step 3.

STEP SIX: *Choose a Border*

Choose a border treatment for your shawl. See pages 234–267 for border possibilities from wavy scallops to intricate lace. Some borders are worked in the same direction and parallel to your work, and in these cases, the rule of compatible stitch multiples from step 2 applies. Other borders are knit perpendicular to the edge of the shawl (see next page), in a sideways manner, so the stitch multiples don't matter. If you use vertical insertions in your design, I suggest using a perpendicular border pattern (or be prepared to do some math).

SHAWL #8

Contrasting colors set off the horizontal insertion and perpendicular border. See page 273 for instructions.

Knitting a Perpendicular Border

A perpendicular border is worked along the bottom of the shawl. Set up for knitting a perpendicular border as follows.

1. End the main part of the shawl after working a wrong-side row. I highly recommend that you put a lifeline in this row. If something goes wrong, you will have a safe place to rip back to. (For how to do this, see page 13.)

2. Cut the yarn when you get to the end of the wrong-side row.

3. With a free needle (double-pointed needles are convenient for this step), cast on the number of stitches required for your perpendicular border, using the cable cast on (see page 278).

4. Attach the border at the opposite end of the row from where you finished knitting, with the wrong side facing you.

Use double joins around the corner

Direction of knitting

Begin perpendicular border here

Cut main body yarn

5. Begin working the border pattern, and at the end of every wrong-side row, attach 1 live stitch from the main body of the shawl to the border in this manner: Slip the last border stitch, knit the next live stitch from the main body, then slip the border stitch over. In this way, every 2 rows of border will incorporate or "eat up" 1 live stitch from the shawl body.

6. When going around the point of the triangle (or any irregular shape), use "double joins" to gather the border and prevent it from puckering. Make a double join as follows: on a wrong-side row, slip the last border stitch and then knit into the previous live shawl stitch — the one you "ate up" in the previous row (see illustrations at right). This way, each live stitch from the body of the shawl will have 4 border rows instead of 2. You may have to experiment to see how many double joins are needed, depending on the silhouette of your shawl.

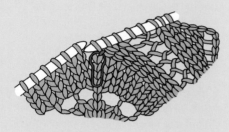

At the end of a wrong-side row, identify the shawl body stitch you just worked and place a locking stitch marker to identify it as the stitch to be double-joined.

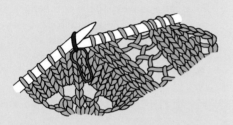

Work the next 2 rows. Put the stitch you marked back on the left needle to work it a second time. Remove the stitch marker and continue as before. After the last live stitch has been eaten up, bind off the remaining border stitches using the super-stretchy bind off (see page 279).

STEP SEVEN: *Choose a Bind Off*

You can select from a simple stretchy finish (a), to a pretty picot edge (b), to an easy (and quick) crocheted bind off (c). It's all about choices. You are the designer. Let your imagination run wild! For options, see pages 278–279.

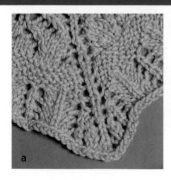

a

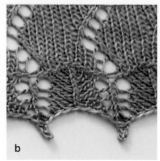

b

c

Gather Your Tools

You can make your shawl a solid color or make each stitch pattern a different color. Try adding stripes or use a different color for the horizontal insertion and border (see shawls #8 and #13 on pages 273 and 275, respectively). Add beads to your border. I caution against using yarns of different weights in the same wedge, as that might throw off the geometry, but really, the sky's the limit! When the piece becomes your desired size — or when the yarn runs out, whichever comes first — the shawl is done!

Any yarn weight is appropriate for a shawl, depending on your goal and personal taste. Finer yarns create lightweight wraps, and chunkier yarns produce heavier ones. Yarn amounts vary depending on the finished size of the shawl and yarn weight. Use the guidelines in the table at right.

YARN REQUIREMENTS		
Yarn Weight	Full-Size Shawl, 35"–40"/ 89–101.5 cm deep	Smaller Shawlette, 25"–30"/63.5–76 cm deep
Lace	1,250–1,550 yds/1,143–1,417 m	550–850 yds/503–777 m
Fingering	1,000–1,300 yds/914–1,189 m	450–750 yds/411–686 m
Sport/DK	925–1,150 yds/846–1,052 m	425–650 yds/389–594 m
Worsted	825–1,050 yds/754–960 m	350–600 yds/320–549 m
Chunky	725–950 yds/663–869 m	325–550 yds/297–503 m

Sport weight   Worsted weight   Chunky weight

Working with Multicolor Yarns

To prevent color pooling when working with multicolor or hand-dyed yarns, work 2-row stripes, alternating from two different balls of yarn. It's best to make the switch just inside the side edging so the floats don't show on the public side of the shawl.

Knitting Needles

Luckily for knitters, shawls are not fitted garments, so gauge is not an issue. You may, however, want to knit a gauge swatch in pattern to make sure you are happy with the drape of the resulting fabric. Here are some tips for choosing the right needle for the yarn you're working with.

- Use needles two or three sizes larger than those called for on the ball band to ensure a nice drape.

- Use circular needles to accommodate the large number of stitches; work back and forth in rows, without joining, except when knitting square or circular shawls.

- Choose needles that match both the yarn and pattern. For lace-weight or fingering-weight yarn in a lace pattern, the needle tips should be pointy, rather than blunt. Slippery yarn like silk is easier to knit on needles with a little texture, like bamboo or wood.

Stitch Markers

Most knitters like to isolate edge and spine stitches with markers. This way, there's less counting involved!

Lifeline

Many knitters have learned the hard way to use a lifeline as a preventive measure, especially with lace knitting. I recommend putting in a lifeline when you have knit a distance that you are unwilling to rip back. Definitely place a lifeline when switching from one pattern to another. Also, when using a perpendicular knitted-on border, having a lifeline on the last row of the main shawl body is very useful.

To incorporate a lifeline, thread a piece of scrap yarn or dental floss through live stitches in a single row of your fabric. If you must rip out later, there's a safe spot to go back to!

Managing Lifelines

Some interchangeable circular needle tips have a small hole near the join of the needle and the cable. While intended for tightening the join, those holes are perfect for threading dental floss or scrap yarn to carry with you across a row of knitting to place your lifeline.

Putting It All Together

The number of wedges you choose in step 1 (page 6) will determine the number of stitches you need to begin and the number of rows you knit for the tab. In general, the number of rows you knit for the tab will be twice the number of stitches you need between the edges of the wedge.

For a two-wedge triangular piece, start with 9 stitches (3 stitches on each side for the edgings, 1 stitch for the tab of each of the two triangles, and 1 spine stitch).

Cast on 3 stitches and work 7 rows of your edging stitch (see page 17) before picking up the stitches around the tab.

You might wonder why you knit 7 rows and not 6 for the basic two-wedge tab. When there are only 6 rows, there just isn't enough room to pick up 3 stitches and still have the 3 provisional cast-on stitches. The extra row makes it easier. For longer tabs, adding that extra row isn't necessary.

For a three-wedge piece, start with 11 stitches (3 stitches on each side for the edgings, 1 stitch for the tab of each of the three triangles, and 2 spine stitches). In this instance, you would cast on 3 stitches and work 10 rows of your edging pattern (see page 17) before picking up 5 stitches around the tab.

For a six-wedge piece, start with 17 stitches (3 stitches on each side for the edgings, 1 stitch for the tab of each of the six triangles, and

SHAWL #5
The picot bind off adds the perfect touch to this silk shawl. See page 272 for instructions.

5 spine stitches). Here, you'd cast on 3 stitches and work 22 rows of your edge stitch before picking up 11 stitches around the tab.

For shawls with vertical insertions, the formula is slightly more involved:

- **Add up the stitches required for Row 1** for all of the pieces of your shawl (the two side edges, the wedges, the vertical insertion/s).

- **Subtract 6** (or the number of edge stitches if you are using something other than a 3-stitch edge).

- **Multiply the result by 2.** That's how many rows of edge stitches you must work before picking up the stitches around the tab.

For instance, to start Shawl #2 on page 270 you need 59 stitches (6 edge stitches, 1 stitch to start the tab of each of the two wedges, three 17-stitch vertical insertions). Cast on 3 stitches and work 106 rows.

$$59 \text{ stitches in Row 1}$$
$$- 6 \text{ edge stitches}$$
$$53 \times 2 = 106 \text{ rows}$$

Rotate the piece 90°, and pick up and knit 53 stitches along the side edge, picking up 1 stitch for each ridge; rotate the piece 90° again, unzip your provisional cast on, and knit the 3 stitches along the cast-on edge (59 stitches). Turn.

To make your knitting easier, don't forget to use markers to separate the different elements of your design. Place a marker just inside the edge stitches and just outside the spine or vertical insertion stitches.

That's it! You're ready to begin your shawl. . . .

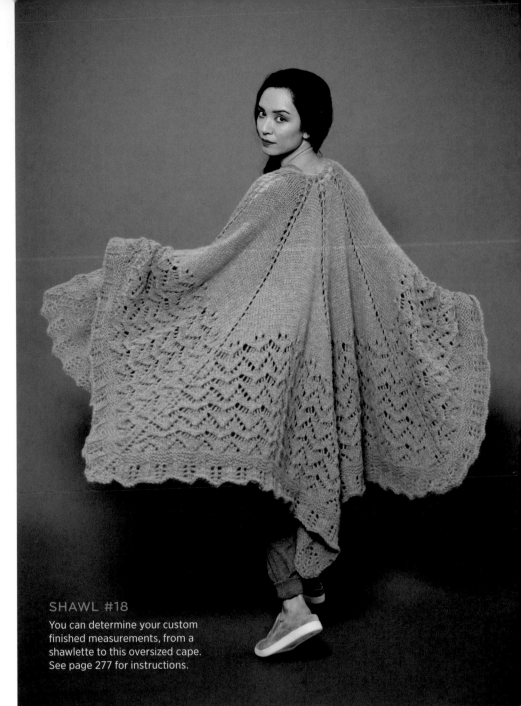

SHAWL #18
You can determine your custom finished measurements, from a shawlette to this oversized cape. See page 277 for instructions.

Turned Around?

The stitch patterns in this book are written and photographed how you'll knit them, from the cast-on tab to the bound-off edge. In wedges, this means starting with the point at the bottom and knitting upward to create an ever-wider triangle. The orientation of your knitted piece will be reversed, though, when you wear it as a garment. (In the photo above, notice that the point of each triangle is at the *top* of the shawl.) This means that depending on how you design your shawl components, the stitch patterns as you wear the finished garment will be upside down from how the swatches appear in the following pages. You did nothing wrong! It's just the reality of knitting from the top down.

PART 2

THE PATTERNS

Use the 185 stitch patterns in this section to fill the wedges of your shawls. From simple and solid to open and lacy, these designs will help you create a stunning custom-made masterpiece to be cherished for a lifetime. See page 285 for a full list of the symbols and abbreviations used in the charts.

SIDE EDGINGS

Choose a pattern for the side edges of your shawl: bumpy garter stitch, smooth stockinette, or a delicate fagoted lace. Note that the patterns are identical whether you work them on the left-hand side or the right-hand side of your shawl. See page 284 for information about how to read knitting charts.

1 Garter Stitch

ROW 1 AND ALL RS ROWS: K3.

ROW 2 AND ALL WS ROWS: K3.

Repeat Rows 1 and 2.

Note: Both left- and right-hand sides are alike.

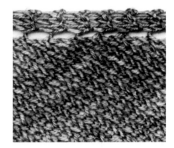

2 Stockinette Stitch

ROW 1 AND ALL RS ROWS: K3.

ROW 2 AND ALL WS ROWS: P3.

Repeat Rows 1 and 2.

Note: Both left- and right-hand sides are alike.

3 Fagoted Lace Pattern

ROW 1 AND ALL RS ROWS: K1, yarn over, k2tog.

ROW 2 AND ALL WS ROWS: K1, yarn over, k2tog.

Repeat Rows 1 and 2.

Note: Both left- and right-hand sides are alike.

SIMPLE FABRICS

Following are some basic options for filling in a wedge. Note that all wedges have yarn-over stitches on each side; these increase stitches shape the wedge. Sometimes the ideal texture is a simple one. Use one of these to highlight a special lace border or fancy edge treatment. ***To help make the knitting easier, be sure to place markers to set off the side edges and spine stitches.***

Start each wedge with the provisional cast on and the tab of your choice (page 10).

 ## Basic Stockinette Stitch

2 (WS) 1 (RS)

ROW 1 AND ALL RS ROWS: Yarn over, knit across to the marker, ending this section with yarn over.

ROW 2 AND ALL WS ROWS: Purl across.

Repeat Rows 1 and 2 for the pattern.

---

5 ## Basic Garter Stitch

2 (WS) 1 (RS)

ROW 1 AND ALL RS ROWS: Yarn over, knit across to the marker, ending this section with yarn over.

ROW 2 AND ALL WS ROWS: Knit across.

Repeat Rows 1 and 2 for the pattern.

SHAWL #14

This lovely wrap was knit with simple garter stitch wedges. See page 275 for instructions.

19

6 Basic Seed Stitch

ROW 1 (RS): Yarn over, p1, yarn over. (3 stitches)

ROW 2: K1, p1, k1.

ROW 3: Yarn over, *k1, p1; repeat from the * to 1 stitch before the marker, ending this section with k1, yarn over. (5 stitches)

ROW 4: P1, k1, *p1, k1; repeat from the * to 1 stitch before the marker, ending this section with p1.

ROW 5: Yarn over, p1, *k1, p1; repeat from the * to 2 stitches before the marker, ending this section with k1, p1, yarn over. (7 stitches)

ROW 6: K1, p1, k1, *p1, k1; repeat from the * to 2 stitches before the marker, ending this section with p1, k1.

Repeat Rows 3–6 for the pattern.

7 Double Seed Stitch

ROW 1 (RS): Yarn over, k1, yarn over. (3 stitches)

ROW 2: K1, p1, k1.

ROW 3: Yarn over, *k1, p1; repeat from the * to 1 stitch before the marker, ending this section with k1, yarn over. (5 stitches)

ROW 4: P2, *k1, p1; repeat from the * to 1 stitch before the marker, ending this section with p1.

ROW 5: Yarn over, k1, *p1, k1; repeat from the * to 2 stitches before the marker, ending this section with p1, k1, yarn over. (7 stitches)

ROW 6: *K1, p1, rep from the * to 1 stitch before the marker, ending this section with k1.

Repeat Rows 3–6 for the pattern.

8 Simple Garter Ridges

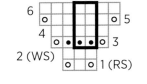

ROW 1 (RS): Yarn over, k1, yarn over. (3 stitches)

ROW 2 AND ALL WS ROWS: Purl across.

ROW 3: Yarn over, purl across to the marker, ending this section with yarn over. (5 stitches)

ROW 5: Yarn over, knit across to the marker, ending this section with yarn over. (7 stitches)

ROW 6: As Row 2.

Repeat Rows 3–6 for the pattern.

9 Wide Garter Ridges

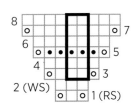

ROW 1 (RS): Yarn over, k1, yarn over. (3 stitches)

ROW 2 AND ALL WS ROWS: Purl across.

ROW 3: Yarn over, knit across to the marker, ending this section with yarn over. (5 stitches)

ROW 5: Yarn over, purl across to the marker, ending this section with yarn over. (7 stitches)

ROW 7: As Row 3.

ROW 8: Purl across.

Repeat Rows 3–8 for the pattern.

MIX 'N' MATCH WEDGES

Choose one — or more! — of these lace patterns to create a truly custom shawl. Just remember: when starting a new lace pattern mid-shawl, count the stitches in each wedge to ensure you have the correct multiple of stitches plus 1 (see page 8).

Stitch counts are given for the first time the row is worked but will change as multiple repeats are worked.

WEDGES with 2-Stitch Multiples

Start each wedge with the provisional cast on and the tab of your choice (page 10).

10

ROW 1 (RS): Yarn over, k1, yarn over. (3 stitches)

ROW 2: Purl across.

ROWS 3 AND 7: Yarn over, knit across to the marker, ending this section with yarn over.

ROWS 4 AND 6: Knit across.

ROW 5: Yarn over, k2tog, *yarn over, k2tog; repeat from the * across to 1 stitch before the marker, ending this section with yarn over, k1, yarn over. (7 stitches)

ROW 8: As Row 2.

Repeat Rows 3–8 for the pattern.

ROW 1 (RS): Yarn over, k1, yarn over. (3 stitches)

ROW 2 AND ALL WS ROWS: Purl across.

ROWS 3, 5, 9, 11, 13, 17, 19, AND 21: Yarn over, knit across to the marker, yarn over.

ROW 7: Yarn over, k1, yarn over, *ssk, yarn over; repeat from the * to 4 stitches before the marker, ending this section with (ssk, yarn over) twice. (9 stitches)

ROW 15: Yarn over, k2, (yarn over, ssk) twice, *yarn over, ssk; repeat from the * to 7 stitches before the marker, ending this section with (yarn over, ssk) 3 times, k1, yarn over. (17 stitches)

ROW 22: As Row 2.

Repeat Rows 3–22 for the pattern.

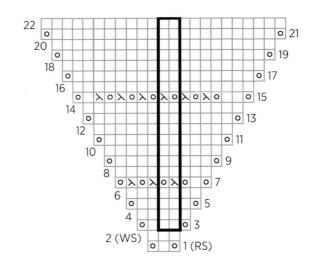

12

ROW 1 (RS): Yarn over, k1, yarn over. (3 stitches)

ROW 2 AND ALL WS ROWS: Purl across.

ROW 3: Yarn over, k1, yarn over, ssk, yarn over. (5 stitches)

ROW 5: Yarn over, k1, k2tog, yarn over, k2, yarn over. (7 stitches)

ROW 7: Yarn over, k1, *yarn over, ssk; repeat from the * to 4 stitches before the marker, ending this section with

(yarn over, ssk) twice, yarn over. (9 stitches)

ROW 9: Yarn over, k1, k2tog, *yarn over, k2tog; repeat from the * to 4 stitches before the marker, ending this section with yarn over, k2tog, yarn over, k2, yarn over. (11 stitches)

ROW 10: As Row 2.

Repeat Rows 7–10 for the pattern.

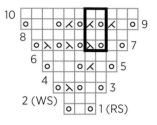

13

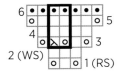

ROW 1 (RS): Yarn over, k1, yarn over.
(3 stitches)

ROWS 2 AND 4: Purl across.

ROW 3: Yarn over, k1, *yarn over, ssk;
repeat from the * to the marker,
ending this section with yarn over.
(5 stitches)

ROW 5: Yarn over, knit across to the
marker, ending this section with
yarn over.

ROW 6: Knit across.

Repeat Rows 3–6 for the pattern.

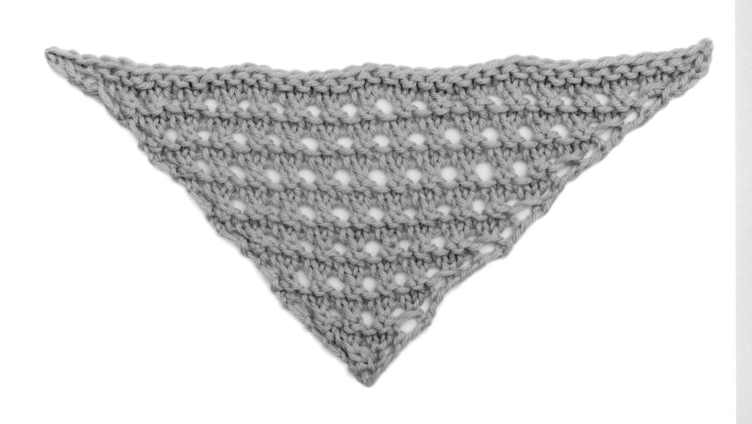

14

ROW 1 (RS): Yarn over, k1, yarn over. (3 stitches)

ROW 2 AND ALL WS ROWS: Purl across.

ROWS 3 AND 13: Yarn over, purl across to the marker, ending this section with yarn over.

ROW 5: Yarn over, k2tog, *yarn over, k2tog; repeat from the * to 1 stitch before the marker, ending this section with yarn over, k1, yarn over. (7 stitches)

ROW 7: Yarn over, k2tog, yarn over, *k2tog, yarn over; repeat from the * to 3 stitches before the marker, ending this section with k2tog, yarn over, k1, yarn over. (9 stitches)

ROW 9: Yarn over, k2tog, yarn over, k2tog, *yarn over, k2tog; repeat from the * to 3 stitches before the marker, ending this section with yarn over, k2tog, yarn over, k1, yarn over. (11 stitches)

ROW 11: (Yarn over, k2tog) twice, yarn over, *k2tog, yarn over; repeat from the * to 5 stitches before the marker, ending this section with (k2tog, yarn over) twice, k1, yarn over. (13 stitches)

ROW 15: Yarn over, k1, (yarn over, ssk) twice, yarn over, *ssk, yarn over; repeat from the * to 8 stitches before the marker, ending this section with (ssk, yarn over) 4 times. (17 stitches)

ROW 17: Yarn over, k1, (yarn over, ssk) 3 times, *yarn over, ssk; repeat from the * to 8 stitches before the marker, ending this section with (yarn over, ssk) 4 times, yarn over. (19 stitches)

ROW 19: Yarn over, k1, (yarn over, ssk) 3 times, yarn over, *ssk, yarn over; repeat from the * to 10 stitches before the marker, ending this section with (ssk, yarn over) 5 times. (21 stitches)

ROW 21: Yarn over, k1, (yarn over, ssk) 4 times, *yarn over, ssk; repeat from the * to 10 stitches before the marker, ending this section with (yarn over, ssk) 5 times, yarn over. (23 stitches)

ROW 22: As Row 2.

Repeat Rows 3–22 for the pattern.

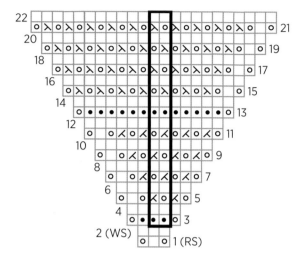

SHAWL #10
Here, a simple textured pattern showcases beautiful lace. See page 274 for instructions.

WEDGES with 4-Stitch Multiples

Start each wedge with the provisional cast on and the tab of your choice (page 10).

ROW 1 (RS): Yarn over, k1, yarn over. (3 stitches)

ROW 2 AND ALL WS ROWS: Purl across.

ROW 3: Yarn over, k3, yarn over. (5 stitches)

ROW 5: Yarn over, ssk, yarn over, k1, yarn over, k2tog, yarn over. (7 stitches)

ROW 7: Yarn over, k2, yarn over, s2kp2 (page 282), yarn over, k2, yarn over. (9 stitches)

ROW 9: Yarn over, k1, *yarn over, s2kp2, yarn over, k1; repeat from the * to 4 stitches before the marker, ending this section with yarn over, s2kp2, yarn over, k1, yarn over. (11 stitches)

ROW 11: Yarn over, k1, k2tog, *yarn over k1, yarn over, s2kp2; repeat from the * to 4 stitches before the marker, ending this section with yarn over, k1, yarn over, ssk, k1, yarn over. (13 stitches)

ROW 13: Yarn over, k2tog, yarn over, k1, *yarn over, s2kp2, yarn over, k1; repeat from the * to 6 stitches before the marker, ending this section with yarn over, s2kp2, yarn over, k1, yarn over, ssk, yarn over. (15 stitches)

ROW 15: Yarn over, k2, yarn over, s2kp2, *yarn over, k1, yarn over, s2kp2; repeat from the * to 6 stitches before the marker, ending this section with yarn over, k1, yarn over, s2kp2, yarn over, k2, yarn over. (17 stitches)

ROW 16: As Row 2.

Repeat Rows 9–16 for the pattern.

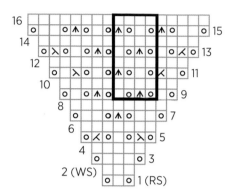

⊼ s2kp2

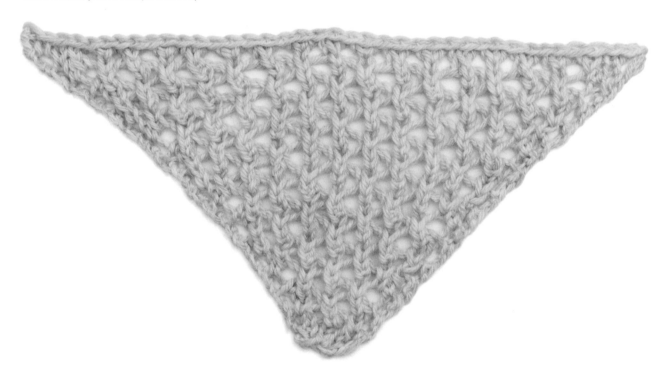

16

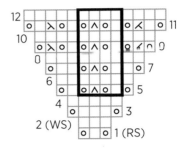

ROW 1 (RS): Yarn over, k1, yarn over. (3 stitches)

ROW 2 AND ALL WS ROWS: Purl across.

ROW 3: Yarn over, k3, yarn over. (5 stitches)

ROW 5: Yarn over, *k1, yarn over, sk2p (page 282), yarn over; repeat from the * to 1 stitch before the marker, ending this section with k1, yarn over. (7 stitches)

ROW 7: Yarn over, k1, *k1, yarn over, sk2p, yarn over; repeat from the * to 2 stitches before the marker, ending this section with k2, yarn over. (9 stitches)

ROW 9: Yarn over, k2tog, yarn over, *k1, yarn over, sk2p, yarn over; repeat from the * to 3 stitches before the marker, ending this section with k1, yarn over, ssk, yarn over. (11 stitches)

ROW 11: Yarn over, k1, k2tog, yarn over, *k1, yarn over, sk2p, yarn over; repeat from the * to 4 stitches before the marker, ending this section with k1, yarn over, ssk, k1, yarn over. (13 stitches)

ROW 12: As Row 2.

Repeat Rows 5–12 for the pattern.

⌃ sk2p

17

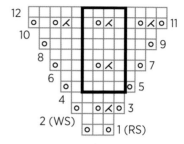

ROW 1 (RS): Yarn over, k1, yarn over. (3 stitches)

ROW 2 AND ALL WS ROWS: Purl across.

ROW 3: Yarn over, k2tog, yarn over, k1, yarn over. (5 stitches)

ROWS 5 AND 9: Yarn over, knit across to the marker, ending this section with yarn over. (7 stitches)

ROW 7: Yarn over, k1, *k1, k2tog, yarn over, k1; repeat from the * to 2 stitches before the marker, ending this section with k2, yarn over. (9 stitches)

ROW 11: Yarn over, k2tog, yarn over, k1, *k1, k2tog, yarn over, k1; repeat from the * to 4 stitches before the marker, ending this section with k1, k2tog, yarn over, k1, yarn over. (13 stitches)

ROW 12: As Row 2.

Repeat Rows 5–12 for the pattern.

WEDGES with 6-Stitch Multiples

Start each wedge with the provisional cast on and the tab of your choice (page 10).

18

ROW 1 (RS): Yarn over, k1, yarn over. (3 stitches)

ROW 2 AND ALL WS ROWS: Purl across.

ROW 3: Yarn over, k3, yarn over. (5 stitches)

ROW 5: Yarn over, k2tog, yarn over, k1, yarn over, ssk, yarn over. (7 stitches)

ROW 7: Yarn over, *k1, yarn over, ssk, k1, k2tog, yarn over; repeat from the * to 1 stitch before the marker, ending this section with k1, yarn over. (9 stitches)

ROW 9: Yarn over, k1, *k1, yarn over, ssk, k1, k2tog, yarn over; repeat from the * to 2 stitches before the marker, ending this section with k2, yarn over. (11 stitches)

ROW 11: Yarn over, k2tog, yarn over, *k1, yarn over, ssk, k1, k2tog, yarn over; repeat from the * to 3 stitches before the marker, ending this section with k1, yarn over, ssk, yarn over. (13 stitches)

ROW 13: Yarn over, k1, yarn over, ssk, *k1, k2tog, yarn over, k1, yarn over, ssk; repeat from the * to 4 stitches before the marker, ending this section with k1, k2tog, yarn over, k1, yarn over. (15 stitches)

ROW 15: Yarn over, k2, yarn over, ssk, *k1, k2tog, yarn over, k1, yarn over, ssk; repeat from the * to 5 stitches before the marker, ending this section with k1, k2tog, yarn over, k2, yarn over. (17 stitches)

ROW 17: Yarn over, k3, yarn over, ssk, *k1, k2tog, yarn over, k1, yarn over, ssk; repeat from the * to 6 stitches before the marker, ending this section with k1, k2tog, yarn over, k3, yarn over. (19 stitches)

ROW 18: As Row 2.

Repeat Rows 7–18 for the pattern.

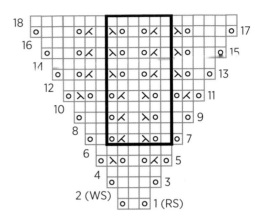

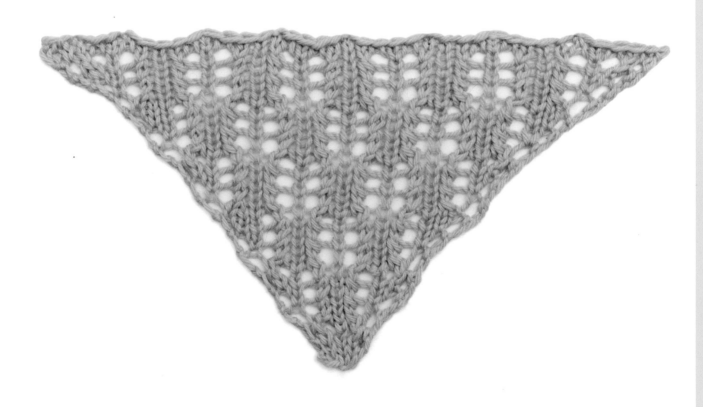

19

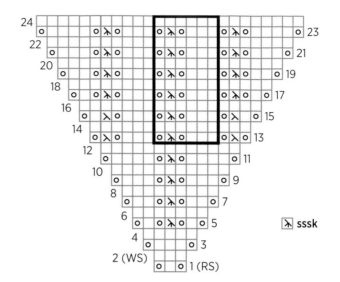

ROW 1 (RS): Yarn over, k1, yarn over. (3 stitches)

ROW 2 AND ALL WS ROWS: Purl across.

ROW 3: Yarn over, k3, yarn over. (5 stitches)

ROW 5: Yarn over, k1, yarn over, sssk (page 285), yarn over, k1, yarn over. (7 stitches)

ROW 7: Yarn over, k2, yarn over, sssk, yarn over, k2, yarn over. (9 stitches)

ROW 9: Yarn over, k3, yarn over, sssk, yarn over, k3, yarn over. (11 stitches)

ROW 11: Yarn over, k4, yarn over, sssk, yarn over, k4, yarn over. (13 stitches)

ROW 13: Yarn over, ssk, yarn over, *k3, yarn over, sssk, yarn over; repeat from the * to 5 stitches before the marker, ending this section with k3, yarn over, ssk, yarn over. (15 stitches)

ROW 15: Yarn over, k1, ssk, yarn over, *k3, yarn over, sssk, yarn over; repeat from the * to 6 stitches before the marker, ending this section with k3, yarn over, ssk, k1, yarn over. (17 stitches)

sssk ⅄ *(chart legend)*

ROW 17: Yarn over, k1, yarn over, sssk, yarn over, *k3, yarn over, sssk, yarn over; repeat from the * to 7 stitches before the marker, ending this section with k3, yarn over, sssk, yarn over, k1, yarn over. (19 stitches)

ROW 19: Yarn over, k2, yarn over, sssk, yarn over, *k3, yarn over, sssk, yarn over; repeat from the * to 8 stitches before the marker, ending this section with k3, yarn over, sssk, yarn over, k2, yarn over. (21 stitches)

ROW 21: Yarn over, k3, yarn over, sssk, yarn over, *k3, yarn over, sssk, yarn over; repeat from the * to 9 stitches before the marker, ending this section with k3, yarn over, sssk, yarn over, k3, yarn over. (23 stitches)

ROW 23: Yarn over, k4, yarn over, sssk, yarn over, *k3, yarn over, sssk, yarn over; repeat from the * to 10 stitches before the marker, ending this section with k3, yarn over, sssk, yarn over, k4, yarn over. (25 stitches)

ROW 24: As Row 2.

Repeat Rows 13–24 for the pattern.

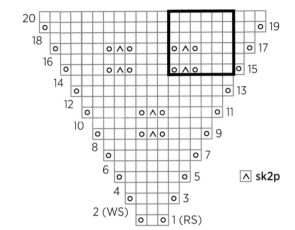

∧ sk2p

ROW 1 (RS): Yarn over, k1, yarn over. (3 stitches)

ROW 2 AND ALL WS ROWS: Purl across.

ROW 3: Yarn over, k3, yarn over. (5 stitches)

ROW 5: Yarn over, k5, yarn over. (7 stitches)

ROW 7: Yarn over, k7, yarn over. (9 stitches)

ROW 9: Yarn over, k3, yarn over, sk2p (page 282), yarn over, k3, yarn over. (11 stitches)

ROW 11: Yarn over, k4, yarn over, sk2p, yarn over, k4, yarn over. (13 stitches)

ROW 13: Yarn over, k13, yarn over. (15 stitches)

ROW 15: Yarn over, *k3, yarn over, sk2p, yarn over; repeat from the * to 9 stitches before the marker, ending this section with k3, yarn over, sk2p, yarn over, k3, yarn over. (17 stitches)

ROW 17: Yarn over, k1, *k3, yarn over, sk2p, yarn over; repeat from the * to 10 stitches before the marker, ending this section with k3, yarn over, sk2p, yarn over, k4, yarn over. (19 stitches)

ROW 19: Yarn over, knit across to the marker, ending this section with yarn over. (21 stitches)

ROW 20: As Row 2.

Repeat Rows 15–20 for the pattern.

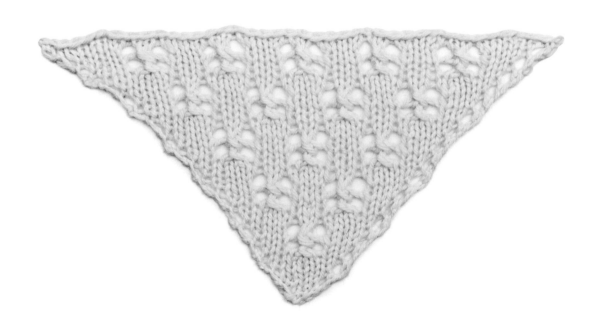

21

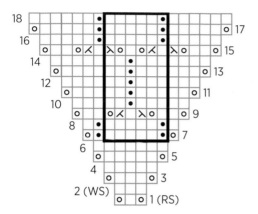

ROW 1 (RS): Yarn over, k1, yarn over. (3 stitches)

ROWS 2, 4, AND 6: Purl across.

ROW 3: Yarn over, k3, yarn over. (5 stitches)

ROW 5: Yarn over, k5, yarn over. (7 stitches)

ROW 7: Yarn over, *p1, k5; repeat from the * to 1 stitch before the marker, ending this section with p1, yarn over. (9 stitches)

ROW 8: P1, k1, *p5, k1; repeat from the * to 1 stitch before the marker, ending this section with p1.

ROW 9: Yarn over, k1, *k1, yarn over, ssk, k1, k2tog, yarn over; repeat from the * to 2 stitches before the marker, ending this section with k2, yarn over. (11 stitches)

ROW 10: P3, *p2, k1, p3; repeat from the * to 2 stitches before the marker, ending this section with p2.

ROW 11: Yarn over, k2, *k3, p1, k2; repeat from the * to 3 stitches before the marker, ending this section with k3, yarn over. (13 stitches)

ROW 12: P4, *p2, k1, p3; repeat from the * to 3 stitches before the marker, ending this section with p3.

ROW 13: Yarn over, k3, *k3, p1, k2; repeat from the * to 4 stitches before the marker, ending this section with k4, yarn over. (15 stitches)

ROW 14: P5, *p2, k1, p3; repeat from the * to 4 stitches before the marker, ending this section with p4.

ROW 15: Yarn over, k2, yarn over, ssk, *k1, k2tog, yarn over, k1, yarn over, ssk; repeat from the * to 5 stitches before the marker, ending this section with k1, k2tog, yarn over, k2, yarn over. (17 stitches)

ROW 16: P5, k1, *p5, k1; repeat from the * to 5 stitches before the marker, ending this section with p5.

ROW 17: Yarn over, k5, *p1, k5; repeat from the * to 6 stitches before the marker, ending this section with p1, k5, yarn over. (19 stitches)

ROW 18: P6, k1, *p5, k1; repeat from the * to 6 stitches before the marker, ending this section with p6.

Repeat Rows 7–18 for the pattern.

22

ROW 1 (RS): Yarn over, k1, yarn over. (3 stitches)

ROW 2: Knit across.

ROW 3: Yarn over, p3, yarn over. (5 stitches)

ROW 4: P1, k3, p1.

ROW 5: Yarn over, k1, p3, k1, yarn over. (7 stitches)

ROW 6: P2, k3, p2.

ROW 7: Yarn over, k2tog, yarn over, k3, yarn over, ssk, yarn over. (9 stitches)

ROW 8: K3, p3, k3.

ROW 9: Yarn over, p3, k3, p3, yarn over. (11 stitches)

ROW 10: P1, k3, p3, k3, p1.

ROW 11: Yarn over, k1, p3, k3, p3, k1, yarn over. (13 stitches)

ROW 12: P2, k3, p3, k3, p2.

ROW 13: Yarn over, k2tog, yarn over, k1, *k2, yarn over, s2kp2 (page 282), yarn over, k1; repeat from the * to 4 stitches before the marker, ending this section with k2, yarn over, ssk, yarn over. (15 stitches)

ROW 14: K3, p2, *p1, k3, p2; repeat from the * to 4 stitches before the marker, ending this section with p1, k3.

ROW 15: Yarn over, p3, k1, *k2, p3, k1; repeat from the * to 5 stitches before the marker, ending this section with k2, p3, yarn over. (17 stitches)

ROW 16: P1, k3, p2, *p1, k3, p2; repeat from the * to 5 stitches before the marker, ending this section with p1, k3, p1.

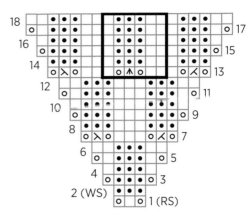

ROW 17: Yarn over, k1, p3, k1, *k2, p3, k1; repeat from the * to 6 stitches before the marker, ending this section with k2, p3, k1, yarn over. (19 stitches)

ROW 18: P2, k3, p2, *p1, k3, p2; repeat from the * to 6 stitches before the marker, ending this section with p1, k3, p2.

Repeat Rows 13–18 for the pattern.

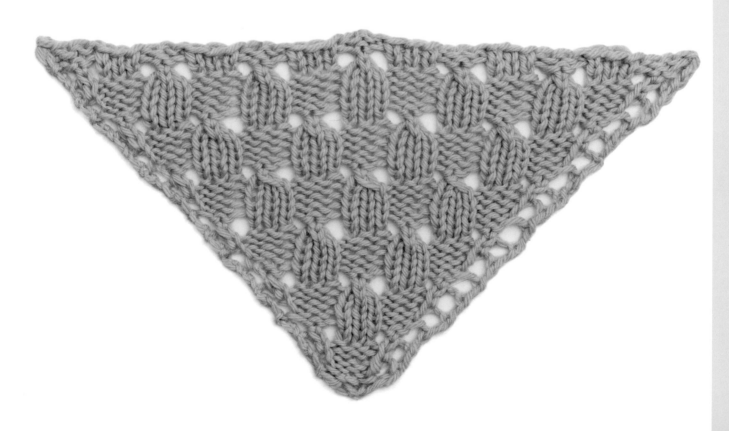

23

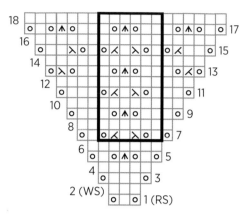

ROW 1 (RS): Yarn over, k1, yarn over. (3 stitches)

ROW 2 AND ALL WS ROWS: Purl across.

ROW 3: Yarn over, k3, yarn over. (5 stitches)

ROW 5: Yarn over, k1, yarn over, s2kp2 (page 282), yarn over, k1, yarn over. (7 stitches)

ROW 7: Yarn over, *k1, yarn over, ssk, k1, k2tog, yarn over; repeat from the * to 1 stitch before the marker, ending this section with k1, yarn over. (9 stitches)

ROW 9: Yarn over, k1, *k2, yarn over, s2kp2, yarn over, k1; repeat from the * to 2 stitches before the marker, ending this section with k2, yarn over. (11 stitches)

ROW 11: Yarn over, k2, *k1, yarn over, ssk, k1, k2tog, yarn over; repeat from the * to 3 stitches before the marker, ending this section with k3, yarn over. (13 stitches)

ROW 13: Yarn over, k2tog, yarn over, k1, *k2, yarn over, s2kp2, yarn over, k1; repeat from the * to 4 stitches before the marker, ending this section with k2, yarn over, ssk, yarn over. (15 stitches)

ROW 15: Yarn over, k2, k2tog, yarn over, *k1, yarn over, ssk, k1, k2tog, yarn over; repeat from the * to 5 stitches before the marker, ending this section with k1, yarn over, ssk, k2, yarn over. (17 stitches)

ROW 17: Yarn over, k1, yarn over, s2kp2, yarn over, k1, *k2, yarn over, s2kp2, yarn over, k1; repeat from the * to 6 stitches before the marker, ending this section with k2, yarn over, s2kp2, yarn over, k1, yarn over. (19 stitches)

ROW 18: As Row 2.

Repeat Rows 7–18 for the pattern.

⬆ s2kp2

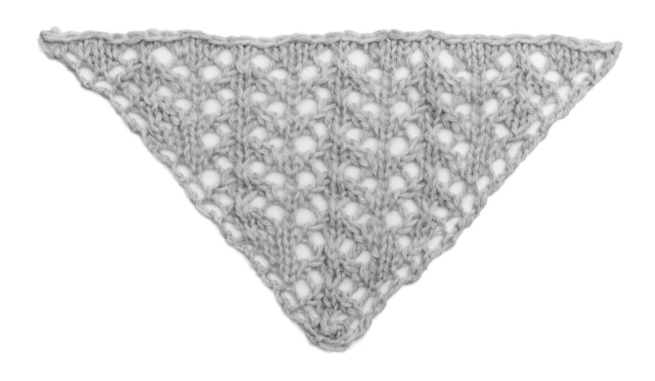

24

ROW 1 (RS): Yarn over, k1, yarn over. (3 stitches)

ROWS 2, 4, 10, 12, 14, AND 16: Purl across.

ROW 3: Yarn over, k3, yarn over. (5 stitches)

ROW 5: Yarn over, k5, yarn over. (7 stitches)

ROWS 6 AND 8: Knit across.

ROW 7: Yarn over, purl across to the marker, ending this section with yarn over. (9 stitches)

ROW 9: Yarn over, knit across to the marker, ending this section with yarn over. (11 stitches)

ROW 11: Yarn over, k2, *k1, k2tog, yarn over, k1, yarn over, ssk; repeat from the * to 3 stitches before the marker, ending this section with k3, yarn over. (13 stitches)

ROW 13: As Row 9. (15 stitches)

ROW 15: Yarn over, k2, yarn over, ssk, *k1, k2tog, yarn over, k1, yarn over, ssk; repeat from the * to 5 stitches before the marker, ending this section with k1, k2tog, yarn over, k2, yarn over. (17 stitches)

ROW 17: As Row 9. (19 stitches)

ROW 18: As Row 6.

Repeat Rows 7–18 for the pattern.

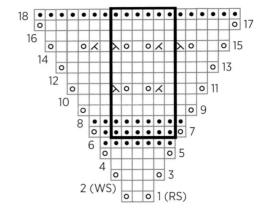

ROW 1 (RS): Yarn over, k1, yarn over. (3 stitches)

ROW 2 AND ALL WS ROWS: Purl across.

ROW 3: Yarn over, k3, yarn over. (5 stitches)

ROW 5: Yarn over, k2, yarn over, ssk, k1, yarn over. (7 stitches)

ROW 7: Yarn over, k1, k2tog, yarn over, k1, yarn over, ssk, k1, yarn over. (9 stitches)

ROW 9: Yarn over, knit across to the marker, ending this section with yarn over. (11 stitches)

ROW 11: Yarn over, k5, yarn over, ssk, k4, yarn over. (13 stitches)

ROW 13: Yarn over, k4, k2tog, yarn over, k1, yarn over, ssk, k4, yarn over. (15 stitches)

ROW 15: As Row 9. (17 stitches)

ROW 17: Yarn over, k3, *k2, yarn over, ssk, k2; repeat from the * to 8 stitches before the marker, ending this section with k2, yarn over, ssk, k4, yarn over. (19 stitches)

ROW 19: Yarn over, k1, yarn over, ssk, k1, *k2tog, yarn over, k1, yarn over, ssk, k1; repeat from the * to 9 stitches before the marker, ending this section with k2tog, yarn over, k1, yarn over, ssk, k4, yarn over. (21 stitches)

ROW 20: As Row 2.

Repeat Rows 15–20 for the pattern.

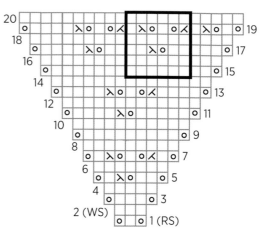

26

ROW 1 (RS): Yarn over, k1, yarn over. (3 stitches)

ROW 2 AND ALL WS ROWS: Purl across.

ROW 3: Yarn over, k3, yarn over. (5 stitches)

ROW 5: Yarn over, k5, yarn over. (7 stitches)

ROW 7: Yarn over, *k1, yarn over, k1, sk2p (page 282), k1, yarn over; repeat from the * to 1 stitch before the marker, ending this section with k1, yarn over. (9 stitches)

ROW 9: Yarn over, k1, *k1, yarn over, k1, sk2p, k1, yarn over; repeat from the * to 2 stitches before the marker, ending this section with k2, yarn over. (11 stitches)

ROW 11: Yarn over, k2, *k1, yarn over, k1, sk2p, k1, yarn over; repeat from the * to 3 stitches before the marker, ending this section with k3, yarn over. (13 stitches)

ROW 13: Yarn over, k2tog, k1, yarn over, *k1, yarn over, k1, sk2p, k1, yarn over; repeat from the * to 4 stitches before the marker, ending this section with k1, yarn over, k1, ssk, yarn over. (15 stitches)

ROW 15: Yarn over, k1, k2tog, k1, yarn over, *k1, yarn over, k1, sk2p, k1, yarn over; repeat from the * to 5 stitches before the marker, ending this section with k1, yarn over, k1, ssk, k1, yarn over. (17 stitches)

ROW 17: Yarn over, k2, k2tog, k1, yarn over, *k1, yarn over, k1, sk2p, k1, yarn over; repeat from the * to 6 stitches before the marker, ending this section with k1, yarn over, k1, ssk, k2, yarn over. (19 stitches)

ROW 18: As Row 2.

Repeat Rows 7–18 for the pattern.

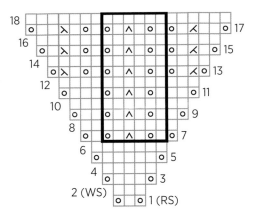

⋀ sk2p

27

NOTE: To create symmetry, this design is different on the right- and left-hand sides. If you are making a two-wedge shawl, follow the instructions for the Right-Hand Side to the center of your shawl, then work the Left-Hand Side instructions. If your shawl has more than two wedges, work the Right-Hand Side instructions first and the Left-Hand Side instructions last, and balance out the wedges in between.

ROW 1 (RS):
Right-Hand Side: Yarn over, k1, yarn over. (3 stitches)
Left-Hand Side: Yarn over, k1, yarn over. (3 stitches)

ROW 2 AND ALL WS ROWS:
Right-Hand and Left-Hand Sides: Purl across.

ROW 3:
Right-Hand Side: Yarn over, k3, yarn over. (5 stitches)
Left-Hand Side: Yarn over, k3, yarn over. (5 stitches)

ROW 5:
Right-Hand Side: Yarn over, k5, yarn over. (7 stitches)
Left-Hand Side: Yarn over, k5, yarn over. (7 stitches)

ROW 7:
Right-Hand Side: Yarn over, *k1, yarn over, ssk, k1, k2tog, yarn over; repeat from the * to 1 stitch before the marker, ending this section with k1, yarn over. (9 stitches)
Left-Hand Side: Yarn over, k1, **yarn over, ssk, k1, k2tog, yarn over, k1; repeat from the ** to the marker, yarn over. (9 stitches)

ROW 9:
Right-Hand Side: Yarn over, k1, *k2, yarn over, k3tog, yarn over, k1; repeat from the * to 2 stitches before the marker, ending this section with k2, yarn over. (11 stitches)
Left-Hand Side: Yarn over, k2 **k1 yarn over, sssk (page 285), yarn over, k2 repeat from the ** to 1 stitch before the marker, ending this section with k1 yarn over. (11 stitches)

ROW 11:
Right-Hand Side: Yarn over, k2, *k2, k2tog, yarn over, k2; repeat from the * to 3 stitches before the marker, ending this section with k3, yarn over. (13 stitches)
Left-Hand Side: Yarn over, k3 **k2, yarn over, ssk, k2; repeat from the ** to 2 stitches before the marker, ending this section with k2, yarn over. (13 stitches)

ROW 12: As Row 2.

Repeat Rows 7–12 for the pattern.

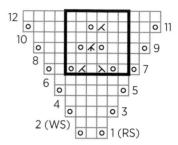

Right-Hand Side

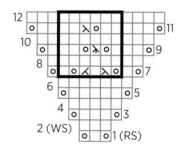

Left-Hand Side

$\overline{\lambda}$ k3tog

$\overline{\lambda}$ sssk

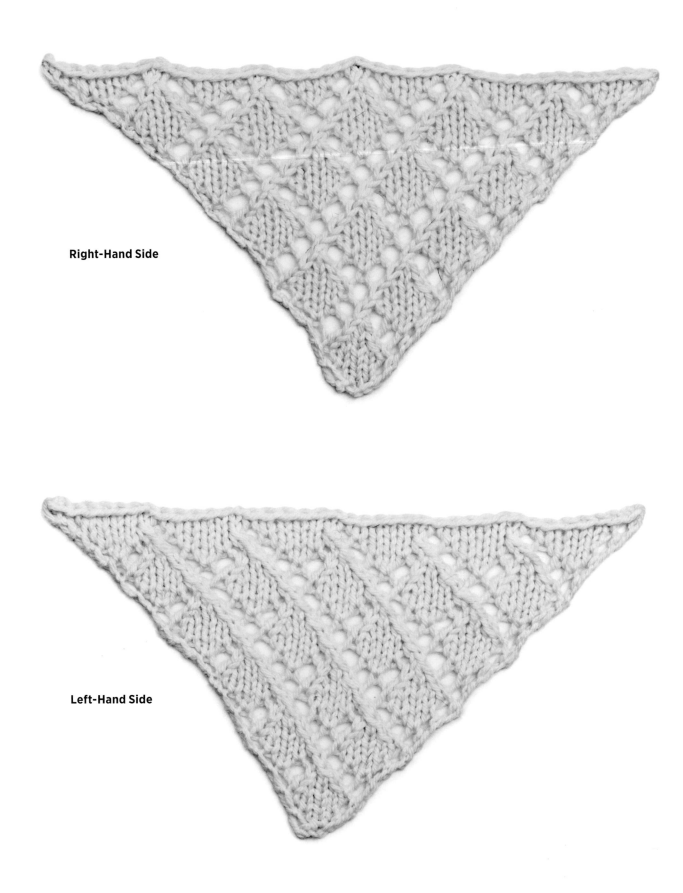

Right-Hand Side

Left-Hand Side

28

ROW 1 (RS): Yarn over, k1, yarn over. (3 stitches)

ROWS 2 AND 4: Purl across.

ROW 3: Yarn over, k3, yarn over. (5 stitches)

ROW 5: Yarn over, k2, yarn over, ssk, k1, yarn over. (7 stitches)

ROW 6: P1, yarn over, p2tog, p1, ssp (page 281), yarn over, p1.

ROW 7: Yarn over, *k2, yarn over, s2kp2 (page 282), yarn over, k1; repeat from the * to 1 stitch before the marker, ending this section with k1, yarn over. (9 stitches)

ROW 8: P2, *ssp, yarn over, p1, yarn over, p2tog, p1; repeat from the * to 1 stitch before the marker, ending this section with p1.

ROW 9: Yarn over, k1, *yarn over, s2kp2, yarn over, k1, yarn over, ssk; repeat from the * to 2 stitches before the marker, ending this section with yarn over, ssk, yarn over. (11 stitches)

ROW 10: P3, *ssp, yarn over, p1, yarn over, p2tog, p1; repeat from the * to 2 stitches before the marker, ending this section with p2.

ROW 11: Yarn over, k1, yarn over, *s2kp2, yarn over, k3, yarn over; repeat from the * to 3 stitches before the marker, ending this section with s2kp2, yarn over, k1, yarn over. (13 stitches)

ROW 12: P1, ssp, yarn over, p1, *yarn over, p2tog, p1, ssp, yarn over, p1; repeat from the * to 3 stitches before the marker, ending this section with yarn over, p2tog, p1.

ROW 13: Yarn over, k1, k2tog, yarn over, *k1, yarn over, ssk, yarn over, s2kp2, yarn over; repeat from the * to 4 stitches before the marker, ending this section with k1, yarn over, ssk, k1, yarn over. (15 stitches)

ROW 14: P2, ssp, yarn over, p1, *yarn over, p2tog, p1, ssp, yarn over, p1; repeat from the * to 4 stitches before the marker, ending this section with yarn over, p2tog, p2.

ROW 15: Yarn over, k1, k2tog, yarn over, k1, *k2, yarn over, s2kp2, yarn over, k1; repeat from the * to 5 stitches before the marker, ending this section with k2, yarn over, ssk, k1, yarn over. (17 stitches)

ROW 16: Ssp, yarn over, p1, yarn over, p2tog, p1, *ssp, yarn over, p1, yarn over, p2tog, p1; repeat from the * to 5 stitches before the marker, ending this sections with ssp, yarn over, p1, yarn over, p2tog.

ROW 17: Yarn over, k2tog, yarn over, k1, yarn over, ssk, *yarn over, s2kp2, yarn over, k1, yarn over, ssk; repeat from the * to 6 stitches before the marker, ending this section with yarn over, s2kp2, yarn over, k1, yarn over, ssk, yarn over. (19 stitches)

ROW 18: P1, ssp, yarn over, p1, yarn over, p2tog, p1, *ssp, yarn over, p1, yarn over, p2tog, p1; repeat from the * to 6 stitches before the marker, ending this section with ssp, yarn over, p1, yarn over, p2tog, p1.

ROW 19: Yarn over, k2tog, yarn over, k3, yarn over, *s2kp2, yarn over, k3, yarn over; repeat from the * to 8 stitches before the marker, ending this section with s2kp2, yarn over, k3, yarn over, ssk, yarn over. (21 stitches)

ROW 20: P2, yarn over, p2tog, p1, ssp, yarn over, p1, *yarn over, p2tog, p1, ssp, yarn over, p1; repeat from the * to 7 stitches before the marker, ending this section with yarn over, p2tog, p1, ssp, yarn over, p2.

ROW 21: Yarn over, k2, yarn over, ssk, yarn over, s2kp2, yarn over, *k1, yarn over, ssk, yarn over, s2kp2, yarn over; repeat from the * to 8 stitches before the marker, ending this section with k1, yarn over, ssk, yarn over, s2kp2, yarn over, k2, yarn over. (23 stitches)

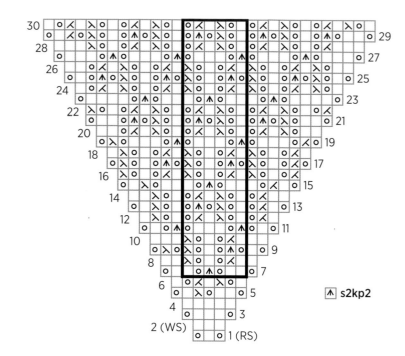

s2kp2

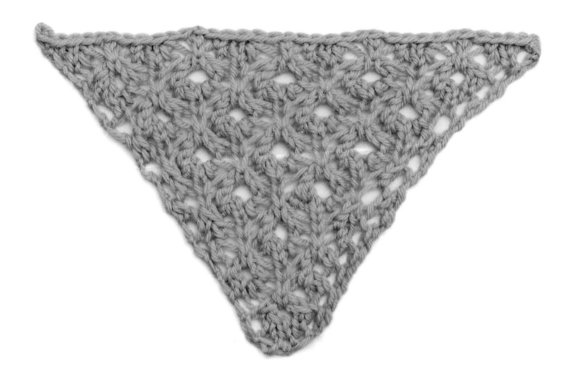

ROW 22: Ssp, yarn over, p1, yarn over, p2tog, p1, ssp, yarn over, p1, *yarn over, p2tog, p1, ssp, yarn over, p1; repeat from the * to 8 stitches before the marker, ending this section with yarn over, p2tog, p1, ssp, yarn over, p1, yarn over, p2tog.

ROW 23: Yarn over, k4, yarn over, s2kp2, yarn over, k1, *k2, yarn over, s2kp2, yarn over, k1; repeat from the * to 9 stitches before the marker, ending this section with k2, yarn over, s2kp2, yarn over, k4, yarn over. (25 stitches)

ROW 24: P1, yarn over, p2tog, p1, ssp, yarn over, p1, yarn over, p2tog, p1, *ssp, yarn over, p1, yarn over, p2tog, p1; repeat from the * to 9 stitches before the marker, ending this section with ssp, yarn over, p1, yarn over, p2tog, p1, ssp, yarn over, p1.

ROW 25: Yarn over, k1, yarn over, ssk, yarn over, s2kp2, yarn over, k1, yarn over, ssk, *yarn over, s2kp2, yarn over, k1, yarn over, ssk; repeat from the * to 9 stitches before the marker, ending this section with yarn over, s2kp2, yarn over, k1, yarn over, ssk, yarn over, s2kp2, yarn over, k1, yarn over. (27 stitches)

ROW 26: P2, yarn over, p2tog, p1, ssp, yarn over, p1, yarn over, p2tog, p1, *ssp, yarn over, p1, yarn over, p2tog, p1; repeat from the * to 10 stitches before the marker, ending this section with ssp, yarn over, p1, yarn over, p2tog, p1, ssp, yarn over, p2.

ROW 27: Yarn over, k3, yarn over, s2kp2, yarn over, k3, yarn over, *s2kp2, yarn over, k3, yarn over; repeat from the * to 12 stitches before the marker, ending this section with (s2kp2, yarn over, k3, yarn over) twice. (29 stitches)

ROW 28: P3, ssp, yarn over, p1, yarn over, p2tog, p1, ssp, yarn over, p1, *yarn over, p2tog, p1, ssp, yarn over, p1; repeat from the * to 11 stitches before the marker, ending this section with yarn over, p2tog, p1, ssp, yarn over, p1, yarn over, p2tog, p3.

ROW 29: Yarn over, k2, yarn over, s2kp2, yarn over, k1, yarn over, ssk, yarn over, s2kp2, yarn over, *k1, yarn over, ssk, yarn over, s2kp2, yarn over; repeat from the * to 12 stitches before the marker, ending this sections with k1, yarn over, ssk, yarn over, s2kp2, yarn over, k1, yarn over, ssk, yarn over, k2tog, k1, yarn over. (31 stitches)

ROW 30: P1, (yarn over, p2tog, p1, ssp, yarn over, p1) twice, *yarn over, p2tog, p1, ssp, yarn over, p1; repeat from the * to 12 stitches before the marker, ending this section with (yarn over, p2tog, p1, ssp, yarn over, p1) twice.

Repeat Rows 7–30 for the pattern.

WEDGES with 8-Stitch Multiples

Start each wedge with the provisional cast on and the tab of your choice (page 10).

29

ROW 1 (RS): Yarn over, k1, yarn over. (3 stitches)

ROW 2 AND ALL WS ROWS: Purl across.

ROW 3: Yarn over, k3, yarn over. (5 stitches)

ROW 5: Yarn over, k5, yarn over. (7 stitches)

ROW 7: Yarn over, k2tog, (k1, yarn over) twice, k1, ssk, yarn over. (9 stitches)

ROW 9: Yarn over, *k1, yarn over, k2tog, k3, ssk, yarn over; repeat from the * to 1 stitch before the marker, ending this section with k1, yarn over. (11 stitches)

ROW 11: Yarn over, k1, *k2, yarn over, k2tog, k1, ssk, yarn over, k1; repeat from the * to 2 stitches before the marker, ending this section with k2, yarn over. (13 stitches)

ROW 13: Yarn over, k2, *k3, yarn over, s2kp2, yarn over, k2; repeat from the * to 3 stitches before the marker, ending this section with k3, yarn over. (15 stitches)

ROW 15: Yarn over, k3, *k1, k2tog, (k1, yarn over) twice, k1, ssk; repeat from the * to 4 stitches before the marker, ending this section with k4, yarn over. (17 stitches)

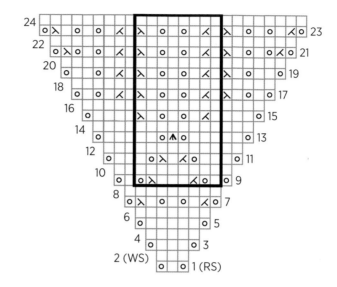

ROW 17: (Yarn over, k1) twice, ssk, *k1, k2tog, (k1, yarn over) twice, k1, ssk; repeat from the * to 5 stitches before the marker, ending this section with k1, k2tog, (k1, yarn over) twice. (19 stitches)

ROW 19: Yarn over, k2, yarn over, k1, ssk, *k1, k2tog, (k1, yarn over) twice, k1, ssk; repeat from the * to 6 stitches before the marker, ending this section with k1, k2tog, k1, yarn over, k2, yarn over. (21 stitches)

ROW 21: Yarn over, k2tog, (yarn over, k1) twice, ssk, *k1, k2tog, (k1, yarn over) twice, k1, ssk; repeat from

the * to 7 stitches before the marker, ending this section with k1, k2tog, (k1, yarn over) twice, ssk, yarn over. (23 stitches)

ROW 23: Yarn over, k2tog, (k1, yarn over) twice, k1, ssk, *k1, k2tog, (k1, yarn over) twice, k1, ssk; repeat from the * to 8 stitches before the marker, ending this section with k1, k2tog, (k1, yarn over) twice, k1, ssk, yarn over. (25 stitches)

ROW 24: As Row 2.

Repeat Rows 9–24 for the pattern.

30

ROW 1 (RS): Yarn over, k1, yarn over. (3 stitches)

ROW 2 AND ALL WS ROWS: Purl across.

ROW 3: Yarn over, k3, yarn over. (5 stitches)

ROW 5: Yarn over, k5, yarn over. (7 stitches)

ROW 7: Yarn over, k7, yarn over. (9 stitches)

ROW 9: Yarn over, k1, *yarn over, k2, s2kp2 (page 282), k2, yarn over, k1; repeat from the * to the marker, ending this section with yarn over. (11 stitches)

ROW 11: Yarn over, k2, *yarn over, k2, s2kp2, k2, yarn over, k1; repeat from the * to 1 stitch before the marker, ending this section with k1, yarn over. (13 stitches)

ROW 13: Yarn over, k3, *yarn over, k2, s2kp2, k2, yarn over, k1; repeat from the * to 2 stitches before the marker, ending this section with k2, yarn over. (15 stitches)

ROW 15: Yarn over, k2tog, k1, yarn over, k1, *yarn over, k2, s2kp2, k2, yarn over, k1; repeat from the * to 3 stitches before the marker, ending this with yarn over, k1, ssk, yarn over. (17 stitches)

ROW 17: Yarn over, k2tog, k2, yarn over, k1, *yarn over, k2, s2kp2, k2, yarn over, k1; repeat from the * to 4 stitches before the marker, ending this section with yarn over, k2, ssk, yarn over. (19 stitches)

ROW 19: Yarn over, k1, k2tog, k2, yarn over, k1, *yarn over, k2, s2kp2, k2, yarn over, k1; repeat from the * to 5 stitches before the marker, ending this section with yarn over, k2, ssk, k1, yarn over. (21 stitches)

ROW 21: Yarn over, k2, k2tog, k2, yarn over, k1, *yarn over, k2, s2kp2, k2, yarn over, k1; repeat from the * to 6 stitches before the marker, ending this section with yarn over, k2, ssk, k2, yarn over. (23 stitches)

ROW 23: Yarn over, k3, k2tog, k2, yarn over, k1, *yarn over, k2, s2kp2, k2, yarn over, k1; repeat from the * to 6 stitches before the marker, ending this section with yarn over, k2, ssk, k3, yarn over. (25 stitches)

ROW 24: As Row 2.

Repeat Rows 9–24 for the pattern.

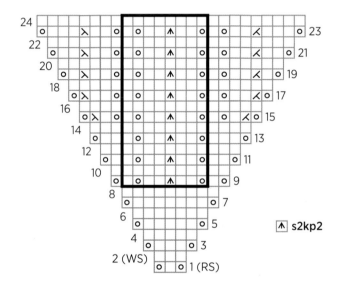

⬆ s2kp2

31

ROW 1 (RS): Yarn over, k1, yarn over. (3 stitches)

ROW 2 AND ALL WS ROWS: Purl across.

ROW 3: Yarn over, k3, yarn over. (5 stitches)

ROW 5: Yarn over, k5, yarn over. (7 stitches)

ROW 7: Yarn over, k2, k2tog, yarn over, k3, yarn over. (9 stitches)

ROW 9: Yarn over, knit across to the marker, ending this section with yarn over. (11 stitches)

ROW 11: Yarn over, k2tog, *yarn over, k6, k2tog; repeat from the * to 1 stitch before the marker, ending this section with yarn over, k1, yarn over. (13 stitches)

ROW 13: As Row 9. (15 stitches)

ROW 15: Yarn over, k3, *k3, k2tog, yarn over, k3; repeat from the * to 4 stitches before the marker, ending this section with k4, yarn over. (17 stitches)

ROW 17: As Row 9. (19 stitches)

ROW 19: Yarn over, k4, k2tog, *yarn over, k6, k2tog; repeat from the * to 5 stitches before the marker, ending this section with yarn over, k5, yarn over. (21 stitches)

ROW 21: As Row 9. (23 stitches)

ROW 23: Yarn over, k7, *k3, k2tog, yarn over, k3; repeat from the * to 8 stitches before the marker, ending this section with k8, yarn over. (25 stitches)

ROW 24: As Row 2.

Repeat Rows 9–24 for the pattern.

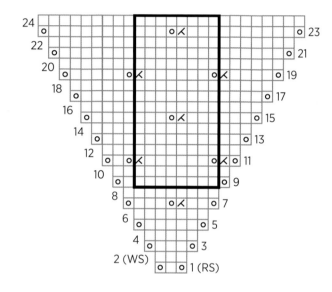

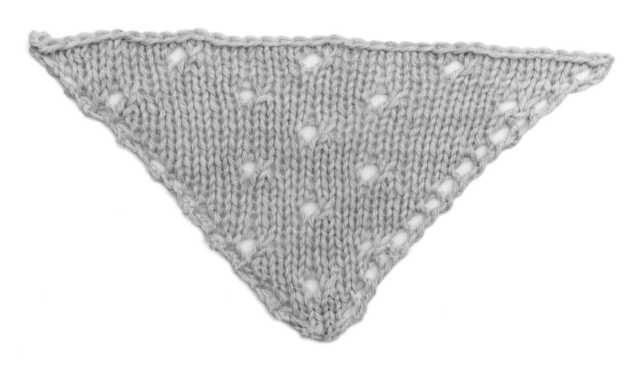

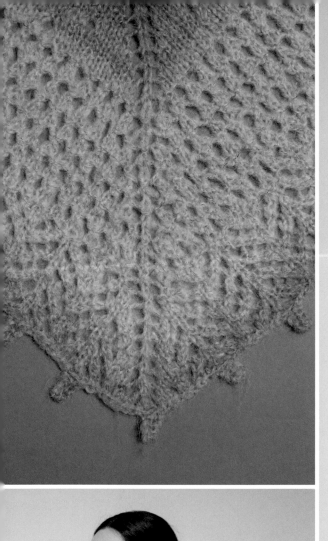

SHAWL #7

In this shawl, a gradient yarn highlights the changing stitch patterns. See page 273 for instructions.

32

ROW 1 (RS): Yarn over, k1, yarn over. (3 stitches)

ROW 2 AND ALL WS ROWS: Purl across.

ROW 3: Yarn over, k3, yarn over. (5 stitches)

ROW 5: Yarn over, k5, yarn over. (7 stitches)

ROW 7: Yarn over, k7, yarn over. (9 stitches)

ROW 9: Yarn over, k1, k2tog, yarn over, k3, yarn over, ssk, k1, yarn over. (11 stitches)

ROW 11: Yarn over, k1, k2tog, yarn over, k1, yarn over, sssk (page 285), yarn over, k1, yarn over, ssk, k1, yarn over. (13 stitches)

ROW 13: Yarn over, k5, yarn over, sssk, yarn over, k5, yarn over. (15 stitches)

ROW 15: Yarn over, k6, yarn over, sssk, yarn over, k6, yarn over. (17 stitches)

ROW 17: Yarn over, k2, *yarn over, ssk, k1, k2tog, yarn over, k3; repeat from the * to 7 stitches before the marker, ending this section with yarn over, ssk, k1, k2tog, yarn over, k2, yarn over. (19 stitches)

ROW 19: Yarn over, k1, ssk, yarn over, *k1, yarn over, s2kp2 (page 282), yarn over, k1, yarn over, sssk, yarn over; repeat from the * to 8 stitches before the marker, ending this section with k1, yarn over, s2kp2, yarn over, k1, yarn over, ssk, k1, yarn over. (21 stitches)

ROW 21: Yarn over, k1, yarn over, sssk, yarn over, *k5, yarn over, sssk, yarn over; repeat from the * to 9 stitches before the marker, ending this section with k5, yarn over, sssk, yarn over, k1, yarn over. (23 stitches)

ROW 23: Yarn over, k2, yarn over, sssk, yarn over, *k5, yarn over, sssk, yarn over; repeat from the * to 10 stitches before the marker, ending this section with k5, yarn over, sssk, yarn over, k2, yarn over. (25 stitches)

ROW 25: Yarn over, k1, k2tog, yarn over, k3, *yarn over, ssk, k1, k2tog, yarn over, k3; repeat from the * to 11 stitches before the marker, ending this section with yarn over, ssk, k1, k2tog, yarn over, k3, yarn over, ssk, k1, yarn over. (27 stitches)

ROW 27: Yarn over, k1, k2tog, yarn over, k1, yarn over, sssk, yarn over, *k1, yarn over, s2kp2, yarn over, k1, yarn over, sssk, yarn over; repeat from the * to 12 stitches before the marker, ending this section with k1, yarn over, s2kp2, yarn over, k1, yarn over, sssk, yarn over, k1, yarn over, ssk, k1, yarn over. (29 stitches)

ROW 29: Yarn over, k5, yarn over, sssk, yarn over, *k5, yarn over, sssk, yarn over; repeat from the * to 13 stitches before the marker, ending this section with k5, yarn over, sssk, yarn over, k5, yarn over. (31 stitches)

ROW 31: Yarn over, k6, yarn over, sssk, yarn over, *k5, yarn over, sssk, yarn over; repeat from the * to 14 stitches before the marker, ending this section with k5, yarn over, sssk, yarn over, k6, yarn over. (33 stitches)

ROW 32: As Row 2.

Repeat Rows 17–32 for the pattern.

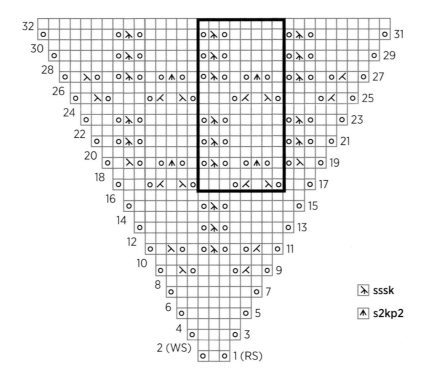

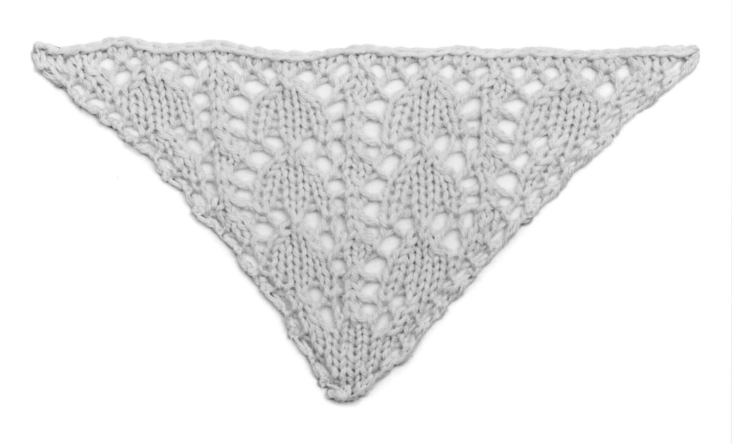

sssk

s2kp2

33

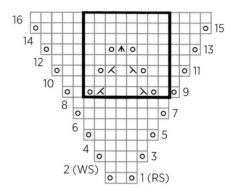

ROW 1 (RS): Yarn over, k1, yarn over. (3 stitches)

ROW 2 AND ALL WS ROWS: Purl across.

ROW 3: Yarn over, k3, yarn over. (5 stitches)

ROW 5: Yarn over, k5, yarn over. (7 stitches)

ROW 7: Yarn over, k7, yarn over. (9 stitches)

ROW 9: Yarn over, *k1, yarn over, ssk, k3, k2tog, yarn over; repeat from the * to 1 stitch before the marker, ending this section with k1, yarn over. (11 stitches)

ROW 11: Yarn over, k1, *k2, yarn over, ssk, k1, k2tog, yarn over, k1; repeat from the * to 2 stitches before the marker, ending this section with k2, yarn over. (13 stitches)

ROW 13: Yarn over, k2, *k3, yarn over, s2kp2 (page 282), yarn over, k2; repeat from the * to 3 stitches before the marker, ending this section with k3, yarn over. (15 stitches)

ROW 15: Yarn over, knit across to the marker, ending this section with yarn over. (17 stitches)

ROW 16: As Row 2.

Repeat Rows 9–16 for the pattern.

⬆ s2kp2

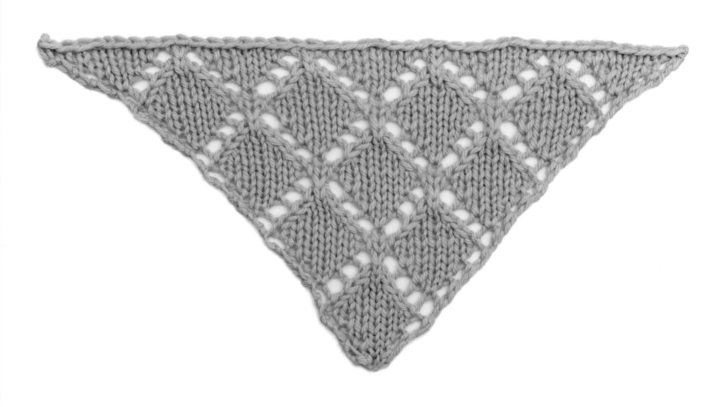

34

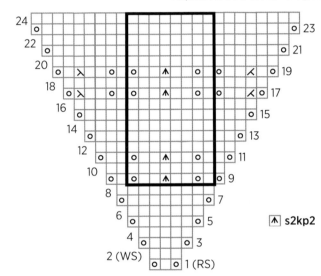

ROW 1 (RS): Yarn over, k1, yarn over. (3 stitches)

ROW 2 AND ALL WS ROWS: Purl across.

ROW 3: Yarn over, k3, yarn over. (5 stitches)

ROW 5: Yarn over, k5, yarn over. (7 stitches)

ROW 7: Yarn over, k7, yarn over. (9 stitches)

ROW 9: Yarn over, *k1, yarn over, k2, s2kp2 (page 282), k2, yarn over; repeat from the * to 1 stitch before the marker, ending this section with k1, yarn over. (11 stitches)

ROW 11: Yarn over, k1, *k1, yarn over, k2, s2kp2, k2, yarn over; repeat from the * to 2 stitches before the marker, ending this section with k2, yarn over. (13 stitches)

ROW 13: Yarn over, knit across to the marker, ending this section with yarn over. (15 stitches)

ROW 15: As Row 13. (17 stitches)

ROW 17: Yarn over, k2tog, k2, yarn over, *k1, yarn over, k2, s2kp2, k2, yarn over; repeat from the * to 5 stitches before the marker, ending this section with k1, yarn over, k2, ssk, yarn over. (19 stitches)

ROW 19: Yarn over, k1, k2tog, k2, yarn over, *k1, yarn over, k2, s2kp2, k2, yarn over; repeat from the * to 6 stitches before the marker, ending this section with k1, yarn over, k2, ssk, k1, yarn over. (21 stitches)

ROW 21: As Row 13. (23 stitches)

ROW 23: As Row 13. (25 stitches)

ROW 24: As Row 2.

Repeat Rows 9–24 for the pattern.

⊼ s2kp2

35

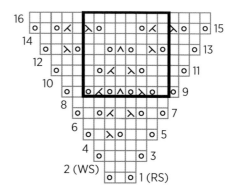

ROW 1 (RS): Yarn over, k1, yarn over. (3 stitches)

ROW 2 AND ALL WS ROWS: Purl across.

ROW 3: Yarn over, k3, yarn over. (5 stitches)

ROW 5: Yarn over, k2, yarn over, ssk, k1, yarn over. (7 stitches)

ROW 7: Yarn over, k1, yarn over, ssk, k1, k2tog, yarn over, k1, yarn over. (9 stitches)

ROW 9: Yarn over, *k1, yarn over, ssk, yarn over, sk2p (page 282), yarn over, k2tog, yarn over; repeat from the * to 1 stitch before the marker, ending this section with k1, yarn over. (11 stitches)

ROW 11: Yarn over, k1, *k2, yarn over, ssk, k1, k2tog, yarn over, k1; repeat from the * to 2 stitches before the marker, ending this section with k2, yarn over. (13 stitches)

ROW 13: Yarn over, k2, *yarn over, ssk, k1, yarn over, sk2p, yarn over, k2; repeat from the * to 3 stitches before the marker, ending this section with yarn over, ssk, k1, yarn over. (15 stitches)

ROW 15: Yarn over, k1, yarn over, ssk, *k1, k2tog, yarn over, k3, yarn over, ssk; repeat from the * to 4 stitches before the marker, ending this section with k1, k2tog, yarn over, k1, yarn over. (17 stitches)

ROW 16: As Row 2.

Repeat Rows 9–16 for the pattern.

⋀ **sk2p**

36

ROW 1 (RS): Yarn over, k1, yarn over. (3 stitches)

ROW 2 AND ALL WS ROWS: Purl across.

ROW 3: Yarn over, k3, yarn over. (5 stitches)

ROW 5: Yarn over, k5, yarn over. (7 stitches)

ROW 7: Yarn over, k7, yarn over. (9 stitches)

ROW 9: Yarn over, *k2, yarn over, ssk, k1, k2tog, yarn over, k1; repeat from the * to 1 stitch before the marker, ending this section with k1, yarn over. (11 stitches)

ROW 11: Yarn over, k1, *ssk, yarn over, k1, yarn over, sssk (page 285), yarn over, k1, yarn over; repeat from the * to 3 stitches before the marker, ending this section with ssk, k1, yarn over. (13 stitches)

ROW 13: Yarn over, k1, yarn over, *sssk, yarn over, k5, yarn over; repeat from the * to 4 stitches before the marker, ending this section with sssk, yarn over, k1, yarn over. (15 stitches)

ROW 15: Yarn over, k2, yarn over, *sssk, yarn over, k5, yarn over; repeat from the * to 5 stitches before the marker, ending this section with sssk, yarn over, k2, yarn over. (17 stitches)

ROW 16: As Row 2.

Repeat Rows 9–16 for the pattern.

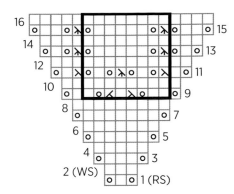

λ sssk

37

ROW 1 (RS): Yarn over, k1, yarn over. (3 stitches)

ROWS 2 AND 4: Purl across.

ROW 3: Yarn over, k3, yarn over. (5 stitches)

ROW 5: Yarn over, k5, yarn over. (7 stitches)

ROW 6: K1, p5, k1.

ROW 7: Yarn over, p1, k5, p1, yarn over. (9 stitches)

ROW 8: P1, k1, p5, k1, p1.

ROW 9: Yarn over, *k1, yarn over, ssk, k3, k2tog, yarn over; repeat from the * to 1 stitch before the marker, ending this section with k1, yarn over. (11 stitches)

ROW 10: P2, *p1, yarn over, p2tog, p1, ssp (page 281), yarn over, p2; repeat from the * to 1 stitch before the marker, p1.

ROW 11: Yarn over, k1, *k3, yarn over, s2kp2 (page 282), yarn over, k2; repeat from the * to 2 stitches before the marker, ending this section with k2, yarn over. (13 stitches)

ROW 12: P3, *p2, k1, p1, k1, p3; repeat from the * to 2 stitches before the marker, ending this section with p2.

ROW 13: Yarn over, k2, *k3, p1, k1, p1, k2; repeat from the * to 3 stitches before the marker, ending this section with k3, yarn over. (15 stitches)

ROW 14: P4, *p2, k1, p1, k1, p3; repeat from the * to 3 stitches before the marker, ending this section with p3.

ROW 15: Yarn over, k3, *k3, p1, k1, p1, k2; repeat from the * to 4 stitches before the marker, ending this section with k4, yarn over. (17 stitches)

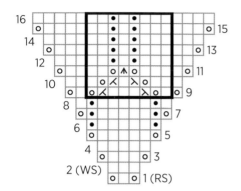

⊼ s2kp2

ROW 16: P5, *p2, k1, p1, k1, p3; repeat from the * to 4 stitches before the marker, ending this section with p4.

Repeat Rows 9–16 for the pattern.

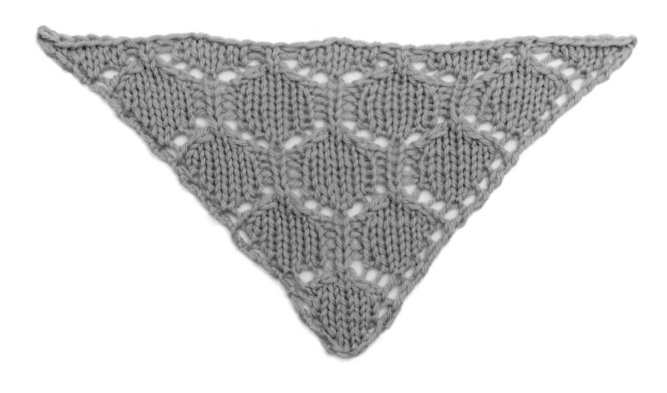

38

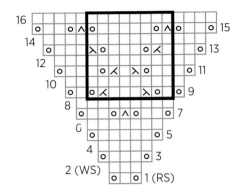

ROW 1 (RS): Yarn over, k1, yarn over. (3 stitches)

ROW 2 AND ALL WS ROWS: Purl across.

ROW 3: Yarn over, k3, yarn over. (5 stitches)

ROW 5: Yarn over, k5, yarn over. (7 stitches)

ROW 7: Yarn over, k2, yarn over, sk2p (page 282), yarn over, k2, yarn over. (9 stitches)

ROW 9: Yarn over, *k1, yarn over, ssk, k3, k2tog, yarn over; repeat from the * to 1 stitch before the marker, ending this section with k1, yarn over. (11 stitches)

ROW 11: Yarn over, k1, *k2, yarn over, ssk, k1, k2tog, yarn over, k1; repeat from the * to 2 stitches before the marker, ending this section with k2, yarn over. (13 stitches)

ROW 13: Yarn over, k2, *k1, k2tog, yarn over, k3, yarn over, ssk; repeat from the * to 3 stitches before the marker, ending this section with k3, yarn over. (15 stitches)

ROW 15: Yarn over, k2, yarn over, *sk2p, yarn over, k5, yarn over; repeat from the * to 5 stitches before the marker, ending this section with sk2p, yarn over, k2, yarn over. (17 stitches)

ROW 16: As Row 2.

Repeat Rows 9–16 for the pattern.

⋀ sk2p

39

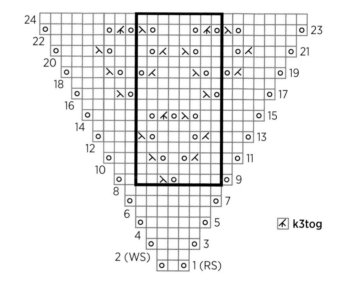

ROW 1 (RS): Yarn over, k1, yarn over. (3 stitches)

ROW 2 AND ALL WS ROWS: Purl across.

ROW 3: Yarn over, k3, yarn over. (5 stitches)

ROW 5: Yarn over, k5, yarn over. (7 stitches)

ROW 7: Yarn over, k7, yarn over. (9 stitches)

ROW 9: Yarn over, *k4, yarn over, ssk, k2; repeat from the * to 1 stitch before the marker, ending this section with k1, yarn over. (11 stitches)

ROW 11: Yarn over, k1, *k2, k2tog, yarn over, k1, yarn over, ssk, k1; repeat from the * to 2 stitches before the marker, ending this section with k2, yarn over. (13 stitches)

ROW 13: Yarn over, k2, *k1, k2tog, yarn over, k3, yarn over, ssk; repeat from the * to 3 stitches before the marker, ending this section with k3, yarn over. (15 stitches)

ROW 15: Yarn over, k3, *k2, yarn over, ssk, yarn over, k3tog, yarn over, k1; repeat from the * to 4 stitches before the marker, ending this section with k4, yarn over. (17 stitches)

ROW 17: Yarn over, k4, *yarn over, ssk, k6; repeat from the * to 5 stitches before the marker, ending this section with yarn over, ssk, k3, yarn over. (19 stitches)

ROW 19: Yarn over, k3, k2tog, yarn over, *k1, yarn over, ssk, k3, k2tog, yarn over; repeat from the * to 6 stitches before the marker, ending this section with k1, yarn over, ssk, k3, yarn over. (21 stitches)

ROW 21: Yarn over, k3, k2tog, yarn over, k1, *k2, yarn over, ssk, k1, k2tog, yarn over, k1; repeat from the * to 7 stitches before the marker, ending this section with k2, yarn over, ssk, k3, yarn over. (23 stitches)

ROW 23: Yarn over, k5, yarn over, ssk, *yarn over, k3tog, yarn over, k3, yarn over, ssk; repeat from the * to 8 stitches before the marker, ending this section with yarn over, k3tog, yarn over, k5, yarn over. (25 stitches)

ROW 24: As Row 2.

Repeat Rows 9–24 for the pattern.

⊼ k3tog

40

ROW 1 (RS): Yarn over, p1, yarn over. (3 stitches)

ROW 2 AND ALL WS ROWS: Purl across.

ROW 3: Yarn over, k3, yarn over. (5 stitches)

ROW 5: Yarn over, k2tog, yarn over, k1, yarn over, ssk, yarn over. (7 stitches)

ROW 7: Yarn over, k1, k2tog, yarn over, k1, yarn over, ssk, k1, yarn over. (9 stitches)

ROW 9: Yarn over, *k2, k2tog, yarn over, k1, yarn over, ssk, k1; repeat from the * to 1 stitch before the marker, ending this section with k1, yarn over. (11 stitches)

ROW 11: Yarn over, k1, *k1, k2tog, yarn over, k3, yarn over, ssk; repeat from the * to 2 stitches before the marker, ending this section with k2, yarn over. (13 stitches)

ROW 13: Yarn over, k2 *k1, ssk, (k1, yarn over) twice, k1, k2tog; repeat from the * to 3 stitches before the marker, ending with k3, yarn over. (15 stitches)

ROW 15: Yarn over, k3, *k1, k2tog, (k1, yarn over) twice, k1, ssk; repeat from the * to 4 stitches before the marker, ending this section with k4, yarn over. (17 stitches)

ROW 17: Yarn over, k2, k2tog, yarn over, *k1, yarn over, ssk, k3, k2tog, yarn over; repeat from the * to 5 stitches before the marker, ending this section with k1, yarn over, ssk, k2, yarn over. (19 stitches)

ROW 19: Yarn over, k1, yarn over, ssk, k2, *k2, yarn over, ssk, k1, k2tog, yarn over, k1; repeat from the * to 6 stitches before the marker, ending this section with k3, k2tog, yarn over, k1, yarn over. (21 stitches)

ROW 21: Yarn over, k3, ssk, k1, yarn over, *k1, yarn over, k1, k2tog, k1, ssk, k1, yarn over; repeat from the * to 7 stitches before the marker, ending this section with k1, yarn over, k1, k2tog, k3, yarn over. (23 stitches)

ROW 23: Yarn over, k4, k2tog, k1, yarn over, *k1, yarn over, k1, ssk, k1, k2tog, k1, yarn over; repeat from the * to 8 stitches before the marker, ending this section with k1, yarn over, k1, ssk, k4, yarn over. (25 stitches)

ROW 24: As Row 2.

Repeat Rows 9–24 for the pattern.

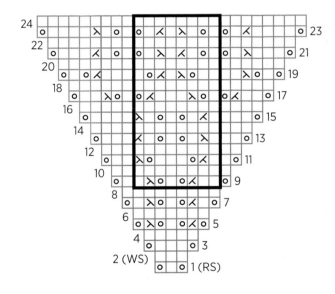

41

NOTE: To create symmetry, this design is different on the right- and left-hand sides. If you are making a two-wedge shawl, follow the instructions for the Right-Hand Side to the center of your shawl, then work the Left-Hand Side instructions. If your shawl has more than two wedges, work the Right-Hand Side instructions first and the Left-Hand Side instructions last, and balance out the wedges in between.

ROW 1 (RS):

Right-Hand Side: Yarn over, k1, yarn over. (3 stitches)

Left-Hand Side: Yarn over, k1, yarn over. (3 stitches)

ROW 2, 6, 8, 10, 14, 16, 18, 22, 24, 26, 30, 32, 34, 38, 40, 42, 46, 48, 50, AND 54:

Right-Hand and Left-Hand Sides: Knit the knit stitches and purl the purl stitches and yarn overs.

ROW 3:

Right-Hand Side: Yarn over, k3, yarn over. (5 stitches)

Left-Hand Side: Yarn over, k3, yarn over. (5 stitches)

ROWS 4, 12, 20, 28, 36, 44, AND 52:

Right-Hand and Left-Hand Sides: K1, knit the knit stitches and purl the purl stitches until 1 stitch remains in the row, k1.

ROW 5:

Right-Hand Side: Yarn over, p1, yarn over, s2kp2 (page 282), yarn over, p1, yarn over. (7 stitches)

Left-Hand Side: Yarn over, p1, yarn over, s2kp2, yarn over, p1, yarn over. (7 stitches)

ROW 7:

Right-Hand Side: Yarn over, k1, p1, yarn over, s2kp2, yarn over, p1, k1, yarn over. (9 stitches)

Left-Hand Side: Yarn over, k1, p1, yarn over, s2kp2, yarn over, p1, k1, yarn over. (9 stitches)

ROW 9:

Right-Hand Side: Yarn over, k2, p1, yarn over, s2kp2, yarn over, p1, k2, yarn over. (11 stitches)

Left-Hand Side: Yarn over, k2, p1, yarn over, s2kp2, yarn over, p1, k2, yarn over. (11 stitches)

ROW 11:

Right-Hand Side: Yarn over, k3, p1, yarn over, s2kp2, yarn over, p1, k3, yarn over. (13 stitches)

Left-Hand Side: Yarn over, k3, p1, yarn over, s2kp2, yarn over, p1, k3, yarn over. (13 stitches)

ROW 13:

Right-Hand Side: Yarn over, p1, C1R (page 285), p1, yarn over, s2kp2, yarn over, p1, C1R, p1, yarn over. (15 stitches)

Left-Hand Side: Yarn over, p1, C1L, p1, yarn over, s2kp2, yarn over, p1, C1L, p1, yarn over. (15 stitches)

ROW 15:

Right-Hand Side: Yarn over, k1, p1, k3, p1, yarn over, s2kp2, yarn over, p1, k3, p1, k1, yarn over. (17 stitches)

Left-Hand Side: Yarn over, k1, p1, k3, p1, yarn over, s2kp2, yarn over, p1, k3, p1, k1, yarn over. (17 stitches)

ROW 17:

Right-Hand Side: Yarn over, k2tog, yarn over, p1, C1R, p1, yarn over, s2kp2, yarn over, p1, C1R, p1, yarn over, ssk, yarn over. (19 stitches)

Left-Hand Side: Yarn over, k2tog, yarn over, p1, C1L, p1, yarn over, s2kp2, yarn over, p1, C1L, p1, yarn over, ssk, yarn over. (19 stitches)

ROW 19:

Right-Hand Side: Yarn over, k1, k2tog, yarn over, p1, k3, p1, yarn over, s2kp2, yarn over, p1, k3, p1, yarn over, ssk, k1, yarn over. (21 stitches)

Left-Hand Side: Yarn over, k1, k2tog, yarn over, p1, k3, p1, yarn over, s2kp2, yarn over, p1, k3, p1, yarn over, ssk, k1, yarn over. (21 stitches)

ROW 21:

Right-Hand Side: Yarn over, p1, (yarn over, s2kp2, yarn over, p1, C1R, p1) twice, yarn over, s2kp2, yarn over, p1, yarn over. (23 stitches)

Left-Hand Side: Yarn over, p1, (yarn over, s2kp2, yarn over, p1, C1L, p1) twice, yarn over, s2kp2, yarn over, p1, yarn over. (23 stitches)

ROW 23:

Right-Hand Side: Yarn over, k1, p1, yarn over, s2kp2, yarn over, p1, *k3, p1, yarn over, s2kp2, yarn over, p1; repeat from the * to 9 stitches before the marker, ending this section with k3, p1, yarn over, s2kp2, yarn over, p1, k1, yarn over. (25 stitches)

Left-Hand Side: Yarn over, k1, p1, yarn over, s2kp2, yarn over, p1, *k3, p1, yarn over, s2kp2, yarn over, p1; repeat from the * to 9 stitches before the marker, ending this section with k3, p1, yarn over, s2kp2, yarn over, p1, k1, yarn over. (25 stitches)

ROW 25:

Right-Hand Side: Yarn over, k2, p1, yarn over, s2kp2, yarn over, p1, *C1R, p1, yarn over, s2kp2, yarn over, p1; repeat from the * to 10 stitches before the marker, ending this section with C1R, p1, yarn over, s2kp2, yarn over, p1, k2, yarn over. (27 stitches)

Left-Hand Side: Yarn over, k2, p1, yarn over, s2kp2, yarn over, p1, *C1L, p1, yarn over, s2kp2, yarn over, p1; repeat from the * to 10 stitches before the marker, ending this section with C1L, p1, yarn over, s2kp2, yarn over, p1, k2, yarn over. (27 stitches)

ROW 27:

Right-Hand Side: Yarn over, k3, p1, yarn over, s2kp2, yarn over, p1, *k3, p1, yarn over, s2kp2, yarn over, p1; repeat from the * to 11 stitches before the marker, ending this section with k3, p1, yarn over, s2kp2, yarn over, p1, k3, yarn over. (29 stitches)

(continued on page 60)

Right-Hand Side

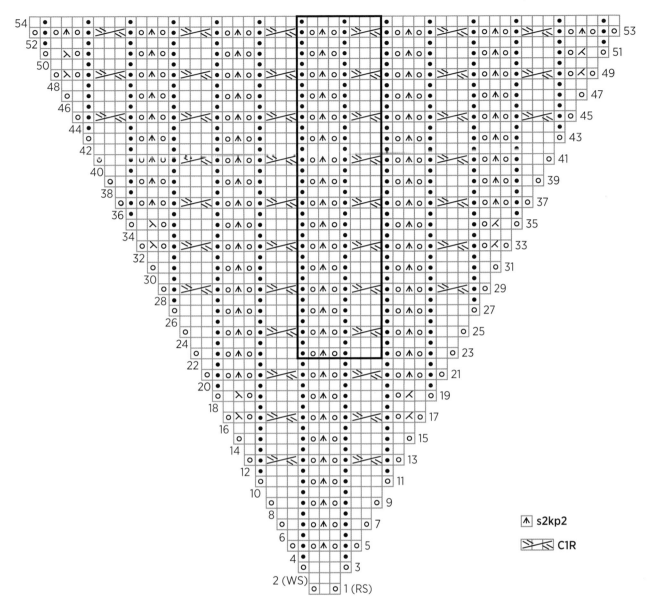

 s2kp2	
 C1R	

WEDGE 41, *continued*

Left-Hand Side: Yarn over, k3, p1, yarn over, s2kp2, yarn over, p1, *k3, p1, yarn over, s2kp2, yarn over, p1; repeat from the * to 11 stitches before the marker, ending this section with k3, p1, yarn over, s2kp2, yarn over, p1, k3, yarn over. (29 stitches)

ROW 29:

Right-Hand Side: Yarn over, p1, C1R, p1, yarn over, s2kp2, yarn over, p1, *C1R, p1, yarn over, s2kp2, yarn over, p1; repeat from the * to 12 stitches before the marker, ending this section with C1R, p1, yarn over, s2kp2, yarn over, p1, C1R, p1, yarn over. (31 stitches)

Left-Hand Side: Yarn over, p1, C1L, p1, yarn over, s2kp2, yarn over, p1, *C1L, p1, yarn over, s2kp2, yarn over, p1; repeat from the * to 12 stitches before the marker, ending this section with C1L, p1, yarn over, s2kp2, yarn over, p1, C1L, p1, yarn over. (31 stitches)

ROW 31:

Right-Hand Side: Yarn over, k1, p1, k3, p1, yarn over, s2kp2, yarn over, p1, *k3, p1, yarn over, s2kp2, yarn over, p1; repeat from the * to 13 stitches before the marker, ending this section with k3, p1, yarn over, s2kp2, yarn over, p1, k3, p1, k1, yarn over. (33 stitches)

Left-Hand Side: Yarn over, k1, p1, k3, p1, yarn over, s2kp2, yarn over, p1, *k3, p1, yarn over, s2kp2, yarn over, p1; repeat from the * to 13 stitches before the marker, ending this section with k3, p1, yarn over, s2kp2, yarn over, p1, k3, p1, k1, yarn over. (33 stitches)

ROW 33:

Right-Hand Side: Yarn over, k2tog, yarn over, p1, C1R, p1, yarn over, s2kp2, yarn over, p1, *C1R, p1, yarn over, s2kp2, yarn over, p1; repeat from the * to 14 stitches before the marker, ending this section with C1R, p1, yarn over, s2kp2, yarn over, p1, C1R, p1, yarn over, ssk, yarn over. (35 stitches)

Left-Hand Side: Yarn over, k2tog, yarn over, p1, C1L, p1, yarn over, s2kp2, yarn over, p1, *C1L, p1, yarn over, s2kp2, yarn over, p1; repeat from the * to 14 stitches before the marker, ending this section with C1L, p1, yarn over, s2kp2, yarn over, p1, C1L, p1, yarn over, ssk, yarn over. (35 stitches)

ROW 35:

Right-Hand Side: Yarn over, k1, k2tog, yarn over, p1, k3, p1, yarn over, s2kp2, yarn over, p1, *k3, p1, yarn over, s2kp2, yarn over, p1; repeat from the * to 15 stitches before the marker, ending this section with k3, p1, yarn over, s2kp2, yarn over, p1, k3, p1, yarn over, ssk, k1, yarn over. (37 stitches)

Left-Hand Side: Yarn over, k1, k2tog, yarn over, p1, k3, p1, yarn over, s2kp2, yarn over, p1, *k3, p1, yarn over, s2kp2, yarn over, p1; repeat from the * to 15 stitches before the marker, ending this section with k3, p1, yarn over, s2kp2, yarn over, p1, k3, p1, yarn over, ssk, k1, yarn over. (37 stitches)

ROW 37:

Right-Hand Side: Yarn over, p1, yarn over, s2kp2, yarn over, p1, C1R, p1, yarn over, s2kp2, yarn over, p1, *C1R, p1, yarn over, s2kp2, yarn over, p1; repeat from the * to 16 stitches before the marker, ending this section with (C1R, p1, yarn over, s2kp2, yarn over, p1) twice, yarn over. (39 stitches)

Left-Hand Side: Yarn over, p1, yarn over, s2kp2, yarn over, p1, C1L, p1, yarn over, s2kp2, yarn over, p1, *C1L, p1, yarn over, s2kp2, yarn over, p1; repeat from the * to 16 stitches before the marker, ending this section with (C1L, p1, yarn over, s2kp2, yarn over, p1) twice, yarn over. (39 stitches)

ROW 39:

Right-Hand Side: Yarn over, k1, p1, yarn over, s2kp2, yarn over, p1, k3, p1, yarn over, s2kp2, yarn over, p1, *k3, p1, yarn over, s2kp2, yarn over, p1; repeat from the * to 17 stitches before the marker, ending this section with (k3, p1, yarn over, s2kp2, yarn over, p1) twice, k1, yarn over. (41 stitches)

Left-Hand Side: Yarn over, k1, p1, yarn over, s2kp2, yarn over, p1, k3, p1, yarn over, s2kp2, yarn over, p1, *k3, p1, yarn over, s2kp2, yarn over, p1; repeat from the * to 17 stitches before the marker, ending this section with (k3, p1, yarn over, s2kp2, yarn over, p1) twice, k1, yarn over. (41 stitches)

ROW 41:

Right-Hand Side: Yarn over, k2, p1, yarn over, s2kp2, yarn over, p1, C1R, p1, yarn over, s2kp2, yarn over, p1, *C1R, p1, yarn over, s2kp2, yarn over, p1; repeat from the * to 18 stitches before the marker, ending this section with (C1R, p1, yarn over, s2kp2, yarn over, p1) twice, k2, yarn over. (43 stitches)

Left-Hand Side: Yarn over, k2, p1, yarn over, s2kp2, yarn over, p1, C1L, p1, yarn over, s2kp2, yarn over, p1, *C1L, p1, yarn over, s2kp2, yarn over, p1; repeat from the * to 18 stitches before the marker, ending this section with (C1L, p1, yarn over, s2kp2, yarn over, p1) twice, k2, yarn over. (43 stitches)

ROW 43:

Right-Hand Side: Yarn over, k3, p1, yarn over, s2kp2, yarn over, p1, k3, p1, yarn over, s2kp2, yarn over, p1, *k3, p1, yarn over, s2kp2, yarn over, p1; repeat from the * to 19 stitches before the marker, ending this section with (k3, p1, yarn over, s2kp2, yarn over, p1) twice, k3, yarn over. (45 stitches)

(continued on page 62)

Left-Hand Side

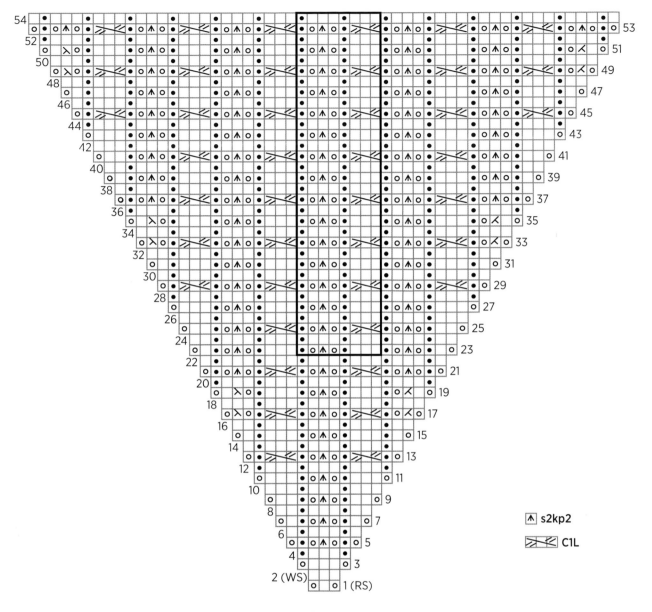

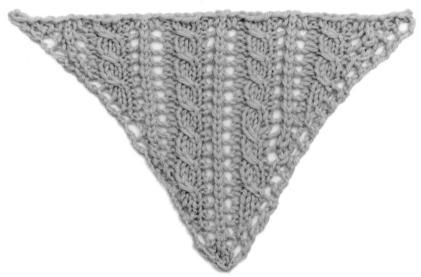

⬆ s2kp2

⤬ C1L

WEDGE 41, *continued*

Left-Hand Side: Yarn over, k3, p1, yarn over, s2kp2, yarn over, p1, k3, p1, yarn over, s2kp2, yarn over, p1, *k3, p1, yarn over, s2kp2, yarn over, p1; repeat from the * to 19 stitches before the marker, ending this section with (k3, p1, yarn over, s2kp2, yarn over, p1) twice, k3, yarn over. (45 stitches)

ROW 45:

Right-Hand Side: Yarn over, p1, (C1R, p1, yarn over, s2kp2, yarn over, p1) twice, *C1R, p1, yarn over, s2kp2, yarn over, p1; repeat from the * to 20 stitches before the marker, ending this section with (C1R, p1, yarn over, s2kp2, yarn over, p1) twice, C1R, p1, yarn over. (47 stitches)

Left-Hand Side: Yarn over, p1, (C1L, p1, yarn over, s2kp2, yarn over, p1) twice, *C1L, p1, yarn over, s2kp2, yarn over, p1; repeat from the * to 20 stitches before the marker, ending this section with (C1L, p1, yarn over, s2kp2, yarn over, p1) twice, C1L, p1, yarn over. (47 stitches)

ROW 47:

Right-Hand Side: Yarn over, k1, p1, k3, p1, yarn over, s2kp2, yarn over, p1, k3, p1, yarn over, s2kp2, yarn over, p1, *k3, p1, yarn over, s2kp2, yarn over, p1; repeat from the * to 21 stitches before the marker, ending this section with (k3, p1, yarn over, s2kp2, yarn over, p1) twice, k3, p1, k1, yarn over. (49 stitches)

Left-Hand Side: Yarn over, k1, p1, k3, p1, yarn over, s2kp2, yarn over, p1, k3, p1, yarn over, s2kp2, yarn over, p1, *k3, p1, yarn over, s2kp2, yarn over, p1; repeat from the * to 21 stitches before the marker, ending this section with (k3, p1, yarn over, s2kp2, yarn over, p1) twice, k3, p1, k1, yarn over. (49 stitches)

ROW 49:

Right-Hand Side: Yarn over, k2tog, yarn over, p1, (C1R, p1, yarn over, s2kp2, yarn over, p1) twice, *C1R, p1, yarn over, s2kp2, yarn over, p1; repeat from the * to 22 stitches before the marker, ending this section with (C1R, p1, yarn over, s2kp2, yarn over, p1) twice, C1R, p1, yarn over, ssk, yarn over. (51 stitches)

Left-Hand Side: Yarn over, k2tog, yarn over, p1, (C1L, p1, yarn over, s2kp2, yarn over, p1) twice, *C1L, p1, yarn over, s2kp2, yarn over, p1; repeat from the * to 22 stitches before the marker, ending this section with (C1L, p1, yarn over, s2kp2, yarn over, p1) twice, C1L, p1, yarn over, ssk, yarn over. (51 stitches)

ROW 51:

Right-Hand Side: Yarn over, k1, k2tog, yarn over, p1, (k3, p1, yarn over, s2kp2, yarn over, p1) twice, *k3, p1, yarn over, s2kp2, yarn over, p1; repeat from the * to 23 stitches before the marker, ending this section with (k3, p1, yarn over, s2kp2, yarn over, p1) twice, k3, p1, yarn over, ssk, k1, yarn over. (53 stitches)

Left-Hand Side: Yarn over, k1, k2tog, yarn over, p1, (k3, p1, yarn over, s2kp2, yarn over, p1) twice, *k3, p1, yarn over, s2kp2, yarn over, p1; repeat from the * to 23 stitches before the marker, ending this section with (k3, p1, yarn over, s2kp2, yarn over, p1) twice, k3, p1, yarn over, ssk, k1, yarn over. (53 stitches)

ROW 53:

Right-Hand Side: Yarn over, p1, yarn over, s2kp2, yarn over, p1, (C1R, p1, yarn over, s2kp2, yarn over, p1) twice, *C1R, p1, yarn over, s2kp2, yarn over, p1; repeat from the * to 24 stitches before the marker, ending this section with (C1R, p1, yarn over, s2kp2, yarn over, p1) twice, C1R, p1, yarn over, s2kp2, yarn over, p1, yarn over. (55 stitches)

Left-Hand Side: Yarn over, p1, yarn over, s2kp2, yarn over, p1, (C1L, p1, yarn over, s2kp2, yarn over, p1) twice, *C1L, p1, yarn over, s2kp2, yarn over, p1; repeat from the * to 24 stitches before the marker, ending this section with (C1L, p1, yarn over, s2kp2, yarn over, p1) twice, C1L, p1, yarn over, s2kp2, yarn over, p1, yarn over. (55 stitches)

ROW 54: As Row 2.

Repeat Rows 23–54 for the pattern.

42

ROW 1 (RS): Yarn over, k1, yarn over. (3 stitches)

ROW 2 AND ALL WS ROWS: Purl across.

ROW 3: Yarn over, k3, yarn over. (5 stitches)

ROW 5: Yarn over, k5, yarn over. (7 stitches)

ROW 7: Yarn over, k7, yarn over. (9 stitches)

ROW 9: Yarn over, *k4, yarn over, ssk, k2; repeat from the * to 1 stitch before the marker, ending this section with k1, yarn over. (11 stitches)

ROW 11: Yarn over, k1, *k2, k2tog, yarn over, k1, yarn over, ssk, k1; repeat from the * to 2 stitches before the marker, ending this section with k2, yarn over. (13 stitches)

ROW 13: Yarn over, k2, *k4, yarn over, ssk, k2; repeat from the * to 3 stitches before the marker, ending this section with k3, yarn over. (15 stitches)

ROW 15: Yarn over, knit across to the marker, ending this section with yarn over. (17 stitches)

ROW 16: As Row 2.

Repeat Rows 9–16 for the pattern.

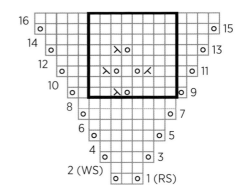

43

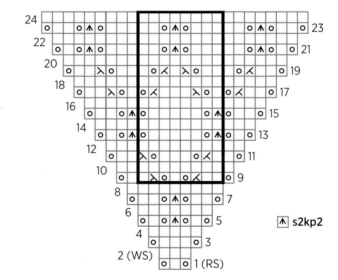

ROW 1 (RS): Yarn over, k1, yarn over. (3 stitches)

ROW 2 AND ALL WS ROWS: Purl across.

ROW 3: Yarn over, k3, yarn over. (5 stitches)

ROW 5: Yarn over, k1, yarn over, s2kp2 (page 282), yarn over, k1, yarn over. (7 stitches)

ROW 7: Yarn over, k2, yarn over, s2kp2, yarn over, k2, yarn over. (9 stitches)

ROW 9: Yarn over, *k2, k2tog, yarn over, k1, yarn over, ssk, k1; repeat from the * to 1 stitch before the marker, ending this section with k1, yarn over. (11 stitches)

ROW 11: Yarn over, k1, *k1, k2tog, yarn over, k3, yarn over, ssk; repeat from the * to 2 stitches before the marker, ending this section with k2, yarn over. (13 stitches)

ROW 13: Yarn over, k1, yarn over, *s2kp2, yarn over, k5, yarn over; repeat from the * to 4 stitches before the marker, ending this section with s2kp2, yarn over, k1, yarn over. (15 stitches)

ROW 15: Yarn over, k2, yarn over, *s2kp2, yarn over, k5, yarn over; repeat from the * to 5 stitches before the marker, ending this section with s2kp2, yarn over, k2, yarn over. (17 stitches)

ROW 17: Yarn over, k2, k2tog, yarn over, *k1, yarn over, ssk, k3, k2tog, yarn over; repeat from the * to 5 stitches before the marker, ending this section with k1, yarn over, ssk, k2, yarn over. (19 stitches)

ROW 19: Yarn over, k2, k2tog, yarn over, k1, *k2, yarn over, ssk, k1, k2tog, yarn over, k1; repeat from the * to 6 stitches before the marker, ending this section with k2, yarn over, ssk, k2, yarn over. (21 stitches)

ROW 21: Yarn over, k1, yarn over, s2kp2, yarn over, k2, *k3, yarn over, s2kp2, yarn over, k2; repeat from the * to 7 stitches before the marker, ending this section with k3, yarn over, s2kp2, yarn over, k1, yarn over. (23 stitches)

ROW 23: Yarn over, k2, yarn over, s2kp2, yarn over, k2, *k3, yarn over, s2kp2, yarn over, k2; repeat from the * to 8 stitches before the marker, ending this section with k3, yarn over, s2kp2, yarn over, k2, yarn over. (25 stitches)

ROW 24: As Row 2.

Repeat Rows 9–24 for the pattern.

⊼ s2kp2

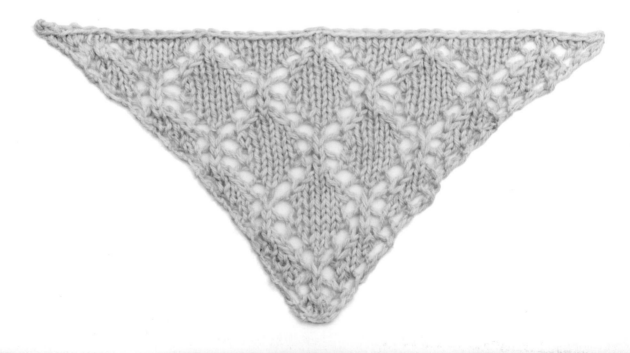

SHAWL #3

Two wedge patterns, a horizontal insertion, and a border demonstrate how the mix-and-match concept creates a one-of-a-kind masterpiece. See page 272 for instructions.

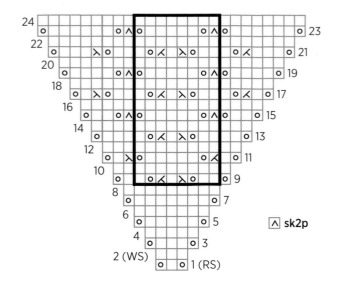

ROW 1 (RS): Yarn over, k1, yarn over. (3 stitches)

ROW 2 AND ALL WS ROWS: Purl across.

ROW 3: Yarn over, k3, yarn over. (5 stitches)

ROW 5: Yarn over, k5, yarn over. (7 stitches)

ROW 7: Yarn over, k7, yarn over. (9 stitches)

ROW 9: Yarn over, *k2, yarn over, ssk, k1, k2tog, yarn over, k1; repeat from the * to 1 stitch before the marker, ending this section with k1, yarn over. (11 stitches)

ROW 11: Yarn over, k1, *k2tog, yarn over, k5, yarn over; repeat from the * to 3 stitches before the marker, ending with ssk, k1, yarn over. (13 stitches)

ROW 13: Yarn over, k2, *k2, yarn over, ssk, k1, k2tog, yarn over, k1; repeat from the * to 3 stitches before the marker, ending this section with k3, yarn over. (15 stitches)

ROW 15: Yarn over, k2, yarn over, *sk2p (page 282), yarn over, k5, yarn over; repeat from the * to 5 stitches before the marker, ending this section with sk2p, yarn over, k2, yarn over. (17 stitches)

ROW 17: Yarn over, k1, k2tog, yarn over, k1, *k2, yarn over, ssk, k1, k2tog, yarn over, k1; repeat from the * to 5 stitches before the marker, ending this section with k2, yarn over, ssk, k1, yarn over. (19 stitches)

ROW 19: Yarn over, k4, yarn over, *sk2p, yarn over, k5, yarn over; repeat from the * to 7 stitches before the marker, ending this section with sk2p, yarn over, k4, yarn over. (21 stitches)

ROW 21: Yarn over, k3, k2tog, yarn over, k1, *k2, yarn over, ssk, k1, k2tog, yarn over, k1; repeat from the * to 7 stitches before the marker, ending this section with k2, yarn over, ssk, k3, yarn over. (23 stitches)

ROW 23: Yarn over, k6, yarn over, *sk2p, yarn over, k5, yarn over; repeat from the * to 9 stitches before the marker, ending this section with sk2p, yarn over, k6, yarn over. (25 stitches)

ROW 24: As Row 2.

Repeat Rows 9–24 for the pattern.

45

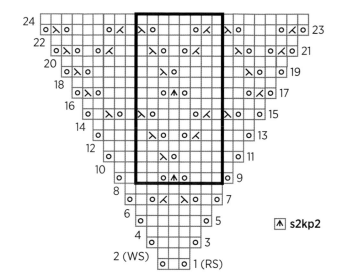

ROW 1 (RS): Yarn over, k1, yarn over. (3 stitches)

ROW 2 AND ALL WS ROWS: Purl across.

ROW 3: Yarn over, k3, yarn over. (5 stitches)

ROW 5: Yarn over, k5, yarn over. (7 stitches)

ROW 7: Yarn over, k1, yarn over, ssk, k1, k2tog, yarn over, k1, yarn over. (9 stitches)

ROW 9: Yarn over, *k3, yarn over, s2kp2 (page 282), yarn over, k2; repeat from the * to 1 stitch before the marker, ending with k1, yarn over. (11 stitches)

ROW 11: Yarn over, k1, *k4, yarn over, ssk, k2; repeat from the * to 2 stitches before the marker, ending with k2, yarn over. (13 stitches)

ROW 13: Yarn over, k2, *k2, k2tog, yarn over, k1, yarn over, ssk, k1; repeat from the * to 3 stitches before the marker, ending this section with k3, yarn over. (15 stitches)

ROW 15: Yarn over, k1, yarn over, ssk, *k1, k2tog, yarn over, k3, yarn over, ssk; repeat from the * to 4 stitches before the marker, ending this section with k1, yarn over, ssk, k1, yarn over. (17 stitches)

ROW 17: Yarn over, k2tog, yarn over, k2, *k3, yarn over, s2kp2, yarn over, k2; repeat from the * to 5 stitches before the marker, ending this section with k3, yarn over, ssk, yarn over. (19 stitches)

ROW 19: Yarn over, k1, yarn over, ssk, k2, *k4, yarn over, ssk, k2; repeat from the * to 6 stitches before the marker, ending this section with k4, yarn over, ssk, yarn over. (21 stitches)

ROW 21: Yarn over, k2tog, yarn over, k1, yarn over, ssk, k1, *k2, k2tog, yarn over, k1, yarn over, ssk, k1; repeat from the * to 7 stitches before the marker, ending this section with k2, k2tog, yarn over, k1, yarn over, ssk, yarn over. (23 stitches)

ROW 23: Yarn over, k2tog, yarn over, k3, yarn over, ssk, *k1, k2tog, yarn over, k3, yarn over, ssk; repeat from the * to 8 stitches before the marker, ending this section with k1, k2tog, yarn over, k3, yarn over, ssk, yarn over. (25 stitches)

ROW 24: As Row 2.

Repeat Rows 9–24 for the pattern.

⊼ s2kp2

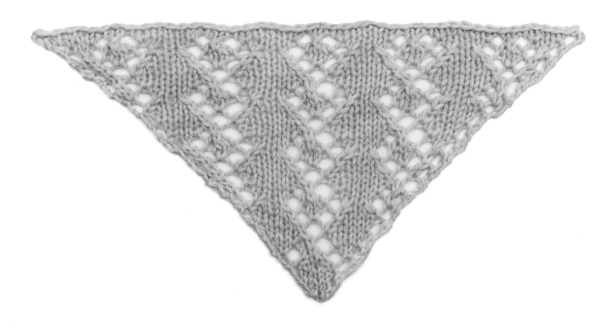

46

ROW 1 (RS): Yarn over, k1, yarn over. (3 stitches)

ROW 2 AND ALL WS ROWS: Purl across.

ROW 3: Yarn over, k3, yarn over. (5 stitches)

ROW 5: Yarn over, k5, yarn over. (7 stitches)

ROW 7: Yarn over, k7, yarn over. (9 stitches)

ROW 9: Yarn over, *k2, k2tog, yarn over, k1, ssk, k1; repeat from the * to 1 stitch before the marker, ending this section with k1, yarn over. (11 stitches)

ROW 11: Yarn over, k1, *k1, k2tog, yarn over, k3, yarn over, ssk; repeat from the * to 2 stitches before the marker, ending this section with k2, yarn over. (13 stitches)

ROW 13: Yarn over, k2, *k1, yarn over, ssk, yarn over, s2kp2 (page 282), yarn over, k2tog, yarn over; repeat from the * to 3 stitches before the marker, ending this section with k3, yarn over. (15 stitches)

ROW 15: Yarn over, k3, *k2, yarn over, ssk, k1, k2tog, yarn over, k1; repeat from the * to 4 stitches before the marker, ending this section with k4, yarn over. (17 stitches)

ROW 17: Yarn over, k4, *k3, yarn over, s2kp2, yarn over, k2; repeat from the * to 5 stitches before the marker, ending this section with k5, yarn over. (19 stitches)

ROW 19: Yarn over, knit across to the marker, ending this section with yarn over. (21 stitches)

ROW 21: Yarn over, k4, k2tog, yarn over, *k1, yarn over, ssk, k3, k2tog, yarn over; repeat from the * to 7 stitches before the marker, ending this section with k1, yarn over, ssk, k4, yarn over. (23 stitches)

ROW 23: Yarn over, k1, yarn over, ssk, k1, k2tog, yarn over, k1, *k2, yarn over, ssk, k1, k2tog, yarn over, k1; repeat from the * to 8 stitches before the marker, ending this section with k2, yarn over, ssk, k1, k2tog, yarn over, k1, yarn over. (25 stitches)

ROW 25: (Yarn over, k2tog) twice, yarn over, k1, yarn over, ssk, yarn over, *s2kp2, yarn over, k2tog, yarn over, k1, yarn over, ssk, yarn over; repeat from the * to 10 stitches before the marker, ending this section with s2kp2, yarn over, k2tog, yarn over, k1, (yarn over, ssk) twice, yarn over. (27 stitches)

ROW 27: Yarn over, k2, k2tog, yarn over, k3, yarn over, ssk, *k1, k2tog, yarn over, k3, yarn over, ssk; repeat from the * to 10 stitches before the marker, ending this section with k1, k2tog, yarn over, k3, yarn over, ssk, k2, yarn over. (29 stitches)

ROW 29: Yarn over, k2, k2tog, yarn over, k5, yarn over, *s2kp2, yarn over, k5, yarn over; repeat from the * to 12 stitches before the marker, ending this section with s2kp2, yarn over, k5, yarn over, s2kp2, yarn over, k1, yarn over. (31 stitches)

ROW 31: As Row 19. (33 stitches)

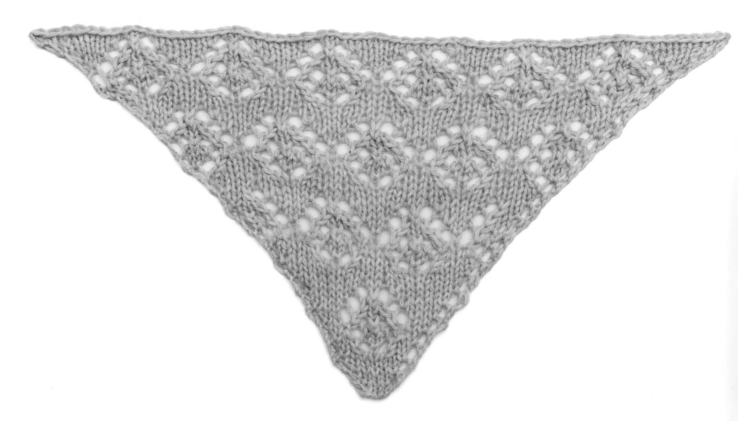

ROW 33: Yarn over, k1, yarn over, ssk, k3, k2tog, yarn over, k1, yarn over, ssk, k1, *k2, k2tog, yarn over, k1, ssk, k1; repeat from the * to 13 stitches before the marker, ending this section with k2, k2tog, yarn over, k1, yarn over, ssk, k3, k2tog, yarn over, k1, yarn over. (35 stitches)

ROW 35: Yarn over, k3, yarn over, ssk, k1, k2tog, yarn over, k3, yarn over, ssk, *k1, k2tog, yarn over, k3, yarn over, ssk; repeat from the * to 14 stitches before the marker, ending this section with k1, k2tog, yarn over, k3, yarn over, ssk, k1, k2tog, yarn over, k3, yarn over. (37 stitches)

ROW 37: Yarn over, k1, yarn over, s2kp2, yarn over, k2tog, yarn over, k1, yarn over, ssk, yarn over, s2kp2, yarn over, k2tog, yarn over, *k1, yarn over, ssk, yarn over, s2kp2, yarn over, k2tog, yarn over; repeat from the * to 16 stitches before the marker, ending this section with (k1, yarn over, ssk, yarn over, s2kp2, yarn over, k2tog, yarn over) twice. (39 stitches)

ROW 39: Yarn over, k1, yarn over, ssk, k1, k2tog, yarn over, k3, yarn over, ssk, k1, k2tog, yarn over, k1, *k2, yarn over, ssk, k1, k2tog, yarn over, k1; repeat from the * to 16 stitches before the marker, ending this section with k2, yarn over, ssk, k1, k2tog, yarn over, k3, yarn over, ssk, k1, k2tog, yarn over, k1, yarn over. (41 stitches)

ROW 41: Yarn over, k3, yarn over, s2kp2, yarn over, k5, yarn over, s2kp2, yarn over, k2, *k3, yarn over, s2kp2, yarn over, k2; repeat from the * to 17 stitches before the marker, ending this section with (k3, yarn over, s2kp2, yarn over, k2) twice, k1, yarn over. (43 stitches)

(continued on the next page)

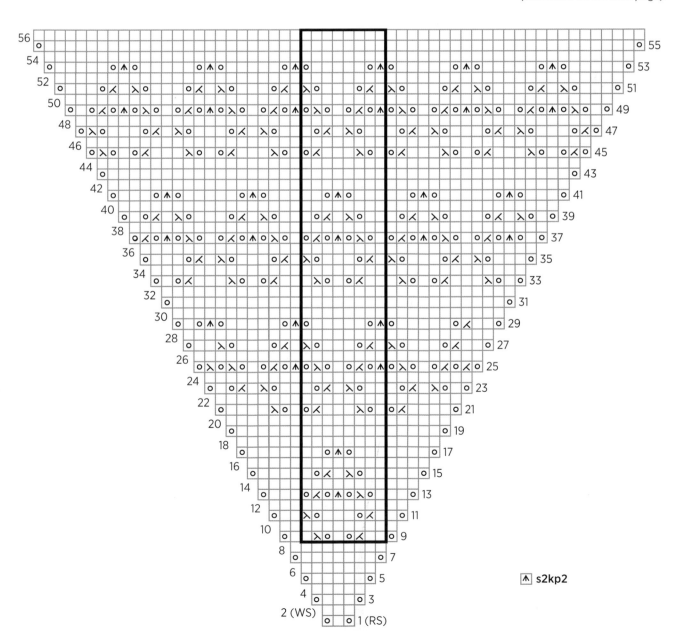

⬆ s2kp2

WEDGE 46, *continued*

ROW 43: As Row 19. (45 stitches)

ROW 45: Yarn over, (k2tog, yarn over, k1, yarn over, ssk, k3) twice, k2tog, yarn over, *k1, yarn over, ssk, k3, k2tog, yarn over; repeat from the * to 19 stitches before the marker, ending this section with k1, yarn over, ssk, k3, k2tog, yarn over, k1, yarn over, ssk, k3, k2tog, yarn over, k1, yarn over, ssk, yarn over. (47 stitches)

ROW 47: Yarn over, (k2tog, yarn over, k3, yarn over, ssk, k1) twice, k2tog, yarn over, k1, *k2, yarn over, ssk, k1, k2tog, yarn over, k1; repeat from the * to 20 stitches before the marker, ending this section with k2, (yarn over, ssk, k1, k2tog, yarn over, k3) twice, yarn over, ssk, yarn over. (49 stitches)

ROW 49: Yarn over, (k1, yarn over, ssk, yarn over, s2kp2, yarn over, k2tog, yarn over) twice, k1, yarn over, ssk, yarn over, *s2kp2, yarn over, k2tog, yarn over, k1, ssk, yarn over; repeat from the * to 22 stitches before the marker, ending this section with (s2kp2, yarn over, k2tog, yarn over, k1, yarn over, ssk, yarn over) twice, s2kp2, yarn over, k2tog, yarn over, k1, yarn over. (51 stitches)

ROW 51: Yarn over, (k3, yarn over, ssk, k1, k2tog, yarn over) twice, k3, yarn over, ssk, *k1, k2tog, yarn over, k3, yarn over, ssk; repeat from the * to 22 stitches before the marker, ending this section with (k1, k2tog, yarn over, k3, yarn over, ssk) twice, k1, k2tog, yarn over, k3, yarn over. (53 stitches)

ROW 53: Yarn over, k5, (yarn over, s2kp2, yarn over, k5) twice, yarn over, *s2kp2, yarn over, k5, yarn over; repeat from the * to 24 stitches before the marker, ending this section with (s2kp2, yarn over, k5, yarn over) 3 times. (55 stitches)

ROW 55: As Row 19. (57 stitches)

ROW 56: As Row 2.

Repeat Rows 9–56 for the pattern.

SHAWL #16

Three triangles provide extra coverage, allowing the shawl to sit well on your shoulders. See page 276 for instructions.

47

ROW 1 (RS): Yarn over, k1, yarn over. (3 stitches)

ROW 2 AND ALL WS ROWS: Purl across.

ROW 3: Yarn over, k3, yarn over. (5 stitches)

ROW 5: Yarn over, k5, yarn over. (7 stitches)

ROW 7: Yarn over, k7, yarn over. (9 stitches)

ROW 9: Yarn over, *k2, k2tog, yarn over, k1, yarn over, ssk, k1; repeat from the * to 1 stitch before the marker, ending this section with k1, yarn over. (11 stitches)

ROW 11: Yarn over, k1, *k1, k2tog, yarn over, k3, yarn over, ssk; repeat from the * to 2 stitches before the marker, ending this section with k2, yarn over. (13 stitches)

ROW 13: Yarn over, k2, *k2, yarn over, ssk, k1, k2tog, yarn over, k1; repeat from the * to 3 stitches before the marker, ending this section with k3, yarn over. (15 stitches)

ROW 15: Yarn over, k3, *k3, yarn over, s2kp2 (page 282), yarn over, k2; repeat from the * to 4 stitches before the marker, ending this section with k4, yarn over. (17 stitches)

ROW 16: As Row 2.

Repeat Rows 9–16 for the pattern.

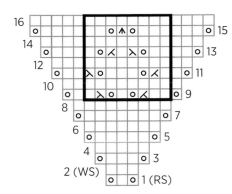

⬆ **s2kp2**

48

ROW 1 (RS): Yarn over, k1, yarn over. (3 stitches)

ROW 2: Purl across.

ROW 3: Yarn over, k3, yarn over. (5 stitches)

ROW 4: P1, yarn over, sssp (page 285), yarn over, p1.

ROW 5: Yarn over, k2tog, yarn over, k1, yarn over, ssk, yarn over. (7 stitches)

ROW 6: Ssp (page 281), yarn over, p3, yarn over, p2tog.

ROW 7: Yarn over, k1, yarn over, ssk, k1, k2tog, yarn over, k1, yarn over. (9 stitches)

ROW 8: P3, yarn over, sssp, yarn over, p3.

ROW 9: Yarn over, *k2, k2tog, yarn over, k1, yarn over, ssk, k1; repeat from the * to 1 stitch before the marker, ending this section with k1, yarn over. (11 stitches)

ROW 10: P2, *ssp, yarn over, p3, yarn over, p2tog, p1; repeat from the * to 1 stitch before the marker, ending this section with p1.

ROW 11: Yarn over, k1, *k2, yarn over, ssk, k1, k2tog, yarn over, k1; repeat from the * to 2 stitches before the marker, ending this section with k2, yarn over. (13 stitches)

ROW 12: P3, *p2, yarn over, sssp, yarn over, p3; repeat from the * to 2 stitches before the marker, ending this section with p2.

ROW 13: Yarn over, k2, *k2, k2tog, yarn over, k1, yarn over, ssk, k1; repeat from the * to 3 stitches before the marker, ending this section with k3, yarn over. (15 stitches)

ROW 14: P1, yarn over, p2tog, p1, *ssp, yarn over, p3, yarn over, p2tog, p1; repeat from the * to 3 stitches before the marker, ending this section with ssp, yarn over, p1.

ROW 15: Yarn over, k2tog, yarn over, k1, *k2, yarn over, ssk, k1, k2tog, yarn over, k1; repeat from the * to 4 stitches before the marker, ending this section with k2, yarn over, ssk, yarn over. (17 stitches)

ROW 16: Ssp, yarn over, p3, *p2, yarn over, sssp, yarn over, p3; repeat from the * to 4 stitches before the marker, ending this section with p2, yarn over, ssp.

ROW 17: Yarn over, k1, yarn over, ssk, k1, *k2, k2tog, yarn over, k1, yarn over, ssk, k1; repeat from the * to 5 stitches before the marker, ending this section with k2, k2tog, yarn over, k1, yarn over. (19 stitches)

ROW 18: P3, yarn over, p2tog, p1, *ssp, yarn over, p3, yarn over, p2tog, p1; repeat from the * to 5 stitches before the marker, ending this section with ssp, yarn over, p3.

ROW 19: Yarn over, k2, k2tog, yarn over, k1, *k2, yarn over, ssk, k1, k2tog, yarn over, k1; repeat from the * to 6 stitches before the marker, ending this section with k2, yarn over, ssk, k2, yarn over. (21 stitches)

ROW 20: P1, yarn over, sssp, yarn over, p3, *p2, yarn over, sssp, yarn over, p3; repeat from the * to 6 stitches before the marker, ending this section with p2, yarn over, sssp, yarn over, p1.

ROW 21: Yarn over, k2tog, yarn over, k1, yarn over, ssk, k1, *k2, k2tog, yarn over, k1, yarn over, ssk, k1; repeat from the * to 7 stitches before the marker, ending this section with k2, k2tog, yarn over, k1, yarn over, ssk, yarn over. (23 stitches)

ROW 22: Ssp, yarn over, p3, yarn over, p2tog, p1, *ssp, yarn over, p3, yarn over, p2tog, p1; repeat from the * to 7 stitches before the marker, ending this section with ssp, yarn over, p3, yarn over, p2tog.

ROW 23: Yarn over, k1, yarn over, ssk, k1, k2tog, yarn over, k1, *k2, yarn over, ssk, k1, k2tog, yarn over, k1; repeat from the * to 8 stitches before the marker, ending this section with k2, yarn over, ssk, k1, k2tog, yarn over, k1, yarn over. (25 stitches)

ROW 24: P3, yarn over, sssp, yarn over, p3, *p2, yarn over, sssp, yarn over, p3; repeat from the* to 8 stitches before the marker, ending this section with p2, yarn over, sssp, yarn over, p3.

Repeat Rows 9–24 for the pattern.

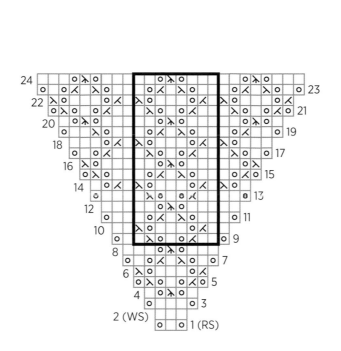

49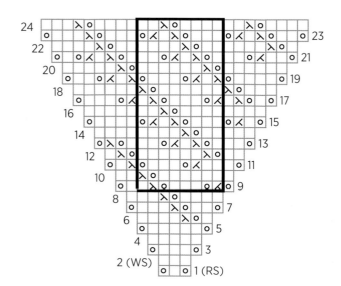

NOTE: To create symmetry, this design is different on the right- and left-hand sides. If you are making a two-wedge shawl, follow the instructions for the Right-Hand Side to the center of your shawl, then work the Left-Hand Side instructions. If your shawl has more than two wedges, work the Right-Hand Side instructions first and the Left-Hand Side instructions last, and balance out the wedges in between.

ROW 1 (RS):

Right-Hand Side: Yarn over, k1, yarn over. (3 stitches)

Left-Hand Side: Yarn over, k1, yarn over. (3 stitches)

ROWS 2 AND 4:

Right-Hand and Left-Hand Sides: Purl across.

ROW 3:

Right-Hand Side: Yarn over, k3, yarn over. (5 stitches)

Left-Hand Side: Yarn over, k3, yarn over. (5 stitches)

ROW 5:

Right-Hand Side: Yarn over, k5, yarn over. (7 stitches)

Left-Hand Side: Yarn over, k5, yarn over. (7 stitches)

ROW 6:

Right-Hand Side: P1, yarn over, p2tog, p4.

Left-Hand Side: P4, ssp (page 281), yarn over, p1.

ROW 7:

Right-Hand Side: Yarn over, k3, k2tog, yarn over, k2, yarn over. (9 stitches)

Left-Hand Side: Yarn over, k2, yarn over, ssk, k3, yarn over. (9 stitches)

ROW 8:

Right-Hand Side: P4, yarn over, p2tog, p3.

Left-Hand Side: P3, ssp, yarn over, p4.

ROW 9:

Right-Hand Side: Yarn over, k1, *k1, k2tog, yarn over, k3, yarn over, ssk; repeat from the * to the marker, ending this section with yarn over. (11 stitches)

Left-Hand Side: Yarn over, *k2tog, yarn over, k3, yarn over, ssk, k1; repeat from the * to 1 stitch before the marker, ending this section with k1, yarn over. (11 stitches)

ROW 10:

Right-Hand Side: P1, *p6, yarn over, p2tog; repeat from the * to 2 stitches before the marker, ending this section with p2.

Left-Hand Side: P2, *ssp, yarn over, p6; repeat from the * to 1 stitch before the marker, ending with p1.

ROW 11:

Right-Hand Side: Yarn over, k1, k2tog, *yarn over, k3, yarn over, ssk, k2; repeat from the * to 1 stitch before the marker, ending this section with k1, yarn over. (13 stitches)

Left-Hand Side: Yarn over, k1, *k2, k2tog, yarn over, k3, yarn over; repeat from the * to 3 stitches before the marker, ending this section with ssk, k1, yarn over. (13 stitches)

(continued on page 77)

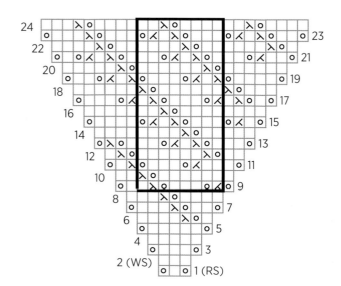

Left-Hand Side

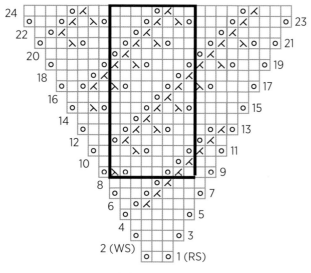

Right-Hand Side

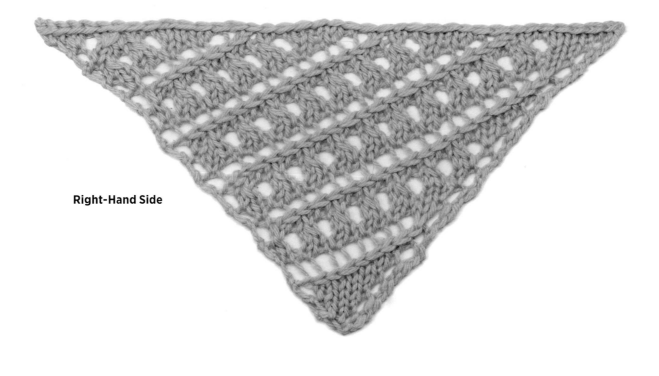

Right-Hand Side

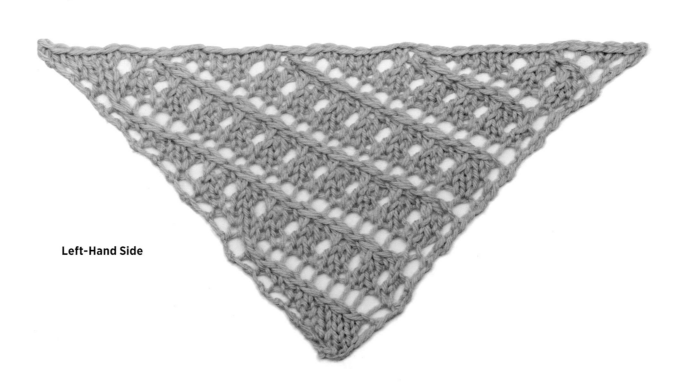

Left-Hand Side

SHAWL #15

A crocheted bind off adds the perfect lacy touch to this design. See page 276 for instructions.

76

ROW 12:

Right-Hand Side: P2, *yarn over, p2tog, p6; repeat from the * to 3 stitches before the marker, ending this section with yarn over, p2tog, p1.

Left-Hand Side: P1, ssp, yarn over, *p6, ssp, yarn over; repeat from the * to 2 stitches before the marker, ending this section with p2.

ROW 13:

Right-Hand Side: Yarn over, k2tog, yarn over, k1, *k2, yarn over, ssk, k1, k2tog, yarn over, k1; repeat from the * to 2 stitches before the marker, ending this section with k2, yarn over. (15 stitches)

Left-Hand Side: Yarn over, k2, *k1, yarn over, ssk, k1, k2tog, yarn over, k2; repeat from the * to 3 stitches before the marker, ending this section with k1, yarn over, ssk, yarn over. (15 stitches)

ROW 14:

Right-Hand Side: P3, *p2, yarn over, p2tog, p4; repeat from the * to 4 stitches before the marker, ending this section with p4.

Left-Hand Side: P4, *p4, ssp, yarn over, p2; repeat from the * to 3 stitches before the marker, ending this section with p3.

ROW 15:

Right-Hand Side: Yarn over, k4, *yarn over, ssk, k1, k2tog, yarn over, k3; repeat from the * to 3 stitches before the marker, ending this section with yarn over, ssk, k1, yarn over. (17 stitches)

Left-Hand Side: Yarn over, k1, k2tog, yarn over, *k3, yarn over, ssk, k1, k2tog, yarn over; repeat from the * to 4 stitches before the marker, ending this section with k4, yarn over. (17 stitches)

ROW 16:

Right-Hand Side: P4, *p4, yarn over, p2tog, p2; repeat from the * to 5 stitches before the marker, ending this section with p5.

Left-Hand Side: P5, *p2, ssp, yarn over, p4; repeat from the * to 4 stitches before the marker, ending this section with p4.

ROW 17:

Right-Hand Side: Yarn over, k3, yarn over, ssk, *k1, k2tog, yarn over, k3, yarn over, ssk; repeat from the * to 4 stitches before the marker, ending this section with k1, k2tog, yarn over, k1, yarn over. (19 stitches)

Left-Hand Side: Yarn over, k1, yarn over, ssk, k1, *k2tog, yarn over, k3, yarn over, ssk, k1; repeat from the * to 5 stitches before the marker, ending this section with k2tog, yarn over, k3, yarn over. (19 stitches)

ROW 18:

Right-Hand Side: P3, yarn over, p2tog, *p6, yarn over, p2tog; repeat from the * to 6 stitches before the marker, ending this section with p6.

Left-Hand Side: P6, *ssp, yarn over, p6; repeat from the * to 5 stitches before the marker, ending this section with ssp, yarn over, p3.

ROW 19:

Right-Hand Side: Yarn over, k2, yarn over, ssk, k1, k2tog, *yarn over, k3, yarn over, ssk, k1, k2tog; repeat from the * to 4 stitches before the marker, ending this section with yarn over, k4, yarn over. (21 stitches)

Left-Hand Side: Yarn over, k4, yarn over, *ssk, k1, k2tog, yarn over, k3, yarn over; repeat from the * to 7 stitches before the marker, ending this section with ssk, k1, k2tog, yarn over, k2, yarn over. (21 stitches)

ROW 20:

Right-Hand Side: P6, *yarn over, p2tog, p6; repeat from the * to 7 stitches before the marker, ending this section with yarn over, p2tog, p5.

Left-Hand Side: P5, ssp, yarn over, *p6, ssp, yarn over; repeat from the * to 6 stitches before the marker, ending this section with p6.

ROW 21:

Right-Hand Side: Yarn over, k1, yarn over, ssk, k1, k2tog, yarn over, k1, *k2, yarn over, ssk, k1, k2tog, yarn over, k1; repeat from the * to 6 stitches before the marker, ending this section with k2, yarn over, ssk, k2, yarn over. (23 stitches)

Left-Hand Side: Yarn over, k2, k2tog, yarn over, k2, *k1, yarn over, ssk, k1, k2tog, yarn over, k2; repeat from the * to 7 stitches before the marker, ending this section with k1, yarn over, ssk, k1, k2tog, yarn over, k1, yarn over. (23 stitches)

ROW 22:

Right-Hand Side: P1, yarn over, p2tog, p4, *p2, yarn over, p2tog, p4; repeat from the * to 8 stitches before the marker, ending this section with p2, yarn over, p2tog, p4.

Left-Hand Side: P4, ssp, yarn over, p2, *p4, ssp, yarn over, p2; repeat from the * to 7 stitches before the marker, ending this section with p4, ssp, yarn over, p1.

ROW 23:

Right-Hand Side: Yarn over, k3, k2tog, yarn over, k3, *yarn over, ssk, k1, k2tog, yarn over, k3; repeat from the * to 7 stitches before the marker, ending this section with yarn over, ssk, k1, k2tog, yarn over, k2, yarn over. (25 stitches)

Left-Hand Side: Yarn over, k2, yarn over, ssk, k1, k2tog, yarn over, *k3, yarn over, ssk, k1, k2tog, yarn over; repeat from the * to 8 stitches before the marker, ending this section with k3, yarn over, ssk, k3, yarn over. (25 stitches)

ROW 24:

Right-Hand Side: P4, yarn over, p2tog, p2, *p4, yarn over, p2tog, p2; repeat from the * to 9 stitches before the marker, ending this section with p4, yarn over, p2tog, p3.

Left-Hand Side: P3, ssp, yarn over, p4, *p2, ssp, yarn over, p4; repeat from the * to 8 stitches before the marker, ending this section with p2, ssp, yarn over, p4.

Repeat Rows 9-24 for pattern.

50

NOTE: To create symmetry, this design is different on the right- and left-hand sides. If you are making a two-wedge shawl, follow the instructions for the Right-Hand Side to the center of your shawl, then work the Left-Hand Side instructions. If your shawl has more than two wedges, work the Right-Hand Side instructions first and the Left-Hand Side instructions last, and balance out the wedges in between.

ROW 1 (RS):

Right-Hand Side: Yarn over, k1, yarn over. (3 stitches)

Left-Hand Side: Yarn over, k1, yarn over. (3 stitches)

ROW 2:

Right-Hand and Left-Hand Sides: Purl across.

ROW 3:

Right-Hand Side: Yarn over, k3, yarn over. (5 stitches)

Left-Hand Side: Yarn over, k3, yarn over. (5 stitches)

ROW 4:

Right-Hand Side: P1, yarn over, p3tog, yarn over, p1.

Left-Hand Side: P1, yarn over, sssp (page 285), yarn over, p1.

ROW 5:

Right-Hand Side: Yarn over, k5, yarn over. (7 stitches)

Left-Hand Side: Yarn over, k5, yarn over. (7 stitches)

ROW 6:

Right-Hand Side: P2, yarn over, p3tog, yarn over, p2

Left-Hand Side: P2, yarn over, sssp, yarn over, p2. (7 stitches)

ROW 7:

Right-Hand Side: Yarn over, k7, yarn over. (9 stitches)

Left-Hand Side: Yarn over, k7, yarn over. (9 stitches)

ROW 8:

Right-Hand Side: P3, yarn over, p3tog, yarn over, p3.

Left-Hand Side: P3, yarn over, sssp, yarn over, p3.

ROW 9:

Right-Hand Side: Yarn over, k1, *k2, k2tog, yarn over, k4; repeat from the * to the marker, ending this section with yarn over. (11 stitches)

Left-Hand Side: Yarn over, *k4, yarn over, ssk, k2; repeat from the * 1 stitch before the marker, ending this section with k1, yarn over. (11 stitches)

ROW 10:

Right-Hand Side: P1, *p2, ssp (page 281), yarn over, p1, yarn over, p2tog, p1; repeat from the * to 2 stitches before the marker, ending this section with p2.

Left-Hand Side: P2, *p1, ssp, yarn over, p1, yarn over, p2tog, p2; repeat from the * to 1 stitch before the marker, ending this section with p1.

ROW 11:

Right-Hand Side: Yarn over, k2, *k2tog, yarn over, k3, yarn over, ssk, k1; repeat from the * to 1 stitch before the marker, ending this section with k1, yarn over. (13 stitches)

Left-Hand Side: Yarn over, k1, *k1, k2tog, yarn over, k3, yarn over, ssk; repeat from the * to 2 stitches before the marker, ending this section with k2, yarn over. (13 stitches)

(continued on page 80)

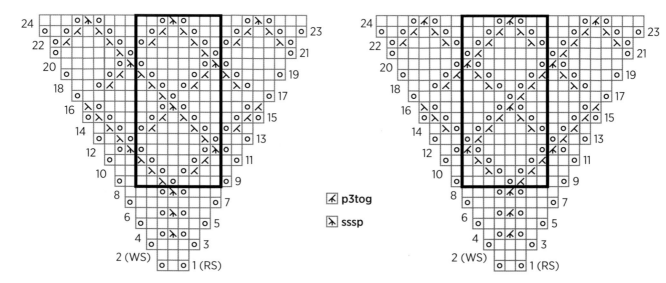

Left-Hand Side

Right-Hand Side

⤚ p3tog

⤜ sssp

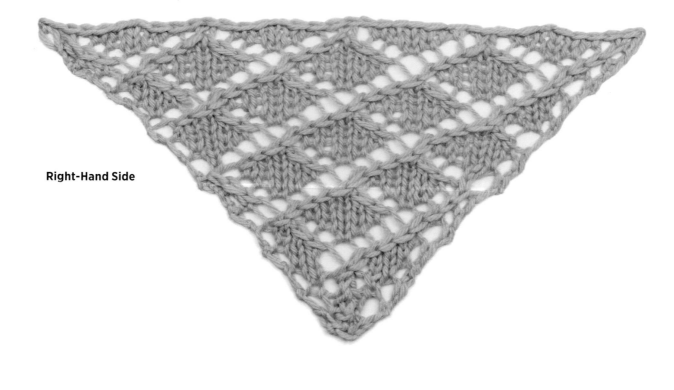

Right-Hand Side

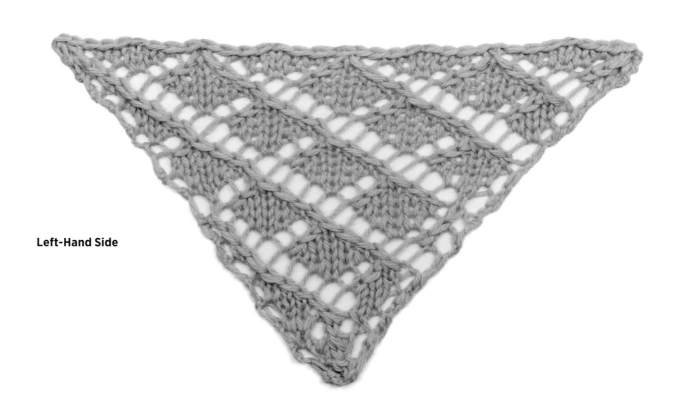

Left-Hand Side

WEDGE 50, *continued*

ROW 12:

Right-Hand Side: P1, yarn over, *p3tog, yarn over, p5, yarn over; repeat from the * to 4 stitches before the marker, ending this section with yarn over, p3tog, yarn over, p1.

Left-Hand Side: P1, yarn over, sssp, *yarn over, p5, yarn over, sssp; repeat from the * to 1 stitch before the marker, ending this section with yarn over, p1.

ROW 13:

Right-Hand Side: Yarn over, k1, k2tog, yarn over, *k6, k2tog, yarn over; repeat from the * to 2 stitches before the marker, ending this section with k2, yarn over. (15 stitches)

Left-Hand Side: Yarn over, k2, *yarn over, ssk, k6; repeat from the * to 3 stitches before the marker, ending this section with yarn over, ssk, k1, yarn over. (15 stitches)

ROW 14:

Right-Hand Side: P1, ssp, yarn over, *p1, yarn over, p2tog, p3, ssp, yarn over; repeat from the * to 3 stitches before the marker, ending this section with yarn over, p1, yarn over, p2tog, p1.

Left-Hand Side: P1, ssp, yarn over, p1, *yarn over, p2tog, p3, ssp, yarn over, p1; repeat from the * to 3 stitches before the marker, ending this section with yarn over, p2tog, p1.

ROW 15:

Right-Hand Side: Yarn over, k2tog, yarn over, k2, *k1, yarn over, ssk, k1, k2tog, yarn over, k2; repeat from the * to 4 stitches before the marker, ending this section with k1, yarn over, ssk, yarn over. (17 stitches)

Left-Hand Side: Yarn over, k2tog, yarn over, k1, *k2, yarn over, ssk, k1, k2tog, yarn over, k1; repeat from the * to 4 stitches before the marker, ending this section with k2, yarn over, ssk, yarn over. (17 stitches)

ROW 16:

Right-Hand Side: Ssp, yarn over, p2, *p3, yarn over, p3tog, yarn over, p2; repeat from the * to 4 stitches before the marker, ending this section with p3, yarn over, p2tog.

Left-Hand Side: Ssp, yarn over, p3, *p2, yarn over, sssp, yarn over, p3; repeat from the * to 4 stitches before the marker, ending this section with p2, yarn over, p2tog.

ROW 17:

Right-Hand Side: Yarn over, k5, *k2, k2tog, yarn over, 43; repeat from the * to 4 stitches before the marker, ending this section with k4, yarn over. (19 stitches)

Left-Hand Side: Yarn over, k4, *k2, yarn over, ssk, k2; repeat from the * to 5 stitches before the marker, ending this section with k5, yarn over. (19 stitches)

ROW 18:

Right-Hand Side: P2, yarn over, p2tog, p1, *p2, ssp, yarn over, p1, yarn over, p2tog, p1; repeat from the * to 6 stitches before the marker, ending this section with p2, ssp, yarn over, p2.

Left-Hand Side: P2, yarn over, p2tog, p2, *p1, ssp, yarn over, p1, yarn over, p2tog, p2; repeat from the * to 5 stitches before the marker, ending this section with p1, ssp, yarn over, p2.

ROW 19:

Right-Hand Side: Yarn over, k3, yarn over, ssk, k1, *k2tog, yarn over, k3, yarn over, ssk, k1; repeat from the * to 5 stitches before the marker, ending this section with k2tog, yarn over, k3, yarn over. (21 stitches)

Left-Hand Side: Yarn over, k3, yarn over, ssk, *k1, k2tog, yarn over, k3, yarn over, ssk; repeat from the * to 6 stitches before the marker, ending this section with k1, k2tog, yarn over, k3, yarn over. (21 stitches)

ROW 20:

Right-Hand Side: P5, yarn over, *p3tog, yarn over, p5, yarn over; repeat from the * to 8 stitches before the marker, ending this section with p3tog, yarn over, p5.

Left-Hand Side: P5, yarn over, sssp, *yarn over, p5, yarn over, sssp; repeat from the * to 5 stitches before the marker, ending this section with yarn over, p5.

ROW 21:

Right-Hand Side: Yarn over, k5, k2tog, yarn over, * k6, k2tog, yarn over; repeat from the * to 6 stitches before the marker, ending this section with k6, yarn over. (23 stitches)

Left-Hand Side: Yarn over, k6, *yarn over, ssk, k6; repeat from the * to 7 stitches before the marker, ending this section with yarn over, ssk, k5, yarn over. (23 stitches)

ROW 22:

Right-Hand Side: Yarn over, p2tog, p3, ssp, yarn over, *p1, yarn over, p2tog, p3, ssp, yarn over; repeat from the * to 8 stitches before the marker, ending this section with p1, yarn over, p2tog, p3, ssp, yarn over.

Left-Hand Side: Yarn over, p2tog, p3, ssp, yarn over, p1, *yarn over, p2tog, p3, ssp, yarn over, p1; repeat from the * to 7 stitches before the marker, ending this section with yarn over, p2tog, p3, ssp, yarn over.

ROW 23:

Right-Hand Side: Yarn over, k1, yarn over, ssk, k1, k2tog, yarn over, k2, *k1, yarn over, ssk, k1, k2tog, yarn over, k2; repeat from the * to 7 stitches before the marker, ending this section with k1, yarn over, ssk, k1, k2tog, yarn over, k1, yarn over. (25 stitches)

Left-Hand Side: Yarn over, k1, yarn over, ssk, k1, k2tog, yarn over, k1, *k2, yarn over, ssk, k1, k2tog, yarn over, k1; repeat from the * to 8 stitches before the marker, ending this section with k2, yarn over, ssk, k1, k2tog, yarn over, k1, yarn over. (25 stitches)

ROW 24:

Right-Hand Side: P3, yarn over, p3tog, yarn over, p2, *p3, yarn over, p3tog, yarn over, p2; repeat from the * to 9 stitches before the marker, ending this section with p3, yarn over, p3tog, yarn over, p3.

Left-Hand Side: P3, yarn over, sssp, yarn over, p3, *p2, yarn over, sssp, yarn over, p3; repeat from the * to 8 stitches before the marker, ending this section with p2, yarn over, sssp, yarn over, p3.

Repeat Rows 9–24 for the pattern.

51

ROW 1 (RS): Yarn over, k1, yarn over. (3 stitches)

ROW 2 AND ALL WS ROWS: Purl across.

ROW 3: Yarn over, k3, yarn over. (5 stitches)

ROW 5: Yarn over, k1, yarn over, s2kp2 (page 282), yarn over, k1, yarn over. (7 stitches)

ROW 7: Yarn over, k1, yarn over, k1, s2kp2, k1, yarn over, k1, yarn over. (9 stitches)

ROW 9: Yarn over, *k1, yarn over, k1, ssk, k1, k2tog, k1, yarn over; repeat from the * to 1 stitch before the marker, ending this section with k1, yarn over. (11 stitches)

ROW 11: Yarn over, k1, *k2, yarn over, k1, s2kp2, k1, yarn over, k1; repeat from the * to 2 stitches before the marker, ending this section with k2, yarn over. (13 stitches)

ROW 13: Yarn over, k2tog, yarn over, *k1, yarn over, k1, ssk, k1, k2tog, k1, yarn over; repeat from the * to 3 stitches before the marker, ending this section with k1, yarn over, ssk, yarn over. (15 stitches)

ROW 15: Yarn over, k2tog, yarn over, k1, *k2, yarn over, k1, s2kp2, k1, yarn over, k1; repeat from the * to 4 stitches before the marker, ending this section with k2, yarn over, ssk, yarn over. (17 stitches)

ROW 17: Yarn over, k1, k2tog, k1, yarn over, *k1, yarn over, k1, ssk, k1, k2tog, k1, yarn over; repeat from the * to 5 stitches before the marker, ending this section with k1, yarn over, k1, ssk, k1, yarn over. (19 stitches)

ROW 19: Yarn over, k1, k2tog, k1, yarn over, k1, *k2, yarn over, k1, s2kp2, k1, yarn over, k1; repeat from the * to 6 stitches before the marker, ending this section with k2, yarn over, k1, ssk, k1, yarn over. (21 stitches)

ROW 21: Yarn over, k3, k2tog, k1, yarn over, *k1, yarn over, k1, ssk, k1, k2tog, k1, yarn over; repeat from the * to 7 stitches before the marker, ending this section with k1, yarn over, k1, ssk, k3, yarn over. (23 stitches)

ROW 23: Yarn over, k1, yarn over, k1, s2kp2, k1, yarn over, k1, *k2, yarn over, k1, s2kp2, k1, yarn over, k1; repeat from the * to 8 stitches before the marker, ending this section with k2, yarn over, k1, s2kp2, k1, yarn over, k1, yarn over. (25 stitches)

ROW 24: As Row 2.

Repeat Rows 9–24 for the pattern.

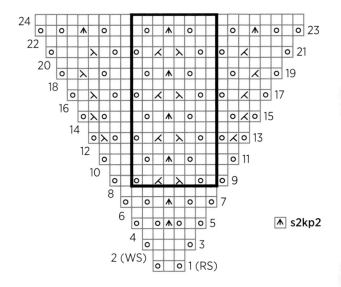

⬆ s2kp2

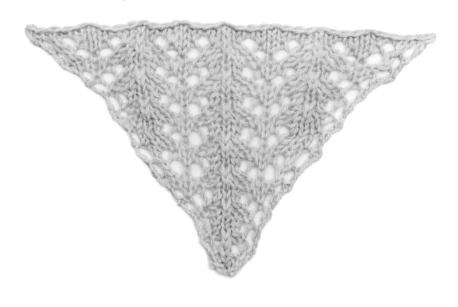

52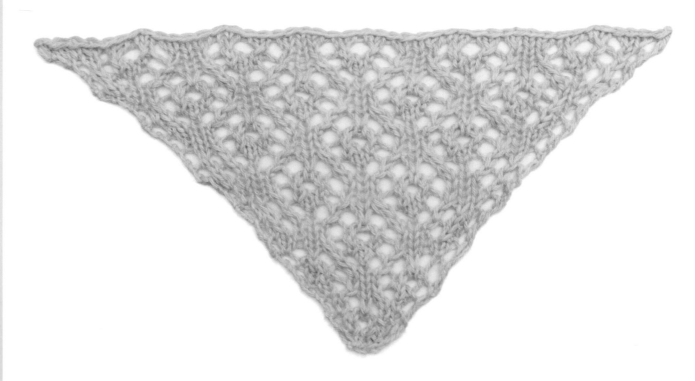

ROW 1 (RS): Yarn over, k1, yarn over. (3 stitches)

ROW 2 AND ALL WS ROWS: Purl across.

ROW 3: Yarn over, k3, yarn over. (5 stitches)

ROW 5: Yarn over, k1, k2tog, yarn over, k2, yarn over. (7 stitches)

ROW 7: Yarn over, k2, yarn over, s2kp2 (page 282), yarn over, k2, yarn over. (9 stitches)

ROW 9: Yarn over, *k2, yarn over, ssk, k1, k2tog, yarn over, k1; repeat from the * to 1 stitch before the marker, ending this section with k1, yarn over. (11 stitches)

ROW 11: Yarn over, k1, *yarn over, s2kp2, yarn over, k3, yarn over, k2tog; repeat from the * to 2 stitches before the marker, ending this section with k2, yarn over. (13 stitches)

ROW 13: Yarn over, k1, yarn over, *s2kp2, yarn over, k2tog, yarn over, k1, yarn over, ssk, yarn over; repeat from the * to 4 stitches before the marker, ending this section with s2kp2, yarn over, k1, yarn over. (15 stitches)

ROW 15: Yarn over, k3, *k1, k2tog, yarn over, k3, yarn over, ssk; repeat from the * to 4 stitches before the marker, ending this section with k4, yarn over. (17 stitches)

ROW 17: Yarn over, k1, k2tog, yarn over, k1, *k2, yarn over, k2tog, yarn over, s2kp2, yarn over, k1; repeat from the * to 5 stitches before the marker, ending this section with k2, yarn over, ssk, k1, yarn over. (19 stitches)

ROW 19: Yarn over, k1, (k2tog, yarn over) twice, *k1, yarn over, ssk, yarn over, s2kp2, yarn over, k2tog, yarn over; repeat from the * to 6 stitches before the marker, ending this section with k1, (yarn over, ssk) twice, k1, yarn over. (21 stitches)

ROW 21: Yarn over, k3, k2tog, yarn over, k1, *k2, yarn over, ssk, k1, k2tog, yarn over, k1; repeat from the * to 7 stitches before the marker, ending this section with k2, yarn over, ssk, k3, yarn over. (23 stitches)

ROW 23: Yarn over, k2tog, yarn over, k3, yarn over, k2tog, *yarn over, s2kp2, yarn over, k3, yarn over, k2tog; repeat from the * to 8 stitches before the marker, ending this section with yarn over, s2kp2, yarn over, k3, yarn over, ssk, yarn over. (25 stitches)

ROW 25: Yarn over, (k2tog, yarn over) twice, k1, yarn over, ssk, yarn over, *s2kp2, yarn over, k2tog, yarn over, k1, yarn over, ssk, yarn over; repeat from the * to 10 stitches before the marker, ending this section with s2kp2, yarn over, k2tog, yarn over, k1, (yarn over, ssk) twice, yarn over. (27 stitches)

ROW 27: Yarn over, k2, k2tog, yarn over, k3, yarn over, ssk, *k1, k2tog, yarn over, k3, yarn over, ssk; repeat from the * to 10 stitches before the marker, ending this section with k1, k2tog, yarn over, k3, yarn over, ssk, k2, yarn over. (29 stitches)

(continued on page 84)

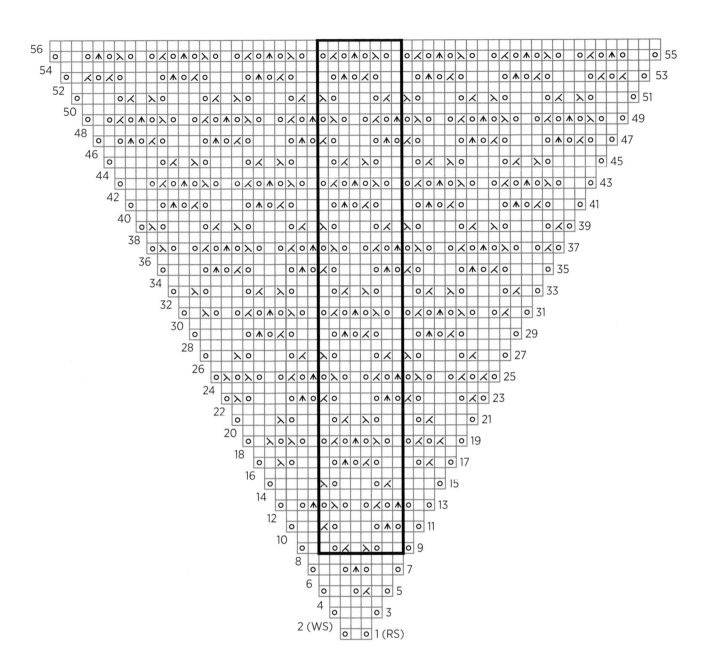

⚛ s2kp2

WEDGE 52, *continued*

ROW 29: Yarn over, k4, yarn over, k2tog, yarn over, s2kp2, yarn over, k1, *k2, yarn over, k2tog, yarn over, s2kp2, yarn over, k1; repeat from the * to 11 stitches before the marker, ending this section with k2, yarn over, k2tog, yarn over, s2kp2, yarn over, k4, yarn over. (31 stitches)

ROW 31: Yarn over, k1, k2tog, yarn over, k1, yarn over, ssk, yarn over, s2kp2, yarn over, k2tog, yarn over, *k1, yarn over, ssk, yarn over, s2kp2, yarn over, k2tog, yarn over; repeat from the * to 12 stitches before the marker, ending this section with k1, yarn over, ssk, yarn over, s2kp2, yarn over, k2tog, yarn over, k1, yarn over, ssk, k1, yarn over. (33 stitches)

ROW 33: Yarn over, k1, k2tog, yarn over, k3, yarn over, ssk, k1, k2tog, yarn over, k1, *k2, yarn over, ssk, k1, k2tog, yarn over, k1; repeat from the * to 13 stitches before the marker ending this sections with k2, yarn over, ssk, k1, k2tog, yarn over, k3, yarn over, ssk, k1, yarn over. (35 stitches)

ROW 35: Yarn over, k3, yarn over, k2tog, yarn over, s2kp2, yarn over, k3, yarn over, k2tog, *yarn over, s2kp2, yarn over, k3, yarn over, k2tog; repeat from the * to 14 stitches before the marker, ending this section with yarn over, s2kp2, yarn over, k3, yarn over, k2tog, yarn over, s2kp2, yarn over, k3, yarn over. (37 stitches)

ROW 37: Yarn over, k2tog, yarn over, k1, yarn over, ssk, yarn over, s2kp2, yarn over, k2tog, yarn over, k1, yarn over, ssk, yarn over, *s2kp2, yarn over, k2tog, yarn over, k1, yarn over, ssk, yarn over; repeat from the * to 16 stitches before the marker, ending this section with s2kp2, yarn over, k2tog, yarn over, k1, yarn over, ssk, yarn over, s2kp2, yarn over, k2tog, yarn over, k1, yarn over, ssk, yarn over. (39 stitches)

ROW 39: Yarn over, k2tog, yarn over, k3, yarn over, ssk, k1, k2tog, yarn over, k3, yarn over, ssk, *k1, k2tog, yarn over, k3, yarn over, ssk; repeat from the * to 16 stitches before the marker, ending this section with (k1, k2tog, yarn over, k3, yarn over, ssk) twice, yarn over. (41 stitches)

ROW 41: Yarn over, (k2, yarn over, k2tog, yarn over, s2kp2, yarn over, k1) twice, *k2, yarn over, k2tog, yarn over, s2kp2, yarn over, k1; repeat from the * to 17 stitches before the marker, ending this section with (k2, yarn over, k2tog, yarn over, s2kp2, yarn over, k1) twice, k1, yarn over. (43 stitches)

ROW 43: Yarn over, k1, (k1, yarn over, ssk, yarn over, s2kp2, yarn over, k2tog, yarn over) twice, *k1, yarn over, ssk, yarn over, s2kp2, yarn over, k2tog, yarn over; repeat from the * to 18 stitches before the marker, ending this section with (k1, yarn over, ssk, yarn over, s2kp2, yarn over, k2tog, yarn over) twice, k2, yarn over. (45 stitches)

ROW 45: Yarn over, k2, (k2, yarn over, ssk, k1, k2tog, yarn over, k1) twice, *k2, yarn over, ssk, k1, k2tog, yarn over, k1; repeat from the * to 19 stitches before the marker, ending this section with (k2, yarn over, ssk, k1, k2tog, yarn over, k1) twice, k3, yarn over. (47 stitches)

ROW 47: Yarn over, k1, (yarn over, k2tog, yarn over, s2kp2, yarn over, k3) twice, yarn over, k2tog, *yarn over, s2kp2, yarn over, k3, yarn over, k2tog; repeat from the * to 20 stitches before the marker, ending this section with yarn over, s2kp2, yarn over, (k3, yarn over, k2tog, yarn over, s2kp2, yarn over) twice, k1, yarn over. (49 stitches)

ROW 49: Yarn over, k1, (yarn over, ssk, yarn over, s2kp2, yarn over, k2tog, yarn over, k1) twice, yarn over, ssk, yarn over, *s2kp2, yarn over, k2tog, yarn over, k1, yarn over, ssk, yarn over; repeat from the * to 22 stitches before the marker, ending this section with s2kp2, yarn over, k2tog, yarn over, (k1, yarn over, ssk, yarn over, s2kp2, yarn over, k2tog, yarn over) twice, k1, yarn over. (51 stitches)

ROW 51: Yarn over, k3, (yarn over, ssk, k1, k2tog, yarn over, k3) twice, yarn over, ssk, *k1, k2tog, yarn over, k3, yarn over, ssk; repeat from the * to 22 stitches before the marker, ending this section with k1, k2tog, yarn over, (k3, yarn over, ssk, k1, k2tog, yarn over) twice, k3, yarn over. (53 stitches)

ROW 53: Yarn over, k1, (k2tog, yarn over) twice, (k3, yarn over, k2tog, yarn over, s2kp2, yarn over) twice, k1, *k2, yarn over, k2tog, yarn over, s2kp2, yarn over, k1; repeat from the * to 23 stitches before the marker, ending this section with k2, (yarn over, k2tog, yarn over, s2kp2, yarn over, k3) twice, (yarn over, k2tog) twice, k1, yarn over. (55 stitches)

ROW 55: Yarn over, k2, yarn over, s2kp2, yarn over, k2tog, yarn over, (k1, yarn over, ssk, yarn over, s2kp2, yarn over, k2tog, yarn over) twice, *k1, yarn over, ssk, yarn over, s2kp2, yarn over, k2tog, yarn over; repeat from the * to 24 stitches before the marker, ending this section with (k1, yarn over, ssk, yarn over, s2kp2, yarn over, k2tog, yarn over) twice, k1, yarn over, ssk, yarn over, s2kp2, yarn over, k2, yarn over. (57 stitches)

ROW 56: As Row 2.

Repeat Rows 9–56 for the pattern.

53

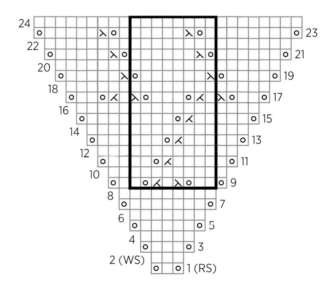

ROW 1 (RS): Yarn over, k1, yarn over. (3 stitches)

ROW 2 AND ALL WS ROWS: Purl across.

ROW 3: Yarn over, k3, yarn over. (5 stitches)

ROW 5: Yarn over, k5, yarn over. (7 stitches)

ROW 7: Yarn over, k7, yarn over. (9 stitches)

ROW 9: Yarn over, *k2, yarn over, ssk, k1, k2tog, yarn over, k1; repeat from the * to 1 stitch before the marker, ending this section with k1, yarn over. (11 stitches)

ROW 11: Yarn over, k1, *k4, k2tog, yarn over, k2; repeat from the * to 2 stitches before the marker, ending this section with k2, yarn over. (13 stitches)

ROW 13: Yarn over, k2, *k3, k2tog, yarn over, k3; repeat from the * to 3 stitches before the marker, ending this section with k3, yarn over. (15 stitches)

ROW 15: Yarn over, k3, *k2, k2tog, yarn over, k4; repeat from the * to 4 stitches before the marker, ending this section with k4, yarn over. (17 stitches)

ROW 17: Yarn over, k2, yarn over, ssk, *k1, k2tog, yarn over, k3, yarn over, ssk; repeat from the * to 5 stitches before the marker, ending this section with k1, k2tog, yarn over, k2, yarn over. (19 stitches)

ROW 19: Yarn over, k4, yarn over, *ssk, k6, yarn over; repeat from the * to 7 stitches before the marker, ending this section with ssk, k5, yarn over. (21 stitches)

ROW 21: Yarn over, k6, *yarn over, ssk, k6; repeat from the * to 7 stitches before the marker, ending this section with yarn over, ssk, k5, yarn over. (23 stitches)

ROW 23: Yarn over, k7, *k1, yarn over, ssk, k5; repeat from the * to 8 stitches before the marker, ending this section with k1, yarn over, ssk, k5, yarn over. (25 stitches)

ROW 24: As Row 2.

Repeat Rows 9–24 for the pattern.

54

NOTE: To execute s2kp2 on a right-side row, see page 282. For wrong-side rows, follow this procedure: insert the needle into the second and then the first stitch (in that order) as if to p2tog-tbl, slip both stitches at once onto the right needle from this position, purl the next stitch, then pass the 2 slipped stitches over the purled stitch. (Abbreviated s2pp2.)

ROW 1 (RS): Yarn over, k1, yarn over. (3 stitches)

ROWS 2, 4, 6, 12, 14, 16, 18, 24, 26, 28, 30, 36, 38, 40, 42, 48, 50, 52, 54, 60, AND 62: Purl across.

ROW 3: Yarn over, k3, yarn over. (5 stitches)

ROW 5: Yarn over, k5, yarn over. (7 stitches)

ROW 7: Yarn over, k3, yarn over, ssk, k2, yarn over. (9 stitches)

ROW 8: P2, ssp (page 281), yarn over, p1, yarn over, p2tog, p2.

ROW 9: Yarn over, k1, k2tog, yarn over, k3, yarn over, ssk, k1, yarn over. (11 stitches)

ROW 10: P1, ssp, yarn over, p5, yarn over, p2tog, p1.

ROW 11: Yarn over, k5, yarn over, ssk, k4, yarn over. (13 stitches)

ROW 13: Yarn over, k4, k2tog, yarn over, k1, yarn over, ssk, k4, yarn over. (15 stitches)

ROW 15: Yarn over, k1, yarn over, ssk, k1, k2tog, yarn over, k3, yarn over, ssk, k1, k2tog, yarn over, k1, yarn over. (17 stitches)

ROW 17: Yarn over, k3, *yarn over, s2kp2, yarn over, k5; repeat from the * to 6 stitches before the marker, ending this section with yarn over, s2kp2, yarn over, k3, yarn over. (19 stitches)

ROW 19: Yarn over, k1, yarn over, ssk, k1, *k5, yarn over, ssk, k1; repeat from the * to 7 stitches before the marker, ending this section with k5, yarn over, ssk, yarn over. (21 stitches)

ROW 20: Ssp, yarn over, p1, yarn over, p2tog, p3, *ssp, yarn over, p1, yarn over, p2tog, p3; repeat from the * to 5 stitches before the marker, ending this section with ssp, yarn over, p1, yarn over, p2tog.

ROW 21: Yarn over, k4, yarn over, *ssk, k1, k2tog, yarn over, k3, yarn over; repeat from the * to the 9 stitches before the marker, ending this section with ssk, k1, k2tog, yarn over, k4, yarn over. (23 stitches)

ROW 22: P6, yarn over, s2pp2 (see note at left), yarn over, *p5, yarn over, s2pp2, yarn over; repeat from the * to 6 stitches before the marker, ending this section with p6.

ROW 23: Yarn over, k3, yarn over, ssk, k1, *k5, yarn over, ssk, k1; repeat from the * to 9 stitches before the marker, ending this section with k5, yarn over, ssk, k2, yarn over. (25 stitches)

ROW 25: Yarn over, k2, k2tog, yarn over, k1, yarn over, ssk, *k3, k2tog, yarn over, k1, yarn over, ssk; repeat from the * to 10 stitches before the marker, ending this section with k3, k2tog, yarn over, k1, yarn over, ssk, k2, yarn over. (27 stitches)

ROW 27: Yarn over, k2, k2tog, yarn over, k3, yarn over, *ssk, k1, k2tog, yarn over, k3, yarn over; repeat from the * to 12 stitches before the marker, ending this section with ssk, k1, k2tog, yarn over, k3, yarn over, ssk, k2, yarn over. (29 stitches)

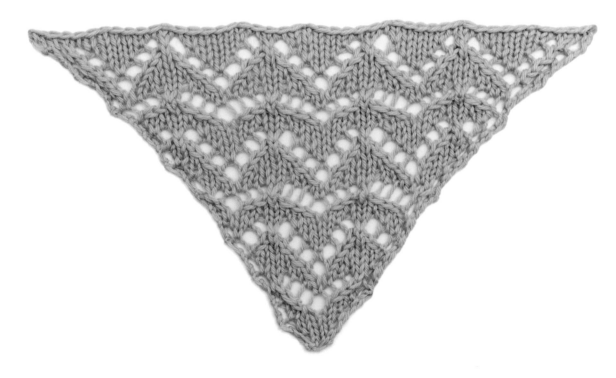

ROW 29: Yarn over, k1, yarn over, s2kp2, yarn over, k5, *yarn over, s2kp2, yarn over, k5; repeat from the * to 12 stitches before the marker, ending this section with yarn over, s2kp2, yarn over, k5, yarn over, s2kp2, yarn over, k1, yarn over. (31 stitches)

ROW 31: Yarn over, k7, yarn over, ssk, k1, *k5, yarn over, ssk, k1; repeat from the * to 13 stitches before the marker, ending this section with k5, yarn over, ssk, k6, yarn over. (33 stitches)

ROW 32: P1, yarn over, p2tog, p3, ssp, yarn over, p1, yarn over, p2tog, p3, *ssp, yarn over, p1, yarn over, p2tog, p3; repeat from the * to 11 stitches before the marker, ending this section with ssp, yarn over, p1, yarn over, p2tog, p3, ssp, yarn over, p1.

ROW 33: Yarn over, k2, yarn over, ssk, k1, k2tog, yarn over, k3, yarn over, *ssk, k1, k2tog, yarn over, k3, yarn over; repeat from the * to 15 stitches before the marker, ending this section with ssk, k1, k2tog, yarn over, k3, yarn over, ssk, k1, k2tog, yarn over, k2, yarn over. (35 stitches)

(continued on page 89)

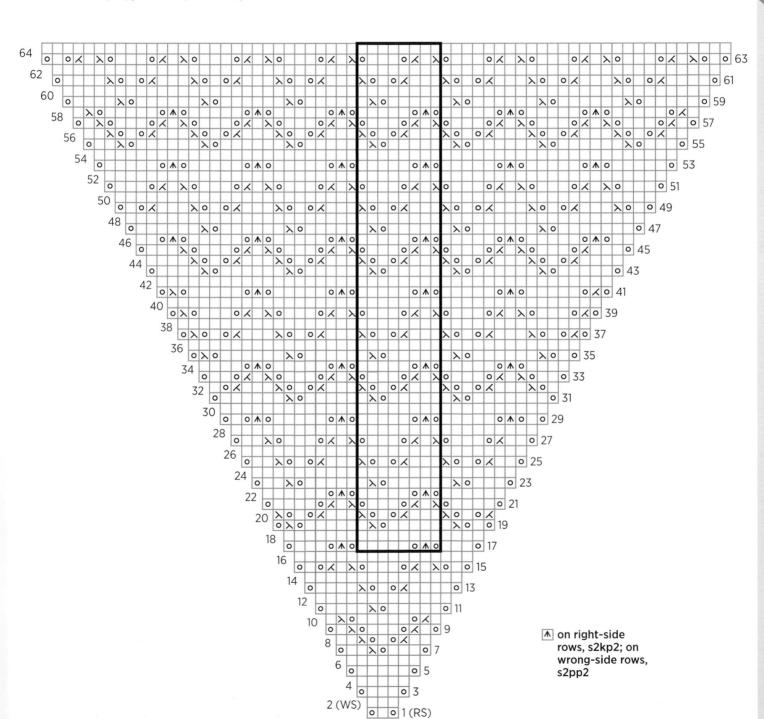

⋀ on right-side rows, s2kp2; on wrong-side rows, s2pp2

SHAWL #18

Six triangles combine to create this full-coverage cape. See page 277 for instructions.

ROW 34: P4, yarn over, s2pp2, yarn over, p5, yarn over, s2pp2, yarn over, *p5, yarn over, s2pp2, yarn over; repeat from the * to 12 stitches before the marker, ending this section with p5, yarn over, s2pp2, yarn over, p4.

ROW 35: Yarn over, k1, yarn over, ssk, k6, yarn over, ssk, k1, *k5, yarn over, ssk, k1; repeat from the * to 15 stitches before the marker, ending this section with k5, yarn over, ssk, k6, yarn over, ssk, yarn over. (37 stitches)

ROW 37: Yarn over, k2tog, yarn over, k1, yarn over, ssk, k3, k2tog, yarn over, k1, yarn over, ssk, *k3, k2tog, yarn over, k1, yarn over, ssk; repeat from the * to 16 stitches before the marker, ending this section with (k3, k2tog, yarn over, k1, yarn over, ssk) twice, yarn over. (39 stitches)

ROW 39: Yarn over, k2tog, yarn over, k3, yarn over, ssk, k1, k2tog, yarn over, k3, yarn over, *ssk, k1, k2tog, yarn over, k3, yarn over; repeat from the * to 18 stitches before the marker, ending this section with (ssk, k1, k2tog, yarn over, k3, yarn over) twice, ssk, yarn over. (41 stitches)

ROW 41: Yarn over, k2tog, yarn over, k5, yarn over, s2kp2, yarn over, k5, *yarn over, s2kp2, yarn over, k5; repeat from the * to 18 stitches before the marker, ending this section with (yarn over, s2kp2, yarn over, k5) twice, yarn over, ssk, yarn over. (43 stitches)

ROW 43: Yarn over, k5, yarn over, ssk, k6, yarn over, ssk, k1, *k5, yarn over, ssk, k1; repeat from the * to 19 stitches before the marker, ending this section with k5, yarn over, ssk, k6, yarn over, ssk, k4, yarn over. (45 stitches)

ROW 44: P4, (ssp, yarn over, p1, yarn over, p2tog, p3) twice, *ssp, yarn over, p1, yarn over, p2tog, p3; repeat from the * to 17 stitches before the marker, ending this section with (ssp, yarn over, p1, yarn over, p2tog, p3) twice, p1.

ROW 45: Yarn over, k3, k2tog, yarn over, k3, yarn over, ssk, k1, k2tog, yarn over, k3, yarn over, *ssk, k1, k2tog, yarn over, k3, yarn over; repeat from the * to 21 stitches before the marker, ending this section with ssk, (k1, k2tog, yarn over, k3, yarn over, ssk) twice, k3, yarn over. (47 stitches)

ROW 46: P2, yarn over, s2pp2, yarn over, (p5, yarn over, s2pp2, yarn over) twice, *p5, yarn over, s2pp2, yarn over; repeat from the * to 18 stitches before the marker, ending this section with (p5, yarn over, s2pp2, yarn over) twice, p2.

ROW 47: Yarn over, k1, (k6, yarn over, ssk) twice, k1, *k5, yarn over, ssk, k1; repeat from the * to 21 stitches before the marker, ending this section with k5, (yarn over, ssk, k6) twice, yarn over. (49 stitches)

ROW 49: Yarn over, k1, (yarn over, ssk, k3, k2tog, yarn over, k1) twice, yarn over, ssk, *k3, k2tog, yarn over, k1, yarn over, ssk; repeat from the * to 22 stitches before the marker, ending this section with (k3, k2tog, yarn over, k1, yarn over, ssk) twice, k3, k2tog, yarn over, k1, yarn over. (51 stitches)

ROW 51: Yarn over, (k3, yarn over, ssk, k1, k2tog, yarn over) twice, k3, yarn over, *ssk, k1, k2tog, yarn over, k3, yarn over; repeat from the * to 24 stitches before the marker, ending this section with ssk, (k1, k2tog, yarn over, k3, yarn over, ssk) twice, k1, k2tog, yarn over, k3, yarn over. (53 stitches)

ROW 53: Yarn over, (k5, yarn over, s2kp2, yarn over) twice, k5, *yarn over, s2kp2, yarn over, k5; repeat from the * to 24 stitches before the marker, ending this section with (yarn over, s2kp2, yarn over, k5) 3 times, yarn over. (55 stitches)

ROW 55: Yarn over, k3, (yarn over, ssk, k6) twice, yarn over, ssk, k1, *k5, yarn over, ssk, k1; repeat from the * to 25 stitches before the marker, ending this section with k5, (yarn over, ssk, k6) twice, yarn over, ssk, k2, yarn over. (57 stitches)

ROW 56: P2, (ssp, yarn over, p1, yarn over, p2tog, p3) 3 times, *ssp, yarn over, p1, yarn over, p2tog, p3; repeat from the * to 23 stitches before the marker, ending this section with (ssp, yarn over, p1, yarn over, p2tog, p3) twice, ssp, yarn over, p1, yarn over, p2tog, p2.

ROW 57: Yarn over, k1, (k2tog, yarn over, k3, yarn over, ssk, k1) twice, k2tog, yarn over, k3, yarn over, *ssk, k1, k2tog, yarn over, k3, yarn over; repeat from the * to 27 stitches before the marker, ending this section with ssk, (k1, k2tog, yarn over, k3, yarn over, ssk) 3 times, k1, yarn over. (59 stitches)

ROW 58: P1, ssp, yarn over, (p5, yarn over, s2pp2, yarn over) 3 times, *p5, yarn over, s2pp2, yarn over; repeat from the * to 24 stitches before the marker, ending this section with p5, yarn over, s2pp2, yarn over) twice, p5, yarn over, p2tog, p1.

ROW 59: Yarn over, k5, (yarn over, ssk, k6) twice, yarn over, ssk, k1, *k5, yarn over, ssk, k1; repeat from the * to 27 stitches before the marker, ending this section with k5, (yarn over, ssk, k6) twice, yarn over, ssk, k4, yarn over. (61 stitches)

ROW 61: Yarn over, k4, (k2tog, yarn over, k1, yarn over, ssk, k3) twice, k2tog, yarn over, k1, yarn over, ssk, *k3, k2tog, yarn over, k1, yarn over, ssk; repeat from the * to 28 stitches before the marker, ending this section with (k3, k2tog, yarn over, k1, yarn over, ssk) 3 times, k4, yarn over. (63 stitches)

ROW 63: Yarn over, k1, (yarn over, ssk, k1, k2tog, yarn over, k3) 3 times, yarn over, *ssk, k1, k2tog, yarn over, k3, yarn over; repeat from the * to 30 stitches before the marker, ending this section with ssk, (k1, k2tog, yarn over, k3, yarn over, ssk) 3 times, k1, k2tog, yarn over, k1, yarn over. (65 stitches)

ROW 64: As Row 2.

Repeat Rows 17–64 for the pattern.

55

ROW 1 (RS): Yarn over, k1, yarn over. (3 stitches)

ROWS 2, 4, 8, 14, 20, 26, 32, 38, 44, AND 50: Purl across.

ROW 3: Yarn over, k3, yarn over. (5 stitches)

ROW 5: Yarn over, k2tog, yarn over, k1, yarn over, ssk, yarn over. (7 stitches)

ROW 6: Ssp (page 281), yarn over, p3, yarn over, p2tog.

ROW 7: Yarn over, k7, yarn over. (9 stitches)

ROW 9: Yarn over, *k3, yarn over, sssk (page 285), yarn over, k2; repeat from the * to 1 stitch before the marker, ending this section with k1, yarn over. (11 stitches)

ROW 10: P2, *p1, yarn over, p2tog, p1, ssp, yarn over, p2; repeat from the * to 1 stitch before the marker, ending this section with p1.

ROW 11: Yarn over, k1, *k1, yarn over, ssk, yarn over, sssk, yarn over, k2tog, yarn over; repeat from the * to 2 stitches before the marker, ending this section with k2, yarn over. (13 stitches)

ROW 12: P3, *p1, yarn over, p2tog, p1, ssp, yarn over, p2; repeat from the * to 2 stitches before the marker, ending this section with p2.

ROW 13: Yarn over, k2, *k3, yarn over, sssk, yarn over, k2; repeat from the * to 3 stitches before the marker, ending this section with k3, yarn over. (15 stitches)

ROW 15: Yarn over, k2, yarn over, *sssk, yarn over, k5, yarn over; repeat from the * to 5 stitches before the marker, ending this section with sssk, yarn over, k2, yarn over. (17 stitches)

ROW 16: P2, yarn over, p2tog, p1, *ssp, yarn over, p3, yarn over, p2tog, p1; repeat from the * to 4 stitches before the marker, ending this section with ssp, yarn over, p2.

ROW 17: Yarn over, k1, yarn over, ssk, yarn over, *sssk, yarn over, k2tog, yarn over, k1, yarn over, ssk, yarn over; repeat from the * to 6 stitches before the marker, ending this section with sssk, yarn over, k2tog, yarn over, k1, yarn over. (19 stitches)

ROW 18: P3, yarn over, p2tog, p1, *ssp, yarn over, k3, yarn over, p2tog, p1; repeat from the * to 5 stitches before the marker, ending this section with ssp, yarn over, p3.

ROW 19: Yarn over, k4, yarn over, *sssk, yarn over, k5, yarn over; repeat from the * to 7 stitches before the marker, ending this section with sssk, yarn over, k4, yarn over. (21 stitches)

ROW 21: Yarn over, k1, yarn over, sssk, yarn over, k2, *k3, yarn over, sssk, yarn over, k2; repeat from the * to 7 stitches before the marker, ending this section with k3, yarn over, sssk, yarn over, k1, yarn over. (23 stitches)

ROW 22: P1, yarn over, p2tog, p1, ssp, yarn over, p2, *p1, yarn over, p2tog, p1, ssp, yarn over, p2; repeat from the * to 7 stitches before the marker, ending this section with p1, yarn over, p2tog, p1, ssp, yarn over, p1.

ROW 23: Yarn over, k2, yarn over, sssk, yarn over, k2tog, yarn over, *k1, yarn over, ssk, yarn over, sssk, yarn over, k2tog, yarn over; repeat from the * to 8 stitches before the marker, ending this section with k1, yarn over, ssk, yarn over, sssk, yarn over, k2, yarn over. (25 stitches)

ROW 24: P2, yarn over, p2tog, p1, ssp, yarn over, p2, *p1, yarn over, p2tog, p1, ssp, yarn over, p2; repeat from the * to 8 stitches before the marker, ending this section with p1, yarn over, p2tog, p1, ssp, yarn over, p2.

ROW 25: Yarn over, k3, yarn over, sssk, yarn over, k2, *k3, yarn over, sssk, yarn over, k2; repeat from the * to 9 stitches before the marker, ending this section with k3, yarn over, sssk, yarn over, k3, yarn over. (27 stitches)

ROW 27: Yarn over, k1, ssk, yarn over, k5, yarn over, *sssk, yarn over, k5, yarn over; repeat from the * to 11 stitches before the marker, ending this section with sssk, yarn over, k5, yarn over, ssk, k1, yarn over. (29 stitches)

ROW 28: Yarn over, p2tog, p1, ssp, yarn over, p3, yarn over, p2tog, p1, *ssp, yarn over, p3, yarn over, p2tog, p1; repeat from the * to 10 stitches before the marker, ending this section with ssp, yarn over, p3, yarn over, p2tog, p1, ssp, yarn over.

ROW 29: Yarn over, k1, yarn over, sssk, yarn over, k2tog, yarn over, k1, yarn over, ssk, yarn over, *sssk, yarn over, k2tog, yarn over, k1, yarn over, ssk, yarn over; repeat from the * to 12 stitches before the marker, ending this section with sssk, yarn over, k2tog, yarn over, k1, yarn over, ssk, yarn over, sssk, yarn over, k1, yarn over. (31 stitches)

ROW 30: P1, yarn over, p2tog, p1, ssp, yarn over, p3, yarn over, p2tog, p1, *ssp, yarn over, p3, yarn over, p2tog, p1; repeat from the * to 11 stitches before the marker, ending this section with ssp, yarn over, p3, yarn over, p2tog, p1, ssp, yarn over, p1.

ROW 31: Yarn over, k2, yarn over, sssk, yarn over, k5, yarn over, *sssk, yarn over, k5, yarn over; repeat from the * to 13 stitches before the marker, ending this section with sssk, yarn over, k5, yarn over, sssk, yarn over, k2, yarn over. (33 stitches)

ROW 33: Yarn over, ssk, yarn over, k5, yarn over, sssk, yarn over, k2, *k3, yarn over, sssk, yarn over, k2; repeat from the * to 13 stitches before the marker, ending this section with k3, yarn over, sssk, yarn over, k5, yarn over, ssk, yarn over. (35 stitches)

(continued on page 92)

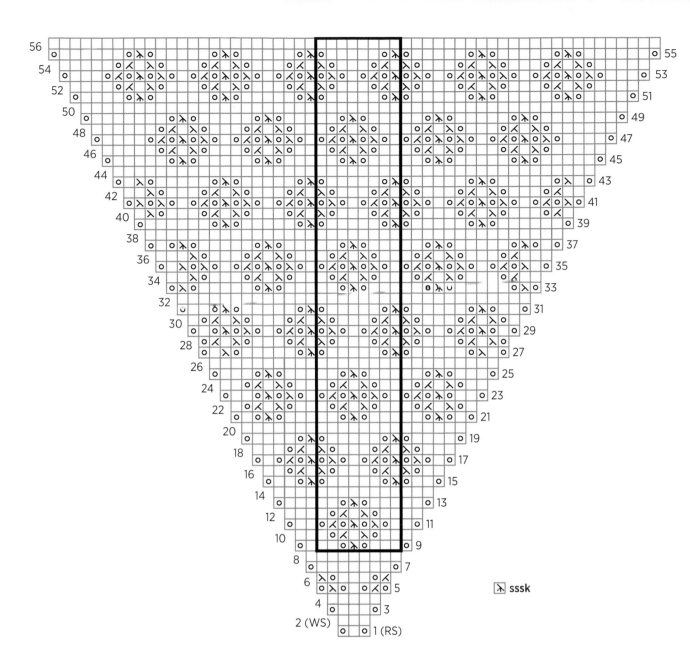

sssk

WEDGE 55, *continued*

ROW 34: P2, ssp, yarn over, p3, yarn over, p2tog, p1, ssp, yarn over, p2, *p1, yarn over, p2tog, p1, ssp, yarn over, p2; repeat from the * to 13 stitches before the marker, ending this section with p1, yarn over, p2tog, p1, ssp, yarn over, p3, yarn over, p2tog, p2.

ROW 35: Yarn over, k1, ssk, yarn over, k2tog, yarn over, k1, yarn over, ssk, yarn over, sssk, yarn over, k2tog, yarn over, *k1, yarn over, ssk, yarn over, sssk, yarn over, k2tog, yarn over; repeat from the * to 14 stitches before the marker, ending this section with k1, yarn over, ssk, yarn over, sssk, yarn over, k2tog, yarn over, k1, (yarn over, ssk) twice, k1, yarn over. (37 stitches)

ROW 36: P3, ssp, yarn over, p3, yarn over, p2tog, p1, ssp, yarn over, p2, *p1, yarn over, p2tog, p1, ssp, yarn over, p2; repeat from the * to 14 stitches before the marker, ending this section with p1, yarn over, p2tog, p1, ssp, yarn over, p3, yarn over, p2tog, p3.

ROW 37: Yarn over, k1, yarn over, sssk, yarn over, k5, yarn over, sssk, yarn over, k2, *k3, yarn over, sssk, yarn over, k2; repeat from the * to 15 stitches before the marker, ending this section with k3, yarn over, sssk, yarn over, k5, yarn over, sssk, yarn over, k1, yarn over. (39 stitches)

ROW 39: Yarn over, k6, yarn over, sssk, yarn over, k5, yarn over, *sssk, yarn over, k5, yarn over; repeat from the * to 17 stitches before the marker, ending this section with sssk, yarn over, k5, yarn over, sssk, yarn over, k6, yarn over. (41 stitches)

ROW 40: P1, ssp, yarn over, p3, yarn over, p2tog, p1, ssp, yarn over, p3, yarn over, p2tog, p1, *ssp, yarn over, p3, yarn over, p2tog, p1; repeat from the * to 16 stitches before the marker, ending this section with ssp, yarn over, p3, yarn over, p2tog, p1, ssp, yarn over, p3, yarn over, p2tog, p1.

ROW 41: Yarn over, ssk, yarn over, k2tog, yarn over, k1, yarn over, ssk, yarn over, sssk, yarn over, k2tog, yarn over, k1, yarn over, ssk, yarn over, *sssk, yarn over, k2tog, yarn over, k1, yarn over, ssk, yarn over; repeat from the * to 18 stitches before the marker, ending this section with sssk, yarn over, k2tog, yarn over, k1, yarn over, ssk, yarn over, sssk, yarn over, k2tog, yarn over, k1, (yarn over, ssk) twice, yarn over. (43 stitches)

ROW 42: P2, ssp, yarn over, p3, yarn over, p2tog, p1, ssp, yarn over, p3, yarn over, p2tog, p1; *ssp, yarn over, p3, yarn over, p2tog, p1, repeat from the * to 17 stitches before the marker, ending this section with ssp, yarn over, p3, yarn over, p2tog, p1, ssp, yarn over, p3, yarn over, p2tog, p2.

ROW 43: Yarn over, k1, ssk, yarn over, k5, yarn over, sssk, yarn over, k5, yarn over, *sssk, yarn over, k5, yarn over; repeat from the * to 19 stitches before the marker, ending this section with sssk, yarn over, k5, yarn over, sssk, yarn over, k5, yarn over, ssk, k1, yarn over. (45 stitches)

ROW 45: Yarn over, (k5, yarn over, sssk, yarn over) twice, k2, *k3, yarn over, sssk, yarn over, k2; repeat from the * to 19 stitches before the marker, ending this section with k3, (yarn over, sssk, yarn over, k5) twice, yarn over. (47 stitches)

ROW 46: P5, yarn over, p2tog, p1, ssp, yarn over, p3, yarn over, p2tog, p1, ssp, yarn over, p2, *p1, yarn over, p2tog, p1, ssp, yarn over, p2; repeat from the * to 19 stitches before the marker, ending this section with p1, yarn over, p2tog, p1, ssp, yarn over, p3, yarn over, p2tog, p1, ssp, yarn over, p5.

ROW 47: Yarn over, k3, (k1, yarn over, ssk, yarn over, sssk, yarn over, k2tog, yarn over) twice, *k1, yarn over, ssk, yarn over, sssk, yarn over, k2tog, yarn over; repeat from the * to 20 stitches before the marker, ending this section with (k1, yarn over, ssk, yarn over, sssk, yarn over, k2tog, yarn over) twice, k4, yarn over. (49 stitches)

ROW 48: P3, (p3, yarn over, p2tog, p1, ssp, yarn over) twice, p2, *p1, yarn over, p2tog, p1, ssp, yarn over, p2; repeat from the * to 20 stitches before the marker, ending this section with p1, (yarn over, p2tog, p1, ssp, yarn over, p3) twice, p3.

ROW 49: Yarn over, k2, (k5, yarn over, sssk, yarn over) twice, k2, *k3, yarn over, sssk, yarn over, k2; repeat from the * to 21 stitches before the marker, ending this section with k3, (yarn over, sssk, yarn over, k5) twice, k2, yarn over. (51 stitches)

ROW 51: Yarn over, k4, (yarn over, sssk, yarn over, k5) twice, yarn over, *sssk, yarn over, k5, yarn over; repeat from the * to 23 stitches before the marker, ending this section with sssk, yarn over, (k5, yarn over, sssk, yarn over) twice, k4, yarn over. (53 stitches)

ROW 52: P4 (yarn over, p2tog, p1, ssp, yarn over, p3) twice, yarn over, p2tog, p1, *ssp, yarn over, p3, yarn over, p2tog, p1; repeat from the * to 22 stitches before the marker, ending this section with (ssp, yarn over, p3, yarn over, p2tog, p1) twice, ssp, yarn over, p4.

ROW 53: Yarn over, k3, (yarn over, ssk, yarn over, sssk, yarn over, k2tog, yarn over, k1) twice, yarn over, ssk, yarn over, *sssk, yarn over, k2tog, yarn over, k1, yarn over, ssk, yarn over; repeat from the * to 24 stitches before the marker, ending this section with sssk, yarn over, k2tog, yarn over, (k1, yarn over, ssk, yarn over, sssk, yarn over, k2tog, yarn over) twice, k3, yarn over. (55 stitches)

ROW 54: P5, (yarn over, p2tog, p1, ssp, yarn over, p3) twice, yarn over, p2tog, p1, *ssp, yarn over, p3, yarn over, p2tog, p1; repeat from the * to 23 stitches before the marker, ending this section with ssp, yarn over, (p3, yarn over, p2tog, p1, ssp, yarn over) twice, p5.

ROW 55: Yarn over, k6, (yarn over, sssk, yarn over, k5) twice, yarn over, *sssk, yarn over, k5, yarn over; repeat from the * to 25 stitches before the marker, ending this section with sssk, yarn over, (k5, yarn over, sssk, yarn over) twice, k6, yarn over. (57 stitches)

ROW 56: Purl across.

Repeat Rows 9–56 for the pattern.

WEDGES with 10-Stitch Multiples

Start each wedge with the provisional cast on and the tab of your choice (page 10).

56

ROW 1 (RS): Yarn over, p1, yarn over. (3 stitches)

ROW 2 AND ALL WS ROWS: Knit the knit stitches and purl the purl stitches and yarn overs.

ROW 3: Yarn over, k1, p1, k1, yarn over. (5 stitches)

ROW 5: Yarn over, k2, p1, k2, yarn over. (7 stitches)

ROW 7: Yarn over, k3, p1, k3, yarn over. (9 stitches)

ROW 9: Yarn over, k4, p1, k4, yarn over. (11 stitches)

ROW 11: Yarn over, *p1, k2tog, k2, yarn over, k1, yarn over, k2, ssk; repeat from the * to 1 stitch before the marker, ending this section with p1, yarn over. (13 stitches)

ROW 13: Yarn over, k1, *p1, k2tog, k1, yarn over, k3, yarn over, k1, ssk; repeat from the * to 2 stitches before the marker, ending this section with p1, k1, yarn over. (15 stitches)

ROW 15: Yarn over, k2, *p1, k2tog, yarn over, k5, yarn over, ssk; repeat from the * to 3 stitches before the marker, ending this section with p1, k2, yarn over. (17 stitches)

ROW 17: Yarn over, k3, *p1, k2, yarn over, ssk, k1, k2tog, yarn over, k2; repeat from the * to 4 stitches before the marker, ending this section with p1, k3, yarn over. (19 stitches)

ROW 19: Yarn over, k4, *p1, k3, yarn over, s2kp2 (page 282), yarn over, k3; repeat from the * to 5 stitches before the marker, ending this section with p1, k4, yarn over. (21 stitches)

ROW 20: As Row 2.

Repeat Rows 11–20 for the pattern.

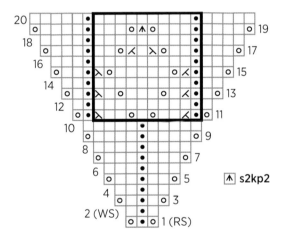

⬆ s2kp2

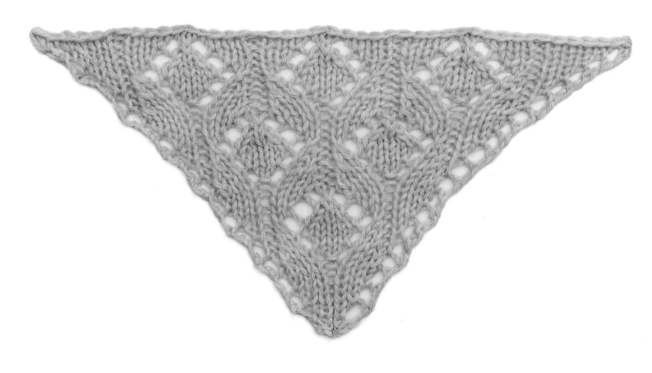

ROW 1 (RS): Yarn over, k1, yarn over. (3 stitches)

ROW 2 AND ALL WS ROWS: Purl across.

ROW 3: Yarn over, k3, yarn over. (5 stitches)

ROW 5: Yarn over, k5, yarn over. (7 stitches)

ROW 7: Yarn over, k1, yarn over, ssk, k1, k2tog, yarn over, k1, yarn over. (9 stitches)

ROW 9: Yarn over, k3, yarn over, s2kp2 (page 282), yarn over, k3, yarn over. (11 stitches)

ROW 11: Yarn over, *k4, k2tog, yarn over, k4; repeat from the * to 1 stitch before the marker, ending this section with k1, yarn over. (13 stitches)

ROW 13: Yarn over, k1, *k3, k2tog, yarn over, k1, yarn over, ssk, k2; repeat from the * to 2 stitches before the marker, ending this section with k2, yarn over. (15 stitches)

ROW 15: Yarn over, k2, *k2, k2tog, yarn over, k3, yarn over, ssk, k1; repeat from the * to 3 stitches before the marker, ending this section with k3, yarn over. (17 stitches)

ROW 17: Yarn over, k1, yarn over, ssk, *k1, k2tog, yarn over, k5, yarn over, ssk; repeat from the * to 4 stitches before the marker, ending this section with k1, k2tog, yarn over, k1, yarn over. (19 stitches)

ROW 19: Yarn over, k3, yarn over, *s2kp2, yarn over, k7, yarn over; repeat from the * to 6 stitches before the marker, ending this section with s2kp2, yarn over, k3, yarn over. (21 stitches)

ROW 20: As Row 2.

Repeat Rows 11–20 for the pattern.

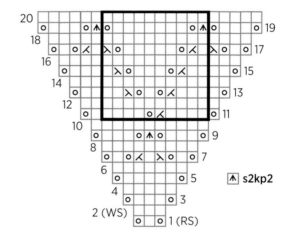

⚊ s2kp2

58

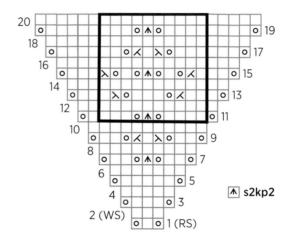

ROW 1 (RS): Yarn over, k1, yarn over. (3 stitches)

ROW 2 AND ALL WS ROWS: Purl across.

ROW 3: Yarn over, k3, yarn over. (5 stitches)

ROW 5: Yarn over, k5, yarn over. (7 stitches)

ROW 7: Yarn over, k2, yarn over, s2kp2 (page 282), yarn over, k2, yarn over. (9 stitches)

ROW 9: Yarn over, k2, yarn over, ssk, k1, k2tog, yarn over, k2, yarn over. (11 stitches)

ROW 11: Yarn over, *k4, yarn over, s2kp2, yarn over, k3; repeat from the * to 1 stitch before the marker, ending this section with k1, yarn over. (13 stitches)

ROW 13: Yarn over, k1, *k2, k2tog, yarn over, k3, yarn over, ssk, k1; repeat from the * to 2 stitches before the marker, ending this section with k2, yarn over. (15 stitches)

ROW 15: Yarn over, k2, *k1, k2tog, yarn over, k1, yarn over, s2kp2, yarn over, k1, yarn over, ssk; repeat from the * to 3 stitches before the marker, ending this section with k3, yarn over. (17 stitches)

ROW 17: Yarn over, k3, *k3, yarn over, ssk, k1, k2tog, yarn over, k2; repeat from the * to 4 stitches before the marker, ending this section with k4, yarn over. (19 stitches)

ROW 19: Yarn over, k4, *k4, yarn over, s2kp2, yarn over, k3; repeat from the * to 5 stitches before the marker, ending this section with k5, yarn over. (21 stitches)

ROW 20: As Row 2.

Repeat Rows 11–20 for the pattern.

⊼ s2kp2

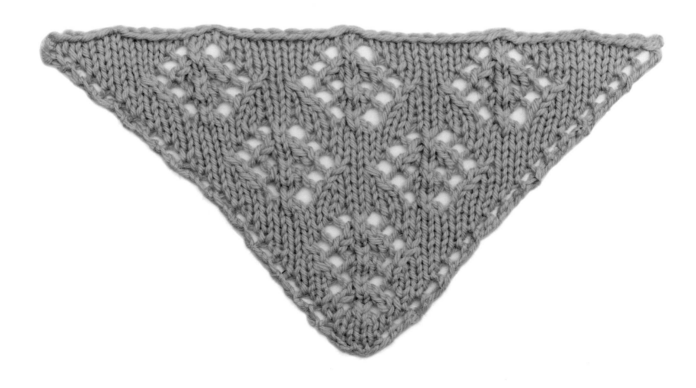

59

ROW 1 (RS): Yarn over, k1, yarn over. (3 stitches)

ROW 2 AND ALL WS ROWS: Purl across.

ROW 3: Yarn over, k3, yarn over. (5 stitches)

ROW 5: Yarn over, k5, yarn over. (7 stitches)

ROW 7: Yarn over, k7, yarn over. (9 stitches)

ROW 9: Yarn over, k9, yarn over. (11 stitches)

ROW 11: Yarn over, k1, yarn over, k3, s2kp2 (page 282), k3, yarn over, k1, yarn over. (13 stitches)

ROW 13: Yarn over, k3, yarn over, k2, s2kp2, k2, yarn over, k3, yarn over. (15 stitches)

ROW 15: Yarn over, k5, yarn over, k1, s2kp2, k1, yarn over, k5, yarn over. (17 stitches)

ROW 17: Yarn over, k7, yarn over, s2kp2, yarn over, k7, yarn over. (19 stitches)

ROW 19: Yarn over, k8, yarn over, s2kp2, yarn over, k8, yarn over. (21 stitches)

ROW 21: Yarn over, k2tog, k3, yarn over, *k1, yarn over, k3, s2kp2, k3, yarn over; repeat from the * to 6 stitches before marker, ending this section with k1, yarn over, k3, ssk, yarn over. (23 stitches)

ROW 23: Yarn over, k1, k2tog, k2, yarn over, k1, *k2, yarn over, k2, s2kp2, k2, yarn over, k1; repeat from the * to 7 stitches before marker, ending this section with k2, yarn over, k2, ssk, k1, yarn over. (25 stitches)

ROW 25: Yarn over, k2, k2tog, k1, yarn over, k2, *k3, yarn over, k1, s2kp2, k1, yarn over, k2; repeat from the * to 8 stitches before marker, ending this section with k3, yarn over, k1, ssk, k2, yarn over. (27 stitches)

ROW 27: Yarn over, k2, yarn over, s2kp2, yarn over, k3, *k4, yarn over, s2kp2, yarn over, k3; repeat from the * to 9 stitches before marker, ending this section with k4, yarn over, s2kp2, yarn over, k2, yarn over. (29 stitches)

ROW 29: Yarn over, k3, yarn over, s2kp2, yarn over, k3, *k4, yarn over, s2kp2, yarn over, k3; repeat from the * to 10 stitches before marker, ending this section with k4, yarn over, s2kp2, yarn over, k3, yarn over. (31 stitches)

ROW 31: Yarn over, k1, yarn over, k3, s2kp2, k3, yarn over, *k1, yarn over, k3, s2kp2, k3, yarn over; repeat from the * to 11 stitches before marker, ending this section with k1, yarn over, k3, s2kp2 k3, yarn over, k1, yarn over. (33 stitches)

ROW 33: Yarn over, k3, yarn over, k2, s2kp2, k2, yarn over, k1, *k2, yarn over, k2, s2kp2, k2, yarn over, k1; repeat from the * to 12 stitches before marker, ending this section with k2, yarn over, k2, s2kp2, k2, yarn over, k3, yarn over. (35 stitches)

ROW 35: Yarn over, k5, yarn over, k1, s2kp2, k1, yarn over, k2, *k3, yarn over, k1, s2kp2, k1, yarn over, k2; repeat from the * to 13 stitches before marker, ending this section with k3, yarn over, k1, s2kp2, k1, yarn over, k5, yarn over. (37 stitches)

ROW 37: Yarn over, k7, yarn over, s2kp2, yarn over, k3, *k4, yarn over, s2kp2, yarn over, k3; repeat from the * to 14 stitches before marker, ending this section with k4, yarn over, s2kp2, yarn over, k7, yarn over. (39 stitches)

ROW 39: Yarn over, k8, yarn over, s2kp2, yarn over, k3, *k4, yarn over, s2kp2, yarn over, k3; repeat from the * to 15 stitches before marker, ending this section with k4, yarn over, s2kp2, yarn over, k8, yarn over. (41 stitches)

ROW 40: As Row 2.

Repeat Rows 21–40 for the pattern.

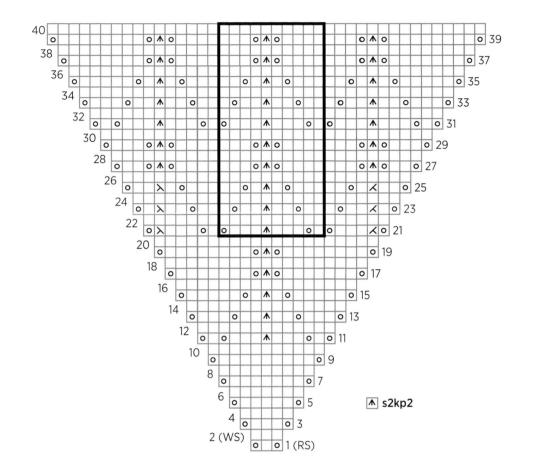

⊼ s2kp2

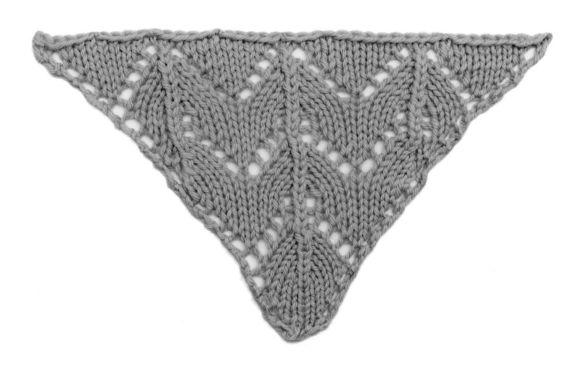

60

ROW 1 (RS): Yarn over, k1, yarn over. (3 stitches)

ROW 2 AND ALL WS ROWS: Purl across.

ROW 3: Yarn over, k3, yarn over. (5 stitches)

ROW 5: Yarn over, k5, yarn over. (7 stitches)

ROW 7: Yarn over, k7, yarn over. (9 stitches)

ROW 9: Yarn over, k9, yarn over. (11 stitches)

ROW 11: Yarn over, k1, yarn over, k3, sssk (page 285), k3, yarn over, k1, yarn over. (13 stitches)

ROW 13: Yarn over, k2, yarn over, k3, sssk, k3, yarn over, k2, yarn over. (15 stitches)

ROW 15: Yarn over, k4, yarn over, k2, sssk, k2, yarn over, k4, yarn over. (17 stitches)

ROW 17: Yarn over, k6, yarn over, k1, sssk, k1, yarn over, k6, yarn over. (19 stitches)

ROW 19: Yarn over, k4, ssk, k3, yarn over, k1, yarn over, k3, ssk, k4, yarn over. (21 stitches)

ROW 21: Yarn over, k1, yarn over, k3, sssk, k3, yarn over, k1, yarn over, k3, sssk, k3, yarn over, k1, yarn over. (23 stitches)

ROW 23: Yarn over, k2, yarn over, k3, sssk, k3, yarn over, k1, yarn over, k3, sssk, k3, yarn over, k2, yarn over. (25 stitches)

ROW 25: Yarn over, k4, yarn over, k2, sssk, k2, yarn over, k3, yarn over, k2, sssk, k2, yarn over, k4, yarn over. (27 stitches)

ROW 27: Yarn over, k6, yarn over, k1, sssk, k1, yarn over, k5, yarn over, k1, sssk, k1, yarn over, k6, yarn over. (29 stitches)

ROW 29: Yarn over, k4, ssk, k3, yarn over, *k1, yarn over, k3, sssk, k3, yarn over; repeat from the * to 10 stitches before marker, ending this section with k1, yarn over, k3, ssk, k4, yarn over. (31 stitches)

ROW 31: Yarn over, k1, yarn over, k3, sssk, k3, yarn over, *k1, yarn over, k3, sssk, k3, yarn over; repeat from the * to 11 stitches before marker, ending this section with k1, yarn over, k3, sssk, k3, yarn over, k1, yarn over. (33 stitches)

ROW 33: Yarn over, k2, yarn over, k3, sssk, k3, yarn over, *k1, yarn over, k3, sssk, k3, yarn over; repeat from the * to 12 stitches before marker, ending this section with k1, yarn over, k3, sssk, k3, yarn over, k2, yarn over. (35 stitches)

ROW 35: Yarn over, k4, yarn over, k2, sssk, k2, yarn over, k1, *k2, yarn over, k2, sssk, k2, yarn over, k1; repeat from the * to 13 stitches before marker, ending this section with k2, yarn over, k2, sssk, k2, yarn over, k4, yarn over. (37 stitches)

ROW 37: Yarn over, k6, yarn over, k1, sssk, k1, yarn over, k2, *k3, yarn over, k1, sssk, k1, yarn over, k2; repeat from the * to 14 stitches before marker, ending this section with k3, yarn over, k1, sssk, k1, yarn over, k6, yarn over. (39 stitches)

ROW 38: As Row 2.

Repeat Rows 29–38 for the pattern.

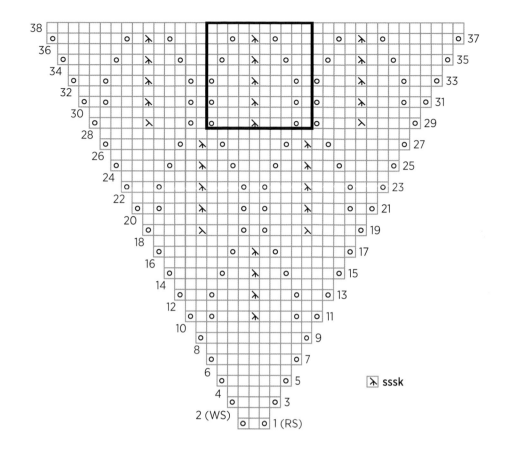

⤬ sssk

61

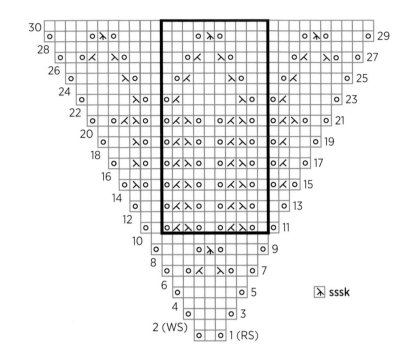

ROW 1 (RS): Yarn over, k1, yarn over. (3 stitches)

ROW 2 AND ALL WS ROWS: Purl across.

ROW 3: Yarn over, k3, yarn over. (5 stitches)

ROW 5: Yarn over, k5, yarn over. (7 stitches)

ROW 7: Yarn over, k1, yarn over, ssk, k1, k2tog, yarn over, k1, yarn over. (9 stitches)

ROW 9: Yarn over, k3, yarn over, sssk (page 285), yarn over, k3, yarn over. (11 stitches)

ROW 11: Yarn over, *(k1, yarn over, ssk, k2tog, yarn over) twice; repeat from the * to 1 stitch before the marker, ending this section with k1, yarn over. (13 stitches)

ROW 13: Yarn over, k1, *(k1, yarn over, ssk, k2tog, yarn over) twice; repeat from the * to 2 stitches before the marker, ending this section with k2, yarn over. (15 stitches)

ROW 15: Yarn over, k2tog, yarn over, *(k1, yarn over, ssk, k2tog, yarn over) twice; repeat from the * to 3 stitches before the marker, ending this section with k1, yarn over, ssk, yarn over. (17 stitches)

ROW 17: Yarn over, k1, k2tog, yarn over, *(k1, yarn over, ssk, k2tog, yarn over) twice; repeat from the * to 4 stitches before the marker, ending this section with k1, yarn over, ssk, k1, yarn over. (19 stitches)

ROW 19: Yarn over, k2, k2tog, yarn over, *(k1, yarn over, ssk, k2tog, yarn over) twice; repeat from the * to 5 stitches before the marker, ending this section with k1, yarn over, ssk, k2, yarn over. (21 stitches)

ROW 21: Yarn over, k1, yarn over, ssk, k2tog, yarn over, *(k1, yarn over, ssk, k2tog, yarn over) twice; repeat from the * to 6 stitches before the marker, ending this section with k1, yarn over, ssk, k2tog, yarn over, k1, yarn over. (23 stitches)

⋋ sssk

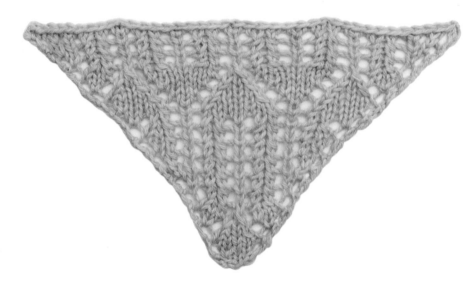

ROW 23: Yarn over, k4, k2tog, yarn over, *k1, yarn over, ssk, k5, k2tog, yarn over; repeat from the * to 7 stitches before the marker, ending this section with k1, yarn over, ssk, k4, yarn over. (25 stitches)

ROW 25: Yarn over, k4, k2tog, yarn over, k1, *k2, yarn over, ssk, k3, k2tog, yarn over, k1; repeat from the * to 8 stitches before the marker, ending this section with k2, yarn over, ssk, k4, yarn over. (27 stitches)

ROW 27: Yarn over, k1, yarn over, ssk, k1, k2tog, yarn over, k2, *k3, yarn over, ssk, k1, k2tog, yarn over, k2; repeat from the * to 9 stitches before the marker, ending this section with k3, yarn over, ssk, k1, k2tog, yarn over, k1, yarn over. (29 stitches)

ROW 29: Yarn over, k3, yarn over, sssk, yarn over, k3, *k4, yarn over, sssk, yarn over, k3; repeat from the * to 10 stitches before the marker, ending this section with k4, yarn over, sssk, yarn over, k3, yarn over. (31 stitches)

ROW 30: As Row 2.

Repeat Rows 11–30 for the pattern.

SHAWL #4
Knitted in the round, this shawl has a versatile square silhouette. See page 272 for instructions.

101

62 ꙮ ꙮ

ROW 1 (RS): Yarn over, k1, yarn over. (3 stitches)

ROW 2 AND ALL WS ROWS: Purl across.

ROW 3: Yarn over, k3, yarn over. (5 stitches)

ROW 5: Yarn over, k1, yarn over, s2kp2 (page 282), yarn over, k1, yarn over. (7 stitches)

ROW 7: Yarn over, k1, yarn over, ssk, k1, k2tog, yarn over, k1, yarn over. (9 stitches)

ROW 9: Yarn over, k1, yarn over, ssk, yarn over, s2kp2, yarn over, k2tog, yarn over, k1, yarn over. (11 stitches)

ROW 11: Yarn over, *k1, (yarn over, ssk) twice, k1, (k2tog, yarn over) twice; repeat from the * to 1 stitch before the marker, ending this section with k1, yarn over. (13 stitches)

ROW 13: Yarn over, k1, *k2, yarn over, ssk, yarn over, s2kp2, yarn over, k2tog, yarn over, k1; repeat from the * to 2 stitches before the marker, ending this section with k2, yarn over. (15 stitches)

ROW 15: Yarn over, k2tog, yarn over, *k1, (yarn over, ssk) twice, k1, (k2tog, yarn over) twice; repeat from the * to 3 stitches before the marker, ending this section with k1, yarn over, ssk, yarn over. (17 stitches)

ROW 17: Yarn over, k2tog, yarn over, k1, *k2, yarn over, ssk, yarn over, s2kp2, yarn over, k2tog, yarn over, k1; repeat from the * to 4 stitches before the marker, ending this section with k2, yarn over, ssk, yarn over. (19 stitches)

ROW 19: Yarn over, (k2tog, yarn over) twice, *k1, (yarn over, ssk) twice, k1, (k2tog, yarn over) twice; repeat from the * to 5 stitches before the marker, ending this section with k1, (yarn over, ssk) twice, yarn over. (21 stitches)

ROW 21: (Yarn over, k2tog) twice, yarn over, k1, *k2, yarn over, ssk, yarn over, s2kp2, yarn over, k2tog, yarn over, k1; repeat from the * to 6 stitches before the marker, ending this section with k2, (yarn over, ssk) twice, yarn over. (23 stitches)

ROW 23: Yarn over, k2, (k2tog, yarn over) twice, *k1, (yarn over, ssk) twice, k1, (k2tog, yarn over) twice; repeat from the * to 7 stitches before the marker, ending this section with k1, (yarn over, ssk) twice, k2, yarn over. (25 stitches)

ROW 25: Yarn over, k1, yarn over, s2kp2, yarn over, k2tog, yarn over, k1, *k2, yarn over, ssk, yarn over, s2kp2, yarn over, k2tog, yarn over, k1; repeat from the * to 8 stitches before the marker, ending this section with k2, yarn over, ssk, yarn over, s2kp2, yarn over, k1, yarn over. (27 stitches)

ROW 27: Yarn over, k1, yarn over, ssk, k1, (k2tog, yarn over) twice, *k1, (yarn over, ssk) twice, k1, (k2tog, yarn over) twice; repeat from the * to 9 stitches before the marker, ending this section with k1, (yarn over, ssk) twice, k1, k2tog, yarn over, k1, yarn over. (29 stitches)

ROW 29: Yarn over, k1, yarn over, ssk, yarn over, s2kp2, yarn over, k2tog, yarn over, k1, *k2, yarn over, ssk, yarn over, s2kp2, yarn over, k2tog, yarn over, k1; repeat from the * to 10 stitches before the marker, ending this section with k2, yarn over, ssk, yarn over, s2kp2, yarn over, k2tog, yarn over, k1, yarn over. (31 stitches)

ROW 30: As Row 2.

Repeat Rows 11–30 for the pattern.

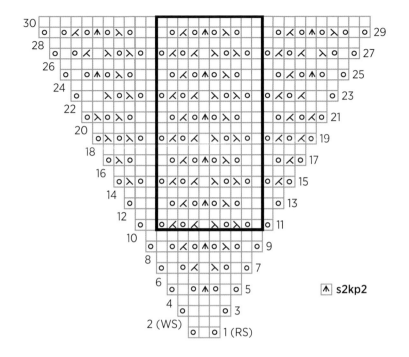

63

ROW 1 (RS): Yarn over, k1, yarn over. (3 stitches)

ROW 2 AND ALL WS ROWS: Purl across.

ROW 3: Yarn over, k3, yarn over. (5 stitches)

ROW 5: Yarn over, k1, yarn over, s2kp2 (page 282), yarn over, k1, yarn over. (7 stitches)

ROW 7: Yarn over, k1, k2tog, yarn over, k1, yarn over, ssk, k1, yarn over. (9 stitches)

ROW 9: Yarn over, k1, k2tog, yarn over, k3, yarn over, ssk, k1, yarn over. (11 stitches)

ROW 11: Yarn over, *k1, (yarn over, ssk) twice, k1, (k2tog, yarn over) twice; repeat from the * to 1 stitch before the marker, ending this section with k1, yarn over. (13 stitches)

ROW 13: Yarn over, k1, *k2, yarn over, ssk, yarn over, s2kp2, yarn over, k2tog, yarn over, k1; repeat from the * to 2 stitches before the marker, ending this section with k2, yarn over. (15 stitches)

ROW 15: Yarn over, k2, *k1, (k2tog, yarn over) twice, k1, (yarn over, ssk) twice; repeat from the * to 3 stitches before the marker, ending this section with k3, yarn over. (17 stitches)

ROW 17: Yarn over, k2, yarn over, *s2kp2, yarn over, k2tog, yarn over, k3, yarn over, ssk, yarn over; repeat from the * to 5 stitches before the marker, ending this section with s2kp2, yarn over, k2, yarn over. (19 stitches)

ROW 19: Yarn over, k4, *k1, (yarn over, ssk) twice, k1, (k2tog, yarn over) twice; repeat from the * to 5 stitches before the marker, ending this section with k5, yarn over. (21 stitches)

ROW 21: (Yarn over, k2tog) twice, yarn over, k1, *k2, yarn over, ssk, yarn over, s2kp2, yarn over, k2tog, yarn over, k1; repeat from the * to 6 stitches before the marker, ending this section with k2, (yarn over, ssk) twice, yarn over. (23 stitches)

ROW 23: Yarn over, k2, (yarn over, ssk) twice, *k1, (k2tog, yarn over) twice, k1, (yarn over, ssk) twice; repeat from the * to 7 stitches before the marker, ending this section with k1, (k2tog, yarn over) twice, k2, yarn over. (25 stitches)

ROW 25: Yarn over, k4, yarn over, ssk, yarn over, *s2kp2, yarn over, k2tog, yarn over, k3, yarn over, ssk, yarn over; repeat from the * to 9 stitches before the marker, ending this section with s2kp2, yarn over, k2tog, yarn over, k4, yarn over. (27 stitches)

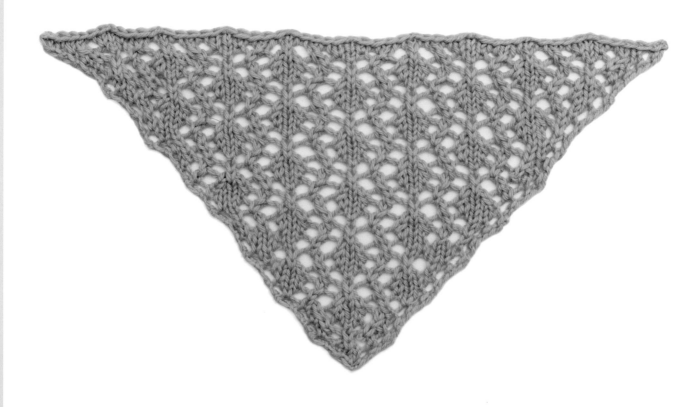

ROW 27: Yarn over, k1, yarn over, ssk, k1, (k2tog, yarn over) twice, *k1, (yarn over, ssk) twice, k1, (k2tog, yarn over) twice; repeat from the * to 9 stitches before the marker, ending this section with k1, (yarn over, ssk) twice, k1, k2tog, yarn over, k1, yarn over. (29 stitches)

ROW 29: Yarn over, k1, yarn over, ssk, yarn over, s2kp2, yarn over, k2tog, yarn over, k1, *k2, yarn over, ssk, yarn over, s2kp2, yarn over, k2tog, yarn over, k1; repeat from the * to 10 stitches before the marker, ending this section with k2, yarn over, ssk, yarn over, s2kp2, yarn over, k2tog, yarn over, k1, yarn over. (31 stitches)

ROW 31: Yarn over, k1, (k2tog, yarn over) twice, k1, (yarn over, ssk) twice, *k1, (k2tog, yarn over) twice, k1, (yarn over, ssk) twice; repeat from the * to 11 stitches before the marker, ending this section with k1, (k2tog, yarn over) twice, k1, (yarn over, ssk) twice, k1, yarn over. (33 stitches)

(continued on the next page)

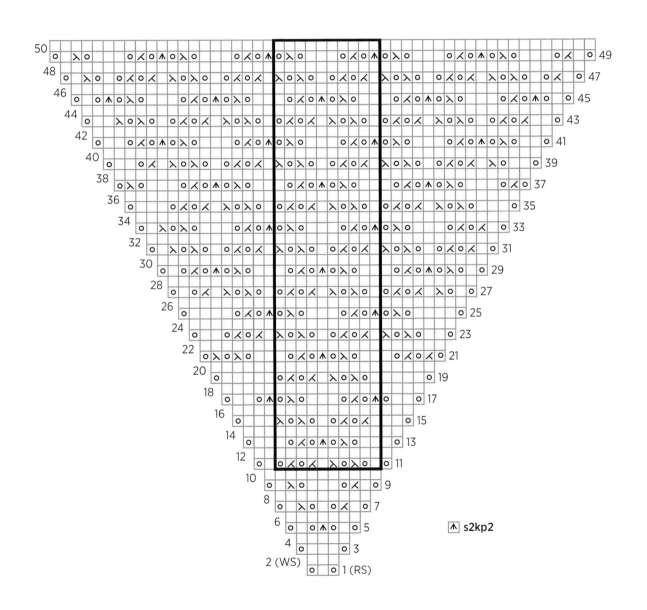

⬆ s2kp2

WEDGE 63, *continued*

ROW 33: Yarn over, k1, (k2tog, yarn over) twice, k3, yarn over, ssk, yarn over, *s2kp2, yarn over, k2tog, yarn over, k3, yarn over, ssk, yarn over; repeat from the * to 13 stitches before the marker, ending this section with s2kp2, yarn over, k2tog, yarn over, k3, (yarn over, ssk) twice, k1, yarn over. (35 stitches)

ROW 35: Yarn over, k3, (yarn over, ssk) twice, k1, (k2tog, yarn over) twice, *k1, (yarn over, ssk) twice, k1, (k2tog, yarn over) twice; repeat from the * to 13 stitches before the marker, ending this section with k1, (yarn over, ssk) twice, k1, (k2tog, yarn over) twice, k3, yarn over. (37 stitches)

ROW 37: Yarn over, k2tog, yarn over, k3, yarn over, ssk, yarn over, s2kp2, yarn over, k2tog, yarn over, k1, *k2, yarn over, ssk, yarn over, s2kp2, yarn over, k2tog, yarn over, k1; repeat from the * to 14 stitches before the marker, ending this section with k2, yarn over, ssk, yarn over, s2kp2, yarn over, k2tog, yarn over, k3, yarn over, ssk, yarn over. (39 stitches)

ROW 39: Yarn over, k2, yarn over, ssk, k1, (k2tog, yarn over) twice, k1, (yarn over, ssk) twice, *k1, (k2tog, yarn over) twice, k1, (yarn over, ssk) twice; repeat from the * to 15 stitches before the marker, ending this section with k1, (k2tog, yarn over) twice, k1, (yarn over, ssk) twice, k1, k2tog, yarn over, k2, yarn over. (41 stitches)

ROW 41: Yarn over, k2, yarn over, ssk, yarn over, s2kp2, yarn over, k2tog, yarn over, k3, yarn over, ssk, yarn over, *s2kp2, yarn over, k2tog, yarn over, k3, yarn over, ssk, yarn over; repeat from the * to 17 stitches before the marker, ending this section with s2kp2, yarn over, k2tog, yarn over, k3, yarn over, ssk, yarn over, s2kp2, yarn over, k2tog, yarn over, k2, yarn over. (43 stitches)

ROW 43: Yarn over, k2, (k2tog, yarn over) twice, k1, (yarn over, ssk) twice, k1, (k2tog, yarn over) twice, *k1, (yarn over, ssk) twice, k1, (k2tog, yarn over) twice; repeat from the * to 17 stitches before the marker, ending this section with k1, (yarn over, ssk) twice, k1, (k2tog, yarn over) twice, k1, (yarn over, ssk) twice, k2, yarn over. (45 stitches)

ROW 45: Yarn over, k1, yarn over, s2kp2, yarn over, k2tog, yarn over, k3, yarn over, ssk, yarn over, s2kp2, yarn over, k2tog, yarn over, k1, *k2, yarn over, ssk, yarn over, s2kp2, yarn over, k2tog, yarn over, k1; repeat from the * to 18 stitches before the marker, ending this section with k2, yarn over, ssk, yarn over, s2kp2, yarn over, k2tog, yarn over, k3, yarn over, ssk, yarn over, s2kp2, yarn over, k1, yarn over. (47 stitches)

ROW 47: Yarn over, k1, k2tog, yarn over, k1, (yarn over, ssk) twice, k1, (k2tog, yarn over) twice, k1, (yarn over, ssk) twice, *k1, (k2tog, yarn over) twice, k1, (yarn over, ssk) twice; repeat from the * to 19 stitches before the marker, ending this section with k1, (k2tog, yarn over) twice, k1, (yarn over, ssk) twice, k1, (k2tog, yarn over) twice, k1, yarn over, ssk, k1, yarn over. (49 stitches)

ROW 49: Yarn over, k1, k2tog, yarn over, k3, yarn over, ssk, yarn over, s2kp2, yarn over, k2tog, yarn over, k3, yarn over, ssk, yarn over, *s2kp2, yarn over, k2tog, yarn over, k3, yarn over, ssk, yarn over; repeat from the * to 21 stitches before the marker, ending this section with s2kp2, yarn over, k2tog, yarn over, k3, yarn over, ssk, yarn over, s2kp2, yarn over, k2tog, yarn over, k3, yarn over, ssk, k1, yarn over. (51 stitches)

ROW 50: As Row 2.

Repeat Rows 11–50 for the pattern.

64

ROW 1 (RS): Yarn over, k1, yarn over. (3 stitches)

ROW 2 AND ALL WS ROWS: Knit the knit stitches and purl the purl stitches and yarn overs.

ROW 3: Yarn over, p3, yarn over. (5 stitches)

ROW 5: Yarn over, k1, p3, k1, yarn over. (7 stitches)

ROW 7: Yarn over, k2, p3, k2, yarn over. (9 stitches)

ROW 9: Yarn over, k3, p3, k3, yarn over. (11 stitches)

ROW 11: Yarn over, knit across to the marker, yarn over. (13 stitches)

ROW 13: Yarn over, p3, k2, yarn over, s2kp2 (page 282), yarn over, k2, p3, yarn over. (15 stitches)

ROW 15: Yarn over, k1, p3, k2, yarn over, s2kp2, yarn over, k2, p3, k1, yarn over. (17 stitches)

ROW 17: Yarn over, k2, p3, k2, yarn over, s2kp2, yarn over, k2, p3, k2, yarn over. (19 stitches)

ROW 19: Yarn over, k3, p3, k7, p3, k3, yarn over. (21 stitches)

ROW 21: Yarn over, knit across to the marker, yarn over. (23 stitches)

ROW 23: Yarn over, p1, *p2, k2, yarn over, s2kp2, yarn over, k2, p1; repeat from the * to 12 stitches before the marker, ending this section with p2, k2, yarn over, s2kp2, yarn over, k2, p3, yarn over. (25 stitches)

ROW 25: Yarn over, k1, p1, *p2, k2, yarn over, s2kp2, yarn over, k2, p1; repeat from the * to 13 stitches before the marker, ending this section with p2, k2, yarn over, s2kp2, yarn over, k2, p3, k1, yarn over. (27 stitches)

ROW 27: Yarn over, k2, p1, *p2, k2, yarn over, s2kp2, yarn over, k2, p1; repeat from the * to 14 stitches before the marker, ending this section with p2, k2, yarn over, s2kp2, yarn over, k2, p3, k2, yarn over. (29 stitches)

ROW 29: Yarn over, k3, p1, *p2, k7, p1; repeat from the * to 15 stitches before the marker, ending this section with p2, k7, p3, k3, yarn over. (31 stitches)

ROW 30: Knit across.

Repeat Rows 21–30 for the pattern.

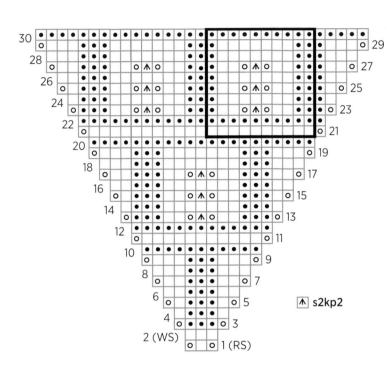

Ⓐ s2kp2

65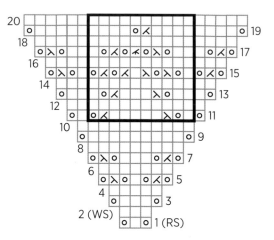

NOTE: To create symmetry, this design is different on the right- and left-hand sides. If you are making a two-wedge shawl, follow the instructions for the Right-Hand Side to the center of your shawl, then work the Left-Hand Side instructions. If your shawl has more than two wedges, work the Right-Hand Side instructions first and the Left-Hand Side instructions last, and balance out the wedges in between.

ROW 1 (RS):

Right-Hand Side: Yarn over, k1, yarn over. (3 stitches)

Left-Hand Side: Yarn over, k1, yarn over. (3 stitches)

ROW 2 AND ALL WS ROWS:

Right-Hand and Left-Hand Sides: Purl across.

ROW 3:

Right-Hand Side: Yarn over, k3, yarn over. (5 stitches)

Left-Hand Side: Yarn over, k3, yarn over. (5 stitches)

ROW 5:

Right-Hand Side: Yarn over, k2tog, yarn over, k1, yarn over, ssk, yarn over. (7 stitches)

Left-Hand Side: Yarn over, k2tog, yarn over, k1, yarn over, ssk, yarn over. (7 stitches)

ROW 7:

Right-Hand Side: Yarn over, k2tog, yarn over, k3, yarn over, ssk, yarn over. (9 stitches)

Left-Hand Side: Yarn over, k2tog, yarn over, k3, yarn over, ssk, yarn over. (9 stitches)

ROW 9:

Right-Hand and Left-Hand Sides: Yarn over, knit across to the marker, ending this section with yarn over. (11 stitches)

ROW 11:

Right-Hand Side: Yarn over, *k1, yarn over, ssk, k5, k2tog, yarn over; repeat from the * to 1 stitch before the marker, ending this section with k1, yarn over. (13 stitches)

Left-Hand Side: Yarn over, k1, *yarn over, ssk, k5, k2tog, yarn over, k1; repeat from the * to the marker, ending this section with yarn over. (13 stitches)

ROW 13:

Right-Hand Side: Yarn over, k1, *k2, yarn over, ssk, k3, k2tog, yarn over, k1; repeat from the * to 2 stitches before the marker, ending this section with k2, yarn over. (15 stitches)

Left-Hand Side: Yarn over, k2, *k1, yarn over, ssk, k3, k2tog, yarn over, k2; repeat from the * to 1 stitch before the marker, ending this section with k1, yarn over. (15 stitches)

ROW 15:

Right-Hand Side: Yarn over, k2tog, yarn over, *k1, (yarn over, ssk) twice, k1, (k2tog, yarn over) twice; repeat from the * to 3 stitches before the marker, ending this section with k1, yarn over, ssk, yarn over. (17 stitches)

Left-Hand Side: Yarn over, k2tog, yarn over, k1, *(yarn over, ssk) twice, k1, (k2tog, yarn over) twice, k1; repeat from the * to 2 stitches before the marker, ending this section with yarn over, ssk, yarn over. (17 stitches)

ROW 17:

Right-Hand Side: Yarn over, k2tog, yarn over, k1, *k2, yarn over, ssk, yarn over, k3tog, yarn over, k2tog, yarn over, k1; repeat from the * to 4 stitches before the marker, ending this section with k2, yarn over, ssk, yarn over. (19 stitches)

Left-Hand Side: Yarn over, k2tog, yarn over, k2, *k1, yarn over, ssk, yarn over, sssk (page 285), yarn over, k2tog, yarn over, k2; repeat from the * to 3 stitches before the marker, ending this section with k1, yarn over, ssk, yarn over. (19 stitches)

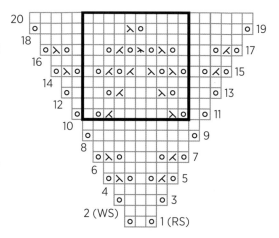

Right-Hand Side

⟋ k3tog

⟍ sssk

Left-Hand Side

ROW 19:

Right-Hand Side: Yarn over, k4, *k4, k2tog, yarn over, k4; repeat from the * to 5 stitches before the marker, ending this section with k5, yarn over. (21 stitches)

Left-Hand Side: Yarn over, k5, *k4, yarn over, ssk, k4; repeat from the * to 4 stitches before the marker, ending this section with k4, yarn over. (21 stitches)

ROW 20: As Row 2.

Repeat Rows 11–20 for the pattern.

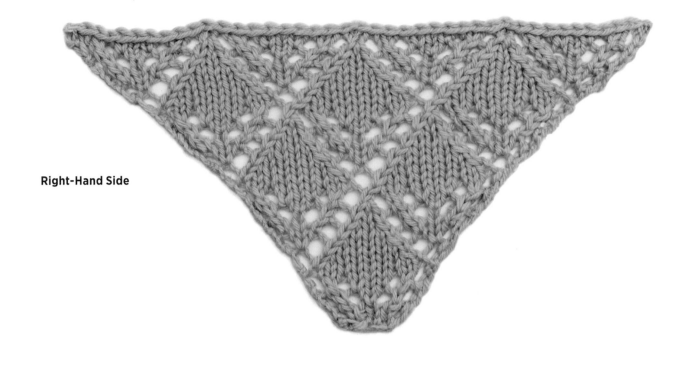

Right-Hand Side

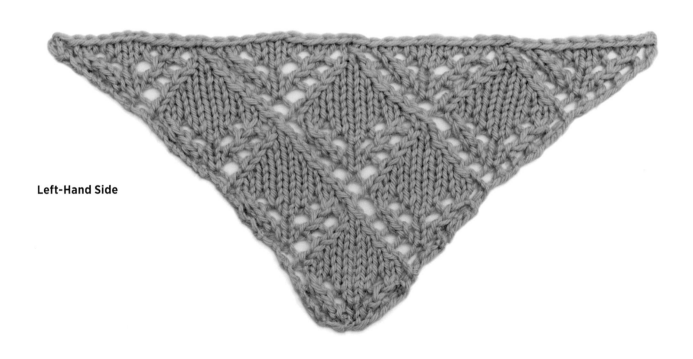

Left-Hand Side

66

ROW 1 (RS): Yarn over, k1, yarn over. (3 stitches)

ROW 2 AND ALL WS ROWS: Purl across.

ROW 3: Yarn over, k3, yarn over. (5 stitches)

ROW 5: Yarn over, k5, yarn over. (7 stitches)

ROW 7: Yarn over, k7, yarn over. (9 stitches)

ROW 9: Yarn over, k9, yarn over. (11 stitches)

ROW 11: Yarn over, *k1, yarn over, ssk, k5, k2tog, yarn over; repeat from the * to 1 stitch before the marker, ending this section with k1, yarn over. (13 stitches)

ROW 13: Yarn over, k1, *k1, yarn over, k1, ssk, k3, k2tog, k1, yarn over; repeat from the * to 2 stitches before the marker, ending this section with k2, yarn over. (15 stitches)

ROW 15: Yarn over, k2, *k1, yarn over, k2, ssk, k1, k2tog, k2, yarn over; repeat from the * to 3 stitches before the marker, ending this section with k3, yarn over, ssk, yarn over. (17 stitches)

ROW 17: Yarn over, k3, *k1, yarn over, k3, sk2p (page 282), k3, yarn over; repeat from the * to 4 stitches before the marker, ending this section with k4, yarn over. (19 stitches)

ROW 19: Yarn over, k2, k2tog, yarn over, *k1, yarn over, ssk, k5, k2tog, yarn over; repeat from the * to 5 stitches before the marker, ending this section with k1, yarn over, ssk, k2, yarn over. (21 stitches)

ROW 21: Yarn over, k2, k2tog, k1, yarn over, *k1, yarn over, k1, ssk, k3, k2tog, k1, yarn over; repeat from the * to 6 stitches before the marker, ending this section with k1, yarn over, k1, ssk, k2, yarn over. (23 stitches)

ROW 23: Yarn over, k2, k2tog, k2, yarn over, *k1, yarn over, k2, ssk, k1, k2tog, k2, yarn over; repeat from the * to 7 stitches before the marker, ending this section with k1, yarn over, k2, ssk, k2, yarn over. (25 stitches)

ROW 25: Yarn over, k2, k2tog, k3, yarn over, *k1, yarn over, k3, sk2p, k3, yarn over; repeat from the * to 8 stitches before the marker, ending this section with k1, yarn over, k3, ssk, k2, yarn over. (27 stitches)

ROW 27: Yarn over, k6, k2tog, yarn over, *k1, yarn over, ssk, k5, k2tog, yarn over; repeat from the * to 9 stitches before the marker, ending this section with k1, yarn over, ssk, k6, yarn over. (29 stitches)

ROW 29: Yarn over, k6, k2tog, k1, yarn over, *k1, yarn over, k1, ssk, k3, k2tog, k1, yarn over; repeat from the * to 10 stitches before the marker, ending this section with k1, yarn over, k1, ssk, k6, yarn over. (31 stitches)

ROW 31: Yarn over, k1, yarn over, k2, ssk, k1, k2tog, k2, yarn over, *k1, yarn over, k2, ssk, k1, k2tog, k2, yarn over; repeat from the * to 11 stitches before the marker, ending this section with k1, yarn over, k2, ssk, k1, k2tog, k2, yarn over, k1, yarn over. (33 stitches)

ROW 33: Yarn over, k2, yarn over, k3, sk2p, k3, yarn over, *k1, yarn over, k3, sk2p, k3, yarn over; repeat from the * to 12 stitches before the marker, ending this section with k1, yarn over, k3, sk2p, k3, yarn over, k2, yarn over. (35 stitches)

ROW 35: Yarn over, k2tog, yarn over, k1, yarn over, ssk, k5, k2tog, yarn over, *k1, yarn over, ssk, k5, k2tog, yarn over; repeat from the * to 13 stitches before the marker, ending this section with k1, yarn over, ssk, k5, k2tog, yarn over, k1, yarn over, ssk, yarn over. (37 stitches)

ROW 37: Yarn over, k2tog, (k1, yarn over) twice, k1, ssk, k3, k2tog, k1, yarn over, *k1, yarn over, k1, ssk, k3, k2tog, k1, yarn over; repeat from the * to 14 stitches before the marker, ending this section with k1, yarn over, k1, ssk, k3, k2tog, (k1, yarn over) twice, k1, ssk, yarn over. (39 stitches)

(continued on page 112)

SHAWL #2
Three vertical insertions add visual interest and additional coverage. See page 270 for instructions.

WEDGE 66, *continued*

ROW 39: Yarn over, k2tog, k2, yarn over, k1, yarn over, k2, ssk, k1, k2tog, k2, yarn over, *k1, yarn over, k2, ssk, k1, k2tog, k2, yarn over; repeat from the * to 15 stitches before the marker, ending this section with k1, yarn over, k2, ssk, k1, k2tog, k2, yarn over, k1, yarn over, k2, ssk, yarn over. (41 stitches)

ROW 41: Yarn over, k2tog, k3, yarn over, k1, yarn over, k3, sk2p, k3, yarn over, *k1, yarn over, k3, sk2p, k3, yarn over; repeat from the * to 16 stitches before the marker, ending this section with k1, yarn over, k3, sk2p, k3, yarn over, k1, yarn over, k3, ssk, yarn over. (43 stitches)

ROW 43: Yarn over, k4, k2tog, yarn over, k1, yarn over, ssk, k5, k2tog, yarn over, *k1, yarn over, ssk, k5, k2tog, yarn over; repeat from the * to 17 stitches before the marker, ending this section with k1, yarn over, ssk, k5, k2tog, yarn over, k1, yarn over, ssk, k4, yarn over. (45 stitches)

ROW 45: Yarn over, k4, k2tog, (k1, yarn over) twice, k1, ssk, k3, k2tog, k1, yarn over, *k1, yarn over, k1, ssk, k3, k2tog, k1, yarn over; repeat from the * to 18 stitches before the marker, ending this section with k1, yarn over, k1, ssk, k3, k2tog, (k1, yarn over) twice, k1, ssk, k4, yarn over. (47 stitches)

ROW 47: Yarn over, k4, k2tog, k2, yarn over, k1, yarn over, k2, ssk, k1, k2tog, k2, yarn over, *k1, yarn over, k2, ssk, k1, k2tog, k2, yarn over; repeat from the * to 19 stitches before the marker, ending this section with k1, yarn over, k2, ssk, k1, k2tog, k2, yarn over, k1, yarn over, k2, ssk, k4, yarn over. (49 stitches)

ROW 49: Yarn over, k4, k2tog, k3, yarn over, k1, yarn over, k3, sk2p, k3, yarn over, *k1, yarn over, k3, sk2p, k3, yarn over; repeat from the * to 20 stitches before the marker, ending this section with k1, yarn over, k3, sk2p, k3, yarn over, k1, yarn over, k3, ssk, k4, yarn over. (51 stitches)

ROW 50: As Row 2.

Repeat Rows 11–50 for the pattern.

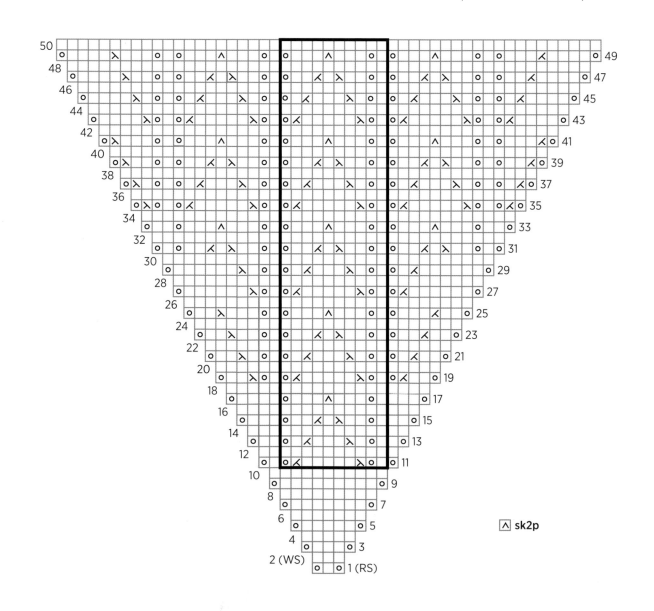

67

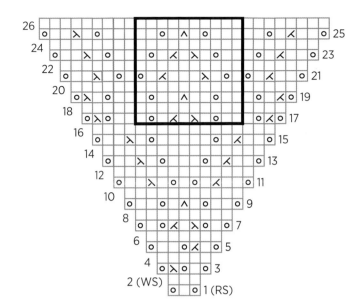

ROW 1 (RS): Yarn over, k1, yarn over. (3 stitches)

ROW 2 AND ALL WS ROWS: Purl across.

ROW 3: Yarn over, k1, yarn over, ssk, yarn over. (5 stitches)

ROW 5: Yarn over, k1, k2tog, yarn over, k2, yarn over. (7 stitches)

ROW 7: Yarn over, k1, yarn over, ssk, k1, k2tog, yarn over, k1, yarn over. (9 stitches)

ROW 9: Yarn over, k2, yarn over, k1, sk2p, k1, yarn over, k2, yarn over. (11 stitches)

ROW 11: Yarn over, k2, k2tog, (k1, yarn over) twice, k1, ssk, k2, yarn over. (13 stitches)

ROW 13: Yarn over, k2, k2tog, k1, yarn over, k3, yarn over, k1, ssk, k2, yarn over. (15 stitches)

ROW 15: Yarn over, k2, k2tog, k1, yarn over, k5, yarn over, k1, ssk, k2, yarn over. (17 stitches)

ROW 17: Yarn over, k2tog, yarn over, k1, *k2, yarn over, k1, ssk, k1, k2tog, k1, yarn over, k1; repeat from the * to 4 stitches before the marker, ending this section with k2, yarn over, ssk, yarn over. (19 stitches)

ROW 19: Yarn over, k2tog, k1, yarn over, k1, *k2, yarn over, k2, sk2p, k2, yarn over, k1; repeat from the * to 5 stitches before the marker, ending this section with k2, yarn over, k1, ssk, yarn over. (21 stitches)

ROW 21: Yarn over, k2, k2tog, k1, yarn over, *k1, yarn over, ssk, k3, k2tog, k1, yarn over; repeat from the * to 6 stitches before the marker, ending this section with k1, yarn over, k1, ssk, k2, yarn over. (23 stitches)

ROW 23: Yarn over, k2, k2tog, k1, yarn over, k1, *k2, yarn over, k1, ssk, k1, k2tog, k1, yarn over, k1; repeat from the * to 7 stitches before the marker, ending this section with k2, yarn over, k1, ssk, k2, yarn over. (25 stitches)

ROW 25: Yarn over, k2, k2tog, k1, yarn over, k2, *k3, yarn over, k1, sk2p, k1, yarn over, k2; repeat from the * to 8 stitches before the marker, ending this section with k3, yarn over, k1, ssk, k2, yarn over. (27 stitches)

ROW 26: As Row 2.

Repeat Rows 17–26 for the pattern.

68

ROW 1 (RS): Yarn over, k1, yarn over. (3 stitches)

ROWS 2, 4, 18, 20, 22, AND 24: Knit the knit stitches and purl the purl stitches and yarn overs.

ROW 3: Yarn over, k3, yarn over. (5 stitches)

ROW 5: Yarn over, k5, yarn over. (7 stitches)

ROWS 6, 8, 10, 12, 14, 16, 26, AND 28: Knit the knit stitches and yarn overs and purl the purl stitches.

ROW 7: Yarn over, p2, k3, p2, yarn over. (9 stitches)

ROW 9: Yarn over, p3, k3, p3, yarn over. (11 stitches)

ROW 11: Yarn over, *p3, k2tog, yarn over, k1, yarn over, ssk, p2; repeat from the * to 1 stitch before the marker, ending this section with p1, yarn over. (13 stitches)

ROW 13: Yarn over, p1, *p2, k2tog, yarn over, k3, yarn over, ssk, p1; repeat from the * to 2 stitches before the marker, ending this section with p2, yarn over. (15 stitches)

ROW 15: Yarn over, p2, *p1, k2tog, yarn over, k5, yarn over, ssk; repeat from the * to 3 stitches before the marker, ending this section with p3, yarn over. (17 stitches)

ROW 17: Yarn over, p3, *p4, k3, p3; repeat from the * to 4 stitches before the marker, ending this section with p4, yarn over. (19 stitches)

ROW 19: Yarn over, k1, p3, *p4, k3, p3; repeat from the * to 5 stitches before the marker, ending this section with p4, k1, yarn over. (21 stitches)

ROW 21: Yarn over, k1, yarn over, ssk, p2, *p3, k2tog, yarn over, k1, yarn over, ssk, p2; repeat from the * to 6 stitches before the marker, ending this section with p3, k2tog, yarn over, k1, yarn over. (23 stitches)

ROW 23: Yarn over, k3, yarn over, ssk, p1, *p2, k2tog, yarn over, k3, yarn over, ssk, p1; repeat from the * to 7 stitches before the marker, ending this section with p2, k2tog, yarn over, k3, yarn over. (25 stitches)

ROW 25: Yarn over, k5, yarn over, ssk, *p1, k2tog, yarn over, k5, yarn over, ssk; repeat from the * to 7 stitches before the marker, ending this section with p1, k2tog, yarn over, k5, yarn over. (27 stitches)

ROW 27: Yarn over, p2, k3, p3, *p4, k3, p3; repeat from the * to 9 stitches before the marker, ending this section with p4, k3, p2, yarn over. (29 stitches)

ROW 29: Yarn over, p3, k3, p3, *p4, k3, p3; repeat from the * to 10 stitches before the marker, ending this section with p4, k3, p3, yarn over. (31 stitches)

ROW 30: As Row 6.

Repeat Rows 11–30 for the pattern.

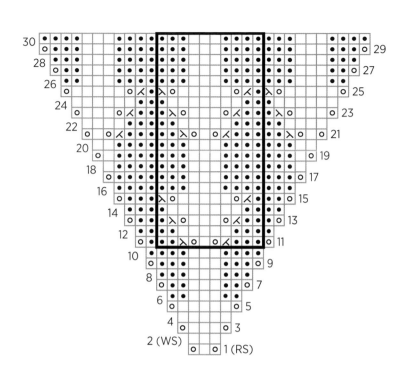

69

ROW 1 (RS): Yarn over, k1, yarn over. (3 stitches)

ROW 2 AND ALL WS ROWS: Purl across.

ROW 3: Yarn over, k3, yarn over. (5 stitches)

ROW 5: Yarn over, k2, yarn over, ssk, k1, yarn over. (7 stitches)

ROW 7: Yarn over, k1, k2tog, yarn over, k1, yarn over, ssk, k1, yarn over. (9 stitches)

ROW 9: Yarn over, k1, k2tog, yarn over, k3, yarn over, ssk, k1, yarn over. (11 stitches)

ROW 11: Yarn over, *k3, yarn over, k2tog, k1, ssk, yarn over, k2; repeat from the * to 1 stitch before the marker, ending this section with k1, yarn over. (13 stitches)

ROW 13: Yarn over, k1, *k3, yarn over, k2tog, k1, ssk, yarn over, k2; repeat from the * to 2 stitches before the marker, ending this section with k2, yarn over. (15 stitches)

ROW 15: Yarn over, k2, *k3, yarn over, k2tog, k1, ssk, yarn over, k2; repeat from the * to 3 stitches before the marker, ending this section with k3, yarn over. (17 stitches)

ROW 17: Yarn over, k3, *k3, yarn over, k2tog, k1, ssk, yarn over, k2; repeat from the * to 4 stitches before the marker, ending this section with k4, yarn over. (19 stitches)

ROW 19: Yarn over, ssk, yarn over, k2, *k3, yarn over, k2tog, k1, ssk, yarn over, k2; repeat from the * to 5 stitches before the marker, ending this section with k3, yarn over, k2tog, yarn over. (21 stitches)

ROW 21: Yarn over, k1, ssk, yarn over, k2, *k3, yarn over, k2tog, k1, ssk, yarn over, k2; repeat from the * to 6 stitches before the marker, ending this section with k3, yarn over, k2tog, k1, yarn over. (23 stitches)

ROW 23: Yarn over, k1, k2tog, yarn over, k3, *k4, yarn over, s2kp2 (page 282), yarn over, k3; repeat from the * to 7 stitches before the marker, ending this section with k4, yarn over, ssk, k1, yarn over. (25 stitches)

ROW 25: Yarn over, k2, yarn over, ssk, k3, *k5, yarn over, ssk, k3; repeat from the * to 8 stitches before the marker, ending this section with k5, yarn over, ssk, k1, yarn over. (27 stitches)

ROW 27: Yarn over, k1, k2tog, yarn over, k1, yarn over, ssk, k2, *k3, k2tog, yarn over, k1, yarn over, ssk, k2; repeat from the * to 9 stitches before the marker, ending this section with k3, k2tog, yarn over, k1, yarn over, ssk, k1, yarn over. (29 stitches)

ROW 29: Yarn over, k1, k2tog, yarn over, k3, yarn over, ssk, k1, *k2, k2tog, yarn over, k3, yarn over, ssk, k1; repeat from the * to 10 stitches before the marker, ending this section with k2, k2tog, yarn over, k3, yarn over, ssk, k1, yarn over. (31 stitches)

ROW 30: As Row 2.

Repeat Rows 11–30 for the pattern.

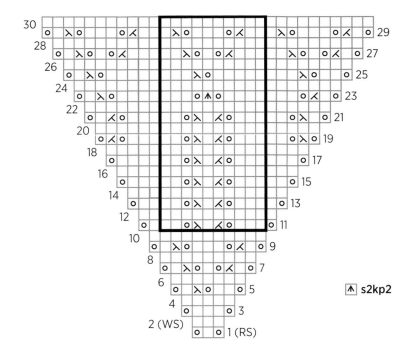

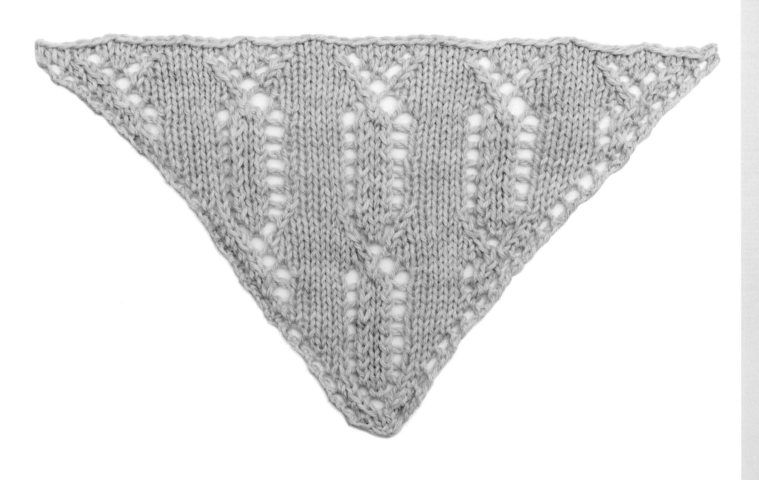

70

ROWS 1, 3, 5, 9, 13, 17, 21, 25, AND 29 (RS): Yarn over, knit across to the marker, ending this section with yarn over.

ROWS 2, 6, 10, 14, 18, 22, AND 26: Purl across.

ROWS 4, 8, 12, 16, 20, 24, AND 28: Knit across.

ROW 7: Yarn over, k1, yarn over, ssk, k1, k2tog, yarn over, k1, yarn over. (9 stitches)

ROW 11: Yarn over, *(k1, yarn over) twice, ssk, s2kp2 (page 282), k2tog, yarn over, k1, yarn over; repeat from the * to 1 stitch before the marker, ending this section with k1, yarn over. (13 stitches)

ROW 15: Yarn over, k2, *(k1, yarn over) twice, ssk, s2kp2, k2tog, yarn over, k1, yarn over; repeat from the * to 3 stitches before the marker, ending this section with k3, yarn over. (17 stitches)

ROW 19: Yarn over, k4, *(k1, yarn over) twice, ssk, s2kp2, k2tog, yarn over, k1, yarn over; repeat from the * to 5 stitches before the marker, ending this section with k5, yarn over. (21 stitches)

ROW 23: Yarn over, k1, (k2tog) twice, yarn over, k1, yarn over, *(k1, yarn over) twice, ssk, s2kp2, k2tog, yarn over, k1, yarn over; repeat from the * to 7 stitches before the marker, ending this section with (k1, yarn over) twice, (ssk) twice, k1, yarn over. (25 stitches)

ROW 27: Yarn over, k1, yarn over, ssk, (k2tog) twice, yarn over, k1, yarn over, *(k1, yarn over) twice, ssk, s2kp2, k2tog, yarn over, k1, yarn over; repeat from the * to 9 stitches before the marker, ending this section with (k1, yarn over) twice, (ssk) twice, k2tog, yarn over, k1, yarn over. (29 stitches)

ROW 30: As Row 2.

Repeat Rows 11–30 for the pattern.

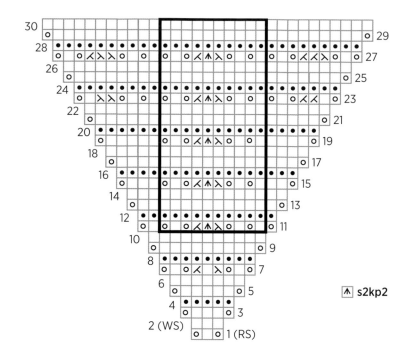

⊼ s2kp2

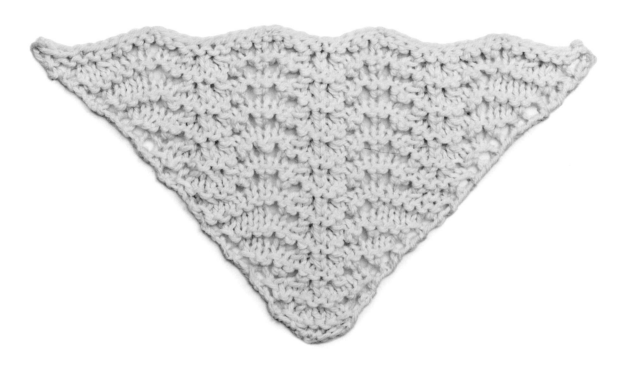

71

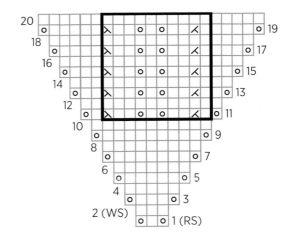

ROWS 1, 3, 5, 7, AND 9 (RS): Yarn over, knit across to the marker, ending this section with yarn over.

ROW 2 AND ALL WS ROWS: Purl across.

ROW 11: Yarn over, *k1, k2tog, k2, yarn over, k1, yarn over, k2, ssk; repeat from the * to 1 stitch before the marker, ending this section with k1, yarn over. (13 stitches)

ROW 13: Yarn over, k1, *k1, k2tog, k2, yarn over, k1, yarn over, k2, ssk; repeat from the * to 2 stitches before the marker, ending this section with k2, yarn over. (15 stitches)

ROW 15: Yarn over, k2, *k1, k2tog, k2, yarn over, k1, yarn over, k2, ssk; repeat from the * to 30 stitches before the marker, ending this section with k3, yarn over. (17 stitches)

ROW 17: Yarn over, k3, *k1, k2tog, k2, yarn over, k1, yarn over, k2, ssk; repeat from the * to 4 stitches before the marker, ending this section with k4, yarn over. (19 stitches)

ROW 19: Yarn over, k4, *k1, k2tog, k2, yarn over, k1, yarn over, k2, ssk; repeat from the * to 5 stitches before the marker, ending this section with k5, yarn over. (21 stitches)

ROW 20: As Row 2.

Repeat Rows 11–20 for the pattern.

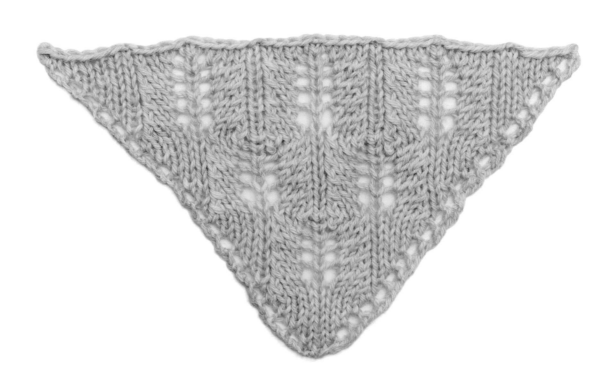

72

NOTE: To create symmetry, this design is different on the right- and left-hand sides. If you are making a two-wedge shawl, follow the instructions for the Right-Hand Side to the center of your shawl, then work the Left-Hand Side instructions. If your shawl has more than two wedges, work the Right-Hand Side instructions first and the Left-Hand Side instructions last, and balance out the wedges in between.

ROWS 1, 3, AND 5 (RS): Yarn over, knit across to the marker, ending this section with yarn over.

ROW 2 AND ALL WS ROWS:
Right-Hand and Left-Hand Sides: Purl across.

ROW 7:
Right-Hand Side: Yarn over, k4, k2tog, yarn over, k1, yarn over. (9 stitches)
Left-Hand Side: Yarn over, k1, yarn over, ssk, k4, yarn over. (9 stitches)

ROW 9:
Right-Hand Side: Yarn over, k4, k2tog, yarn over, k3, yarn over. (11 stitches)
Left-Hand Side: Yarn over, k3, yarn over. (11 stitches)

ROW 11:
Right-Hand Side: Yarn over, k1, *k3, k2tog, yarn over, k5; repeat from the * to the marker, ending this section with yarn over. (13 stitches)
Left-Hand Side: Yarn over, *k5, yarn over, ssk, k3; repeat from the * to 1 stitch before the marker, ending this section with k1, yarn over. (13 stitches)

ROW 13:
Right-Hand Side: Yarn over, k2, *k2, k2tog, yarn over, k6; repeat from the * to 1 stitch before the marker, ending this section with k1, yarn over. (15 stitches)
Left-Hand Side: Yarn over, k1, *k6, yarn over, ssk, k2; repeat from the * to 2 stitches before the marker, ending this section with k2, yarn over. (15 stitches)

ROW 15:
Right-Hand Side: Yarn over, k3, *k1, k2tog, yarn over, k7; repeat from the * to 2 stitches before the marker, ending this section with k2, yarn over. (17 stitches)

Left-Hand Side: Yarn over, k2, *k7, yarn over, ssk, k1; repeat from the * to 3 stitches before the marker, ending this section with k3, yarn over. (17 stitches)

ROW 17:
Right-Hand Side: Yarn over, k4, *k2tog, yarn over, k8; repeat from the * to 3 stitches before the marker, ending this section with k2tog, yarn over, k1, yarn over. (19 stitches)
Left-Hand Side: Yarn over, k1, yarn over, ssk, *k8, yarn over, ssk; repeat from the * to 4 stitches before the marker, ending this section with k4, yarn over. (19 stitches)

ROW 19:
Right-Hand Side: Yarn over, k4, k2tog, *yarn over, k8, k2tog; repeat from the * to 3 stitches before the marker, ending this section with yarn over, k2, yarn over. (21 stitches)
Left-Hand Side: Yarn over, k3, yarn over, *ssk, k8, yarn over; repeat from the * to 6 stitches before the marker, ending this section with ssk, k4, yarn over. (21 stitches)

ROW 20: As Row 2.

Repeat Rows 11–20 for the pattern.

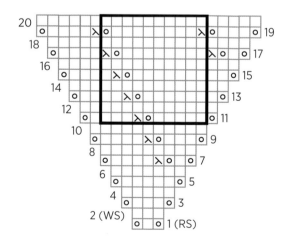

Left-Hand Side

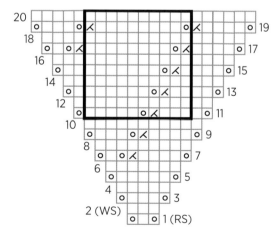

Right-Hand Side

Right-Hand Side

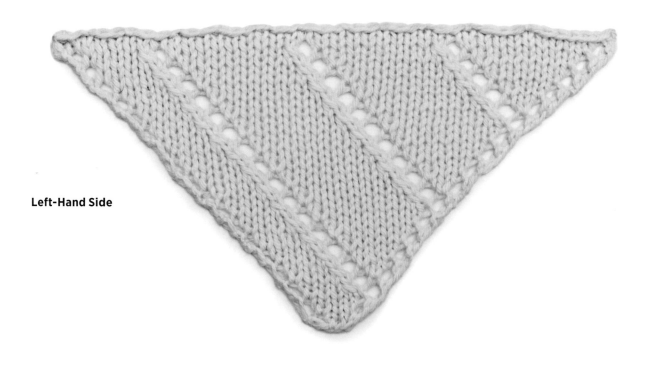

Left-Hand Side

73

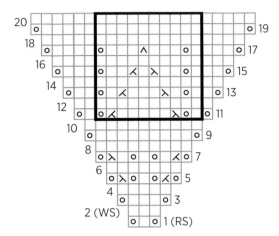

ROW 1 (RS): Yarn over, k1, yarn over. (3 stitches)

ROW 2 AND ALL WS ROWS: Purl across.

ROW 3: Yarn over, k3, yarn over. (5 stitches)

ROW 5: Yarn over, k2tog, yarn over, k1, yarn over, ssk, yarn over. (7 stitches)

ROW 7: Yarn over, k2tog, (k1, yarn over) twice, k1, ssk, yarn over. (9 stitches)

ROW 9: Yarn over, knit across to the marker, ending this section with yarn over. (11 stitches)

ROW 11: Yarn over, *k1, yarn over, ssk, k5, k2tog, yarn over; repeat from the * to 1 stitch before the marker, ending this section with k1, yarn over. (13 stitches)

ROW 13: Yarn over, k1, *k1, yarn over, k1, ssk, k3, k2tog, k1, yarn over; repeat from the * to 2 stitches before the marker, ending this section with k2, yarn over. (15 stitches)

ROW 15: Yarn over, k2, *k1, yarn over, k2, ssk, k1, k2tog, k2, yarn over; repeat from the * to 3 stitches before the marker, ending this section with k3, yarn over. (17 stitches)

ROW 17: Yarn over, k3, *k1, yarn over, k3, sk2p (page 282), k3, yarn over; repeat from the * to 4 stitches before the marker, ending this section with k4, yarn over. (19 stitches)

ROW 19: Yarn over, knit across to the marker, ending this section with yarn over. (21 stitches)

ROW 20: As Row 2.

Repeat Rows 11–20 for the pattern.

∧ **sk2p**

74

ROWS 1, 3, 5, 7, 9, 17, AND 19 (RS): Yarn over, knit across to the marker, ending this section with yarn over.

ROW 2 AND ALL WS ROWS: Purl across.

ROW 11: Yarn over, *k3, yarn over, ssk, k1, k2tog, yarn over, k2; repeat from the * to 1 stitch before the marker, ending this section with k1, yarn over. (13 stitches)

ROW 13: Yarn over, k1, *k4, yarn over, s2kp2 (page 282), yarn over, k3; repeat from the * to 2 stitches before the marker, ending this section with k2, yarn over. (15 stitches)

ROW 15: Yarn over, k2, *k5, bobble (page 279), k4; repeat from the * to 3 stitches before the marker, ending this section with k3, yarn over. (17 stitches)

ROW 20: As Row 2.

Repeat Rows 11–20 for the pattern.

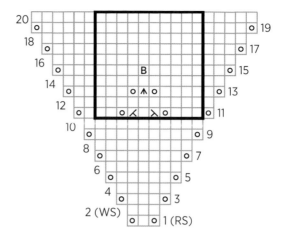

↑ s2kp2

B Bobble

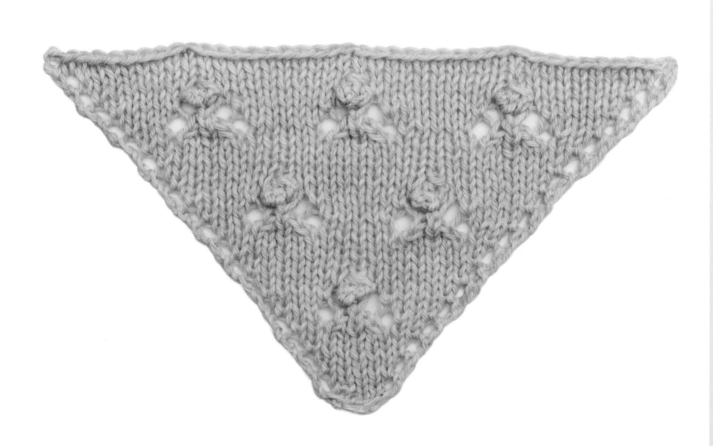

75 ₩

ROW 1 (RS): Yarn over, k1, yarn over. (3 stitches)

ROW 2 AND ALL WS ROWS: Purl across.

ROW 3: Yarn over, k1, yarn over, ssk, yarn over. (5 stitches)

ROW 5: Yarn over, k2tog, yarn over, k1, yarn over, ssk, yarn over. (7 stitches)

ROW 7: Yarn over, k2tog, yarn over, k2, k2tog, yarn over, k1, yarn over. (9 stitches)

ROW 9: Yarn over, k2tog, yarn over, k4, k2tog, yarn over, k1, yarn over. (11 stitches)

ROW 11: Yarn over, *k2tog, yarn over, k3, yarn over, ssk, k1, k2tog, yarn over; repeat from the * to 1 stitch before the marker, ending this section with k1, yarn over. (13 stitches)

ROW 13: Yarn over, k2tog, *yarn over, k3, (yarn over, ssk) twice, k1, k2tog; repeat from the * to 1 stitch before the marker, ending this section with yarn over, k1, yarn over. (15 stitches)

ROW 15: Yarn over, k2, *k3, (yarn over, ssk) 3 times, k1; repeat from the * to 3 stitches before the marker, ending this section with k3, yarn over. (17 stitches)

ROW 17: Yarn over, k1, yarn over, ssk, *k2, (yarn over, ssk) 4 times; repeat from the * to 4 stitches before the marker, ending this section with k2, yarn over, ssk, yarn over. (19 stitches)

ROW 19: Yarn over, k1, yarn over, ssk, k1, *k3, (yarn over, ssk) 3 times, k1; repeat from the * to 5 stitches before the marker, ending this section with k3, yarn over, ssk, yarn over. (21 stitches)

ROW 21: Yarn over, k1, yarn over, ssk, k1, k2tog, *yarn over, k3, (yarn over, ssk) twice, k1, k2tog; repeat from the * to 5 stitches before the marker, ending this section with yarn over, k3, yarn over, ssk, yarn over. (23 stitches)

ROW 23: Yarn over, k1, yarn over, ssk, k1, k2tog, yarn over, *k2tog, yarn over, k3, yarn over, ssk, k1, k2tog, yarn over; repeat from the * to 7 stitches before the marker, ending this section with k2tog, yarn over, k3, yarn over, ssk, yarn over. (25 stitches)

ROW 25: Yarn over, k4, k2tog, yarn over, k2tog, *yarn over, k2tog, yarn over, k4, k2tog, yarn over, k2tog; repeat from the * to 7 stitches before the marker, ending this section with yarn over, k2tog, yarn over, k5, yarn over. (27 stitches)

ROW 27: Yarn over, k2tog, yarn over, k2, (k2tog, yarn over) twice, *(k2tog, yarn over) twice, k2, (k2tog, yarn over) twice; repeat from the * to 9 stitches before the marker, ending this section with (k2tog, yarn over) twice, k2, k2tog, yarn over, k1, yarn over. (29 stitches)

ROW 29: Yarn over, k2tog, yarn over, k4, k2tog, yarn over, k2tog, *yarn over, k2tog, yarn over, k4, k2tog, yarn over, k2tog; repeat from the * to 9 stitches before the marker, ending this section with yarn over, k2tog, yarn over, k4, k2tog, yarn over, k1, yarn over. (31 stitches)

ROW 30: As Row 2.

Repeat Rows 11–30 for the pattern.

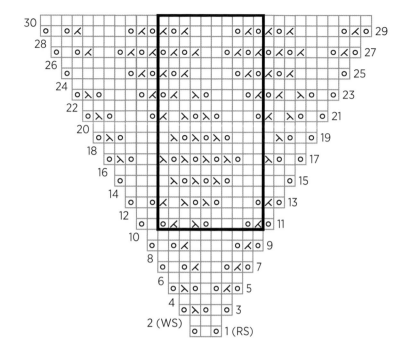

76

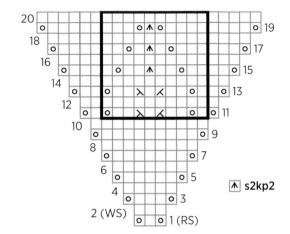

ROW 1 (RS): Yarn over, k1, yarn over. (3 stitches)

ROW 2 AND ALL WS ROWS: Purl across.

ROW 3: Yarn over, k3, yarn over. (5 stitches)

ROW 5: Yarn over, k5, yarn over. (7 stitches)

ROW 7: Yarn over, k7, yarn over. (9 stitches)

ROW 9: Yarn over, k9, yarn over. (11 stitches)

ROW 11: Yarn over, *k1, yarn over, k2, k2tog, k1, ssk, k2, yarn over; repeat from the * to 1 stitch before the marker, ending this section with k1, yarn over. (13 stitches)

ROW 13: Yarn over, k1, *k1, yarn over, k2, k2tog, k1, ssk, k2, yarn over; repeat from the * to 2 stitches before the marker, ending this section with k2, yarn over. (15 stitches)

⊼ s2kp2

ROW 15: Yarn over, k2, *k2, yarn over, k2, s2kp2 (page 282), k2, yarn over, k1; repeat from the * to 3 stitches before the marker, ending this section with k3, yarn over. (17 stitches)

ROW 17: Yarn over, k3, *k3, yarn over, k1, s2kp2, k1, yarn over, k2; repeat from the * to 4 stitches before the marker, ending this section with k4, yarn over. (19 stitches)

ROW 19: Yarn over, k4, *k4, yarn over, s2kp2, yarn over, k3; repeat from the * to 5 stitches before the marker, ending this section with k5, yarn over. (21 stitches)

ROW 20: As Row 2.

Repeat Rows 11–20 for the pattern.

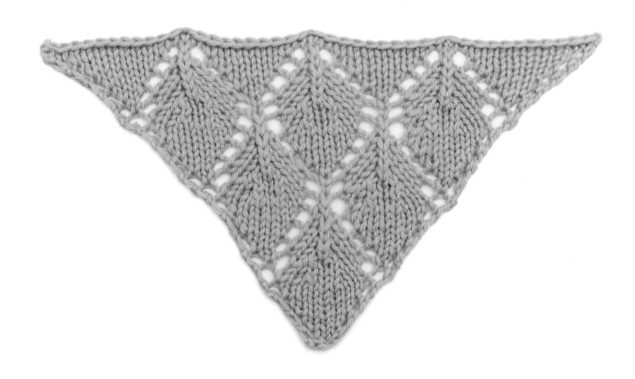

NOTE: To execute s2kp2 on a right-side row, see page 282. For wrong-side rows, follow this procedure: insert the needle into the second and then the first stitch (in that order) as if to p2tog-tbl, slip both stitches at once onto the right needle from this position, purl the next stitch, then pass the 2 slipped stitches over the purled stitch. (Abbreviated s2pp2.)

ROW 1: Yarn over, k1, yarn over. (3 stitches)

ROW 2, 4, 6, 8, 20, 22, 24, 26, 28: Purl across.

ROW 3: Yarn over, k3, yarn over. (5 stitches)

ROW 5: Yarn over, k5, yarn over. (7 stitches)

ROW 7: Yarn over, k7, yarn over. (9 stitches)

ROW 9: Yarn over, k9, yarn over. (11 stitches)

ROW 10: P4, yarn over, s2pp2 (see note at left), yarn over, p4.

ROW 11: Yarn over, *k3, k2tog, yarn over, k1, yarn over, ssk, k2; repeat from the * to 1 stitch before marker, ending this section with k1, yarn over. (13 stitches)

ROW 12: P2, *p1, ssp (page 281), yarn over, p3, yarn over, p2tog, p2; repeat from the * to 1 stitch before the marker, ending this section with p1.

ROW 13: Yarn over, k1, *k1, k2tog, yarn over, k5, yarn over, ssk; repeat from the * to 2 stitches before the marker, ending this section with k2, yarn over. (15 stitches)

ROW 14: P1, yarn over, s2pp2, *yarn over, p7, yarn over, s2pp2; repeat from the * to 1 stitch before the marker, ending this section with yarn over, p1.

ROW 15: Yarn over, k2, *k4, yarn over, s2kp2 (page 282), yarn over, k3; repeat from the * to 3 stitches before the marker, ending this section with k3, yarn over. (17 stitches)

ROW 16: P4, *yarn over, p2tog, p5, ssp, yarn over, p1; repeat from the * to 3 stitches before the marker, ending this section with p3.

ROW 17: Yarn over, k3, *k2, yarn over, ssk, k3, k2tog yarn over, k1; repeat from the * to 4 stitches before the marker, ending this section with k4, yarn over. (19 stitches)

ROW 18: P5, *p2, yarn over, p2tog, p1, ssp, yarn over, p3; repeat from the * to 4 stitches before the marker, ending this section with p4.

ROW 19: Yarn over, k4, *k4, yarn over, s2kp2, yarn over, k3; repeat from the * to 5 stitches before the marker, ending this section with k5, yarn over. (21 stitches)

(continued on the next page)

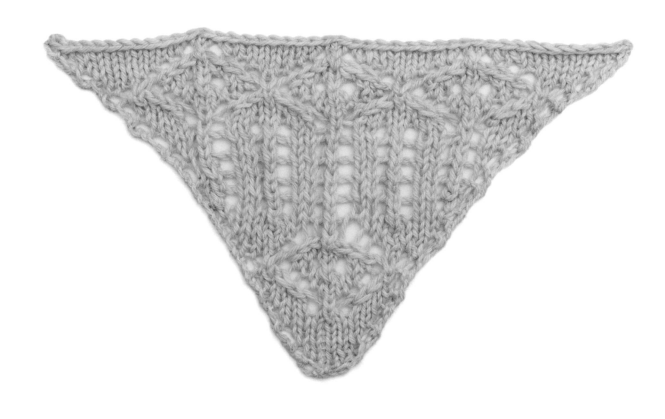

WEDGE 77, *continued*

ROW 21: Yarn over, k2tog, yarn over, k2, yarn over, *s2kp2, yarn over, k2, yarn over, s2kp2, yarn over, k2, yarn over; repeat from the * to 7 stitches before the marker, ending this section with s2kp2, yarn over, k2, yarn over, ssk, yarn over. (23 stitches)

ROW 23: Yarn over, k1, k2tog, yarn over, k2, yarn over, *s2kp2, yarn over, k2, yarn over, s2kp2, yarn over, k2, yarn over; repeat from the * to 8 stitches before the marker, ending this section with s2kp2, yarn over, k2, yarn over, ssk, k1, yarn over. (25 stitches)

ROW 25: Yarn over, k1, yarn over, s2kp2, yarn over, k2, yarn over, *s2kp2, yarn over, k2, yarn over, s2kp2, yarn over, k2, yarn over; repeat from the * to 9 stitches before the marker, ending this section with s2kp2, yarn over, k2, yarn over, s2kp2, yarn over, k1, yarn over. (27 stitches)

ROW 27: Yarn over, k2, yarn over, s2kp2, yarn over, k2, yarn over, *s2kp2, yarn over, k2, yarn over, s2kp2, yarn over, k2, yarn over; repeat from the * to 10 stitches before the marker, ending this section with s2kp2, yarn over, k2, yarn over, s2kp2, yarn over, k2, yarn over. (29 stitches)

ROW 29: Yarn over, k3, yarn over, s2kp2, yarn over, k2, yarn over, *s2kp2, yarn over, k2, yarn over, s2kp2, yarn over, k2, yarn over; repeat from the * to 11 stitches before the marker, ending this section with s2kp2, yarn over, k2, yarn over, s2kp2, yarn over, k3, yarn over. (31 stitches)

ROW 30: As Row 2.

Repeat Rows 11–30 for the pattern.

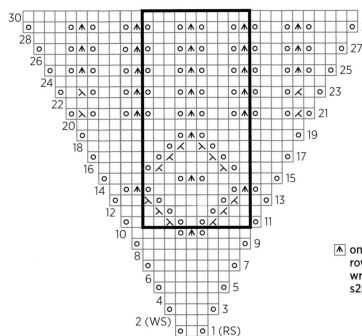

⋀ on right-side rows, s2kp2; on wrong-side rows, s2pp2

SHAWL #19

A gradient yarn and a beaded border make this delicate piece pop! See page 277 for instructions.

78

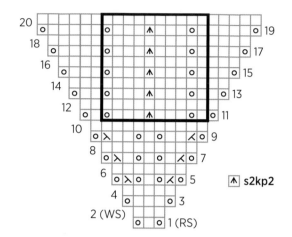

ROW 1 (RS): Yarn over, k1, yarn over. (3 stitches)

ROW 2 AND ALL WS ROWS: Purl across.

ROW 3: Yarn over, k3, yarn over. (5 stitches)

ROW 5: Yarn over, k2tog, yarn over, k1, yarn over, ssk, yarn over. (7 stitches)

ROW 7: Yarn over, k2tog, (k1, yarn over) twice, k1, ssk, yarn over. (9 stitches)

ROW 9: Yarn over, k2tog, k2, yarn over, k1, yarn over, k2, ssk, yarn over. (11 stitches)

ROW 11: Yarn over, *k1, yarn over, k3, s2kp2 (page 282), k3, yarn over; repeat from the * to 1 stitch before the marker, ending this section with k1, yarn over. (13 stitches)

ROW 13: Yarn over, k1, *k1, yarn over, k3, s2kp2, k3, yarn over; repeat from the * to 2 stitches before the marker, ending this section with k2, yarn over. (15 stitches)

ROW 15: Yarn over, k2, *k1, yarn over, k3, s2kp2, k3, yarn over; repeat from the * to 3 stitches before the marker, ending this section with k3, yarn over. (17 stitches)

ROW 17: Yarn over, k3, *k1, yarn over, k3, s2kp2, k3, yarn over; repeat from the * to 4 stitches before the marker, ending this section with k4, yarn over. (19 stitches)

ROW 19: Yarn over, k4, *k1, yarn over, k3, s2kp2, k3, yarn over; repeat from the * to 5 stitches before the marker, ending this section with k5, yarn over. (21 stitches)

ROW 20: As Row 2.

Repeat Rows 11–20 for the pattern.

⊼ s2kp2

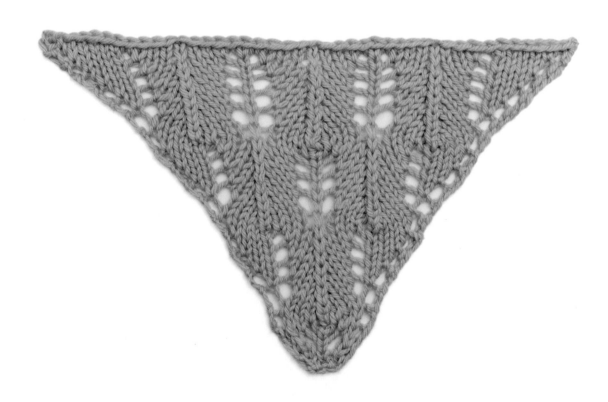

WEDGES with 12-Stitch Multiples

Start each wedge with the provisional cast on and the tab of your choice (page 10).

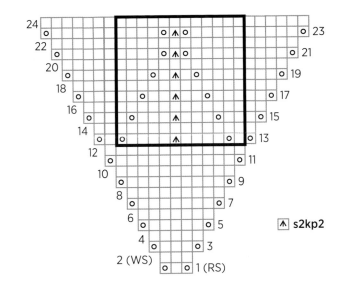

s2kp2

ROW 1 (RS): Yarn over, k1, yarn over. (3 stitches)

ROW 2 AND ALL WS ROWS: Purl across.

ROW 3: Yarn over, k3, yarn over. (5 stitches)

ROW 5: Yarn over, k5, yarn over. (7 stitches)

ROW 7: Yarn over, k7, yarn over. (9 stitches)

ROW 9: Yarn over, k9, yarn over. (11 stitches)

ROW 11: Yarn over, k11, yarn over. (13 stitches)

ROW 13: Yarn over, *k1, yarn over, k4, s2kp2 (page 282), k4, yarn over; repeat from the * to 1 stitch before the marker, ending this section with k1, yarn over. (15 stitches)

ROW 15: Yarn over, k1, *k2, yarn over, k3, s2kp2, k3, yarn over, k1; repeat from the * to 2 stitches before the marker, ending this section with k2, yarn over. (17 stitches)

ROW 17: Yarn over, k2, *k3, yarn over, k2, s2kp2, k2, yarn over, k2; repeat from the * to 3 stitches before the marker, ending this section with k3, yarn over. (19 stitches)

ROW 19: Yarn over, k3, *k4, yarn over, k1, s2kp2, k1, yarn over, k3; repeat from the * to 4 stitches before the marker, ending this section with k4, yarn over. (21 stitches)

ROW 21: Yarn over, k4, *k5, yarn over, s2kp2, yarn over, k4; repeat from the * to 5 stitches before the marker, ending this section with k5, yarn over. (23 stitches)

ROW 23: Yarn over, k5, *k5, yarn over, s2kp2, yarn over, k4; repeat from the * to 6 stitches before the marker, ending this section with k6, yarn over. (25 stitches)

ROW 24: As Row 2.

Repeat Rows 13–24 for the pattern.

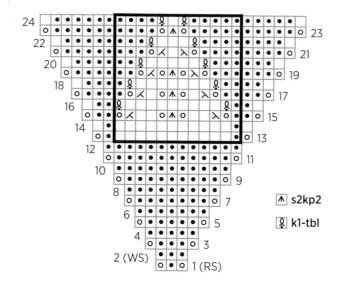

ROW 1 (RS): Yarn over, p1, yarn over. (3 stitches)

ROWS 2, 4, 6, 8, 10, AND 12: Knit across.

ROW 3: Yarn over, p3, yarn over. (5 stitches)

ROW 5: Yarn over, p5, yarn over. (7 stitches)

ROW 7: Yarn over, p7, yarn over. (9 stitches)

ROW 9: Yarn over, p9, yarn over. (11 stitches)

ROW 11: Yarn over, p11, yarn over. (13 stitches)

ROW 13: Yarn over, *p1, k11; repeat from the * to 1 stitch before the marker, ending this section with p1, yarn over. (15 stitches)

ROW 14: P1, k1, *p11, k1; repeat from the * to 1 stitch before the marker, ending this section with p1.

ROW 15: Yarn over, p1, *p1, yarn over, ssk, k2, yarn over, s2kp2 (page 282), yarn over, k2, k2tog, yarn over; repeat from the * to 2 stitches before the marker, ending this section with p2, yarn over. (17 stitches)

ROW 16: P1, k2, *k1-tbl (page 285), p9, k1-tbl, k1; repeat from the * to 2 stitches before the marker, ending with k1, p1.

ROW 17: Yarn over, p2, *p2, yarn over, ssk, k1, yarn over, s2kp2, yarn over, k1, k2tog, yarn over, p1; repeat from the * to 3 stitches before the marker, ending this section with p3, yarn over. (19 stitches)

ROW 18: P1, k3, *k1, k1-tbl, p7, k1-tbl, k2; repeat from the * to 3 stitches before the marker, ending this section with k2, p1.

ROW 19: Yarn over, p3, *p3, yarn over, ssk, yarn over, s2kp2, yarn over, k2tog, yarn over, p2; repeat from the * to 4 stitches before the marker, ending this section with p4, yarn over. (21 stitches)

ROW 20: P1, k4, *k2, k1-tbl, p5, k1-tbl, k3; repeat from the * to 4 stitches before the marker, ending this section with k3, p1.

ROW 21: Yarn over, p4, *p4, yarn over, ssk, k1, k2tog, yarn over, p3; repeat from the * to 5 stitches before the marker, ending this section with p5, yarn over. (23 stitches)

ROW 22: P1, k5, *k3, k1-tbl, p3, k1-tbl, k4; repeat from the * to 5 stitches before the marker, ending this section with k4, p1.

ROW 23: Yarn over, p5, *p5, yarn over, s2kp2, yarn over, p4; repeat from the * to 6 stitches before the marker, ending this section with p6, yarn over. (25 stitches)

ROW 24: P1, k6, *k4, k1-tbl, p1, k1-tbl, k5; repeat from the * to 6 stitches before the marker, ending this section with k5, p1.

Repeat Rows 13–24 for the pattern.

⋏ s2kp2

ᛩ k1-tbl

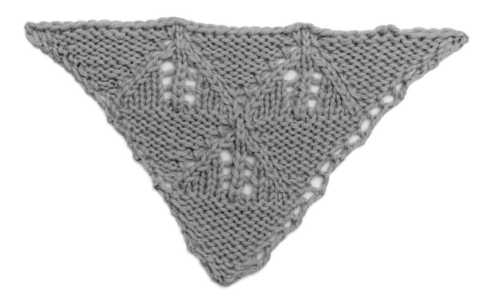

81

ROW 1 (RS): Yarn over, k1, yarn over. (3 stitches)

ROW 2 AND ALL WS ROWS: Knit the knit stitches and purl the purl stitches and yarn overs.

ROW 3: Yarn over, k1, p1, k1, yarn over. (5 stitches)

ROW 5: Yarn over, k2tog, yarn over, p1, yarn over, ssk, yarn over. (7 stitches)

ROW 7: Yarn over, k2tog, yarn over, p3, yarn over, ssk, yarn over. (9 stitches)

ROW 9: Yarn over, k2tog, yarn over, p5, yarn over, ssk, yarn over. (11 stitches)

ROW 11: Yarn over, k2tog, yarn over, p7, yarn over, ssk, yarn over. (13 stitches)

ROW 13: Yarn over, *p1, ssk, k3, yarn over, k1, yarn over, k3, k2tog; repeat from the * to 1 stitch before the marker, ending this section with p1, yarn over. (15 stitches)

ROW 15: Yarn over, k1, *p1, ssk, k3, yarn over, k1, yarn over, k3, k2tog; repeat from the * to 2 stitches before the marker, ending this section with p1, k1, yarn over. (17 stitches)

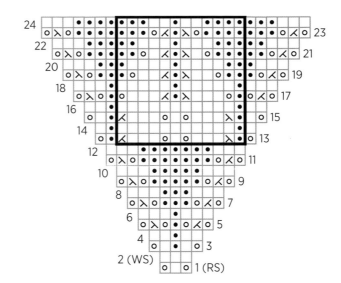

ROW 17: Yarn over, k2tog, yarn over, *p1, yarn over, k3, ssk, p1, k2tog, k3, yarn over; repeat from the * to 3 stitches before the marker, ending this section with p1, yarn over, ssk, yarn over. (19 stitches)

ROW 19: Yarn over, k2tog, yarn over, p1, *p2, yarn over, k2, ssk, p1, k2tog, k2, yarn over, p1; repeat from the * to 4 stitches before the marker, ending this section with p2, yarn over, ssk, yarn over. (21 stitches)

ROW 21: Yarn over, k2tog, yarn over, p2, *p3, yarn over, k1, ssk, p1, k2tog, k1, yarn over, p2; repeat from the * to 5 stitches before the marker, ending this section with p3, yarn over, ssk, yarn over. (23 stitches)

ROW 23: Yarn over, k2tog, yarn over, p3, *p4, yarn over, ssk, p1, k2tog, yarn over, p3; repeat from the * to 6 stitches before the marker, ending this section with p4, yarn over, ssk, yarn over. (25 stitches)

ROW 24: As Row 2.

Repeat Rows 13–24 for the pattern.

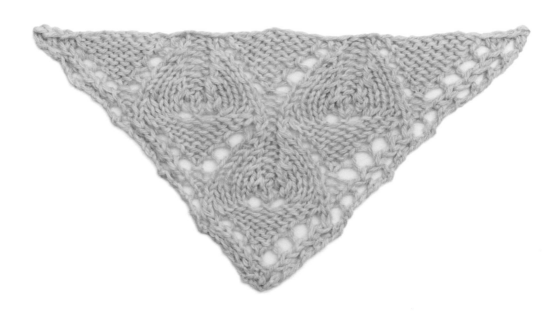

82

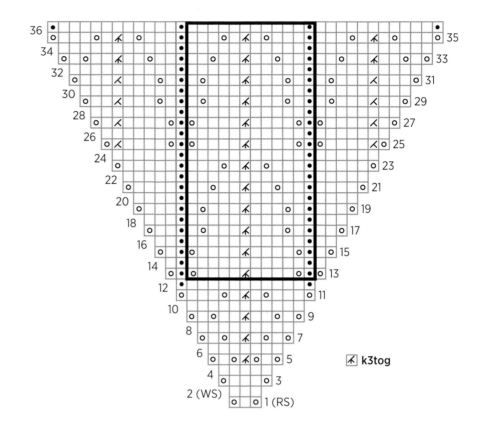

ROW 1 (RS): Yarn over, k1, yarn over. (3 stitches)

ROWS 2, 4, 6, 8, 10, 14, 16, 18, 20, 22, 24, 26, 28, 30, 32, AND 34: Knit the knit stitches and purl the purl stitches and yarn overs.

ROW 3: Yarn over, k3, yarn over. (5 stitches)

ROW 5: Yarn over, k1, yarn over, k3tog, yarn over, k1, yarn over. (7 stitches)

ROW 7: (Yarn over, k1) twice, k3tog, (k1, yarn over) twice. (9 stitches)

ROW 9: Yarn over, k1, yarn over, k2, k3tog, k2, yarn over, k1, yarn over. (11 stitches)

ROW 11: Yarn over, k3, yarn over, k1, k3tog, k1, yarn over, k3, yarn over. (13 stitches)

ROW 12: K1, p11, k1.

ROW 13: Yarn over, *p1, yarn over, k4, k3tog, k4, yarn over; repeat from the * to 1 stitch before the marker, ending this section with p1, yarn over. (15 stitches)

ROW 15: Yarn over, k1, *p1, yarn over, k4, k3tog, k4, yarn over; repeat from the * to 2 stitches before the marker, ending this section with p1, k1, yarn over. (17 stitches)

ROW 17: Yarn over, k2, *p1, k1, yarn over, k3, k3tog, k3, yarn over, k1; repeat from the * to 3 stitches before the marker, ending this section with p1, k2, yarn over. (19 stitches)

ROW 19: Yarn over, k3, *p1, k1, yarn over, k3, k3tog, k3, yarn over, k1; repeat from the * to 4 stitches before the marker, ending this section with p1, k3, yarn over. (21 stitches)

ROW 21: Yarn over, k4, *p1, k2, yarn over, k2, k3tog, k2, yarn over, k2; repeat from the * to 5 stitches before the marker, ending this section with p1, k4, yarn over. (23 stitches)

k3tog

ROW 23: Yarn over, k5, *p1, k3, yarn over, k1, k3tog, k1, yarn over, k3; repeat from the * to 6 stitches before the marker, ending this section with p1, k5, yarn over. (25 stitches)

ROW 25: Yarn over, k2tog, k4, yarn over, *p1, yarn over, k4, k3tog, k4, yarn over; repeat from the * to 7 stitches before the marker, ending this section with p1, yarn over, k4, k2tog, yarn over. (27 stitches)

ROW 27: Yarn over, k1, k2tog, k4, yarn over, *p1, yarn over, k4, k3tog, k4, yarn over; repeat from the * to 8 stitches before the marker, ending this section with p1, yarn over, k4, k2tog, k1, yarn over. (29 stitches)

ROW 29: Yarn over, k2, k2tog, k3, yarn over, k1, *p1, k1, yarn over, k3, k3tog, k3, yarn over, k1; repeat from the * to 9 stitches before the marker, ending this section with p1, k1, yarn over, k3, k2tog, k2, yarn over. (31 stitches)

ROW 31: Yarn over, k3, k2tog, k3, yarn over, k1, *p1, k1, yarn over, k3, k3tog, k3, yarn over, k1; repeat from the * to 10 stitches before the marker, ending this section with p1, k1, yarn over, k3, k2tog, k3, yarn over. (33 stitches)

ROW 33: Yarn over, k1, yarn over, k2, k3tog, k2, yarn over, k2, *p1, k2, yarn over, k2, k3tog, k2, yarn over, k2; repeat from the * to 11 stitches before the marker, ending this section with p1, k2, yarn over, k2, k3tog, k2, yarn over, k1, yarn over. (35 stitches)

ROW 35: Yarn over, k3, yarn over, k1, k3tog, k1, yarn over, k3, *p1, k3, yarn over, k1, k3tog, k1, yarn over, k3; repeat from the * to 12 stitches before the marker, ending this section with p1, k3, yarn over, k1, k3tog, k1, yarn over, k3, yarn over. (37 stitches)

ROW 36: K1, p11, k1, *p11, k1; repeat from the * to 12 stitches before the marker, ending this section with p11, k1.

Repeat Rows 13–36 for the pattern.

SHAWL #1
Using variegated yarn adds interest to a simple stockinette pattern. See page 268 for instructions.

83

ROW 1 (RS): Yarn over, k1, yarn over. (3 stitches)

ROW 2 AND ALL WS ROWS: Purl across.

ROW 3: Yarn over, k3, yarn over. (5 stitches)

ROW 5: Yarn over, k5, yarn over. (7 stitches)

ROW 7: Yarn over, k1, k2tog, yarn over, k1, yarn over, ssk, k1, yarn over. (9 stitches)

ROW 9: Yarn over, k1, k2tog, yarn over, k3, yarn over, ssk, k1, yarn over. (11 stitches)

ROW 11: Yarn over, k4, yarn over, sk2p (page 282), yarn over, k4, yarn over. (13 stitches)

ROW 13: Yarn over, *k1, yarn over, ssk, k7, k2tog, yarn over; repeat from the * to 1 stitch before the marker, ending this section with k1, yarn over. (15 stitches)

ROW 15: Yarn over, k1, *k2, yarn over, ssk, k5, k2tog, yarn over, k1; repeat from the * to 2 stitches before the marker, ending this section with k2, yarn over. (17 stitches)

ROW 17: Yarn over, k1, yarn over, *sk2p, yarn over, k9, yarn over; repeat from the * to 4 stitches before the marker, ending this section with sk2p, yarn over, k1, yarn over. (19 stitches)

ROW 19: Yarn over, k3, *k4, k2tog, yarn over, k1, yarn over, ssk, k3; repeat from the * to 4 stitches before the marker, ending this section with k4, yarn over. (21 stitches)

ROW 21: Yarn over, k4, *k3, k2tog, yarn over, k3, yarn over, ssk, k2; repeat from the * to 5 stitches before the marker, ending this section with k5, yarn over. (23 stitches)

ROW 23: Yarn over, k5, *k5, yarn over, sk2p, yarn over, k4; repeat from the * to 6 stitches before the marker, ending this section with k6, yarn over. (25 stitches)

ROW 25: Yarn over, k4, k2tog, yarn over, *k1, yarn over, ssk, k7, k2tog, yarn over; repeat from the * to 7 stitches before the marker, ending this section with k1, yarn over, ssk, k4, yarn over. (27 stitches)

ROW 27: Yarn over, k4, k2tog, yarn over, k1, *k2, yarn over, ssk, k5, k2tog, yarn over, k1; repeat from the * to 8 stitches before the marker, ending this section with k2, yarn over, ssk, k4, yarn over. (29 stitches)

ROW 29: Yarn over, k7, yarn over, *sk2p, yarn over, k9, yarn over; repeat from the * to 10 stitches before the marker, ending this section with sk2p, yarn over, k7, yarn over. (31 stitches)

ROW 31: Yarn over, k1, k2tog, yarn over, k1, yarn over, ssk, k3, *k4, k2tog, yarn over, k1, yarn over, ssk, k3; repeat from the * to 10 stitches before the marker, ending this section with k4, k2tog, yarn over, k1, yarn over, ssk, k1, yarn over. (33 stitches)

ROW 33: Yarn over, k1, k2tog, yarn over, k3, yarn over, ssk, k2, *k3, k2tog, yarn over, k3, yarn over, ssk, k2; repeat from the * to 11 stitches before the marker, ending this section with k3, k2tog, yarn over, k3, yarn over, ssk, k1, yarn over. (35 stitches)

ROW 35: Yarn over, k4, yarn over, sk2p, yarn over, k4, *k5, yarn over, sk2p, yarn over, k4; repeat from the * to 12 stitches before the marker, ending this section with k5, yarn over, sk2p, yarn over, k4, yarn over. (37 stitches)

ROW 36: As Row 2.

Repeat Rows 13–36 for the pattern.

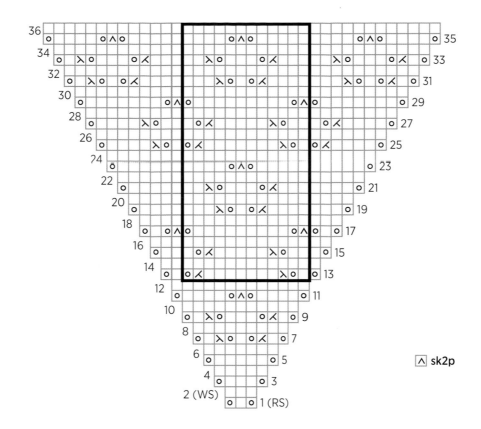

∧ sk2p

84

ROW 1 (RS): Yarn over, k1, yarn over. (3 stitches)

ROW 2 AND ALL WS ROWS: Purl across.

ROW 3: Yarn over, k3, yarn over. (5 stitches)

ROW 5: Yarn over, k5, yarn over. (7 stitches)

ROW 7: Yarn over, k3, nupp (page 279), k3, yarn over. (9 stitches)

ROW 9: Yarn over, k1, yarn over, ssk, k3, k2tog, yarn over, k1, yarn over. (11 stitches)

ROW 11: Yarn over, k3, yarn over, ssk, k1, k2tog, yarn over, k3, yarn over. (13 stitches)

ROW 13: Yarn over, *k5, yarn over, sk2p (page 282), yarn over, k4; repeat from the * to 1 stitch before the marker, ending this section with k1, yarn over. (15 stitches)

ROW 15: Yarn over, k1, *k2, k2tog, yarn over, k5, yarn over, ssk, k1; repeat from the * to 2 stitches before the marker, ending this section with k2, yarn over. (17 stitches)

ROW 17: Yarn over, k2, *k1, k2tog, yarn over, k7, yarn over, ssk; repeat from the * to 3 stitches before the marker, ending this section with k3, yarn over. (19 stitches)

ROW 19: Yarn over, k2, yarn over, *sk2p, yarn over, k4, nupp, k4, yarn over; repeat from the * to 5 stitches before the marker, ending this section with sk2p, yarn over, k2, yarn over. (21 stitches)

ROW 21: Yarn over, k2tog, yarn over, k2, *k3, yarn over, ssk, k3, k2tog, yarn over, k2; repeat from the * to 5 stitches before the marker, ending this section with k3, yarn over, ssk, yarn over. (23 stitches)

ROW 23: Yarn over, k2tog, yarn over, k3, *k4, yarn over, ssk, k1, k2tog, yarn over, k3; repeat from the * to 6 stitches before the marker, ending this section with k4, yarn over, ssk, yarn over. (25 stitches)

ROW 25: Yarn over, k2tog, yarn over, k4, *nupp, k4, yarn over, sk2p, yarn over, k4; repeat from the * to 7 stitches before marker, ending this section with nupp, k4, yarn over, ssk, yarn over. (27 stitches)

ROW 27: Yarn over, k4, yarn over, ssk, k1, *k2, k2tog, yarn over, k5, yarn over, ssk, k1; repeat from the * to 8 stitches before marker, ending this section with k2, k2tog, yarn over, k4, yarn over. (29 stitches)

ROW 29: Yarn over, k6, yarn over, ssk, *k1, k2tog, yarn over, k7, yarn over, ssk; repeat from the * to 9 stitches before marker, ending this section with k1, k2tog, yarn over, k6, yarn over. (31 stitches)

ROW 31: Yarn over, k3, nupp, k4, yarn over, *sk2p, yarn over, k4, nupp, k4, yarn over; repeat from the * to 11 stitches before the marker, ending this section with sk2p, yarn over, k4, nupp, k3, yarn over. (33 stitches)

ROW 33: Yarn over, k1, yarn over, ssk, k3, k2tog, yarn over, k2, *k3, yarn over, ssk, k3, k2tog, yarn over, k2; repeat from the * to 11 stitches before the marker, ending this section with k3, yarn over, ssk, k3, k2tog, yarn over, k1, yarn over. (35 stitches)

ROW 35: Yarn over, k3, yarn over, ssk, k1, k2tog, yarn over, k3, *k4, yarn over, ssk, k1, k2tog, yarn over, k3; repeat from the * to 12 stitches before the marker, ending this section with k4, yarn over, ssk, k1, k2tog, yarn over, k3, yarn over. (37 stitches)

ROW 36: As Row 2.

Repeat Rows 13–36 for the pattern.

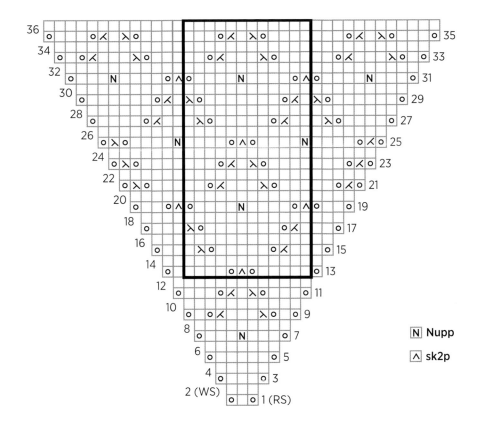

N Nupp

∧ sk2p

85

ROW 1 (RS): Yarn over, k1, yarn over. (3 stitches)

ROW 2 AND ALL WS ROWS: Purl across.

ROW 3: Yarn over, k3, yarn over. (5 stitches)

ROW 5: Yarn over, k5, yarn over. (7 stitches)

ROW 7: Yarn over, k7, yarn over. (9 stitches)

ROW 9: Yarn over, k9, yarn over. (11 stitches)

ROW 11: Yarn over, k11, yarn over. (13 stitches)

ROW 13: Yarn over, knit across to the marker, ending this section with yarn over. (15 stitches)

ROW 15: As Row 13. (17 stitches)

ROW 17: Yarn over, k2tog, yarn over, *k1, yarn over, ssk, k7, k2tog, yarn over; repeat from the * to 3 stitches before the marker, ending this section with k1, yarn over, ssk, yarn over. (19 stitches)

ROW 19: Yarn over, k2tog, yarn over, k1, *k2, yarn over, ssk, k5, k2tog, yarn over, k1; repeat from the * to 4 stitches before the marker, ending this section with k2, yarn over, ssk, yarn over. (21 stitches)

ROW 21: Yarn over, k2tog, yarn over, k2, *k3, yarn over, ssk, k3, k2tog, yarn over, k2; repeat from the * to 5 stitches before the marker, ending this section with k3, yarn over, ssk, yarn over. (23 stitches)

ROW 23: Yarn over, k2tog, yarn over, k1, k2tog, yarn over, *(k1, yarn over, ssk) twice, k1, k2tog, yarn over, k1, k2tog, yarn over; repeat from the * to 6 stitches before the marker, ending this section with (k1, yarn over, ssk) twice, yarn over. (25 stitches)

ROW 25: Yarn over, (k2tog yarn over, k1) twice, *k2, yarn over, ssk, k1, yarn over, s2kp2 (page 282), yarn over, k1, k2tog, yarn over, k1; repeat from the * to 7 stitches to the marker, ending this section with k2, yarn over, ssk, k1, yarn over, ssk, yarn over. (27 stitches)

ROW 27: Yarn over, k3, k2tog, yarn over, k2, *k3, yarn over, ssk, k3, k2tog, yarn over, k2; repeat from the * to 8 stitches before the marker, ending this section with k3, yarn over, ssk, k3, yarn over. (29 stitches)

ROW 29: Yarn over, k3, k2tog, yarn over, k3, *k4, yarn over, ssk, k1, k2tog, yarn over, k3; repeat from the * to 9 stitches before the marker, ending this section with k4, yarn over, ssk, k3, yarn over. (31 stitches)

ROW 31: Yarn over, k3, k2tog, yarn over, k4, *k5, yarn over, s2kp2, yarn over, k4; repeat from the * to 10 stitches before the marker, ending this section with k5, yarn over, ssk, k3, yarn over. (33 stitches)

ROW 33: As Row 13. (35 stitches)

ROW 35: As Row 13. (37 stitches)

ROW 36: As Row 2.

Repeat Rows 13–36 for the pattern.

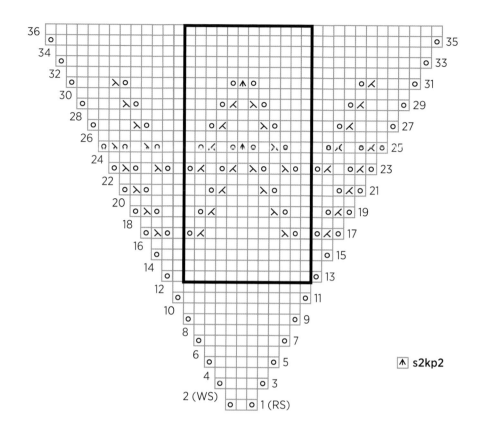

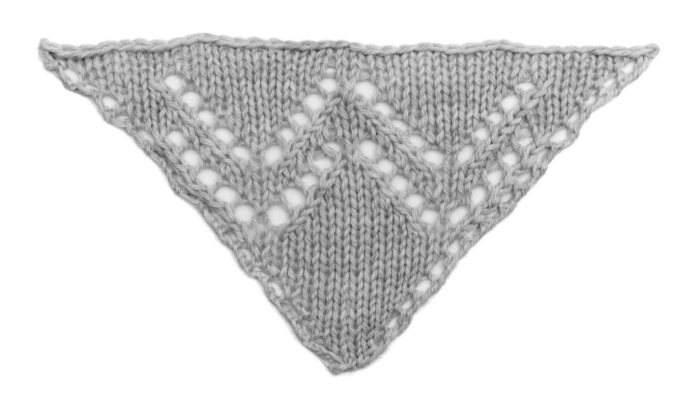

86

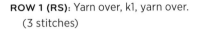

ROW 1 (RS): Yarn over, k1, yarn over. (3 stitches)

ROW 2 AND ALL WS ROWS: Purl across.

ROW 3: Yarn over, k3, yarn over. (5 stitches)

ROW 5: Yarn over, k5, yarn over. (7 stitches)

ROW 7: Yarn over, k7, yarn over. (9 stitches)

ROW 9: Yarn over, k2, yarn over, ssk, k1, k2tog, yarn over, k2, yarn over. (11 stitches)

ROW 11: Yarn over, k4, yarn over, sk2p (page 282), yarn over, k4, yarn over. (13 stitches)

ROWS 13, 19, 25, AND 31: Yarn over, knit across to the marker, ending this section with yarn over.

ROW 15: Yarn over, k1, *k1, k2tog, yarn over, k7, yarn over, ssk; repeat from the * to 2 stitches before the marker, ending this section with k2, yarn over. (17 stitches)

ROW 17: Yarn over, k1, yarn over, *sk2p, yarn over, k9, yarn over; repeat from the * to 4 stitches before the marker, ending with sk2p, yarn over, k1, yarn over. (19 stitches)

ROW 21: Yarn over, k4, *k4, yarn over, ssk, k1, k2tog, yarn over, k3; repeat from the * to 5 stitches before the marker, ending this section with k5, yarn over. (23 stitches)

ROW 23: Yarn over, k5, *k5, yarn over, sk2p, yarn over, k4; repeat from the * to 6 stitches before the marker, ending this section with k6, yarn over. (25 stitches)

ROW 27: Yarn over, k5, yarn over, ssk, *k1, k2tog, yarn over, k7, yarn over, ssk; repeat from the * to 8 stitches before the marker, ending this section with k1, k2tog, yarn over, k5, yarn over. (29 stitches)

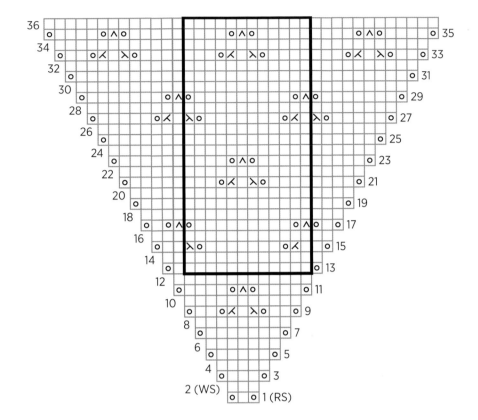

ROW 29: Yarn over, k7, yarn over, *sk2p, yarn over, k9, yarn over; repeat from the * to 10 stitches before the marker, ending this section with sk2p, yarn over, k7, yarn over. (31 stitches)

ROW 33: Yarn over, k2, yarn over, ssk, k1, k2tog, yarn over, k3, *k4, yarn over, ssk, k1, k2tog, yarn over, k3; repeat from the * to 11 stitches before the marker, ending this section with k4, yarn over, ssk, k1, k2tog, yarn over, k2, yarn over. (35 stitches)

ROW 35: Yarn over, k4, yarn over, sk2p, yarn over, k4, *k5, yarn over, sk2p, yarn over, k4; repeat from the * to 12 stitches before the marker, ending this section with k5, yarn over, sk2p, yarn over, k4, yarn over. (37 stitches)

ROW 36: As Row 2.

Repeat Rows 13–36 for the pattern.

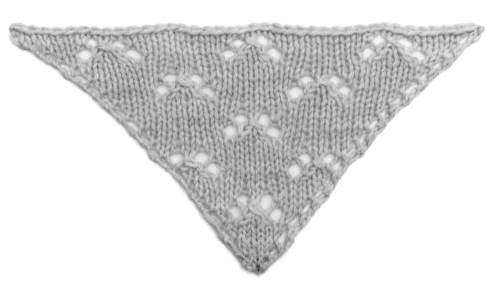

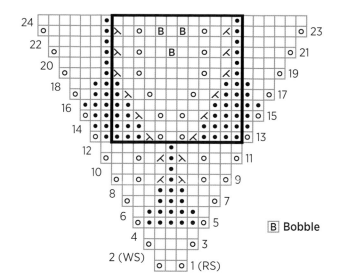

B Bobble

ROW 1 (RS): Yarn over, k1, yarn over. (3 stitches)

ROW 2 AND ALL WS ROWS: Knit the knit stitches and purl the purl stitches and yarn overs.

ROW 3: Yarn over, k3, yarn over. (5 stitches)

ROW 5: Yarn over, purl to the marker, ending this section with yarn over. (7 stitches)

ROW 7: Yarn over, k2, p3, k2, yarn over. (9 stitches)

ROW 9: (Yarn over, k1) twice, ssk, p1, k2tog, (k1, yarn over) twice. (11 stitches)

ROW 11: Yarn over, k2, yarn over, k1, ssk, p1, k2tog, k1, yarn over, k2, yarn over. (13 stitches)

ROW 13: Yarn over, *p4, k2tog, yarn over, k1, yarn over, ssk, p3; repeat from the * to 1 stitch before the marker, ending this section with p1, yarn over. (15 stitches)

ROW 15: Yarn over, p1, *p3, k2tog, (k1, yarn over) twice, k1, ssk, p2; repeat from the * to 2 stitches before the marker, ending this section with p2, yarn over. (17 stitches)

ROW 17: Yarn over, k1, p1, *p2, k2tog, k1, yarn over, k3, yarn over, k1, ssk, p1; repeat from the * to 3 stitches before the marker, ending this section with p2, k1, yarn over. (19 stitches)

ROW 19: Yarn over, k3, *p1, k2tog, k1, yarn over, k5, yarn over, k1, ssk; repeat from the * to 4 stitches before the marker, ending this section with p1, k3, yarn over. (21 stitches)

ROW 21: Yarn over, k4, *p1, k2tog, k1, yarn over, k2, bobble (page 279), k2, yarn over, k1, ssk; repeat from the * to 5 stitches before the marker, ending this section with p1, k4, yarn over. (23 stitches)

ROW 23: Yarn over, k5, *p1, k2tog, k1, yarn over, (k1, bobble) twice, k1, yarn over, k1, ssk; repeat from the * to 6 stitches before the marker, ending this section with p1, k5, yarn over. (25 stitches)

ROW 24: As Row 2.

Repeat Rows 13–24 for the pattern.

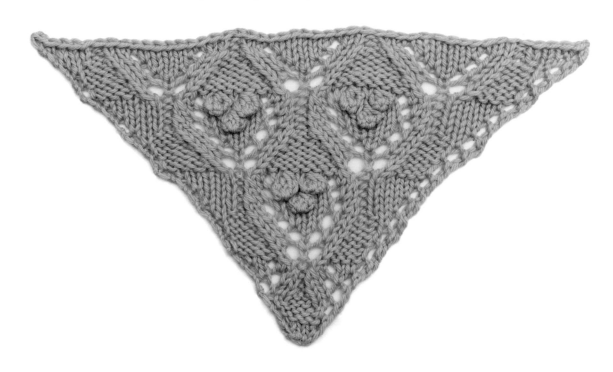

88

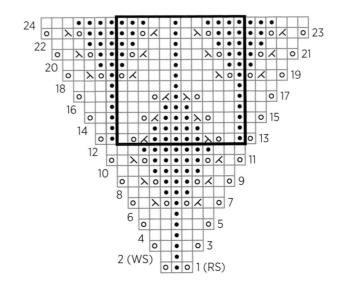

ROW 1 (RS): Yarn over, p1, yarn over. (3 stitches)

ROW 2 AND ALL WS ROWS: K1, knit the knit stitches and purl the purl stitches and the yarn overs until the last stitch before the marker, k1.

ROW 3: Yarn over, k1, p1, k1, yarn over. (5 stitches)

ROW 5: Yarn over, k2, p1, k2, yarn over. (7 stitches)

ROW 7: Yarn over, k1, k2tog, yarn over, p1, yarn over, ssk, k1, yarn over. (9 stitches)

ROW 9: Yarn over, k1, k2tog, yarn over, p3, yarn over, ssk, k1, yarn over. (11 stitches)

ROW 11: Yarn over, k1, k2tog, yarn over, p5, yarn over, ssk, k1, yarn over. (13 stitches)

ROW 13: Yarn over, *p1, k1, yarn over, ssk, p5, k2tog, yarn over, k1; repeat from the * to 1 stitch before the marker, ending this section with p1, yarn over. (15 stitches)

ROW 15: Yarn over, k1, *p1, k2, yarn over, ssk, p3, k2tog, yarn over, k2; repeat from the * across to 2 stitches before the marker, ending this section with p1, k1, yarn over. (17 stitches)

ROW 17: Yarn over, k2, *p1, k3, yarn over, ssk, p1, k2tog, yarn over, k3; repeat from the * to 3 stitches before the marker, ending this section with p1, k2, yarn over. (19 stitches)

ROW 19: Yarn over, k1, k2tog, yarn over, *p1, yarn over, ssk, k3, p1, k3, k2tog, yarn over; repeat from the * to 5 stitches before the marker, ending this section with p1, yarn over, ssk, k1, yarn over. (21 stitches)

ROW 21: Yarn over, k1, k2tog, yarn over, p1, *p2, yarn over, ssk, k2, p1, k2, k2tog, yarn over, p1; repeat from the * to 6 stitches before the marker, ending this section with p2, yarn over, ssk, k1, yarn over. (23 stitches)

ROW 23: Yarn over, k1, k2tog, yarn over, p2, *p3, yarn over, ssk, k1, p1, k1, k2tog, yarn over, p2; repeat from the * to 6 stitches before the marker, ending this section with p3, yarn over, ssk, k1, yarn over. (25 stitches)

ROW 24: As Row 2.

Repeat Rows 13–24 for the pattern.

89

ROW 1 (RS): Yarn over, k1, yarn over. (3 stitches)

ROW 2 AND ALL WS ROWS: Knit the knit stitches and purl the purl stitches and yarn overs.

ROW 3: Yarn over, k3, yarn over. (5 stitches)

ROW 5: Yarn over, k5, yarn over. (7 stitches)

ROW 7: Yarn over, k7, yarn over. (9 stitches)

ROW 9: Yarn over, k3, p3, k3, yarn over. (11 stitches)

ROW 11: Yarn over, k4, p3, k4, yarn over. (13 stitches)

ROW 13: Yarn over, *p2, k3tog, (yarn over, k1) 3 times, yarn over, sssk (page 285), p1; repeat from the * to 1 stitch before the marker, ending this section with p1, yarn over. (15 stitches)

ROW 15: Yarn over, p1, *p2, k9, p1; repeat from the * to 2 stitches before the marker, ending this section with p2, yarn over. (17 stitches)

ROW 17: Yarn over, k2, *(k1, yarn over) twice, sssk, p3, k3tog, yarn over, k1, yarn over; repeat from the * to 3 stitches before the marker, ending this section with k3, yarn over. (19 stitches)

ROW 19: Yarn over, k3, *k5, p3, k4; repeat from the * to 4 stitches before the marker, ending this section with k4, yarn over. (21 stitches)

ROW 21: Yarn over, k1, yarn over, ssk, p1, *p2, k3tog, (yarn over, k1) 3 times, yarn over, sssk, p1; repeat from the * to 5 stitches before the marker, ending this section with p2, k2tog, yarn over, k1, yarn over. (23 stitches)

ROW 23: Yarn over, k4, p1, *p2, k9, p1; repeat from the * to 6 stitches before the marker, ending this section with p2, k4. (25 stitches)

ROW 24: As Row 2.

Repeat Rows 13–24 for the pattern.

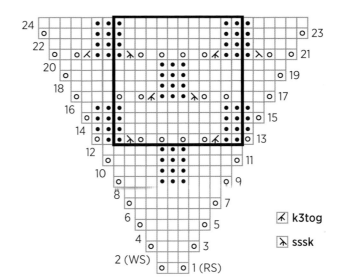

⊼ k3tog

⊼ sssk

90 ▼▼

ROW 1 (RS): Yarn over, k1, yarn over. (3 stitches)

ROW 2 AND ALL WS ROWS: Purl across.

ROW 3: Yarn over, k3, yarn over. (5 stitches)

ROW 5: Yarn over, k1, yarn over, s2kp2 (page 282), yarn over, k1, yarn over. (7 stitches)

ROW 7: Yarn over, k1, yarn over, k2tog, k1, ssk, yarn over, k1, yarn over. (9 stitches)

ROW 9: (Yarn over, k1) twice, k2tog, k1, ssk, (k1, yarn over) twice. (11 stitches)

ROW 11: Yarn over, k2, yarn over, k1, k2tog, k1, ssk, k1, yarn over, k2, yarn over. (13 stitches)

ROW 13: Yarn over, *k1, ssk, k1, yarn over, k2tog, yarn over, k1, yarn over, ssk, yarn over, k1, k2tog; repeat from the * to 1 stitch before the marker, ending this section with k1, yarn over. (15 stitches)

ROW 15: Yarn over, k1, *k1, ssk, k2, yarn over, k3, yarn over, k2, k2tog; repeat from the * to 2 stitches before the marker, ending this section with k2, yarn over. (17 stitches)

ROW 17: Yarn over, k2, *k1, ssk, k1, yarn over, k5, yarn over, k1, k2tog; repeat from the * to 3 stitches before the marker, ending this section with k3, yarn over. (19 stitches)

ROW 19: Yarn over, k1, k2tog, yarn over, *k1, yarn over, ssk, yarn over, k1, k2tog, k1, ssk, k1, yarn over, k2tog, yarn over; repeat from the * to 4 stitches before the marker, ending this section with k1, yarn over, ssk, k1, yarn over. (21 stitches)

ROW 21: Yarn over, ssk, k1, yarn over, k1, *k2, yarn over, k2, k2tog, k1, ssk, k2, yarn over, k1; repeat from the * to 5 stitches before the marker, ending this section with k2, yarn over, k1, k2tog, yarn over. (23 stitches)

ROW 23: Yarn over, ssk, k1, yarn over, k2, *k3, yarn over, k1, k2tog, k1, ssk, k1, yarn over, k2; repeat from the * to 6 stitches before the marker, ending this section with k3, yarn over, k1, k2tog, yarn over. (25 stitches)

ROW 25: Yarn over, k1, yarn over, ssk, yarn over, k1, k2tog, *k1, ssk, k1, yarn over, k2tog, yarn over, k1, yarn over, ssk, yarn over, k1, k2tog; repeat from the * to 7 stitches before the marker, ending this section with k1, ssk, k1, yarn over, k2tog, yarn over, k1, yarn over. (27 stitches)

ROW 27: Yarn over, k3, yarn over, k2, k2tog, *k1, ssk, k2, yarn over, k3, yarn over, k2, k2tog; repeat from the * to 8 stitches before the marker, ending this section with k1, ssk, k2, yarn over, k3, yarn over. (29 stitches)

ROW 29: Yarn over, k5, yarn over, k1, k2tog, *k1, ssk, k1, yarn over, k5, yarn over, k1, k2tog; repeat from the * to 9 stitches before the marker, ending this section with k1, ssk, k1, yarn over, k5, yarn over. (31 stitches)

ROW 31: Yarn over, k4, ssk, k1, yarn over, k2tog, yarn over, *k1, yarn over, ssk, yarn over, k1, k2tog, k1, ssk, k1, yarn over, k2tog, yarn over; repeat from the * to 10 stitches before the marker, ending this section with k1, yarn over, ssk, yarn over, k1, k2tog, k4, yarn over. (33 stitches)

ROW 33: Yarn over, k5, ssk, k2, yarn over, k1, *k2, yarn over, k2, k2tog, k1, ssk, k2, yarn over, k1; repeat from the * to 11 stitches before the marker, ending this section with k2, yarn over, k2, k2tog, k5, yarn over. (35 stitches)

ROW 35: Yarn over, k2, yarn over, k1, k2tog, k1, ssk, k1, yarn over, k2, *k3, yarn over, k1, k2tog, k1, ssk, k1, yarn over, k2; repeat from the * to 12 stitches before the marker, ending this section with k3, yarn over, k1, k2tog, k1, ssk, k1, yarn over, k2, yarn over. (37 stitches)

ROW 36: As Row 2.

Repeat Rows 13–36 for the pattern.

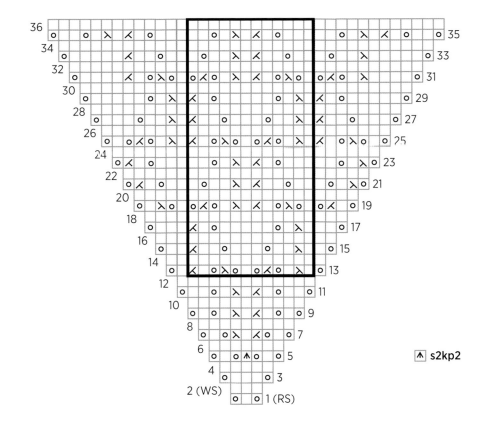

⩓ s2kp2

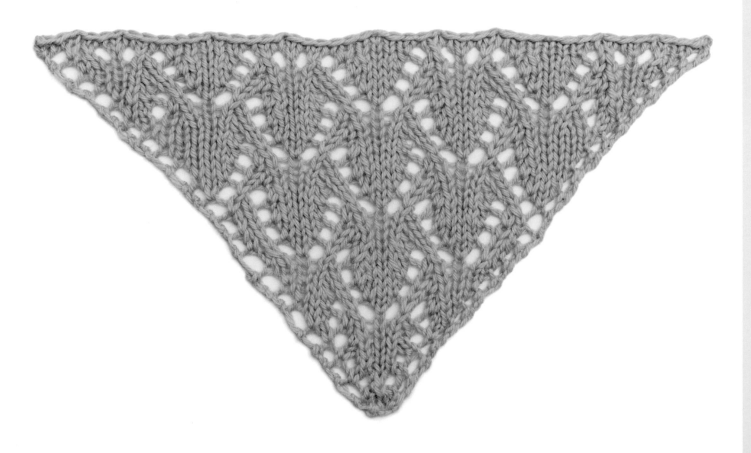

91

ROW 1 (RS): Yarn over, k1, yarn over. (3 stitches)

ROWS 2, 4, 6, 8, 10, 14, 16, 18, 20, 22, 26, 28, 30, 32, AND 34: Knit the knit stitches and purl the purl stitches and yarn overs.

ROW 3: Yarn over, k3, yarn over. (5 stitches)

ROW 5: Yarn over, k1, yarn over, s2kp2 (page 282), yarn over, k1, yarn over. (7 stitches)

ROW 7: Yarn over, k2, yarn over, s2kp2, yarn over, k2, yarn over. (9 stitches)

ROW 9: Yarn over, k1, yarn over, ssk, yarn over, s2kp2, yarn over, k2tog, yarn over, k1, yarn over. (11 stitches)

ROW 11: Yarn over, purl across to the marker, ending this section with yarn over. (13 stitches)

ROWS 12 AND 24: Knit across.

ROW 13: Yarn over, *k1, (yarn over, ssk) twice, yarn over, s2kp2, (yarn over, k2tog) twice, yarn over; repeat from the * to 1 stitch before the marker, ending this section with k1, yarn over. (15 stitches)

ROW 15: Yarn over, k1, *k2, yarn over, ssk, k1, yarn over, s2kp2, yarn over, k1, k2tog, yarn over, k1; repeat from the * to 2 stitches before the marker, ending this section with k2, yarn over. (17 stitches)

ROW 17: Yarn over, k2tog, yarn over, *k1, (yarn over, ssk) twice, yarn over, s2kp2, (yarn over, k2tog) twice, yarn over; repeat from the * to 3 stitches before the marker, ending this section with k1, yarn over, ssk, yarn over. (19 stitches)

ROW 19: Yarn over, k2tog, yarn over, k1, *k2, yarn over, ssk, k1, yarn over, s2kp2, yarn over, k1, k2tog, yarn over, k1; repeat from the * to 4 stitches before the marker, ending this section with k2, yarn over, ssk, yarn over. (21 stitches)

ROW 21: (Yarn over, k2tog) twice, yarn over, *k1, (yarn over, ssk) twice, yarn over, s2kp2, (yarn over, k2tog) twice, yarn over; repeat from the * to 5 stitches before the marker, ending this section with k1, (yarn over, ssk) twice, yarn over. (23 stitches)

ROW 23: As Row 11. (25 stitches)

ROW 25: (Yarn over, k2tog) 3 times, yarn over, *k1, (yarn over, ssk) twice, yarn over, s2kp2, (yarn over, k2tog) twice, yarn over; repeat from the * to 7 stitches before the marker, ending this section with k1, (yarn over, ssk) 3 times, yarn over. (27 stitches)

ROW 27: Yarn over, (k1, k2tog, yarn over) twice, k1, *k2, yarn over, ssk, k1, yarn over, s2kp2, yarn over, k1, k2tog, yarn over, k1; repeat from the * to 8 stitches before the marker, ending this section with k2, (yarn over, ssk, k1) twice, yarn over. (29 stitches)

ROW 29: Yarn over, k1, yarn over, s2kp2, (yarn over, k2tog) twice, yarn over, *k1, (yarn over, ssk) twice, yarn over, s2kp2, (yarn over, k2tog) twice, yarn over; repeat from the * to 9 stitches before the marker, ending this section with k1, (yarn over, ssk) twice, yarn over, s2kp2, yarn over, k1, yarn over. (31 stitches)

ROW 31: Yarn over, k2, yarn over, s2kp2 yarn over, k1, k2tog, yarn over, k1, *k2, yarn over, ssk, k1, yarn over, s2kp2, yarn over, k1, k2tog, yarn over, k1; repeat from the * to 10 stitches before the marker, ending this section with k2, yarn over, ssk, k1, yarn over, s2kp2, yarn over, k2, yarn over. (33 stitches)

ROW 33: Yarn over, k1, yarn over, ssk, yarn over, s2kp2, (yarn over, k2tog) twice, yarn over, *k1, (yarn over, ssk) twice, yarn over, s2k2p, (yarn over, k2tog) twice, yarn over; repeat from the * to 11 stitches before the marker, ending this section with k1, (yarn over, ssk) twice, yarn over, s2kp2, yarn over, k2tog, yarn over, k1, yarn over. (35 stitches)

ROW 35: As Row 13. (37 stitches)

ROW 36: As Row 12.

Repeat Rows 13–36 for the pattern.

MIX 'N' MATCH WEDGES

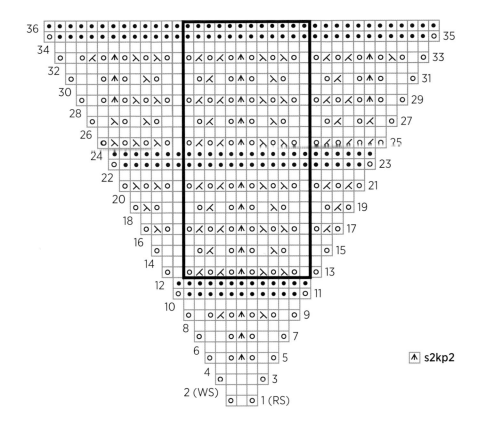

⊼ s2kp2

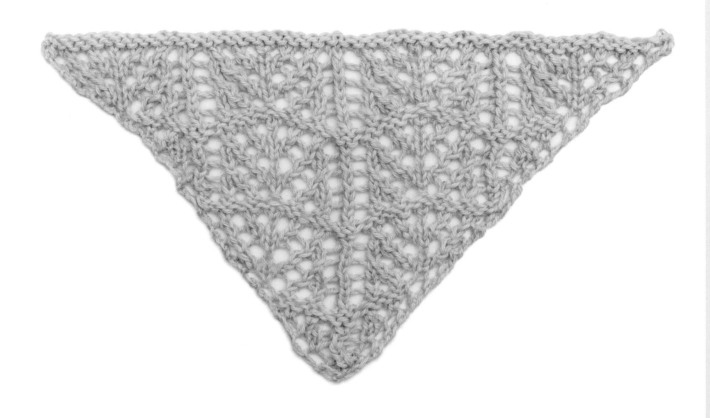

92

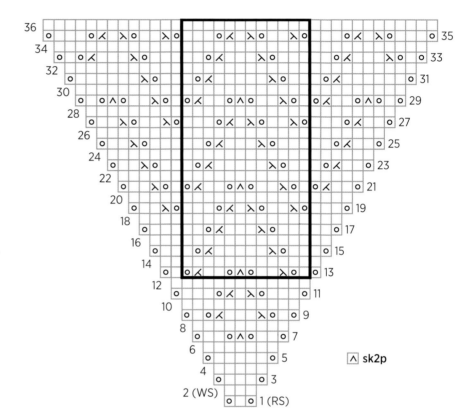

ROW 1 (RS): Yarn over, k1, yarn over. (3 stitches)

ROW 2 AND ALL WS ROWS: Purl across.

ROW 3: Yarn over, k3, yarn over. (5 stitches)

ROW 5: Yarn over, k5, yarn over. (7 stitches)

ROW 7: Yarn over, k2, yarn over, sk2p (page 282), yarn over, k2, yarn over. (9 stitches)

ROW 9: Yarn over, k1, yarn over, ssk, k3, k2tog, yarn over, k1, yarn over. (11 stitches)

ROW 11: Yarn over, k3, yarn over, ssk, k1, k2tog, yarn over, k3, yarn over. (13 stitches)

ROW 13: Yarn over, *k1, yarn over, ssk, k2, yarn over, sk2p, yarn over, k2, k2tog, yarn over; repeat from the * to 1 stitch before the marker, ending this section with k1, yarn over. (15 stitches)

ROW 15: Yarn over, k1, *k2, yarn over, ssk, k5, k2tog, yarn over, k1; repeat from the * to 2 stitches before the marker, ending this section with k2, yarn over. (17 stitches)

ROW 17: Yarn over, k2, *k3, yarn over, ssk, k3, k2tog, yarn over, k2; repeat from the * to 3 stitches before the marker, ending this section with k3, yarn over. (19 stitches)

ROW 19: Yarn over, k3, *yarn over, ssk, k2, yarn over, ssk, k1, k2tog, yarn over, k3; repeat from the * to 4 stitches before the marker, ending this section with yarn over, ssk, k2, yarn over. (21 stitches)

ROW 21: Yarn over, k2, k2tog, yarn over, *k1, yarn over, ssk, k2, yarn over, sk2p, yarn over, k2, k2tog, yarn over; repeat from the * to 5 stitches before the marker, ending this section with k1, yarn over, ssk, k2, yarn over. (23 stitches)

ROW 23: Yarn over, k2, k2tog, yarn over, k1, *k2, yarn over, ssk, k5, k2tog, yarn over, k1; repeat from the * to 6 stitches before the marker, ending this section with k2, yarn over, ssk, k2, yarn over. (25 stitches)

⋀ sk2p

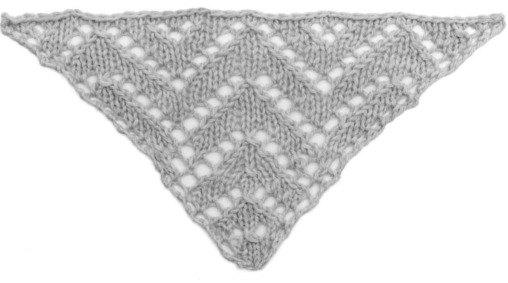

ROW 25: Yarn over, k2, k2tog, yarn over, k2, *k3, yarn over, ssk, k3, k2tog, yarn over, k2; repeat from the * to 7 stitches before the marker, ending this section with k3, yarn over, ssk, k2, yarn over. (27 stitches)

ROW 27: Yarn over, k2, k2tog, yarn over, k3, *yarn over, ssk, k2, yarn over, ssk, k1, k2tog, yarn over, k3; repeat from the * to 8 stitches before the marker, ending this section with yarn over, ssk, k2, yarn over, ssk, k2, yarn over. (29 stitches)

ROW 29: Yarn over, k1, yarn over, sk2p, yarn over, k2, k2tog, yarn over, *k1, yarn over, ssk, k2, yarn over, sk2p, yarn over, k2, k2tog, yarn over; repeat from the * to 9 stitches before the marker, ending this section with k1, yarn over, ssk, k2, yarn over, sk2p, yarn over, k1, yarn over. (31 stitches)

ROW 31: Yarn over, k6, k2tog, yarn over, k1, *k2, yarn over, ssk, k5, k2tog, yarn over, k1; repeat from the * to 10 stitches before the marker, ending this section with k2, yarn over, ssk, k6, yarn over. (33 stitches)

ROW 33: Yarn over, k1, yarn over, ssk, k3, k2tog, yarn over, k2, *k3, yarn over, ssk, k3, k2tog, yarn over, k2; repeat from the * to 11 stitches before the marker, ending this section with k3, yarn over, ssk, k3, k2tog, yarn over, k1, yarn over. (35 stitches)

ROW 35: Yarn over, k3, yarn over, ssk, k1, k2tog, yarn over, k3, *yarn over, ssk, k2, yarn over, ssk, k1, k2tog, yarn over, k3; repeat from the * to 12 stitches before the marker, ending this section with yarn over, ssk, k2, yarn over, ssk, k1, k2tog, yarn over, k3, yarn over. (37 stitches)

ROW 36: As Row 2.

Repeat Rows 13–36 for the pattern.

SHAWL #12
Tassels create a boho look and can be added to any shawl. See page 275 for instructions.

93

ROW 1 (RS): Yarn over, k1, yarn over. (3 stitches)

ROW 2 AND ALL WS ROWS: Purl across.

ROW 3: Yarn over, k3, yarn over. (5 stitches)

ROW 5: Yarn over, k5, yarn over. (7 stitches)

ROW 7: Yarn over, k7, yarn over. (9 stitches)

ROW 9: Yarn over, k1, yarn over, ssk, k3, k2tog, yarn over, k1, yarn over. (11 stitches)

ROW 11: Yarn over, k1, (yarn over, ssk) twice, k1, (k2tog, yarn over) twice, k1, yarn over. (13 stitches)

ROW 13: Yarn over, *bobble (page 279), k2, yarn over, ssk, yarn over, s2kp2 (page 282), yarn over, k2tog, yarn over, k2; repeat from the * to 1 stitch before the marker, ending this section with bobble, yarn over. (15 stitches)

ROW 15: Yarn over, k1, *k2, (k2tog, yarn over) twice, k1, (yarn over, ssk) twice, k1; repeat from the * to 2 stitches before the marker, ending this section with k2, yarn over. (17 stitches)

ROW 17: Yarn over, k2, *k1, (k2tog, yarn over) twice, k3, (yarn over, ssk) twice; repeat from the * to 3 stitches before the marker, ending this section with k3, yarn over. (19 stitches)

ROW 19: Yarn over, k2, yarn over, *s2kp2, yarn over, k2tog, yarn over, k2, bobble, k2, yarn over, ssk, yarn over; repeat from the * to 5 stitches before the marker, ending this section with s2kp2, yarn over, k2, yarn over. (21 stitches)

ROW 21: (Yarn over, k2tog) twice, yarn over, *k1, (yarn over, ssk) twice, k3, (k2tog, yarn over) twice; repeat from the * to 5 stitches before the marker, ending this section with k1, yarn over, (ssk, yarn over) twice. (23 stitches)

ROW 23: (Yarn over, k2tog) twice, yarn over, k1, *k2, (yarn over, ssk) twice, k1, (k2tog, yarn over) twice, k1; repeat from the * to 6 stitches before the marker, ending this section with k2, (yarn over, ssk) twice, yarn over. (25 stitches)

ROW 25: (Yarn over, k2tog) twice, yarn over, k2, *bobble, k2, yarn over, ssk, yarn over, s2kp2, yarn over, k2tog, yarn over, k2; repeat from the * to 7 stitches before the marker, ending this section with bobble, k2, (yarn over, ssk) twice, yarn over. (27 stitches)

ROW 27: Yarn over, k2, (yarn over, ssk) twice, k1, *k2, (k2tog, yarn over) twice, k1, (yarn over, ssk) twice, k1; repeat from the * to 8 stitches before the marker, ending this section with k2, (k2tog, yarn over) twice, k2, yarn over. (29 stitches)

ROW 29: Yarn over, k4, (yarn over, ssk) twice, *k1, (k2tog, yarn over) twice, k3, (yarn over, ssk) twice; repeat from the * to 9 stitches before the marker, ending this section with k1, (k2tog, yarn over) twice, k4, yarn over. (31 stitches)

ROW 31: Yarn over, k3, bobble, k2, yarn over, ssk, yarn over, *s2kp2, yarn over, k2tog, yarn over, k2, bobble, k2, yarn over, ssk, yarn over; repeat from the * to 11 stitches before the marker, ending this section with s2kp2, yarn over, k2tog, yarn over, k2, bobble, k3, yarn over. (33 stitches)

ROW 33: Yarn over, k1, yarn over, ssk, k3, (k2tog, yarn over) twice, *k1, (yarn over, ssk) twice, k3, (k2tog, yarn over) twice; repeat from the * to 11 stitches before the marker, ending this section with k1, (yarn over, ssk) twice, k3, k2tog, yarn over, k1, yarn over. (35 stitches)

ROW 35: Yarn over, k1, yarn over, (ssk, yarn over) twice, k1, (k2tog, yarn over) twice, k1, *k2, (yarn over, ssk) twice, k1, (k2tog, yarn over) twice, k1; repeat from the * to 12 stitches before the marker, ending this section with k2, (yarn over, ssk) twice, k1, (k2tog, yarn over) twice, k1, yarn over. (37 stitches)

ROW 36: As Row 2.

Repeat Rows 13–36 for the pattern.

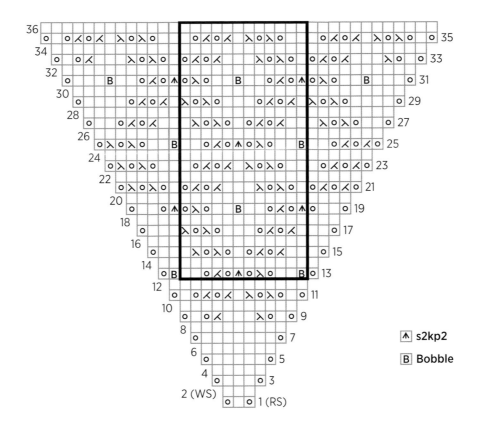

s2kp2

B Bobble

94 ♈

ROW 1 (RS): Yarn over, k1, yarn over. (3 stitches)

ROW 2 AND ALL WS ROWS: Purl across.

ROW 3: Yarn over, k3, yarn over. (5 stitches)

ROW 5: Yarn over, k1, yarn over, s2kp2 (page 282), yarn over, k1, yarn over. (7 stitches)

ROW 7: Yarn over, k1, yarn over, ssk, k1, k2tog, yarn over, k1, yarn over. (9 stitches)

ROW 9: Yarn over, k1, yarn over, ssk, yarn over, s2kp2, yarn over, k2tog, yarn over, k1, yarn over. (11 stitches)

ROW 11: Yarn over, k1, yarn over, ssk, yarn over, k1, s2kp2, k1, yarn over, k2tog, yarn over, k1, yarn over. (13 stitches)

ROW 13: Yarn over, *k1, yarn over, k4, s2kp2, k4, yarn over; repeat from the * to 1 stitch before the marker, ending this section with k1, yarn over. (15 stitches)

ROW 15: Yarn over, k1, *k2, yarn over, p3, s2kp2, p3, yarn over, k1; repeat from the * to 2 stitches before the marker, ending this section with k2, yarn over. (17 stitches)

ROW 17: Yarn over, k2, *k1, yarn over, ssk, yarn over, k2, s2kp2, k2, yarn over, k2tog, yarn over; repeat from the * to 3 stitches before the marker, ending this section with k3, yarn over. (19 stitches)

ROW 19: Yarn over, k3, *k1, yarn over, k1, ssk, yarn over, p1, s2kp2, p1, yarn over, k2tog, k1, yarn over; repeat from the * to 4 stitches before the marker, ending this section with k4, yarn over. (21 stitches)

ROW 21: Yarn over, k4, *k4, p1, k3, p1, k3; repeat from the * to 5 stitches before the marker, ending this section with k5, yarn over. (23 stitches)

ROW 23: Yarn over, k5, *k4, p1, k3, p1, k3; repeat from the * to 6 stitches before the marker, ending this section with k6, yarn over. (25 stitches)

ROW 25: Yarn over, k1, yarn over, ssk, yarn over, k2, *s2kp2, k2, yarn over, k2tog, yarn over, k1, yarn over, ssk, yarn over, k2; repeat from the * to 8 stitches before the marker, ending this section with s2kp2, k2, yarn over, k2tog, yarn over, k1, yarn over. (27 stitches)

ROW 27: Yarn over, k3, yarn over, ssk, yarn over, k1, *s2kp2, k1, yarn over, k2tog, yarn over, k3, yarn over, ssk, yarn over, k1; repeat from the * to 9 stitches before the marker, ending this section with s2kp2, k1, yarn over, k2tog, yarn over, k3, yarn over. (29 stitches)

ROW 29: Yarn over, k5, yarn over, ssk, yarn over, *s2kp2, yarn over, k2tog, yarn over, k5, yarn over, ssk, yarn over; repeat from the * to 10 stitches before the marker, ending this section with s2kp2, yarn over, k2tog, yarn over, k5, yarn over. (31 stitches)

ROW 31: Yarn over, k7, yarn over, ssk, *k1, k2tog, yarn over, k7, yarn over, ssk; repeat from the * to 10 stitches before the marker, ending this section with k1, k2tog, yarn over, k7, yarn over. (33 stitches)

ROW 33: Yarn over, k9, yarn over, *s2kp2, yarn over, k9, yarn over; repeat from the * to 12 stitches before the marker, ending this section with s2kp2, yarn over, k9, yarn over. (35 stitches)

ROW 35: Yarn over, knit across to the marker, ending this section with yarn over. (37 stitches)

ROW 36: As Row 2.

Repeat Rows 13–36 for the pattern.

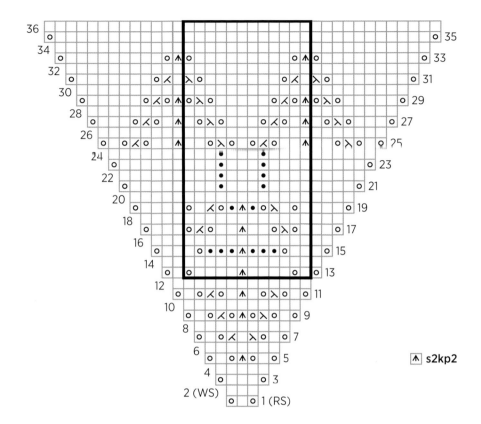

s2kp2

95

ROW 1 (RS): Yarn over, k1, yarn over. (3 stitches)

ROW 2 AND ALL WS ROWS: Purl across.

ROW 3: Yarn over, k3, yarn over. (5 stitches)

ROW 5: Yarn over, k2, yarn over, ssk, k1, yarn over. (7 stitches)

ROW 7: Yarn over, k1, k2tog, yarn over, k1, yarn over, ssk, k1, yarn over. (9 stitches)

ROW 9: Yarn over, k1, k2tog, yarn over, k3, yarn over, ssk, k1, yarn over. (11 stitches)

ROW 11: Yarn over, knit across to the marker, ending this section with yarn over. (13 stitches)

ROW 13: Yarn over, *k1, yarn over, ssk, k3, yarn over, ssk, k2, k2tog, yarn over; repeat from the * to 1 stitch before the marker, ending this section with k1, yarn over. (15 stitches)

ROW 15: Yarn over, k1, *(k1, yarn over, ssk, k1, k2tog, yarn over) twice; repeat from the * to 2 stitches before the marker, ending this section with k2, yarn over. (17 stitches)

ROW 17: Yarn over, k2tog, yarn over, *k1, yarn over, ssk, k2tog, yarn over, k3, yarn over, ssk, k2tog, yarn over; repeat from the * to 3 stitches before the marker, ending this section with k1, yarn over, ssk, yarn over. (19 stitches)

ROW 19: Yarn over, k1, k2tog, yarn over, *k1, yarn over, ssk, k7, k2tog, yarn over; repeat from the * to 4 stitches before the marker, ending this section with k1, yarn over, ssk, k1, yarn over. (21 stitches)

ROW 21: Yarn over, k2, k2tog, yarn over, *k1, yarn over, ssk, k3, yarn over, ssk, k2, k2tog, yarn over; repeat from the * to 5 stitches before the marker, ending this section with k1, yarn over, ssk, k2, yarn over. (23 stitches)

ROW 23: Yarn over, k3, k2tog, yarn over, *(k1, yarn over, ssk, k1, k2tog, yarn over) twice; repeat from the * to 6 stitches before the marker, ending this section with k1, yarn over, ssk, k3, yarn over. (25 stitches)

ROW 25: Yarn over, k2, yarn over, ssk, k2tog, yarn over, *k1, yarn over, ssk, k2tog, yarn over, k3, yarn over, ssk, k2tog, yarn over; repeat from the * to 7 stitches before the marker, ending this section with k1, yarn over, ssk, k2tog, yarn over, k2, yarn over. (27 stitches)

ROW 27: Yarn over, k5, k2tog, yarn over, *k1, yarn over, ssk, k7, k2tog, yarn over; repeat from the * to 8 stitches before the marker, ending this section with k1, yarn over, ssk, k5, yarn over. (29 stitches)

ROW 29: Yarn over, k2, yarn over, ssk, k2, k2tog, yarn over, *k1, yarn over, ssk, k3, yarn over, ssk, k2, k2tog, yarn over; repeat from the * to 9 stitches before the marker, ending this section with k1, yarn over, ssk, k3, yarn over, ssk, k1, yarn over. (31 stitches)

ROW 31: Yarn over, k1, k2tog, yarn over, k1, yarn over, ssk, k1, k2tog, yarn over, *(k1, yarn over, ssk, k1, k2tog, yarn over) twice; repeat from the * to 10 stitches before the marker, ending this section with k1, yarn over, ssk, k1, k2tog, yarn over, k1, yarn over, ssk, k1, yarn over. (33 stitches)

ROW 33: Yarn over, k1, k2tog, yarn over, k3, yarn over, ssk, k2tog, yarn over, *k1, yarn over, ssk, k2tog, yarn over, k3, yarn over, ssk, k2tog, yarn over; repeat from the * to 11 stitches before the marker, ending this section with k1, yarn over, ssk, k2tog, yarn over, k3, yarn over, ssk, k1, yarn over. (35 stitches)

ROW 35: Yarn over, k9, k2tog, yarn over, *k1, yarn over, ssk, k7, k2tog, yarn over; repeat from the * to 12 stitches before the marker, ending this section with k1, yarn over, ssk, k9, yarn over. (37 stitches)

ROW 36: As Row 2.

Repeat Rows 13–36 for the pattern.

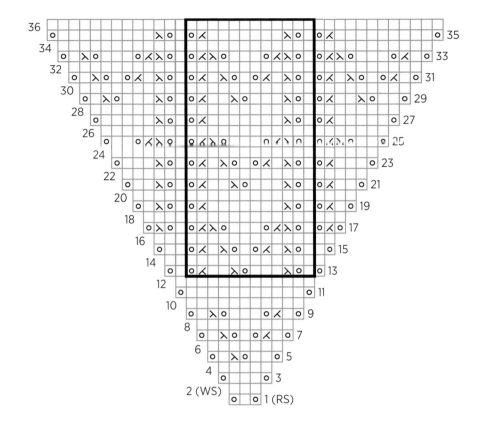

96 ⬩⬩⬩

NOTE: To execute s2kp2 on a right-side row, see page 282. For wrong-side rows, follow this procedure: insert the needle into the second and then the first stitch (in that order) as if to p2tog-tbl, slip both stitches at once onto the right needle from this position, purl the next stitch, then pass the 2 slipped stitches over the purled stitch. (Abbreviated s2pp2.)

ROW 1 (RS): Yarn over, k1, yarn over. (3 stitches)

ROWS 2, 4, 6, 8, 18, 20, 30, AND 32: Purl across.

ROW 3: Yarn over, k3, yarn over. (5 stitches)

ROW 5: Yarn over, k1, yarn over, s2kp2 (page 282), yarn over, k1, yarn over. (7 stitches)

ROW 7: Yarn over, knit across to the marker, yarn over. (9 stitches)

ROW 9: Yarn over, knit across to the marker, yarn over. (11 stitches)

ROWS 10, 12, 22, 24, AND 34: Knit across.

ROW 11: As Row 9. (13 stitches)

ROW 13: Yarn over, *k1, yarn over, k4, s2kp2, k4, yarn over; repeat from the * to 1 st before the marker, ending this section with k1, yarn over. (15 stitches)

ROW 14: P2, *p1, yarn over, p3, s2pp2 (see note at left), k3, yarn over, k2; repeat from the * to 1 stitch before the marker, ending this section with p1.

ROW 15: Yarn over, k1 *k3, yarn over, k2, s2kp2, k2, yarn over, k2; repeat from the * to 2 stitches before the marker, ending this section with k2, yarn over. (17 stitches)

ROW 16: P3, *p3, yarn over, p1, s2pp2, p1, yarn over, p4; repeat from the * to 2 stitches before the marker, ending this section with p2.

ROW 17: Yarn over, k2, *k5, yarn over, s2kp2, yarn over, k4; repeat from the * to 3 stitches before the marker, ending this section with k3, yarn over. (19 stitches)

ROW 19: As Row 9. (21 stitches)

ROW 21: As Row 9. (23 stitches)

ROW 23: As Row 9. (25 stitches)

ROW 25: Yarn over, k2tog, k4, yarn over, *k1, yarn over, k4, s2kp2, k4, yarn over; repeat from the * to 7 stitches before the marker, ending this section with k1, yarn over, k4, ssk, yarn over. (27 stitches)

ROW 26: P1, ssp, p3, yarn over, p2, *p1, yarn over, p3, s2pp2, p3, yarn over, p2; repeat from the * to 7 stitches before the marker, ending this section with p1, yarn over, p3, p2tog, p1.

ROW 27: Yarn over, k1, k2tog, k2, yarn over, k2, *k3, yarn over, k2, s2kp2, k2, yarn over, k2; repeat from the * to 8 stitches before the marker, ending this section with k3, yarn over, k2, ssk, k1, yarn over. (29 stitches)

ROW 28: P2, ssp, p1, yarn over, p4, *p3, yarn over, p1, s2pp2, p1, yarn over, p4; repeat from the * to 8 stitches before the marker, ending this section with p3, yarn over, p1, p2tog, p2.

ROW 29: Yarn over, k1, yarn over, s2kp2, yarn over, k4, *k5, yarn over, s2kp2, yarn over, k4; repeat from the * to 9 stitches before the marker, ending this section with k5, yarn over, s2kp2, yarn over, k1, yarn over. (31 stitches)

ROW 31: As Row 9. (33 stitches)

ROW 33: As Row 9. (35 stitches)

ROW 35: As Row 9. (37 stitches)

ROW 36: Knit across.

Repeat Rows 13–36 for the pattern.

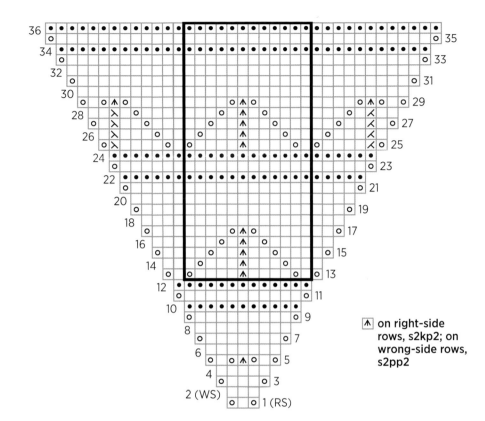

⚠ on right-side rows, s2kp2; on wrong-side rows, s2pp2

97

ROW 1 (RS): Yarn over, k1, yarn over. (3 stitches)

ROW 2 AND ALL WS ROWS: Purl across.

ROW 3: Yarn over, k3, yarn over. (5 stitches)

ROW 5: Yarn over, k5, yarn over. (7 stitches)

ROW 7: Yarn over, k1, yarn over, k1, s2kp2 (page 282), k1, yarn over, k1, yarn over. (9 stitches)

ROW 9: Yarn over, k2, yarn over, k1, s2kp2, k1, yarn over, k2, yarn over. (11 stitches)

ROW 11: Yarn over, k2, yarn over, k2tog, yarn over, s2kp2, yarn over, ssk, yarn over, k2, yarn over. (13 stitches)

ROW 13: Yarn over, *k1, yarn over, k4, s2kp2, k4, yarn over; repeat from the * to 1 stitch before the marker, ending this section with k1, yarn over. (15 stitches)

ROW 15: Yarn over, k1, *k1, yarn over, k4, s2kp2, k4, yarn over; repeat from the * to 2 stitches before the marker, ending this section with k2, yarn over. (17 stitches)

ROW 17: Yarn over, k2, *k2, yarn over, k3, s2kp2, k3, yarn over, k1; repeat from the * to 3 stitches before the marker, ending this section with k3, yarn over. (19 stitches)

ROW 19: Yarn over, k3, *k1, yarn over, k2tog, yarn over, k2, s2kp2, k2, yarn over, ssk, yarn over; repeat from the * to 4 stitches before the marker, ending this section with k4, yarn over. (21 stitches)

ROW 21: Yarn over, k4, *k2, yarn over, k2tog, yarn over, k1, s2kp2, k1, yarn over, ssk, yarn over, k1; repeat from the * to 5 stitches before the marker, ending this section with k5, yarn over. (23 stitches)

ROW 23: Yarn over, k1, (ssk, yarn over) twice, *k1, (yarn over, k2tog) twice, yarn over, s2kp2, yarn over, (ssk, yarn over) twice; repeat from the * to 6 stitches before the marker, ending this section with k1, (yarn over, k2tog) twice, k1, yarn over. (25 stitches)

ROW 25: Yarn over, ssk, k4, yarn over, *k1, yarn over, k4, s2kp2, k4, yarn over; repeat from the * to 7 stitches before the marker, ending this section with k1, yarn over, k4, k2tog, yarn over. (27 stitches)

ROW 27: Yarn over, k1, ssk, k4, yarn over, *k1, yarn over, k4, s2kp2, k4, yarn over; repeat from the * to 8 stitches before the marker, ending this section with k1, yarn over, k4, k2tog, k1, yarn over. (29 stitches)

ROW 29: Yarn over, k2, ssk, k3, yarn over, k1, *k2, yarn over, k3, s2kp2, k3, yarn over, k1; repeat from the * to 9 stitches before the marker, ending this section with k2, yarn over, k3, k2tog, k2, yarn over. (31 stitches)

ROW 31: Yarn over, k3, ssk, k2, yarn over, ssk, yarn over, *k1, yarn over, k2tog, yarn over, k2, s2kp2, k2, yarn over, ssk, yarn over; repeat from the * to 10 stitches before the marker, ending this section with k1, yarn over, k2tog, yarn over, k2, k2tog, k3, yarn over. (33 stitches)

ROW 33: Yarn over, k2, yarn over, k1, s2kp2, k1, yarn over, ssk, yarn over, k1, *k2, yarn over, k2tog, yarn over, k1, s2kp2, k1, yarn over, ssk, yarn over, k1; repeat from the * to 11 stitches before the marker, ending this section with k2, yarn over, k2tog, yarn over, k1, s2kp2, k1, yarn over, k2, yarn over. (35 stitches)

ROW 35: Yarn over, k2, yarn over, k2tog, yarn over, s2kp2, yarn over, (yarn over, ssk) twice, *k1, (yarn over, k2tog) twice, yarn over, s2kp2, yarn over, (ssk, yarn over) twice; repeat from the * to 12 stitches before the marker, ending this section with k1, (yarn over, k2tog) twice, yarn over, s2kp2, yarn over, ssk, yarn over, k2, yarn over. (37 stitches)

ROW 36: As Row 2.

Repeat Rows 13–36 for the pattern.

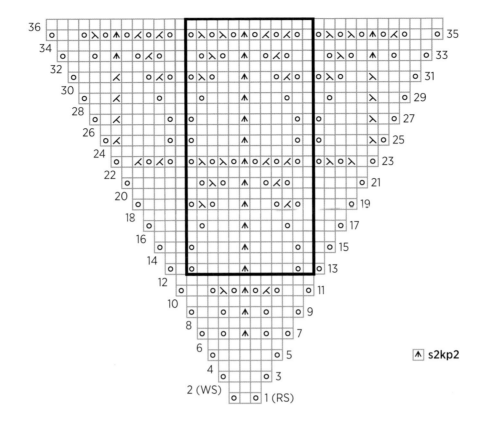

⊼ s2kp2

98 ♥♥♥

ROW 1 (RS): Yarn over, k1, yarn over. (3 stitches)

ROW 2 AND ALL WS ROWS: Purl across.

ROW 3: Yarn over, k3, yarn over. (5 stitches)

ROW 5: Yarn over, k5, yarn over. (7 stitches)

ROW 7: Yarn over, k3, yarn over, ssk, k2, yarn over. (9 stitches)

ROW 9: Yarn over, k2, k2tog, yarn over, k1, yarn over, ssk, k2, yarn over. (11 stitches)

ROW 11: Yarn over, k2, k2tog, yarn over, k3, yarn over, ssk, k2, yarn over. (13 stitches)

ROW 13: Yarn over, k2tog, yarn over, k4, yarn over, ssk, k3, yarn over, ssk, yarn over. (15 stitches)

ROW 15: Yarn over, k1, k2tog, yarn over, k2, k2tog, yarn over, k1, yarn over, ssk, k2, yarn over, ssk, k1, yarn over. (17 stitches)

ROW 17: Yarn over, k1, yarn over, s2kp2 (page 282), yarn over, k1, k2tog, yarn over, k3, yarn over, ssk, k1, yarn over, s2kp2, yarn over, k1, yarn over. (19 stitches)

ROW 19: Yarn over, k2, yarn over, s2kp2, yarn over, k4, yarn over, ssk, k3, yarn over, s2kp2, yarn over, k2, yarn over. (21 stitches)

ROW 21: Yarn over, k3, yarn over, s2kp2, yarn over, k2, k2tog, yarn over, k1, yarn over, ssk, k2, yarn over, s2kp2, yarn over, k3, yarn over. (23 stitches)

ROW 23: Yarn over, k1, yarn over, ssk, k1, yarn over, s2kp2, yarn over, k1, k2tog, yarn over, k3, yarn over, ssk, k1, yarn over, s2kp2, yarn over, k1, k2tog, yarn over, k1, yarn over. (25 stitches)

ROW 25: Yarn over, k5, *yarn over, s2kp2, yarn over, k4, yarn over, ssk, k3; repeat from the * to 8 stitches before the marker, ending this section with yarn over, s2kp2, yarn over, k5, yarn over. (27 stitches)

ROW 27: Yarn over, k2, yarn over, ssk, k2, *yarn over, s2kp2, yarn over, k2, k2tog, yarn over, k1, yarn over, ssk, k2; repeat from the * to 9 stitches before the marker, ending this section with yarn over, s2kp2, yarn over, k2, k2tog, yarn over, k2, yarn over. (29 stitches)

ROW 29: Yarn over, k4, yarn over, ssk, k1, *yarn over, s2kp2, yarn over, k1, k2tog, yarn over, k3, yarn over, ssk, k1; repeat from the * to 10 stitches before the marker, ending this section with yarn over, s2kp2, yarn over, k1, k2tog, yarn over, k4, yarn over. (31 stitches)

ROW 31: Yarn over, k3, yarn over, ssk, k3, *yarn over, s2kp2, yarn over, k4, yarn over, ssk, k3; repeat from the * to 11 stitches before the marker, ending this section with yarn over, s2k2p, yarn over, k4, yarn over, ssk, k2, yarn over. (33 stitches)

ROW 33: Yarn over, k2, k2tog, yarn over, k1, yarn over, ssk, k2, *yarn over, s2kp2, yarn over, k2, k2tog, yarn over, k1, yarn over, ssk, k2; repeat from the * to 12 stitches before the marker, ending this section with yarn over, s2kp2, yarn over, k2, k2tog, yarn over, k1, yarn over, ssk, k2, yarn over. (35 stitches)

ROW 35: Yarn over, k2, k2tog, yarn over, k3, yarn over, ssk, k1, *yarn over, s2kp2, yarn over, k1, k2tog, yarn over, k3, yarn over, ssk, k1; repeat from the * to 13 stitches before the marker, ending this section with yarn over, s2k2p, yarn over, k1, k2tog, yarn over, k3, yarn over, ssk, k2, yarn over. (37 stitches)

ROW 37: Yarn over, k2tog, yarn over, k4, yarn over, ssk, k3, *yarn over, s2kp2, yarn over, k4, yarn over, ssk, k3; repeat from the * to 14 stitches before the marker, ending this section with yarn over, s2kp2, yarn over, k4, yarn over, ssk, k3, yarn over, ssk, yarn over. (39 stitches)

ROW 39: Yarn over, k1, k2tog, yarn over, k2, k2tog, yarn over, k1, yarn over, ssk, k2, *yarn over, s2kp2, yarn over, k2, k2tog, yarn over, k1, yarn over, ssk, k2; repeat from the * to 15 stitches before the marker, ending this section with yarn over, s2kp2, yarn over, k2, k2tog, yarn over, k1, yarn over, ssk, k2, yarn over, ssk, k1, yarn over. (41 stitches)

ROW 41: Yarn over, k1, yarn over, s2kp2, yarn over, k1, k2tog, yarn over, k3, yarn over, ssk, k1, *yarn over, s2kp2, yarn over, k1, k2tog, yarn over, k3, yarn over, ssk, k1; repeat from the * to 16 stitches before the marker, ending this section with yarn over, s2kp2, yarn over, k1, k2tog, yarn over, k3, yarn over, ssk, k1, yarn over, s2kp2, yarn over, k1, yarn over. (43 stitches)

ROW 43: Yarn over, k2, yarn over, s2kp2, yarn over, k4, yarn over, ssk, k3, *yarn over, s2kp2, yarn over, k4, yarn over, ssk, k3; repeat from the * to 17 stitches before the marker, ending this section with yarn over, s2kp2, yarn over, k4, yarn over, ssk, k3, yarn over, s2kp2, yarn over, k2, yarn over. (45 stitches)

ROW 45: Yarn over, k3, yarn over, s2kp2, yarn over, k2, k2tog, yarn over, k1, yarn over, ssk, k2, *yarn over, s2kp2, yarn over, k2, k2tog, yarn over, k1, yarn over, ssk, k2; repeat from the * to 18 stitches before the marker, ending this section with yarn over, s2kp2, yarn over, k2, k2tog, yarn over, k1, yarn over, ssk, k2, yarn over, s2kp2, yarn over, k3, yarn over. (47 stitches)

ROW 47: Yarn over, k4, yarn over, s2kp2, yarn over, k1, k2tog, yarn over, k3, yarn over, ssk, k1, *yarn over, s2kp2, yarn over, k1, k2tog, yarn over, k3, yarn over, ssk, k1; repeat from the * to 19 stitches before the marker, ending this section with yarn over, s2kp2, yarn over, k1, k2tog, yarn over, k3, yarn over, ssk, k1, yarn over, s2kp2, yarn over, k4, yarn over. (49 stitches)

ROW 48: As Row 2.

Repeat Rows 25–48 for the pattern.

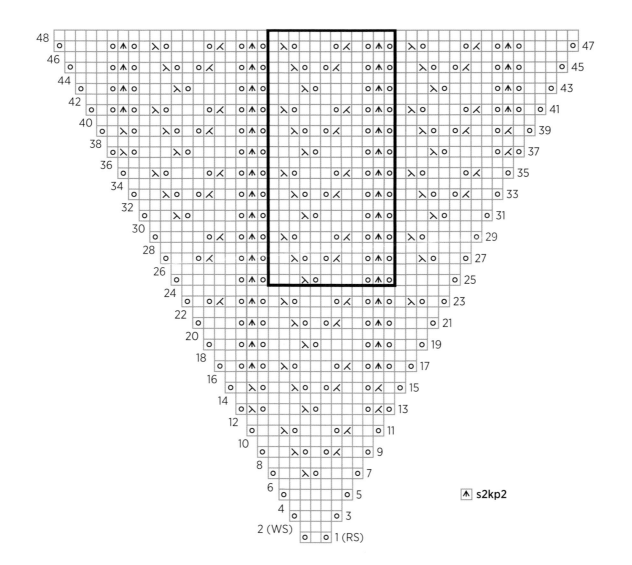

⚠ s2kp2

99

ROW 1 (RS): Yarn over, p1, yarn over. (3 stitches)

ROWS 2, 4, 6, 8, 10, 12, 14, 16, 18, 20, 28, 30, 32, AND 34: Knit the knit stitches and purl the purl stitches and yarn overs.

ROW 3: Yarn over, p3, yarn over. (5 stitches)

ROW 5: Yarn over, k2, p1, k2, yarn over. (7 stitches)

ROW 7: Yarn over, k1, p5, k1, yarn over. (9 stitches)

ROW 9: (Yarn over, k1) twice, p1, p3tog, p1, (k1, yarn over) twice. (11 stitches)

ROW 11: Yarn over, k3, yarn over, k1, p3tog, k1, yarn over, k3, yarn over. (13 stitches)

ROW 13: Yarn over, *k1, yarn over, k2, p2, p3tog, p2, k2, yarn over; repeat from the * to 1 stitch before the marker, ending this section with k1, yarn over. (15 stitches)

ROW 15: Yarn over, k1, *k1, yarn over, p1, k2, p1, p3tog, p1, k2, p1, yarn over; repeat from the * to 2 stitches before the marker, ending this section with k2, yarn over. (17 stitches),

ROW 17: Yarn over, k2, *k1, yarn over, p2, k2, p3tog, k2, p2, yarn over; repeat from the * to 3 stitches before the marker, ending this section with k3, yarn over. (19 stitches)

ROW 19: Yarn over, k3, *k1, yarn over, k2, p2, p3tog, p2, k2, yarn over; repeat from the * to 4 stitches before the marker, ending this section with k4, yarn over. (21 stitches)

ROW 21: Yarn over, k2tog, k1, p1, yarn over, *k1, yarn over, p1, k2, p1, p3tog, p1, k2, p1, yarn over; repeat from the * to 5 stitches before the marker, ending this section with k1, yarn over, p1, k1, ssk, yarn over. (23 stitches)

ROW 22: P3, k1, p2, *p1, k1, p2, k3, p2, k1, p2; repeat from the * to 5 stitches before the marker, ending this section with p1, k1, p3.

ROW 23: Yarn over, k2tog, k1, p2, yarn over, *k1, yarn over, p2, k2, p3tog, k2, p2, yarn over; repeat from the * to 6 stitches before the marker, ending this section with k1, yarn over, p2, k1, ssk, yarn over. (25 stitches)

ROW 24: K1, p2, k2, p2, *p1, k2, p2, k1, p2, k2, p2; repeat from the * to 6 stitches before the marker, ending this section with p1, k2, p2, k1.

ROW 25: Yarn over, p2tog, p2, k2, yarn over, *k1, yarn over, k2, p2, p3tog, p2, k2, yarn over; repeat from the * to 7 stitches before the marker, ending this section with k1, yarn over, k2, p2, p2tog, yarn over. (27 stitches)

ROW 26: K4, p4, *p3, k5, p4; repeat from the * to 7 stitches before the marker, ending with p3, k4.

ROW 27: Yarn over, p1, p2tog, p1, k2, p1, yarn over, *k1, yarn over, p1, k2, p1, p3tog, p1, k2, p1, yarn over; repeat from the * to 8 stitches before the marker, ending this section with k1, yarn over, p1, k2, p1, p2tog, p1, yarn over. (29 stitches)

ROW 29: Yarn over, k2, p2tog, k2, p2, yarn over, *k1, yarn over, p2, k2, p3tog, k2, p2, yarn over; repeat from the * to 9 stitches before the marker, ending this section with k1, yarn over, p2, k2, p2tog, k2, yarn over. (31 stitches)

ROW 31: Yarn over, k1, p2, p2tog, p2, k2, yarn over, *k1, yarn over, k2, p2, p3tog, p2, k2, yarn over; repeat from the * to 10 stitches before the marker, ending this section with k1, yarn over, k2, p2, p2tog, p2, k1, yarn over. (33 stitches)

ROW 33: Yarn over, p1, k2, p1, p2tog, p1, k2, p1, yarn over; *k1, yarn over, p1, k2, p1, p3tog, p1, k2, p1, yarn over; repeat from the * to 11 stitches before the marker, ending this section with k1, yarn over, p1, k2, p1, p2tog, p1, k2, p1, yarn over. (35 stitches)

ROW 35: Yarn over, k1, p2, k2, p2tog, k2, p2, yarn over, *k1, yarn over, p2, k2, p3tog, k2, p2, yarn over; repeat from the * to 12 stitches before the marker, ending this section with k1, yarn over, p2, k2, p2tog, k2, p2, k1, yarn over. (37 stitches)

ROW 36: As Row 2.

Repeat Rows 13–36 for the pattern.

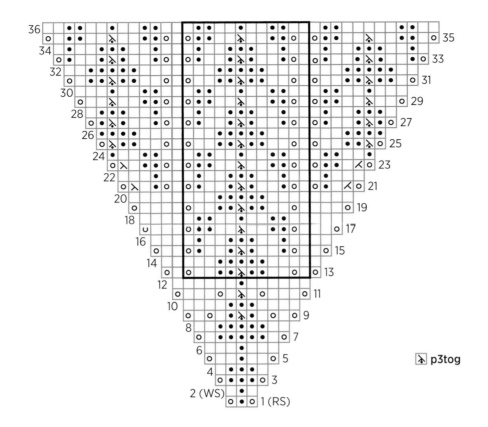

100

ROW 1 (RS): Yarn over, k1, yarn over. (3 stitches)

ROWS 2, 4, 6, 8, 10, 12, 18, 24, AND 30: Purl across.

ROW 3: Yarn over, k3, yarn over. (5 stitches)

ROW 5: Yarn over, k5, yarn over. (7 stitches)

ROW 7: Yarn over, k2tog, k1, yarn over, k1, yarn over, k1, ssk, yarn over. (9 stitches)

ROW 9: Yarn over, ssk, k1, yarn over, k3, yarn over, k1, k2tog, yarn over. (11 stitches)

ROW 11: Yarn over, k1, ssk, yarn over, k5, yarn over, k2tog, k1, yarn over. (13 stitches)

ROW 13: Yarn over, *k1, yarn over, k2, k2tog, p3, ssk, k2, yarn over; repeat from the * to 1 stitch before the marker, ending this section with k1, yarn over. (15 stitches)

ROWS 14, 16, 20, 22, 28, 32, AND 34: Knit the knit stitches and purl the purl stitches and yarn overs.

ROW 15: Yarn over, k1, *k2, yarn over, k1, k2tog, p3, ssk, k1, yarn over, k1; repeat from the * to 2 stitches before the marker, ending this section with k2, yarn over. (17 stitches)

ROW 17: Yarn over, k2, *k3, yarn over, k2tog, p3, ssk, yarn over, k2; repeat from the * to 3 stitches before the marker, ending this section with k3, yarn over. (19 stitches)

ROW 19: Yarn over, k2, p1, *p2, ssk, k2, yarn over, k1, yarn over, k2, k2tog, p1; repeat from the * to 4 stitches before the marker, ending this section with p2, k2, yarn over. (21 stitches)

ROW 21: Yarn over, k3, p1, *p2, ssk, k1, yarn over, k3, yarn over, k1, k2tog, p1; repeat from the * to 5 stitches before the marker, ending this section with p2, k3, yarn over. (23 stitches)

ROW 23: Yarn over, k4, p1, *p2, ssk, yarn over, k5, yarn over, k2tog, p1; repeat from the * to 6 stitches before the marker, ending this section with p2, k4, yarn over. (25 stitches)

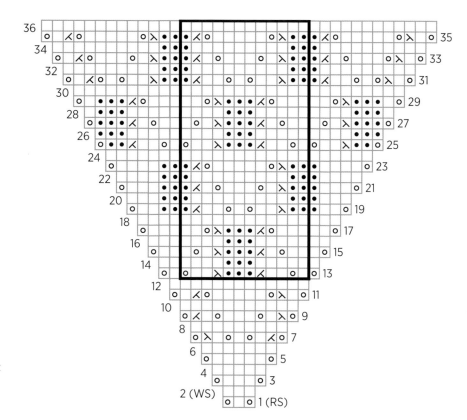

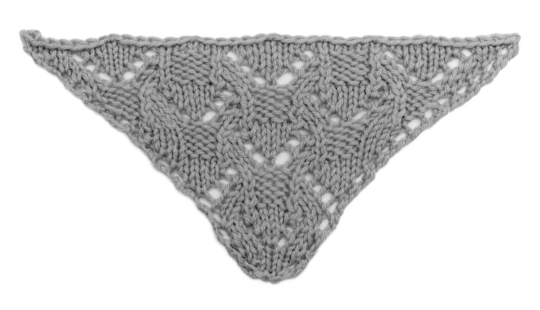

ROW 25: Yarn over, p2, ssk, k2, yarn over, *k1, yarn over, k2, k2tog, p3, ssk, k2, yarn over; repeat from the * to 7 stitches before the marker, ending this section with k1, yarn over, k2, k2tog, p2, yarn over. (27 stitches)

ROW 26: K3, p5, *p4, k3, p5; repeat from the * to 7 stitches before the marker, ending this section with p4, k3.

ROW 27: Yarn over, p3, ssk, k1, yarn over, k1, *k2, yarn over, k1, k2tog, p3, ssk, k1, yarn over, k1; repeat from the * to 8 stitches before the marker, ending this section with k2, yarn over, k1, k2tog, p3, yarn over. (29 stitches)

ROW 29: Yarn over, k1, p3, ssk, yarn over, k2, *k3, yarn over, k2tog, p3, ssk, yarn over, k2; repeat from the * to 9 stitches before the marker, ending this section with k3, yarn over, k2tog, p3, k1, yarn over. (31 stitches)

ROW 31: Yarn over, k1, ssk, yarn over, k1, yarn over, k2, k2tog, p1, *p2, ssk, k2, yarn over, k1, yarn over, k2, k2tog, p1; repeat from the * to 10 stitches before the marker, ending this section with p2, ssk, k2, yarn over, k1, yarn over, k2tog, k1, yarn over. (33 stitches)

ROW 33: Yarn over, k1, ssk, yarn over, k3, yarn over, k1, k2tog, p1, *p2, ssk, k1, yarn over, k3, yarn over, k1, k2tog, p1; repeat from the * to 11 stitches before the marker, ending this section with p2, ssk, k1, yarn over, k3, yarn over, k2tog, k1, yarn over. (35 stitches)

ROW 35: Yarn over, k1, ssk, yarn over, k5, yarn over, k2tog, p1, *p2, ssk, yarn over, k5, yarn over, k2tog, p1; repeat from the * to 12 stitches before the marker, ending this section with p2, ssk, yarn over, k5, yarn over, k2tog, k1, yarn over. (37 stitches)

ROW 36: As Row 2.

Repeat Rows 13–36 for the pattern.

SHAWL #8
When knitting a perpendicular border, use double joins (page 12) around the corners to prevent puckering. See page 273 for instructions.

101 ᵂᵂ

ROW 1 (RS): Yarn over, k1, yarn over. (3 stitches)

ROW 2 AND ALL WS ROWS: Purl across.

ROW 3: Yarn over, k3, yarn over. (5 stitches)

ROW 5: Yarn over, k1, yarn over, s2kp2 (page 282), yarn over, k1, yarn over. (7 stitches)

ROW 7: Yarn over, k1, yarn over, ssk, k1, k2tog, yarn over, k1, yarn over. (9 stitches)

ROW 9: Yarn over, k1, yarn over, ssk, yarn over, s2kp2, yarn over, k2tog, yarn over, k1, yarn over. (11 stitches)

ROW 11: Yarn over, knit across to the next marker, yarn over. (13 stitches)

ROW 13: Yarn over, *k1, (yarn over, ssk) twice, k3, (k2tog, yarn over) twice; repeat from the * to 1 stitch before the marker, ending this section with k1, yarn over. (15 stitches)

ROW 15: Yarn over, k1, *k2, (yarn over, ssk) twice, k1, (k2tog, yarn over) twice, k1; repeat from the * to 2 stitches before the marker, ending the section with k2, yarn over. (17 stitches)

ROW 17: Yarn over, k2tog, yarn over, *k1, (yarn over, ssk) twice, yarn over, s2kp2, yarn over (k2tog, yarn over) twice; repeat from the * to 3 stitches before the marker, ending this section with k1, yarn over, ssk, yarn over. (19 stitches)

ROW 19: Yarn over, k2tog, yarn over, k1, *k2, (yarn over, ssk) twice, k1, (k2tog, yarn over) twice, k1; repeat from the * to 4 stitches before the marker, ending this section with k2, yarn over, ssk, yarn over. (21 stitches)

ROW 21: Yarn over, k2tog, yarn over, k2, *k3, yarn over, ssk, yarn over, s2kp2, yarn over, k2tog, yarn over, k2; repeat from the * to 5 stitches before the marker, ending this section with k3, yarn over, ssk, yarn over. (23 stitches)

ROW 23: As Row 11. (25 stitches)

ROW 25: Yarn over, k2, (k2tog, yarn over) twice, *k1, (yarn over, ssk) twice, k3, (k2tog, yarn over) twice; repeat from the * to 7 stitches before the marker, ending this section with k1, (yarn over, ssk) twice, k2, yarn over. (27 stitches)

ROW 27: Yarn over, k2, (k2tog, yarn over) twice, k1, *k2, (yarn over, ssk) twice, k1, (k2tog, yarn over) twice, k1; repeat from the * to 8 stitches before the marker, ending this section with k2, (yarn over, ssk) twice, k2, yarn over. (29 stitches)

ROW 29: Yarn over, k1, yarn over, s2kp2, yarn over, (k2tog, yarn over) twice, *k1, (yarn over, ssk) twice, yarn over, s2kp2, yarn over, (k2tog, yarn over) twice; repeat from the * to 9 stitches before the marker, ending this section with k1, (yarn over, ssk) twice, yarn over, s2kp2, yarn over, k1, yarn over. (31 stitches)

ROW 31: Yarn over, k1, yarn over, ssk, k1, (k2tog, yarn over) twice, k1, *k2, (yarn over, ssk) twice, k1, (k2tog, yarn over) twice, k1; repeat from the * to 10 stitches before the marker, ending this section with k2, (yarn over, ssk) twice, k1, k2tog, yarn over, k1, yarn over. (33 stitches)

ROW 33: Yarn over, k1, yarn over, ssk, yarn over, s2kp2, yarn over, k2tog, yarn over, k2, *k3, yarn over, ssk, yarn over, s2kp2, yarn over, k2tog, yarn over, k2; repeat from the * to 11 stitches before the marker, ending this section with k3, yarn over, ssk, yarn over, s2kp2, yarn over, k2tog, yarn over, k1, yarn over. (35 stitches)

ROW 35: As Row 11. (37 stitches)

ROW 36: As Row 2.

Repeat Rows 13–36 for the pattern.

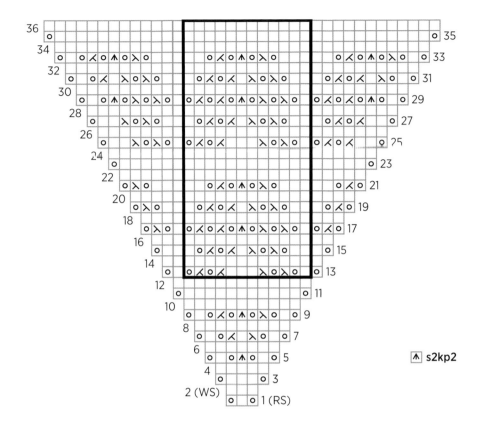

s2kp2

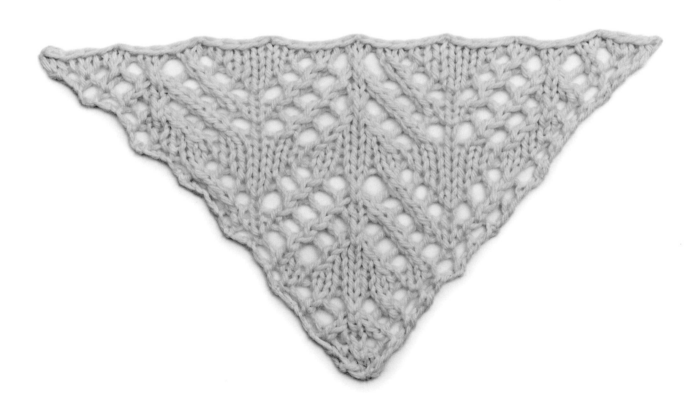

102

ROW 1 (RS): Yarn over, k1, yarn over. (3 stitches)

ROW 2 AND ALL WS ROWS: Purl across.

ROW 3: Yarn over, k3, yarn over. (5 stitches)

ROW 5: Yarn over, k5, yarn over. (7 stitches)

ROW 7: Yarn over, k1, k2tog, yarn over, k1, yarn over, ssk, k1, yarn over. (9 stitches)

ROW 9: Yarn over, k1, k2tog, yarn over, k3, yarn over, ssk, k1, yarn over. (11 stitches)

ROW 11: Yarn over, k1, (k2tog, yarn over) twice, k1, (yarn over, ssk) twice, k1, yarn over. (13 stitches)

ROW 13: Yarn over, *k1, (yarn over, ssk) twice, yarn over, s2kp2 (page 282), yarn over, (k2tog, yarn over) twice; repeat from the * to 1 stitch before the marker, ending this section with k1, yarn over. (15 stitches)

ROW 15: Yarn over, k1, *k2, (yarn over, ssk) twice, k1, (k2tog, yarn over) twice, k1; repeat from the * to 2 stitches before the marker, ending this section with k2, yarn over. (17 stitches)

ROW 17: Yarn over, k2tog, yarn over, *k1, (yarn over, ssk) twice, yarn over, s2kp2, yarn over, (k2tog, yarn over) twice; repeat from the * to 3 stitches before the marker, ending this section with k1, yarn over, ssk, yarn over. (19 stitches)

ROW 19: Yarn over, k2tog, yarn over, k1, *k2, (yarn over, ssk) twice, k1, (k2tog, yarn over) twice, k1; repeat from the * to 4 stitches before the marker, ending this section with k2, yarn over, ssk, yarn over. (21 stitches)

ROW 21: Yarn over, (k2tog, yarn over) twice, *k1, (yarn over, ssk) twice, yarn over, s2kp2, yarn over, (k2tog, yarn over) twice; repeat from the * to 5 stitches before the marker, ending this section with k1, (yarn over, ssk) twice, yarn over. (23 stitches)

ROW 23: Yarn over, k2, yarn over, ssk, yarn over, *s2kp2, yarn over, (k2tog, yarn over) twice, k1, (yarn over, ssk) twice, yarn over; repeat from the * to 7 stitches before the marker, ending this section with s2kp2, yarn over, k2tog, yarn over, k2, yarn over. (25 stitches)

ROW 25: Yarn over, k2, (yarn over, ssk) twice, *k1, (k2tog, yarn over) twice, k3, (yarn over, ssk) twice; repeat from the * to 7 stitches before the marker, ending this section with k1, (k2tog, yarn over) twice, k2, yarn over. (27 stitches)

ROW 27: Yarn over, k2, (yarn over, ssk) twice, yarn over, *s2kp2, yarn over, (k2tog, yarn over) twice, k1, (yarn over, ssk) twice, yarn over; repeat from the * to 9 stitches before the marker, ending this section with s2kp2, yarn over, (k2tog, yarn over) twice, k2, yarn over. (29 stitches)

ROW 29: Yarn over, k4, (yarn over, ssk) twice, *k1, (k2tog, yarn over) twice, k3, (yarn over, ssk) twice; repeat from the * to 9 stitches before the marker, ending this section with k1, (k2tog, yarn over) twice, k4, yarn over. (31 stitches)

ROW 31: Yarn over, k1, k2tog, yarn over, k1, (yarn over, ssk) twice, yarn over, *s2kp2, yarn over, (k2tog, yarn over) twice, k1, (yarn over, ssk) twice, yarn over; repeat from the * to 11 stitches before the marker, ending this section with s2kp2, yarn over, (k2tog, yarn over) twice, k1, yarn over, ssk, k1, yarn over. (33 stitches)

ROW 32: As Row 2.

Repeat Rows 13–32 for pattern.

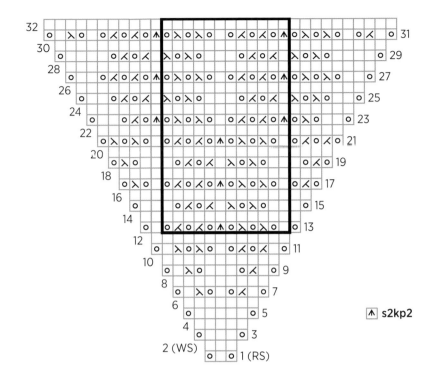

⊼ s2kp2

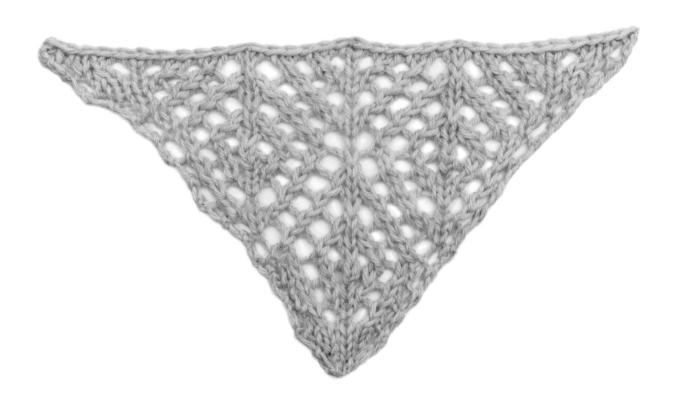

103

ROW 1 (RS): Yarn over, k1, yarn over. (3 stitches)

ROW 2 AND ALL WS ROWS: Purl across.

ROW 3: Yarn over, k3, yarn over. (5 stitches)

ROW 5: Yarn over, k1, yarn over, s2kp2 (page 282), yarn over, k1, yarn over. (7 stitches)

ROW 7: Yarn over, k2, yarn over, s2kp2, yarn over, k2, yarn over. (9 stitches)

ROW 9: Yarn over, k2, yarn over, ssk, k1, k2tog, yarn over, k2, yarn over. (11 stitches)

ROW 11: Yarn over, k1, k2tog, yarn over, k1, yarn over, s2kp2, yarn over, k1, yarn over, ssk, k1, yarn over. (13 stitches)

ROW 13: Yarn over, k1, k2tog, yarn over, k7, yarn over, ssk, k1, yarn over. (15 stitches)

ROW 15: Yarn over, k1, k2tog, yarn over, k1, yarn over, ssk, k3, k2tog, yarn over, k1, yarn over, ssk, k1, yarn over. (17 stitches)

ROW 17: Yarn over, k1, yarn over, s2kp2, yarn over, k2, yarn over, ssk, k1, k2tog, yarn over, k2, yarn over, s2kp2, yarn over, k1, yarn over. (19 stitches)

ROW 19: Yarn over, k2, yarn over, s2kp2, yarn over, k3, yarn over, s2kp2, yarn over, k3, yarn over, s2kp2, yarn over, k2, yarn over. (21 stitches)

ROW 21: Yarn over, k1, k2tog, yarn over, k3, yarn over, ssk, k1, yarn over, s2kp2, yarn over, k1, k2tog, yarn over, k3, yarn over, ssk, k1, yarn over. (23 stitches)

ROW 23: Yarn over, k1, k2tog, yarn over, k5, yarn over, ssk, yarn over, s2kp2, yarn over, k2tog, yarn over, k5, yarn over, ssk, k1, yarn over. (25 stitches)

ROW 25: Yarn over, k1, k2tog, yarn over, k3, *k4, yarn over, ssk, k1, k2tog, yarn over, k3; repeat from the * to 7 stitches before the marker, ending this section with k4, yarn over, ssk, k1, yarn over. (27 stitches)

ROW 27: Yarn over, k1, k2tog, yarn over, k1, yarn over, ssk, k1, *k2, k2tog, yarn over, k1, yarn over, s2kp2, yarn over, k1, yarn over, ssk, k1; repeat from the * to 8 stitches before the marker, ending this section with k2, k2tog, yarn over, k1, yarn over, ssk, k1, yarn over. (29 stitches)

ROW 29: Yarn over, k1, yarn over, s2kp2, yarn over, k2, yarn over, ssk, *k1, k2tog, yarn over, k2, yarn over, s2kp2, yarn over, k2, yarn over, ssk; repeat from the * to 9 stitches before the marker, ending this section with k1, k2tog, yarn over, k2, yarn over, s2kp2, yarn over, k1, yarn over. (31 stitches)

ROW 31: Yarn over, k2, yarn over, s2kp2, yarn over, k3, yarn over, *s2kp2, yarn over, k3, yarn over, s2kp2, yarn over, k3, yarn over; repeat from the * to 11 stitches before the marker, ending this section with s2kp2, yarn over, k3, yarn over, s2kp2, yarn over, k2, yarn over. (33 stitches)

ROW 33: Yarn over, k1, k2tog, yarn over, k3, yarn over, ssk, k1, yarn over, *s2kp2, yarn over, k1, k2tog, yarn over, k3, yarn over, ssk, k1, yarn over; repeat from the * to 12 stitches before the marker, ending this section with s2kp2, yarn over, k1, k2tog, yarn over, k3, yarn over, ssk, k1, yarn over. (35 stitches)

ROW 35: Yarn over, k1, k2tog, yarn over, k5, yarn over, ssk, yarn over, *s2kp2, yarn over, k2tog, yarn over, k5, yarn over, ssk, yarn over; repeat from the * to 13 stitches before the marker, ending this section with s2kp2, yarn over, k2tog, yarn over, k5, yarn over, ssk, k1, yarn over. (37 stitches)

ROW 36: As Row 2.

Repeat Rows 25–36 for the pattern.

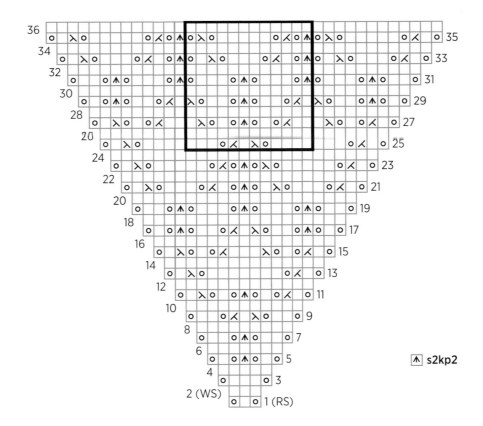

⩓ s2kp2

104

ROW 1 (RS): Yarn over, k1, yarn over. (3 stitches)

ROW 2 AND ALL WS ROWS: Purl across.

ROW 3: Yarn over, k3, yarn over. (5 stitches)

ROW 5: Yarn over, k5, yarn over. (7 stitches)

ROW 7: Yarn over, k3, ssk, yarn over, k2, yarn over. (9 stitches)

ROW 9: Yarn over, k3, (ssk, yarn over) twice, k2, yarn over. (11 stitches)

ROW 11: Yarn over, k1, yarn over, k2tog, k8, yarn over. (13 stitches)

ROW 13: Yarn over, *k1, (yarn over, k2tog) twice, k7; repeat from the * to 1 stitch before the marker, ending this section with k1, yarn over. (15 stitches)

ROW 15: Yarn over, k1, *k2, (yarn over, k2tog) twice, k6; repeat from the * to 2 stitches before the marker, ending this section with k2, yarn over. (17 stitches)

ROW 17: Yarn over, ssk, yarn over, *k8, (ssk, yarn over) twice; repeat from the * to 3 stitches before the marker, ending this section with k3, yarn over. (19 stitches)

ROW 19: Yarn over, ssk, yarn over, k1, *k7, (ssk, yarn over) twice, k1; repeat from the * to 4 stitches before the marker, ending this section with k4, yarn over. (21 stitches)

ROW 21: Yarn over, ssk, yarn over, k2, *k6, (ssk, yarn over) twice, k2; repeat from the * to 5 stitches before the marker, ending this section with k5, yarn over. (23 stitches)

ROW 23: Yarn over, ssk, yarn over, k3, *k5, (ssk, yarn over) twice, k3; repeat from the * to 6 stitches before the marker, ending this section with k6, yarn over. (25 stitches)

ROW 25: Yarn over, k5, yarn over, *k2tog, yarn over, k2tog, k8, yarn over; repeat from the * to 8 stitches before the marker, ending this section with k2tog, yarn over, k2tog, k4, yarn over. (27 stitches)

ROW 27: Yarn over, k7, *(yarn over, k2tog) twice, k8; repeat from the * to 8 stitches before the marker, ending this section with (yarn over, k2tog) twice, k4, yarn over. (29 stitches)

ROW 29: Yarn over, k8, *k1, (yarn over, k2tog) twice, k7; repeat from the * to 9 stitches before the marker, ending this section with k1, (yarn over, k2tog) twice, k4, yarn over. (31 stitches)

ROW 31: Yarn over, k1, yarn over, k2tog, k6, *k2, (yarn over, k2tog) twice, k6; repeat from the * to 10 stitches before the marker, ending this section with k2, (yarn over, k2tog) twice, k4, yarn over. (33 stitches)

ROW 33: Yarn over, k6, (ssk, yarn over) twice, *k8, (ssk, yarn over) twice; repeat from the * to 11 stitches before the marker, ending this section with k8, ssk, yarn over, k1, yarn over. (35 stitches)

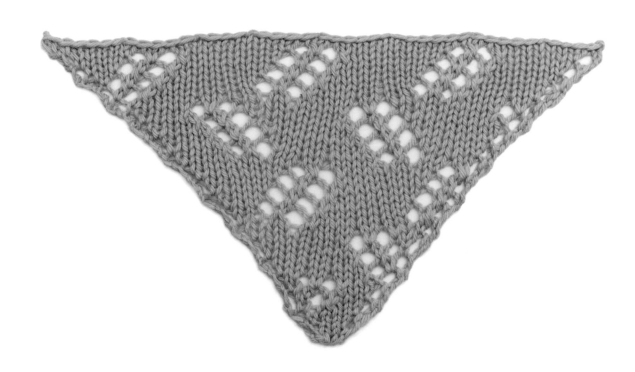

ROW 35: Yarn over, k6, (ssk, yarn over) twice, k1, *k7, (ssk, yarn over) twice, k1; repeat from the * to 12 stitches before the marker, ending this section with k7, (ssk, yarn over) twice, k1, yarn over. (37 stitches)

ROW 37: Yarn over, k6, (ssk, yarn over) twice, k2, *k6, (ssk, yarn over) twice, k2; repeat from the * to 13 stitches before the marker, ending this section with k6, (ssk, yarn over) twice, k3, yarn over. (39 stitches)

ROW 39: Yarn over, k6, (ssk, yarn over) twice, k3, *k5, (ssk, yarn over) twice, k3; repeat from the * to 14 stitches before the marker, ending this section with k5, (ssk, yarn over) twice, k5, yarn over. (41 stitches)

ROW 41: Yarn over, k1, (yarn over, k2tog) twice, k8, yarn over, *k2tog, yarn over, k2tog, k8, yarn over; repeat from the * to 16 stitches before the marker, ending this section with k2tog, yarn over, k2tog, k8, (yarn over, k2tog) twice, yarn over. (43 stitches)

(continued on the next page)

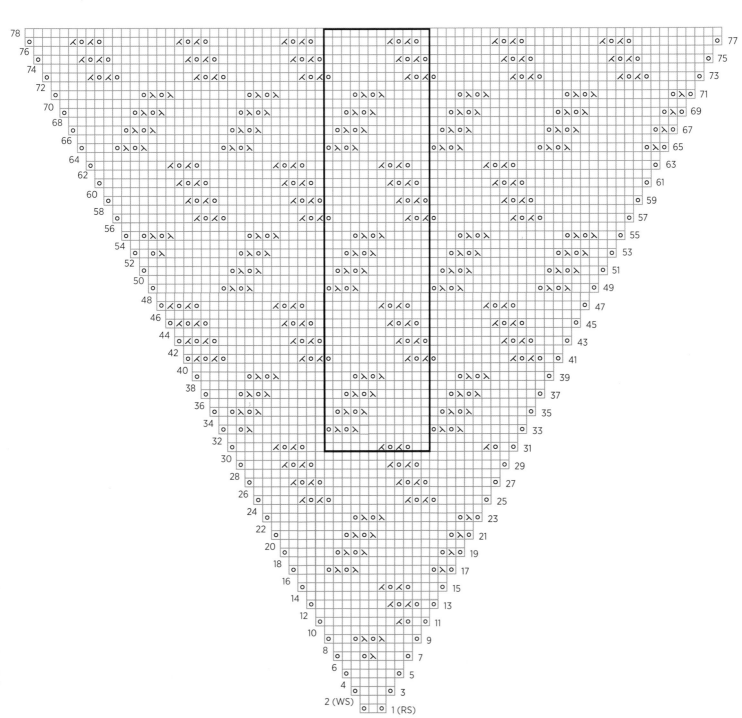

WEDGE 104, *continued*

ROW 43: Yarn over, k3, (yarn over, k2tog) twice, k8, *(yarn over, k2tog) twice, k8; repeat from the * to 16 stitches before the marker, ending this section with (yarn over, k2tog) twice, k8, (yarn over, k2tog) twice, yarn over. (45 stitches)

ROW 45: Yarn over, k5, (yarn over, k2tog) twice, k7, *k1, (yarn over, k2tog) twice, k7; repeat from the * to 17 stitches before the marker, ending this section with k1, (yarn over, k2tog) twice, k8, (yarn over, k2tog) twice, yarn over. (47 stitches)

ROW 47: Yarn over, k7, (yarn over, k2tog) twice, k6, *k2, (yarn over, k2tog) twice, k6; repeat from the * to 18 stitches before the marker, ending this section with k2, (yarn over, k2tog) twice, k8, (yarn over, k2tog) twice, yarn over. (49 stitches)

ROW 49: Yarn over, k2, (ssk, yarn over) twice, k8, (ssk, yarn over) twice, *k8, (ssk, yarn over) twice; repeat from the * to 19 stitches before the marker, ending this section with k8, (ssk, yarn over) twice, k7, yarn over. (51 stitches)

ROW 51: Yarn over, k2, (ssk, yarn over) twice, k8, (ssk, yarn over) twice, k1, *k7, (ssk, yarn over) twice, k1; repeat from the * to 20 stitches before the marker, ending this section with k7, (ssk, yarn over) twice, k9, yarn over. (53 stitches)

ROW 53: Yarn over, k2, (ssk, yarn over) twice, k8, (ssk, yarn over) twice, k2, *k6, (ssk, yarn over) twice, k2; repeat from the * to 21 stitches before the marker, ending this section with k6, (ssk, yarn over) twice, k8, ssk, yarn over, k1, yarn over. (55 stitches)

ROW 55: Yarn over, k2, (ssk, yarn over) twice, k8, (ssk, yarn over) twice, k3, *k5, (ssk, yarn over) twice, k3; repeat from the * to 22 stitches before the marker, ending this section with k5, (ssk, yarn over) twice, k8, (ssk, yarn over) twice, k1, yarn over. (57 stitches)

ROW 57: Yarn over, k9, (yarn over, k2tog) twice, k8, yarn over, *k2tog, yarn over, k2tog, k8, yarn over; repeat from the * to 24 stitches before the marker, ending this section with k2tog, yarn over, k2tog, k8, (yarn over, k2tog) twice, k8, yarn over. (59 stitches)

ROW 59: Yarn over, k11, (yarn over, k2tog) twice, k8, *(yarn over, k2tog) twice, k8; repeat from the * to 24 stitches before the marker, ending this section with (yarn over, k2tog) twice, k8, (yarn over, k2tog) twice, k8, yarn over. (61 stitches)

ROW 61: Yarn over, k13, (yarn over, k2tog) twice, k7, *k1, (yarn over, k2tog) twice, k7; repeat from the * to 25 stitches before the marker, ending this section with k1, (yarn over, k2tog) twice, k8, (yarn over, k2tog) twice, k8, yarn over. (63 stitches)

ROW 63: Yarn over, k15, (yarn over, k2tog) twice, k6, *k2, (yarn over, k2tog) twice, k6; repeat from the * to 26 stitches before the marker, ending this section with k2, (yarn over, k2tog) twice, k8, (yarn over, k2tog) twice, k8, yarn over. (65 stitches)

ROW 65: Yarn over, ssk, yarn over, k8, (ssk, yarn over) twice, k8, (ssk, yarn over) twice, *k8, (ssk, yarn over) twice; repeat from the * to 27 stitches before the marker, ending this section with k8, (ssk, yarn over) twice, k8, (ssk, yarn over) twice, k3, yarn over. (67 stitches)

ROW 67: Yarn over, ssk, yarn over, k8, (ssk, yarn over) twice, k8, (ssk, yarn over) twice, k1, *k7, (ssk, yarn over) twice, k1; repeat from the * to 28 stitches before the marker, ending this section with k7, (ssk, yarn over) twice, k8, (ssk, yarn over) twice, k5, yarn over. (69 stitches)

ROW 69: Yarn over, ssk, yarn over, k8, (ssk, yarn over) twice, k8, (ssk, yarn over) twice, k2, *k6, (ssk, yarn over) twice, k2; repeat from the * to 29 stitches before the marker, ending this section with k6, (ssk, yarn over) twice, k8, (ssk, yarn over) twice, k7, yarn over. (71 stitches)

ROW 71: Yarn over, ssk, yarn over, k8, (ssk, yarn over) twice, k8, (ssk, yarn over) twice, k3, *k5, (ssk, yarn over) twice, k3; repeat from the * to 30 stitches before the marker, ending this section with k5, (ssk, yarn over) twice, k8, (ssk, yarn over) twice, k9, yarn over. (73 stitches)

ROW 73: Yarn over, k5, (yarn over, k2tog) twice, k8, (yarn over, k2tog) twice, k8, yarn over, *k2tog, yarn over, k2tog, k8, yarn over; repeat from the * to 32 stitches before the marker, ending this section with k2tog, yarn over, k2tog, k8, (yarn over, k2tog) twice, k8, (yarn over k2tog) twice, k4, yarn over. (75 stitches)

ROW 75: Yarn over, k7, (yarn over, k2tog) twice, k8, (yarn over, k2tog) twice, k8, *(yarn over, k2tog) twice, k8; repeat from the * to 32 stitches before the marker, ending this section with (yarn over, k2tog) twice, k8, (yarn over, k2tog) twice, k8, (yarn over, k2tog) twice, k4, yarn over. (77 stitches)

ROW 77: Yarn over, k9, (yarn over, k2tog) twice, k8, (yarn over, k2tog) twice, k7, *k1, (yarn over, k2tog) twice, k7; repeat from the * to 33 stitches before the marker, ending this section with k1, (yarn over, k2tog) twice, k8, (yarn over, k2tog) twice, k8, (yarn over, k2tog) twice, k4, yarn over. (79 stitches)

ROW 78: As Row 2.

Repeat Rows 31–78 for the pattern.

105

ROW 1 (RS): Yarn over, k1, yarn over. (3 stitches)

ROW 2 AND ALL WS ROWS: Knit the knit stitches and purl the purl stitches and yarn overs.

ROW 3: Yarn over, k3, yarn over. (5 stitches)

ROW 5: Yarn over, k1, yarn over, s2kp2 (page 282), yarn over, k1, yarn over. (7 stitches)

ROW 7: Yarn over, ssk, yarn over, k3, yarn over, k2tog, yarn over. (9 stitches)

ROW 9: Yarn over, k3, yarn over, s2kp2, yarn over, k3, yarn over. (11 stitches)

ROW 11: Yarn over, knit across to the marker, ending this section with yarn over. (13 stitches)

ROW 13: Yarn over, *k5, p3, k4; repeat from the * to 1 stitch before the marker, ending this section with k1, yarn over. (15 stitches)

ROW 15: Yarn over, k1, *k5, p3, k4; repeat from the * to 2 stitches before the marker, ending this section with k2, yarn over. (17 stitches)

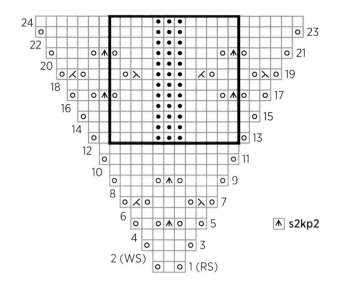

⍓ s2kp2

ROW 17: Yarn over, k1, yarn over, *s2kp2, yarn over, k3, p3, k3, yarn over; repeat from the * to 4 stitches before the marker, ending this section with s2kp2, yarn over, k1, yarn over. (19 stitches)

ROW 19: Yarn over, ssk, yarn over, k1, *k2, yarn over, k2tog, k1, p3, k1, ssk, yarn over, k1; repeat from the * to 4 stitches before the marker, ending this section with k2, yarn over, k2tog, yarn over. (21 stitches)

ROW 21: Yarn over, k3, yarn over, *s2kp2, yarn over, k3, p3, k3, yarn over; repeat from the * to 6 stitches before the marker, ending this section with s2kp2, yarn over, k3, yarn over. (23 stitches)

ROW 23: Yarn over, k5, *k5, p3, k4; repeat from the * to 6 stitches before the marker, ending this section with k6, yarn over. (27 stitches)

ROW 24: As Row 2.

Repeat Rows 13–24 for the pattern.

WEDGES with 14-Stitch Multiples

Start each wedge with the provisional cast on and the tab of your choice (page 10).

106

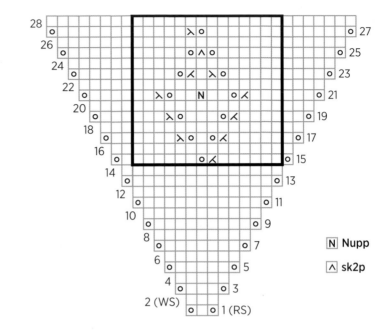

N Nupp

∧ sk2p

ROW 1 (RS): Yarn over, k1, yarn over. (3 stitches)

ROW 2 AND ALL WS ROWS: Purl across.

ROW 3: Yarn over, k3, yarn over. (5 stitches)

ROW 5: Yarn over, k5, yarn over. (7 stitches)

ROW 7: Yarn over, k7, yarn over. (9 stitches)

ROW 9: Yarn over, k9, yarn over. (11 stitches)

ROW 11: Yarn over, k11, yarn over. (13 stitches)

ROW 13: Yarn over, k13, yarn over. (15 stitches)

ROW 15: Yarn over, *k6, k2tog, yarn over, k6; repeat from the * to 1 stitch before the marker, ending this section with k1, yarn over. (17 stitches)

ROW 17: Yarn over, *k5, k2tog, yarn over, k1, yarn over, ssk, k4; repeat from the * to 2 stitches before the marker, ending this section with k2, yarn over. (19 stitches)

ROW 19: Yarn over, k2, *k4, k2tog, yarn over, k3, yarn over, ssk, k3; repeat from the * to 3 stitches before the marker, ending this section with k3, yarn over. (21 stitches)

ROW 21: Yarn over, k3, *k3, k2tog, yarn over, k2, nupp (page 279), k2, yarn over, ssk, k2; repeat from the * to 4 stitches before the marker, ending this section with k4, yarn over. (23 stitches)

ROW 23: Yarn over, k4, *k5, yarn over, ssk, k1, k2tog, yarn over, k4; repeat from the * to 5 stitches before the marker, ending this section with k5, yarn over. (25 stitches)

ROW 25: Yarn over, k5, *k6, yarn over, sk2p (page 282), yarn over, k5; repeat from the * to 6 stitches before the marker, ending this section with k6, yarn over. (27 stitches)

ROW 27: Yarn over, k6, *k7, yarn over, ssk, k5; repeat from the * to 7 stitches before the marker, ending this section with k7, yarn over. (29 stitches)

ROW 28: As Row 2.

Repeat Rows 15–28 for the pattern.

107

ROW 1 (RS): Yarn over, k1, yarn over. (3 stitches)

ROW 2 AND ALL WS ROWS: Purl across.

ROWS 3, 5, 7, 9, 11, 13, 23, 25, AND 27: Yarn over, knit to marker, yarn over.

ROW 15: Yarn over, *k5, k2tog, yarn over, k1, yarn over, ssk, k4; repeat from the * to 1 stitch before the marker, ending this section with k1, yarn over. (17 stitches)

ROW 17: Yarn over, k1, *k4, k2tog, yarn over, k3, yarn over, ssk, k3; repeat from the * to 2 stitches before the marker, ending this section with k2, yarn over. (19 stitches)

ROW 19: Yarn over, k2, *k5, yarn over, ssk, yarn over, k3tog, yarn over, k4; repeat from the * to 3 stitches before the marker, ending this section with k3, yarn over. (21 stitches)

ROW 21: Yarn over, k3, *k6, yarn over, sk2p (page 282), yarn over, k5; repeat from the * to 4 stitches before the marker, ending this section with k4, yarn over. (23 stitches)

ROW 28: As Row 2.

Repeat Rows 15–28 for the pattern.

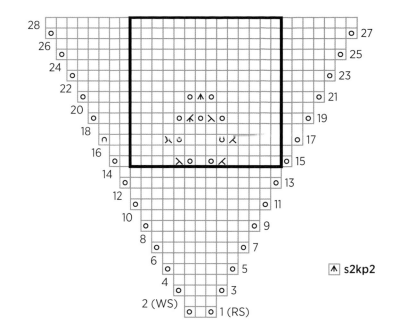

⋀ s2kp2

108

ROW 1 (RS): Yarn over, k1, yarn over. (3 stitches)

ROW 2 AND ALL WS ROWS: Purl across.

ROW 3: Yarn over, k3, yarn over. (5 stitches)

ROW 5: Yarn over, k5, yarn over. (7 stitches)

ROW 7: Yarn over, k3, yarn over, ssk, k2, yarn over. (9 stitches)

ROW 9: Yarn over, k2, k2tog, yarn over, k1, yarn over, ssk, k2, yarn over. (11 stitches)

ROW 11: Yarn over, k2, k2tog, yarn over, k3, yarn over, ssk, k2, yarn over. (13 stitches)

ROW 13: Yarn over, k2, k2tog, yarn over, k5, yarn over, ssk, k2, yarn over. (15 stitches)

ROW 15: Yarn over, *k2, (k2tog, yarn over, k1, yarn over, ssk, k1) twice; repeat from the * to 1 stitch before the marker, ending this section with k1, yarn over. (17 stitches)

ROW 17: Yarn over, k1, *k1, k2tog, yarn over, k3, yarn over, s2kp2 (page 282), yarn over, k3, yarn over, ssk; repeat from the * to 2 stitches before the marker, ending this section with k2, yarn over. (19 stitches)

ROW 19: Yarn over, k2, *k2tog, yarn over, k1, yarn over, ssk, k2, yarn over, ssk, k1, k2tog, yarn over, k1, yarn over; repeat from the * to 4 stitches before the marker, ending with ssk, k2, yarn over. (21 stitches)

ROW 21: Yarn over, k3, *(yarn over, ssk, k2) twice, k1, k2tog, yarn over, k3; repeat from the * to 4 stitches before the marker, ending this section with yarn over, ssk, k2, yarn over. (23 stitches)

ROW 23: Yarn over, k2, k2tog, yarn over, *k1, yarn over, ssk, k2, yarn over, ssk, k1, k2tog, yarn over, k2, k2tog, yarn over; repeat from the * to 5 stitches before the marker, ending this section with k1, yarn over, ssk, k2, yarn over. (25 stitches)

ROW 25: Yarn over, k2, k2tog, yarn over, k1, *k2, yarn over, ssk, k2, yarn over, s2kp2, yarn over, k2, k2tog, yarn over, k1; repeat from the * to 6 stitches before the marker, ending this section with k2, yarn over, ssk, k2, yarn over. (27 stitches)

ROW 27: Yarn over, k2, k2tog, yarn over, k2, *k3, yarn over, ssk, k2, yarn over, ssk, k1, k2tog, yarn over, k2; repeat from the * to 7 stitches before the marker, ending this section with k3, yarn over, ssk, k2, yarn over. (29 stitches)

ROW 29: Yarn over, k2, k2tog, yarn over, k1, yarn over, ssk, *k1, k2tog, yarn over, k1, yarn over, ssk, k3, k2tog, yarn over, k1, yarn over, ssk; repeat from the * to 8 stitches before the marker, ending this section with k1, k2tog, yarn over, k1, yarn over, ssk, k2, yarn over. (31 stitches)

ROW 31: Yarn over, k2, k2tog, yarn over, k3, yarn over, *s2kp2, yarn over, k3, yarn over, ssk, k1, k2tog, yarn over, k3, yarn over; repeat from the * to 10 stitches before the marker, ending this section with s2kp2, yarn over, k3, yarn over, ssk, k2, yarn over. (33 stitches)

ROW 33: Yarn over, k2, k2tog, yarn over, k1, yarn over, ssk, k2, *yarn over, ssk, k1, k2tog, yarn over, k1, yarn over, s2kp2, yarn over, k1, yarn over, ssk, k2; repeat from the * to 10 stitches before the marker, ending this section with yarn over, ssk, k1, k2tog, yarn over, k1, yarn over, ssk, k2, yarn over. (35 stitches)

ROW 35: Yarn over, k3, yarn over, ssk, k2, yarn over, ssk, k1, *k2, k2tog, yarn over, k3, yarn over, ssk, k2, yarn over, ssk, k1; repeat from the * to 11 stitches before the marker, ending this section with k2, k2tog, yarn over, k3, yarn over, ssk, k2, yarn over. (37 stitches)

ROW 37: Yarn over, k2, k2tog, yarn over, k1, yarn over, ssk, k2, yarn over, ssk, *k1, k2tog, yarn over, k2, k2tog, yarn over, k1, yarn over, ssk, k2, yarn over, ssk; repeat from the * to 12 stitches before the marker, ending this section with k1, k2tog, yarn over, k2, k2tog, yarn over, k1, yarn over, ssk, k2, yarn over. (39 stitches)

ROW 39: Yarn over, k2, k2tog, yarn over, k3, yarn over, ssk, k2, yarn over, *s2kp2, yarn over, k2, k2tog, yarn over, k3, yarn over, ssk, k2, yarn over; repeat from the * to 14 stitches before the marker, ending this section with s2kp2, yarn over, k2, k2tog, yarn over, k3, yarn over, ssk, k2, yarn over. (41 stitches)

ROW 41: Yarn over, k2, k2tog, yarn over, k5, yarn over, ssk, k2, *yarn over, ssk, k1, k2tog, yarn over, k5, yarn over, ssk, k2; repeat from the * to 14 stitches before the marker, ending this section with yarn over, ssk, k1, k2tog, yarn over, k5, yarn over, ssk, k2, yarn over. (43 stitches)

ROW 42: As Row 2.

Repeat Rows 29–42 for the pattern.

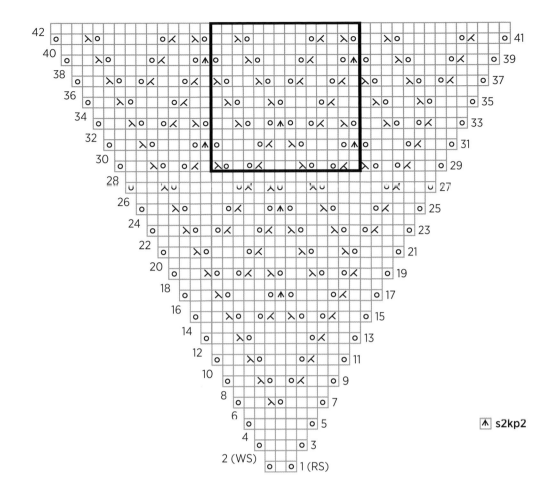

⩚ s2kp2

109

NOTE: To create symmetry, this design is different on the right- and left-hand sides. If you are making a two-wedge shawl, follow the instructions for the Right-Hand Side to the center of your shawl, then work the Left-Hand Side instructions. If your shawl has more than two wedges, work the Right-Hand Side instructions first and the Left-Hand Side instructions last, and balance out the wedges in between.

ROW 1 (RS):

Right-Hand Side: Yarn over, k1, yarn over. (3 stitches)

Left-Hand Side: Yarn over, k1, yarn over. (3 stitches)

ROW 2 AND ALL WS ROWS:

Right-Hand and Left-Hand Sides: Purl across.

ROW 3:

Right-Hand Side: Yarn over, k3, yarn over. (5 stitches)

Left-Hand Side: Yarn over, k3, yarn over. (5 stitches)

ROW 5:

Right-Hand Side: Yarn over, k5, yarn over. (7 stitches)

Left-Hand Side: Yarn over, k5, yarn over. (7 stitches)

ROW 7:

Right-Hand Side: Yarn over, k3, k2tog, yarn over, k2, yarn over. (9 stitches)

Left-Hand Side: Yarn over, k2, yarn over, ssk, k3, yarn over. (9 stitches)

ROW 9:

Right-Hand Side: Yarn over, k3, k2tog, yarn over, k2, yarn over, ssk, yarn over. (11 stitches)

Left-Hand Side: Yarn over, k2tog, yarn over, k2, yarn over, ssk, k3, yarn over. (11 stitches)

(continued on page 184)

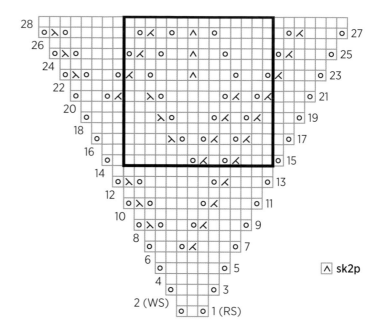

∧ sk2p

Right-Hand Side

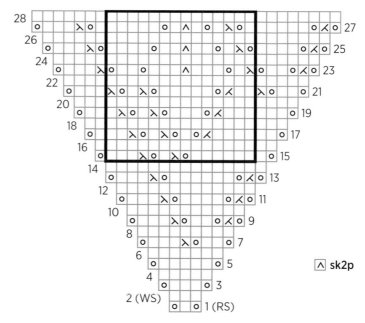

∧ sk2p

Left-Hand Side

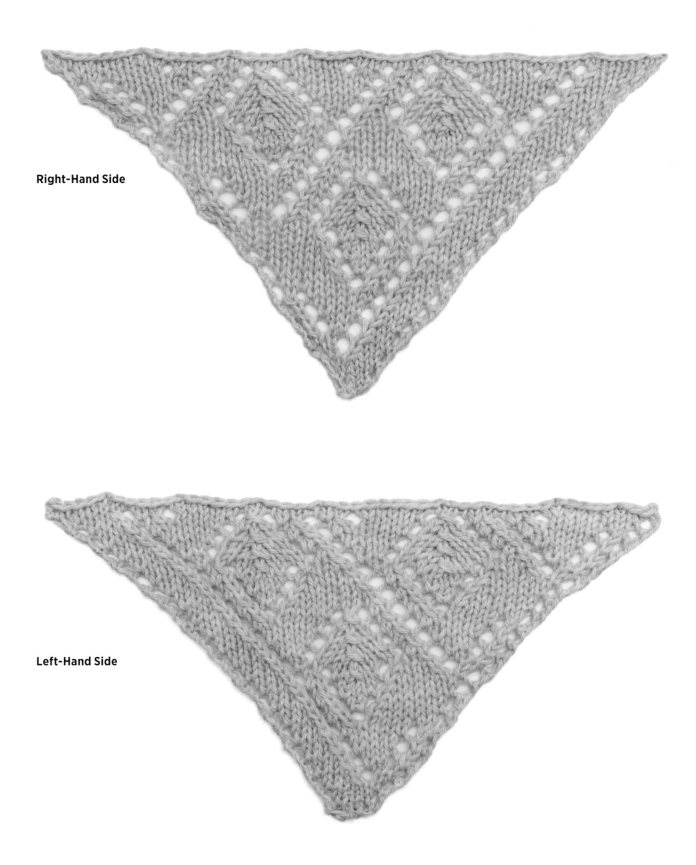

Right-Hand Side

Left-Hand Side

WEDGE 109, *continued*

ROW 11:

Right-Hand Side: Yarn over, k3, k2tog, yarn over, k4, yarn over, ssk, yarn over. (13 stitches)

Left-Hand Side: Yarn over, k2tog, yarn over, k4, yarn over, ssk, k3, yarn over. (13 stitches)

ROW 13:

Right-Hand Side: Yarn over, k3, k2tog, yarn over, k6, yarn over, ssk, yarn over. (15 stitches)

Left-Hand Side: Yarn over, k2tog, yarn over, k6, yarn over, ssk, k3, yarn over. (15 stitches)

ROW 15:

Right-Hand Side: Yarn over, *k3, (k2tog, yarn over, k1) twice, k5; repeat from the * to 1 stitch before the marker, ending this section with k1, yarn over. (17 stitches)

Left-Hand Side: Yarn over, k1, *k6, yarn over, ssk, k1, yarn over, ssk, k3; repeat from the * to the marker, ending this section with yarn over. (17 stitches)

ROW 17:

Right-Hand Side: Yarn over, k1, *k2, (k2tog, yarn over, k1) twice, yarn over, ssk, k4; repeat from the * to 2 stitches before the marker, ending this section with k2, yarn over. (19 stitches)

Left-Hand Side: Yarn over, k2, *k4, k2tog, yarn over, (k1, yarn over, ssk) twice, k2; repeat from the * to 1 stitch before the marker, ending this section with k1, yarn over. (19 stitches)

ROW 19:

Right-Hand Side: Yarn over, k2, *(k1, k2tog, yarn over) twice, k3, yarn over, ssk, k3; repeat from the * to 3 stitches before the marker, ending this section with k3, yarn over. (21 stitches)

Left-Hand Side: Yarn over, k3, *k3, k2tog, yarn over, k3, (yarn over, ssk, k1) twice; repeat from the * to 2 stitches before the marker, ending this section with k2, yarn over. (21 stitches)

ROW 21:

Right-Hand Side: Yarn over, k3, *(k2tog, yarn over, k1) twice, k4, yarn over, ssk, k2; repeat from the * to 4 stitches before the marker, ending this section with k2tog, yarn over, k2, yarn over. (23 stitches)

Left-Hand Side: Yarn over, k2, yarn over, ssk, *k2, k2tog, yarn over, k5, yarn over, ssk, k1, yarn over, ssk; repeat from the * to 3 stitches before the marker, ending this section with k3, yarn over. (23 stitches)

ROW 23:

Right-Hand Side: Yarn over, k3, k2tog, *yarn over, k2, yarn over, k3, sk2p (page 282), k3, yarn over, k1, k2tog; repeat from the * to 4 stitches before the marker, ending this section with yarn over, k2, yarn over, ssk, yarn over. (25 stitches)

Left-Hand Side: Yarn over, k2tog, yarn over, k2, yarn over, *ssk, k1, yarn over, k3, sk2p, k3, yarn over, k2, yarn over; repeat from the * to 5 stitches before the marker, ending this section with ssk, k3, yarn over. (25 stitches)

ROW 25:

Right-Hand Side: Yarn over, k3, k2tog, yarn over, *k4, yarn over, k2, sk2p, k2, yarn over, k1, k2tog, yarn over; repeat from the * to 6 stitches before the marker, ending this section with k4, yarn over, ssk, yarn over. (27 stitches)

Left-Hand Side: Yarn over, k2tog, yarn over, k4, *yarn over, ssk, k1, yarn over, k2, sk2p, k2, yarn over, k4; repeat from the * to 5 stitches before the marker, ending this section with yarn over, ssk, k3, yarn over. (27 stitches)

ROW 27:

Right-Hand Side: Yarn over, k3, k2tog, yarn over, k1, *k5, yarn over, k1, sk2p, k1, yarn over, k1, k2tog, yarn over, k1; repeat from the * to 7 stitches before the marker, ending this section with k5, yarn over, ssk, yarn over. (29 stitches)

Left-Hand Side: Yarn over, k2tog, yarn over, k5, *k1, yarn over, ssk, k1, yarn over, k1, sk2p, k1, yarn over, k5; repeat from the * to 6 stitches before the marker, ending this section with k1, yarn over, ssk, k3, yarn over. (29 stitches)

ROW 28: As Row 2.

Repeat Rows 15–28 for the pattern.

SHAWL #20

Some wedge patterns have a left-hand and right-hand version to create overall symmetry. See page 277 for instructions.

110

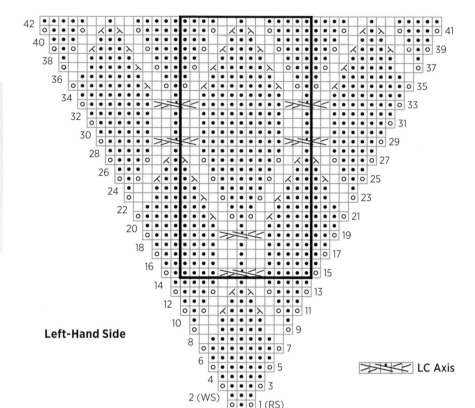

Left-Hand Side

⨯⨯⨉⨞ LC Axis

ROW 1 (RS):

Right-Hand Side: Yarn over, p1, yarn over. (3 stitches)

Left-Hand Side: Yarn over, p1, yarn over. (3 stitches)

ROWS 2, 4, AND 6:

Right-Hand and Left-Hand Sides: Knit across.

ROW 3:

Right-Hand Side: Yarn over, p3, yarn over. (5 stitches)

Left-Hand Side: Yarn over, p3, yarn over. (5 stitches)

ROW 5:

Right-Hand Side: Yarn over, p5, yarn over. (7 stitches)

Left-Hand Side: Yarn over, p5, yarn over. (7 stitches)

ROW 7:

Right-Hand Side: Yarn over, p7, yarn over. (9 stitches)

Left-Hand Side: Yarn over, p7, yarn over. (9 stitches)

ROW 8:

Right-Hand Side: P1, k7, p1.

Left-Hand Side: P1, k7, p1.

ROW 9:

Right-Hand Side: Yarn over, k2, p5, k2, yarn over. (11 stitches)

Left-Hand Side: Yarn over, k2, p5, k2, yarn over. (11 stitches)

ROW 10:

Right-Hand Side: K1, p2, k5, p2, k1.

Left-Hand Side: K1, p2, k5, p2, k1.

ROW 11:

Right-Hand Side: Yarn over, p1, yarn over, k1, ssk, p3, k2tog, k1, yarn over, p1, yarn over. (13 stitches)

Left-Hand Side: Yarn over, p1, yarn over, k1, ssk, p3, k2tog, k1, yarn over, p1, yarn over. (13 stitches)

ROW 12:

Right-Hand Side: K3, (p2, k3) twice.

Left-Hand Side: K3, (p2, k3) twice.

ROW 13:

Right-Hand Side: Yarn over, p3, yarn over, k1, ssk, p1, k2tog, k1, yarn over, p3, yarn over. (15 stitches)

Left-Hand Side: Yarn over, p3, yarn over, k1, ssk, p1, k2tog, k1, yarn over, p3, yarn over. (15 stitches)

ROW 14:

Right-Hand Side: K5, p2, k1, p2, k5.

Left-Hand Side: K5, p2, k1, p2, k5.

ROW 15:

Right-Hand Side: Yarn over, *p5, RC Axis (page 285), p4; repeat from the * to 1 stitch before the marker, ending this section with p1, yarn over. (17 stitches)

Left-Hand Side: Yarn over, *p5, LC Axis (page 285), p4; repeat from the * to 1 stitch before the marker, ending this section with p1, yarn over. (17 stitches)

ROW 16:

Right-Hand Side: K2, *k4, p2, k1, p2, k5; repeat from the * to 1 stitch before the marker, ending this section with k1.

Left-Hand Side: K2, *k4, p2, k1, p2, k5; repeat from the * to 1 stitch before the marker, ending this section with k1.

ROW 17:

Right-Hand Side: Yarn over, p1, *p5, k2, p1, k2, p4; repeat from the * to 2 stitches before the marker, ending this section with p2, yarn over. (19 stitches)

Left-Hand Side: Yarn over, p1, *p5, k2, p1, k2, p4; repeat from the * to 2 stitches before the marker, ending this section with p2, yarn over. (19 stitches)

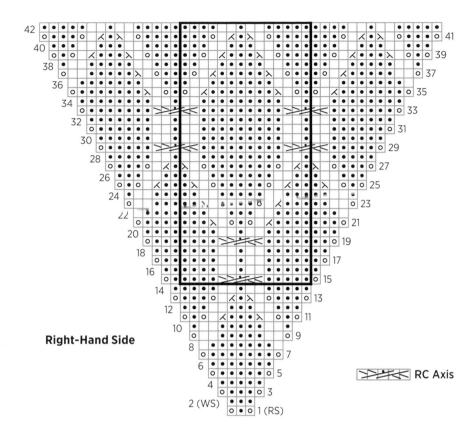

Right-Hand Side

⊠⊠⊠⊠ RC Axis

ROW 18:

> **Right-Hand Side:** K3, *k4, p2, k1, p2, k5; repeat from the * to 2 stitches before the marker, ending this section with k2.
>
> **Left-Hand Side:** K3, *k4, p2, k1, p2, k5; repeat from the * to 2 stitches before the marker, ending this section with k2.

ROW 19:

> **Right-Hand Side:** Yarn over, p2, *p5, RC Axis, p4; repeat from the * to 3 stitches before the marker, ending this section with p3, yarn over. (21 stitches)
>
> **Left-Hand Side:** Yarn over, p2, *p5, LC Axis, p4; repeat from the * to 3 stitches before the marker, ending this section with p3, yarn over. (21 stitches)

ROW 20:

> **Right-Hand Side:** K4, *k4, p2, k1, p2, k5; repeat from the * to 3 stitches before the marker, ending this section with k3.
>
> **Left-Hand Side:** K4, *k4, p2, k1, p2, k5; repeat from the * to 3 stitches before the marker, ending this section with k3.

ROW 21:

> **Right-Hand Side:** Yarn over, p3, *p4, k2tog, k1, yarn over, p1, yarn over, k1, ssk, p3; repeat from the * to 4 stitches before the marker, ending this section with p4, yarn over. (23 stitches)
>
> **Left-Hand Side:** Yarn over, p3, *p4, k2tog, k1, yarn over, p1, yarn over, k1, ssk, p3; repeat from the * to 4 stitches before the marker, ending this section with p4, yarn over. (23 stitches)

ROW 22:

> **Right-Hand Side:** P1, k4, *(k3, p2) twice, k4; repeat from the * to 4 stitches before the marker, ending this section with k3, p1.
>
> **Left-Hand Side:** P1, k4, *(k3, p2) twice, k4; repeat from the * to 4 stitches before the marker, ending this section with k3, p1.

ROW 23:

> **Right-Hand Side:** Yarn over, k2, p2, *p3, k2tog, k1, yarn over, p3, yarn over, k1, ssk, p2; repeat from the * to 5 stitches before the marker, ending this section with p3, k2, yarn over. (25 stitches)
>
> **Left-Hand Side:** Yarn over, k2, p2, *p3, k2tog, k1, yarn over, p3, yarn over, k1, ssk, p2; repeat from the * to 5 stitches before the marker, ending this section with p3, k2, yarn over. (25 stitches)

ROW 24:

> **Right-Hand Side:** K1, p2, k3, *k2, p2, k5, p2, k3; repeat from the * to 5 stitches before the marker, ending this section with k2, p2, k1.
>
> **Left-Hand Side:** K1, p2, k3, *k2, p2, k5, p2, k3; repeat from the * to 5 stitches before the marker, ending this section with k2, p2, k1.

(continued on the next page)

WEDGE 110, *continued*

ROW 25:

Right-Hand Side: Yarn over, p1, yarn over, k1, ssk, p1, *p2, k2tog, k1, yarn over, p5, yarn over, k1, ssk, p1; repeat from the * to 6 stitches before the marker, ending this section with p2, k2tog, k1, yarn over, p1, yarn over. (27 stitches)

Left-Hand Side: Yarn over, p1, yarn over, k1, ssk, p1, *p2, k2tog, k1, yarn over, p5, yarn over, k1, ssk, p1; repeat from the * to 6 stitches before the marker, ending this section with p2, k2tog, k1, yarn over, p1, yarn over. (27 stitches)

ROW 26:

Right-Hand Side: K3, p2, k2, *k1, p2, k7, p2, k2; repeat from the * to 6 stitches before the marker, ending this section with k1, p2, k3.

Left-Hand Side: K3, p2, k2, *k1, p2, k7, p2, k2; repeat from the * to 6 stitches before the marker, ending this section with k1, p2, k3.

ROW 27:

Right-Hand Side: Yarn over, p3, yarn over, k1, ssk, *p1, k2tog, k1, yarn over, p7, yarn over, k1, ssk; repeat from the * to 7 stitches before the marker, ending this section with p1, k2tog, k1, yarn over, p3, yarn over. (29 stitches)

Left-Hand Side: Yarn over, p3, yarn over, k1, ssk, *p1, k2tog, k1, yarn over, p7, yarn over, k1, ssk; repeat from the * to 7 stitches before the marker, ending this section with p1, k2tog, k1, yarn over, p3, yarn over. (29 stitches)

ROW 28:

Right-Hand Side: K5, p2, k1, *p2, k9, p2, k1; repeat from the * to 7 stitches before the marker, ending this section with p2, k5.

Left-Hand Side: K5, p2, k1, *p2, k9, p2, k1; repeat from the * to 7 stitches before the marker, ending this section with p2, k5.

ROW 29:

Right-Hand Side: Yarn over, p5, *RC Axis, p9; repeat from the * to 10 stitches before the marker, ending this section with RC Axis, p5, yarn over. (31 stitches)

Left-Hand Side: Yarn over, p5, *LC Axis, p9; repeat from the * to 10 stitches before the marker, ending this section with LC Axis, p5, yarn over. (31 stitches)

ROW 30:

Right-Hand Side: K6, p2, k1, *p2, k9, p2, k1; repeat from the * to 8 stitches before the marker, ending this section with p2, k6.

Left-Hand Side: K6, p2, k1, *p2, k9, p2, k1; repeat from the * to 8 stitches before the marker, ending this section with p2, k6.

ROW 31:

Right-Hand Side: Yarn over, p6, k2, *p1, k2, p9, k2; repeat from the * to 9 stitches before the marker, ending this section with p1, k2, p6, yarn over. (33 stitches)

Left-Hand Side: Yarn over, p6, k2, *p1, k2, p9, k2; repeat from the * to 9 stitches before the marker, ending this section with p1, k2, p6, yarn over. (33 stitches)

ROW 32:

Right-Hand Side: K7, p2, k1, *p2, k9, p2, k1; repeat from the * to 9 stitches before the marker, ending this section with p2, k7.

Left-Hand Side: K7, p2, k1, *p2, k9, p2, k1; repeat from the * to 9 stitches before the marker, ending this section with p2, k7.

ROW 33:

Right-Hand Side: Yarn over, p7, *RC Axis, p9; repeat from the * to 12 stitches before the marker, ending this section with RC Axis, p7, yarn over. (35 stitches)

Left-Hand Side: Yarn over, p7, *LC Axis, p9; repeat from the * to 12 stitches before the marker, ending this section with LC Axis, p7, yarn over. (35 stitches)

ROW 34:

Right-Hand Side: K8, p2, k1, *p2, k9, p2, k1; repeat from the * to 10 stitches before the marker, ending this section with p2, k8.

Left-Hand Side: K8, p2, k1, *p2, k9, p2, k1; repeat from the * to 10 stitches before the marker, ending this section with p2, k8.

ROW 35:

Right-Hand Side: Yarn over, p7, k2tog, k1, yarn over, *p1, yarn over, k1, ssk, p7, k2tog, k1, yarn over; repeat from the * to 11 stitches before the marker, ending this section with p1, yarn over, k1, ssk, p7, yarn over. (37 stitches)

Left-Hand Side: Yarn over, p7, k2tog, k1, yarn over, *p1, yarn over, k1, ssk, p7, k2tog, k1, yarn over; repeat from the * to 11 stitches before the marker, ending this section with p1, yarn over, k1, ssk, p7, yarn over. (37 stitches)

ROW 36:

Right-Hand Side: P1, k7, p2, k2, *k1, p2, k7, p2, k2; repeat from the * to 11 stitches before the marker, ending this section with k1, p2, k7, p1.

Left-Hand Side: P1, k7, p2, k2, *k1, p2, k7, p2, k2; repeat from the * to 11 stitches before the marker, ending this section with k1, p2, k7, p1.

ROW 37:

Right-Hand Side: Yarn over, k2, p5, k2tog, k1, yarn over, p1, *p2, yarn over, k1, ssk, p5, k2tog, k1, yarn over, p1; repeat from the * to 12 stitches before the marker, ending this section with p2, yarn over, k1, ssk, p5, k2, yarn over. (39 stitches)

Left-Hand Side: Yarn over, k2, p5, k2tog, k1, yarn over, p1, *p2, yarn over, k1, ssk, p5, k2tog, k1, yarn over, p1; repeat from the * to 12 stitches before the marker, ending this section with p2, yarn over, k1, ssk, p5, k2, yarn over. (39 stitches)

ROW 38:

Right-Hand Side: K1, p2, k5, p2, k3, *k2, p2, k5, p2, k3; repeat from the * to 12 stitches before the marker, ending this section with k2, p2, k5, p2, k1.

Left-Hand Side: K1, p2, k5, p2, k3, *k2, p2, k5, p2, k3; repeat from the * to 12 stitches before the marker, ending this section with k2, p2, k5, p2, k1.

ROW 39:

Right-Hand Side: Yarn over, p1, yarn over, k1, ssk, p3, k2tog, k1, yarn over, p2, *p3, yarn over, k1, ssk, p3, k2tog, k1, yarn over, p2; repeat from the * to 13 stitches before the marker, ending this section with p3, yarn over, k1, ssk, p3, k2tog, k1, yarn over, p1, yarn over. (41 stitches)

Left-Hand Side: Yarn over, p1, yarn over, k1, ssk, p3, k2tog, k1, yarn over, p2, *p3, yarn over, k1, ssk, p3, k2tog, k1, yarn over, p2; repeat from the * to 13 stitches before the marker, ending this section with p3, yarn over, k1, ssk, p3, k2tog, k1, yarn over, p1, yarn over. (41 stitches)

ROW 40:

Right-Hand Side: K3, p2, k3, p2, k4, *(k3, p2) twice, k4; repeat from the * to 13 stitches before the marker, ending this section with (k3, p2) twice, k3.

Left-Hand Side: K3, p2, k3, p2, k4, *(k3, p2) twice, k4; repeat from the * to 13 stitches before the marker, ending this section with (k3, p2) twice, k3.

ROW 41:

Right-Hand Side: Yarn over, p3, yarn over, k1, ssk, p1, k2tog, k1, yarn over, p3, *p4, yarn over, k1, ssk, p1, k2tog, k1, yarn over, p3; repeat from the * to 14 stitches before the marker, ending this section with p4, yarn over, k1, ssk, p1, k2tog, k1, yarn over, p3, yarn over. (43 stitches)

Left-Hand Side: Yarn over, p3, yarn over, k1, ssk, p1, k2tog, k1, yarn over, p3, *p4, yarn over, k1, ssk, p1, k2tog, k1, yarn over, p3; repeat from the * to 14 stitches before the marker, ending this section with p4, yarn over, k1, ssk, p1, k2tog, k1, yarn over, p3, yarn over. (43 stitches)

ROW 42:

Right-Hand Side: K5, p2, k1, p2, k5, *k4, p2, k1, p2, k5; repeat from the * to 14 stitches before the marker, ending this section with k4, p2, k1, p2, k5.

Left-Hand Side: K5, p2, k1, p2, k5, *k4, p2, k1, p2, k5; repeat from the * to 14 stitches before the marker, ending this section with k4, p2, k1, p2, k5.

Repeat Rows 15–42 for the pattern.

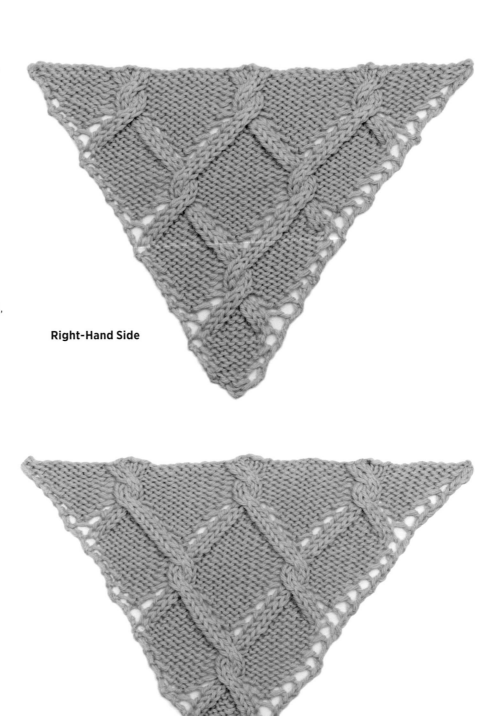

Right-Hand Side

Left-Hand Side

111

ROW 1 (RS): Yarn over, k1, yarn over. (3 stitches)

ROW 2 AND ALL WS ROWS: Purl across.

ROW 3: Yarn over, k3, yarn over. (5 stitches)

ROW 5: Yarn over, k5, yarn over. (7 stitches)

ROW 7: Yarn over, k7, yarn over. (9 stitches)

ROW 9: Yarn over, k1, yarn over, ssk, k3, k2tog, yarn over, k1, yarn over. (11 stitches)

ROW 11: Yarn over, k1, (yarn over, ssk) twice, k1, (k2tog, yarn over) twice, k1, yarn over. (13 stitches)

ROW 13: Yarn over, k1, (yarn over, ssk) twice, yarn over, s2kp2 (page 282), yarn over, (k2tog, yarn over) twice, k1, yarn over. (15 stitches)

ROW 15: Yarn over, *k1, yarn over, ssk, k9, k2tog, yarn over; repeat from the * to 1 stitch before the marker, ending this section with k1, yarn over. (17 stitches)

ROW 17: Yarn over, k1, *k1, yarn over, ssk, k9, k2tog, yarn over; repeat from the * to 2 stitches before the marker, ending this section with k2, yarn over. (19 stitches)

ROW 19: Yarn over, k2, *k2, yarn over, ssk, k7, k2tog, yarn over, k1; repeat from the * to 3 stitches before the marker, ending this section with k3, yarn over. (21 stitches)

ROW 21: Yarn over, k3, *k1, (yarn over, ssk) twice, k5, (k2tog, yarn over) twice; repeat from the * to 4 stitches before the marker, ending this section with k4, yarn over. (23 stitches)

ROW 23: Yarn over, k4, *k2, (yarn over, ssk) twice, k3, (k2tog, yarn over) twice, k1; repeat from the * to 5 stitches before the marker, ending this section with k5, yarn over. (25 stitches)

ROW 25: Yarn over, k5, *k1, (yarn over, ssk) 3 times, k1, (k2tog, yarn over) 3 times; repeat from the * to 6 stitches before the marker, ending this section with k6, yarn over. (27 stitches)

ROW 27: Yarn over, k6, *k2, (yarn over, ssk) twice, yarn over, s2kp2, yarn over, (k2tog, yarn over) twice, k1; repeat from the * to 7 stitches before the marker, ending this section with k7, yarn over. (29 stitches)

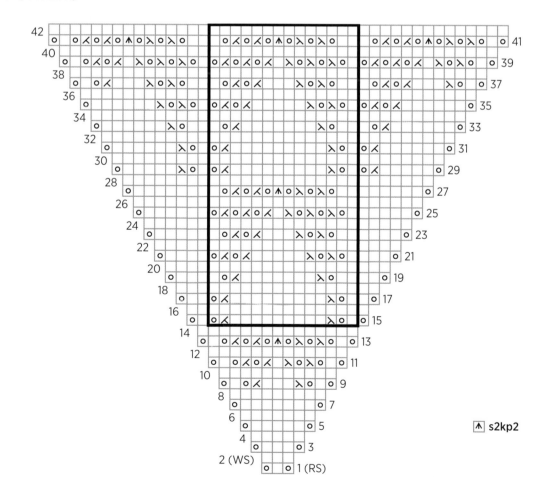

⩗ s2kp2

ROW 29: Yarn over, k5, k2tog, yarn over, *k1, yarn over, ssk, k9, k2tog, yarn over; repeat from the * to 8 stitches before the marker, ending this section with k1, yarn over, ssk, k5, yarn over. (31 stitches)

ROW 31: Yarn over, k6, k2tog, yarn over, *k1, yarn over, ssk, k9, k2tog, yarn over; repeat from the * to 9 stitches before the marker, ending this section with k1, yarn over, ssk, k6, yarn over. (33 stitches)

ROW 33: Yarn over, k6, k2tog, yarn over, k1, *k2, yarn over, ssk, k7, k2tog, yarn over, k1; repeat from the * to 10 stitches before the marker, ending this section with k2, yarn over, ssk, k6, yarn over. (35 stitches)

ROW 35: Yarn over, k6, (k2tog, yarn over) twice, *k1, (yarn over, ssk) twice, k5, (k2tog, yarn over) twice; repeat from the * to 11 stitches before the marker, ending this section with k1, (yarn over, ssk) twice, k6, yarn over. (37 stitches)

ROW 37: Yarn over, k1, yarn over, ssk, k3, (k2tog, yarn over) twice, k1, *k2, (yarn over, ssk) twice, k3, (k2tog, yarn over) twice, k1; repeat from the * to 12 stitches before the marker, ending this section with k2, (yarn over, ssk) twice, k3, k2tog, yarn over, k1, yarn over. (39 stitches)

ROW 39: Yarn over, k1, (yarn over, ssk) twice, k1, (k2tog, yarn over) 3 times, *k1, (yarn over, ssk) 3 times, k1, (k2tog, yarn over) 3 times; repeat from the * to 13 stitches before the marker, ending this section with k1, (yarn over, ssk) 3 times, k1, (k2tog, yarn over) twice, k1, yarn over. (41 stitches)

ROW 41: Yarn over, k1, (yarn over, ssk) twice, yarn over, s2kp2, (yarn over, k2tog) twice, yarn over, k1, *k2, (yarn over, ssk) twice, yarn over, s2kp2, (yarn over, k2tog) twice, yarn over, k1; repeat from the * to 14 stitches before the marker, ending this section with k2, (yarn over, ssk) twice, yarn over, s2kp2, (yarn over, k2tog) twice, yarn over, k1, yarn over. (43 stitches)

ROW 42: As Row 2.

Repeat Rows 15–42 for the pattern.

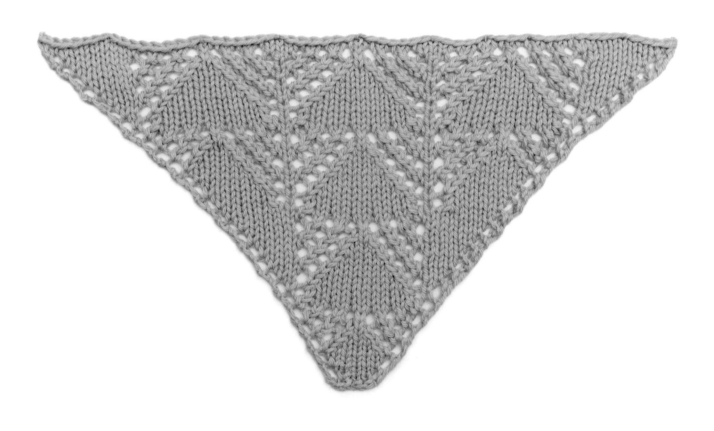

112

ROW 1 (RS): Yarn over, k1, yarn over. (3 stitches)

ROW 2 AND ALL WS ROWS: Purl across.

ROW 3: Yarn over, k3, yarn over. (5 stitches)

ROW 5: Yarn over, k5, yarn over. (7 stitches)

ROW 7: Yarn over, k7, yarn over. (9 stitches)

ROW 9: Yarn over, k9, yarn over. (11 stitches)

ROW 11: Yarn over, k2, yarn over, k2, sssk (page 285), k2, yarn over, k2, yarn over. (13 stitches)

ROW 13: Yarn over, k2, yarn over, ssk, yarn over, k1, sssk, k1, yarn over, k2tog, yarn over, k2, yarn over. (15 stitches)

ROW 15: Yarn over, *k4, yarn over, ssk, yarn over, sssk, yarn over, k2tog, yarn over, k3; repeat from the * to 1 stitch before the marker, ending this section with k1, yarn over. (17 stitches)

ROW 17: Yarn over, k1, *ssk, k2, yarn over, k1, yarn over, ssk, yarn over, k3tog, yarn over, k1, yarn over, k2; repeat from the * to 3 stitches before the marker, ending this section with ssk, k1, yarn over. (19 stitches)

ROW 19: Yarn over, k1, yarn over, *sssk, k1, yarn over, k2tog, yarn over, k1, yarn over, sssk, yarn over, k1, yarn over, ssk, yarn over, k1; repeat from the * to 4 stitches before the marker, ending this section with sssk, yarn over, k1, yarn over. (21 stitches)

ROW 21: Yarn over, k2, yarn over, *sssk, yarn over, k2tog, yarn over, k7, yarn over, ssk, yarn over; repeat from the * to 5 stitches before the marker, ending this section with sssk, yarn over, k2, yarn over. (23 stitches)

ROW 23: Yarn over, k2, yarn over, ssk, *yarn over, k3tog, yarn over, k1, yarn over, k2, sssk, k2, yarn over, k1, yarn over, ssk; repeat from the * to 5 stitches before the marker, ending this section with yarn over, k3tog, yarn over, k2, yarn over. (25 stitches)

ROW 25: Yarn over, k1, k2tog, yarn over, k1, yarn over, *sssk, yarn over, k1, yarn over, ssk, yarn over, k1, sssk, k1, yarn over, k2tog, yarn over, k1, yarn over; repeat from the * to 7 stitches before the marker, ending this section with sssk, yarn over, k1, yarn over, ssk, k1, yarn over. (27 stitches)

ROW 27: Yarn over, k1, k2tog, yarn over, k3, *k4, yarn over, ssk, yarn over, sssk, yarn over, k2tog, yarn over, k3; repeat from the * to 7 stitches before the marker, ending this section with k4, yarn over, ssk, k1, yarn over. (29 stitches)

ROW 29: Yarn over, k1, k2tog, yarn over, k1, yarn over, k2, *sssk, k2, yarn over, k1, yarn over, ssk, yarn over, k3tog, yarn over, k1, yarn over, k2; repeat from the * to 9 stitches before the marker, ending this section with sssk, k2, yarn over, k1, yarn over, ssk, k1, yarn over. (31 stitches)

ROW 31: Yarn over, k3, yarn over, ssk, yarn over, k2, *sssk, k1, yarn over, k2tog, yarn over, k1, yarn over, sssk, yarn over, k1, yarn over, ssk, yarn over, k1; repeat from the * to 10 stitches before the marker, ending this section with sssk, k2, yarn over, k2tog, yarn over, k3, yarn over. (33 stitches)

ROW 33: Yarn over, k6, yarn over, ssk, yarn over, *sssk, yarn over, k2tog, yarn over, k7, yarn over, ssk, yarn over; repeat from the * to 11 stitches before the marker, ending this section with sssk, yarn over, k2tog, yarn over, k6, yarn over. (35 stitches)

ROW 35: Yarn over, k3, k2tog, k2, yarn over, k1, yarn over, ssk, *yarn over, k3tog, yarn over, k1, yarn over, k2, sssk, k2, yarn over, k1, yarn over, ssk; repeat from the * to 11 stitches before the marker, ending this section with yarn over, k3tog, yarn over, k1, yarn over, k2, ssk, k3, yarn over. (37 stitches)

ROW 37: Yarn over, k1, ssk, yarn over, k1, sssk, k1, yarn over, k2tog, yarn over, k1, yarn over, *sssk, yarn over, k1, yarn over, ssk, yarn over, k1, sssk, k1, yarn over, k2tog, yarn over, k1, yarn over; repeat from the * to 14 stitches before the marker, ending this section with sssk, yarn over, k1, yarn over, ssk, yarn over, k1, sssk, k1, yarn over, k2tog, k1, yarn over. (39 stitches)

(continued on the next page)

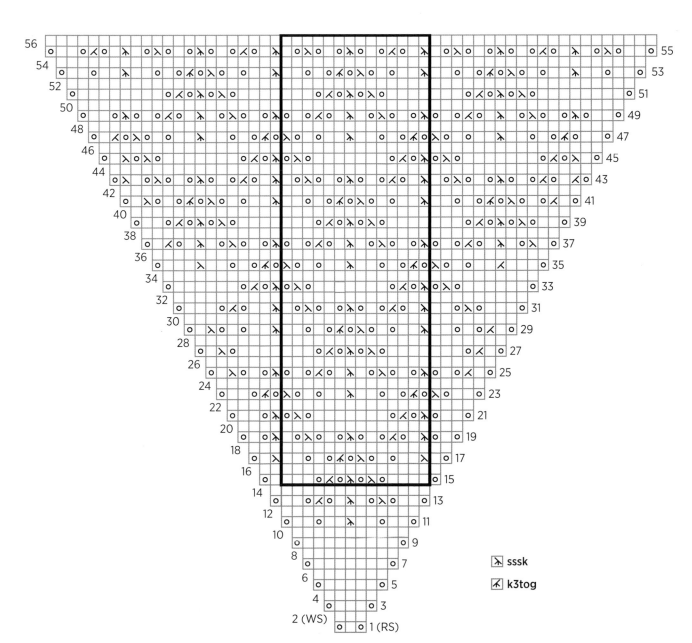

⊼ sssk

⊿ k3tog

ROW 39: Yarn over, k2, yarn over, ssk, yarn over, sssk, yarn over, k2tog, yarn over, k3, *k4, yarn over, ssk, yarn over, sssk, yarn over, k2tog, yarn over, k3; repeat from the * to 13 stitches before the marker, ending this section with k4, yarn over, ssk, yarn over, sssk, yarn over, k2tog, yarn over, k2, yarn over. (41 stitches)

ROW 41: Yarn over, k1, k2tog, yarn over, k1, yarn over, ssk, yarn over, k3tog, yarn over, k1, yarn over, k2, *sssk, k2, yarn over, k1, yarn over, ssk, yarn over, k3tog, yarn over, k1, yarn over, k2; repeat from the * to 15 stitches before the marker, ending this section with sssk, k2, yarn over, k1, yarn over, ssk, yarn over, k3tog, yarn over, k1, yarn over, ssk, k1, yarn over. (43 stitches)

ROW 43: Yarn over, k2tog, k1, yarn over, k2tog, yarn over, k1, yarn over, sssk, yarn over, k1, yarn over, ssk, yarn over, k1, *sssk, k1, yarn over, k2tog, yarn over, k1, yarn over, sssk, yarn over, k1, yarn over, ssk, yarn over, k1; repeat from the * to 16 stitches before the marker, ending this section with sssk, k1, yarn over, k2tog, yarn over, k1, yarn over, sssk, yarn over, k1, yarn over, ssk, yarn over, k1, ssk, yarn over. (45 stitches)

ROW 45: Yarn over, k1, ssk, yarn over, k2tog, yarn over, k7, yarn over, ssk, yarn over, *sssk, yarn over, k2tog, yarn over, k7, yarn over, ssk, yarn over; repeat from the * to 17 stitches before the marker, ending this section with sssk, yarn over, k2tog, yarn over, k7, yarn over, ssk, yarn over, ssk, k1, yarn over. (47 stitches)

ROW 47: Yarn over, k2, yarn over, k3tog, yarn over, k1, yarn over, k2, sssk, k2, yarn over, k1, yarn over, ssk, *yarn over, k3tog, yarn over, k1, yarn over, k2, sssk, k2, yarn over, k1, yarn over, ssk; repeat from the * to 17 stitches before the marker, ending this section with yarn over, k3tog, yarn over, k1, yarn over, k2, sssk, k2, yarn over, k1, yarn over, ssk, yarn over, k2tog, k1, yarn over. (49 stitches)

ROW 49: Yarn over, k2, yarn over, sssk, yarn over, k1, yarn over, ssk, yarn over, k1, sssk, k1, yarn over, k2tog, yarn over, k1, yarn over, *sssk, yarn over, k1, yarn over, ssk, yarn over, k1, sssk, k1, yarn over, k2tog, yarn over, k1, yarn over; repeat from the * to 19 stitches before the marker, ending this section with sssk, yarn over, k1, yarn over, ssk, yarn over, k1, sssk, k1, yarn over, k2tog, yarn over, k1, yarn over, sssk, yarn over, k2, yarn over. (51 stitches)

ROW 51: Yarn over, k8, yarn over, ssk, yarn over, sssk, yarn over, k2tog, yarn over, k3, *k4, yarn over, ssk, yarn over, sssk, yarn over, k2tog, yarn over, k3; repeat from the * to 19 stitches before the marker, ending this section with k4, yarn over, ssk, yarn over, sssk, yarn over, k2tog, yarn over, k8, yarn over. (53 stitches)

ROW 53: Yarn over, k2, yarn over, k2, sssk, k2, yarn over, k1, yarn over, ssk, yarn over, k3tog, yarn over, k1, yarn over, k2, *sssk, k2, yarn over, k1, yarn over, ssk, yarn over, k3tog, yarn over, k1, yarn over, k2; repeat from the * to 21 stitches before the marker, ending this section with sssk, k2, yarn over, k1, yarn over, ssk, yarn over, k3tog, yarn over, k1, yarn over, k2, sssk, k2, yarn over, k2, yarn over. (55 stitches)

ROW 55: Yarn over, k2, yarn over, ssk, yarn over, k1, sssk, k1, yarn over, k2tog, yarn over, k1, yarn over, sssk, yarn over, k1, yarn over, ssk, yarn over, k1, *sssk, k1, yarn over, k2tog, yarn over, k1, yarn over, sssk, yarn over, k1, yarn over, ssk, yarn over, k1; repeat from the * to 22 stitches before the marker, ending this section with sssk, k1, yarn over, k2tog, yarn over, k1, yarn over, sssk, yarn over, k1, yarn over, ssk, yarn over, k1, sssk, k1, yarn over, k2tog, yarn over, k2, yarn over. (57 stitches)

ROW 56: As Row 2.

Repeat Rows 15–56 for the pattern.

WEDGES with 16-Stitch Multiples

Start each wedge with the provisional cast on and the tab of your choice (page 10).

113

ROW 1 (RS): Yarn over, k1, yarn over. (3 stitches)

ROW 2 AND ALL WS ROWS: Purl across.

ROW 3: Yarn over, k3, yarn over. (5 stitches)

ROW 5: Yarn over, k5, yarn over. (7 stitches)

ROW 7: Yarn over, k7, yarn over. (9 stitches)

ROW 9: Yarn over, k2, yarn over, ssk, k1, k2tog, yarn over, k2, yarn over. (11 stitches)

ROW 11: Yarn over, k4, yarn over, sk2p (page 282), yarn over, k4, yarn over. (13 stitches)

ROW 13: Yarn over, k1, yarn over, ssk, k7, k2tog, yarn over, k1, yarn over. (15 stitches)

ROW 15: Yarn over, k1, k2tog, yarn over, k9, yarn over, ssk, k1, yarn over. (17 stitches)

ROW 17: Yarn over, *k1, k2tog, yarn over, k3, k2tog, yarn over, k1, yarn over, ssk, k3, yarn over, ssk; repeat from the * to 1 stitch before the marker, ending this section with k1, yarn over. (19 stitches)

ROW 19: Yarn over, k1, *(k2tog, yarn over, k3) twice, yarn over, ssk, k3, yarn over; repeat from the * to 3 stitches before the marker, ending this section with ssk, k1, yarn over. (21 stitches)

ROW 21: Yarn over, k2, *k4, k2tog, yarn over, k5, yarn over, ssk, k3; repeat from the * to 3 stitches before the marker, ending this section with k3, yarn over. (23 stitches)

ROW 23: Yarn over, k3, *k5, yarn over, ssk, k3, k2tog, yarn over, k4; repeat from the * to 4 stitches before the marker, ending this section with k4, yarn over. (25 stitches)

ROW 25: Yarn over, k2, k2tog, yarn over, *k1, yarn over, ssk, k3, yarn over, ssk, k1, k2tog, yarn over, k3, k2tog, yarn over; repeat from the * to 5 stitches before the marker, ending this section with k1, yarn over, ssk, k2, yarn over. (27 stitches)

ROW 27: Yarn over, k2, k2tog, yarn over, k1, *k2, yarn over, ssk, k3, yarn over, sk2p, yarn over, k3, k2tog, yarn over, k1; repeat from the * to 6 stitches before the marker, ending this section with k2, yarn over, ssk, k2, yarn over. (29 stitches)

ROW 29: Yarn over, k2, k2tog, yarn over, k2, *k3, yarn over, ssk, k7, ssk, yarn over, k2; repeat from the * to 7 stitches before the marker, ending this section with k3, yarn over, ssk, k2, yarn over. (31 stitches)

ROW 31: Yarn over, k4, yarn over, ssk, k1, *k2, k2tog, yarn over, k9, yarn over, ssk, k1; repeat from the * to 8 stitches before the marker, ending with k2, k2tog, yarn over, k4, yarn over. (33 stitches)

ROW 33: Yarn over, k1, yarn over, ssk, k3, yarn over, ssk, *k1, k2tog, yarn over, k3, k2tog, yarn over, k1, yarn over, ssk, k3, yarn over, ssk; repeat from the * to 9 stitches before the marker, ending this section with k1, k2tog, yarn over, k3, k2tog, yarn over, k1, yarn over. (35 stitches)

ROW 35: Yarn over, k3, yarn over, ssk, k3, yarn over, *sk2p, yarn over, k3, k2tog, yarn over, k3, yarn over, ssk, k3, yarn over; repeat from the * to 11 stitches before the marker, ending this section with sk2p, yarn over, k3, k2tog, yarn over, k3, yarn over. (37 stitches)

(continued on the next page)

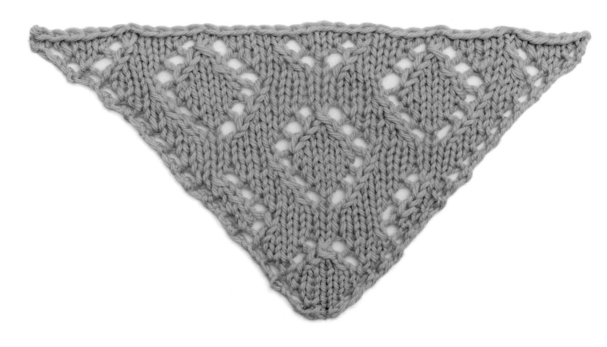

WEDGE 113, *continued*

ROW 37: Yarn over, k5, yarn over, ssk, k3, *k4, k2tog, yarn over, k5, yarn over, ssk, k3; repeat from the * to 11 stitches before the marker, ending this section with k4, k2tog, yarn over, k5, yarn over. (39 stitches)

ROW 39: Yarn over, k5, k2tog, yarn over, k4, *k5, yarn over, ssk, k3, k2tog, yarn over, k4; repeat from the * to 12 stitches before the marker, ending this section with k5, yarn over, ssk, k5, yarn over. (41 stitches)

ROW 41: Yarn over, k2, yarn over, ssk, k1, k2tog, yarn over, k3, k2tog, yarn over, *k1, yarn over, ssk, k3, yarn over, ssk, k1, k2tog, yarn over, k3, k2tog, yarn over; repeat from the * to 13 stitches before the marker, ending this section with k1, yarn over, ssk, k3, yarn over, ssk, k1, k2tog, yarn over, k2, yarn over. (43 stitches)

ROW 43: Yarn over, k4, yarn over, sk2p, yarn over, k3, k2tog, yarn over, k1, *k2, yarn over, ssk, k3, yarn over, sk2p, yarn over, k3, k2tog, yarn over, k1; repeat from the * to 14 stitches before the marker, ending with k2, yarn over, ssk, k3, yarn over, sk2p, yarn over, k4, yarn over. (45 stitches)

ROW 45: Yarn over, k1, yarn over, ssk, k7, k2tog, yarn over, k2, *k3, yarn over, ssk, k7, k2tog, yarn over, k2; repeat from the * to 15 stitches before the marker, ending this section with k3, yarn over, ssk, k7, k2tog, yarn over, k1, yarn over. (47 stitches)

ROW 47: Yarn over, k1, k2tog, yarn over, k9, yarn over, ssk, k1, *k2, k2tog, yarn over, k9, yarn over, ssk, k1; repeat from the * to 16 stitches before the marker, ending this section with k2, k2tog, yarn over, k9, yarn over, ssk, k1, yarn over. (49 stitches)

ROW 48: As Row 2.

Repeat Rows 17–48 for the pattern.

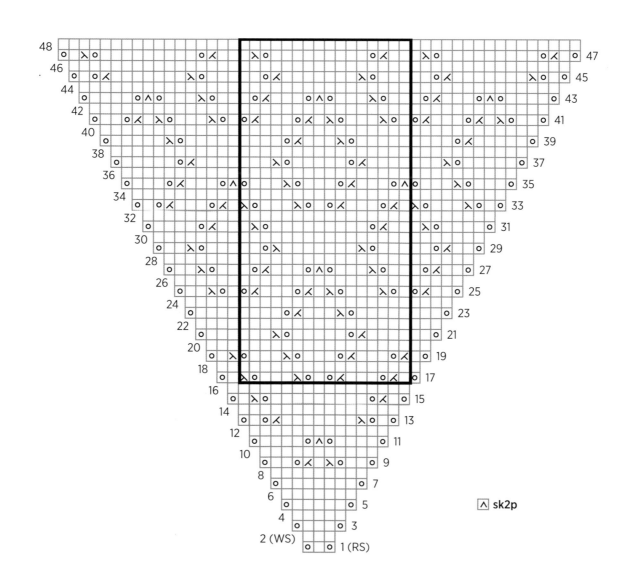

⌃ sk2p

SHAWL #11

Using garter stitch for the background texture creates a different look. See page 274 for instructions.

114

ROW 1 (RS): Yarn over, k1, yarn over. (3 stitches)

ROW 2 AND ALL WS ROWS: Purl across.

ROW 3: Yarn over, knit across to the marker, ending this section with yarn over. (5 stitches)

ROW 5: Yarn over, k1, yarn over, s2kp2 (page 282), yarn over, k1, yarn over. (7 stitches)

ROW 7: As Row 3. (9 stitches)

ROW 9: Yarn over, k3, yarn over, s2kp2, yarn over, k3, yarn over. (11 stitches)

ROW 11: As Row 3. (13 stitches)

ROW 13: Yarn over, k5, yarn over, s2kp2, yarn over, k5, yarn over. (15 stitches)

ROW 15: As Row 3. (17 stitches)

ROW 17: Yarn over, *k7, yarn over, s2kp2, yarn over, k6; repeat from the * to 1 stitch before the marker, ending this section with k1, yarn over. (19 stitches)

ROW 19: As Row 3. (21 stitches)

ROW 21: Yarn over, k2, *k7, yarn over, s2kp2, yarn over, k6; repeat from the * to 3 stitches before the marker, ending this section with k3, yarn over. (23 stitches)

ROW 23: As Row 3. (25 stitches)

ROW 25: Yarn over, k4, *k7, yarn over, s2kp2, yarn over, k6; repeat from the * to 5 stitches before the marker, ending this section with k5, yarn over. (27 stitches)

ROW 27: As Row 3. (29 stitches)

ROW 29: Yarn over, k6, *k7, yarn over, s2kp2, yarn over, k6; repeat from the * to 7 stitches before the marker, ending this section with k7, yarn over. (31 stitches)

ROW 31: As Row 3. (33 stitches)

ROW 33: Yarn over, k2tog, yarn over, k6, *k7, yarn over, s2kp2, yarn over, k6; repeat from the * to 9 stitches before the marker, ending this section with k7, yarn over, ssk, yarn over. (35 stitches)

ROW 35: As Row 3. (37 stitches)

ROW 37: Yarn over, k1, yarn over, s2kp2, yarn over, k6, *k7, yarn over, s2kp2, yarn over, k6; repeat from the * to 11 stitches before the marker, ending this section with k7, yarn over, s2kp2, yarn over, k1, yarn over. (39 stitches)

ROW 39: As Row 3. (41 stitches)

ROW 41: Yarn over, k3, yarn over, s2kp2, yarn over, k6, *k7, yarn over, s2kp2, yarn over, k6; repeat from the * to 13 stitches before the marker, ending this section with k7, yarn over, s2kp2, yarn over, k3, yarn over. (43 stitches)

ROW 43: As Row 3. (45 stitches)

ROW 45: Yarn over, k5, yarn over, s2kp2, yarn over, k6, *k7, yarn over, s2kp2, yarn over, k6; repeat from the * to 15 stitches before the marker, ending this section with k7, yarn over, s2kp2, yarn over, k5, yarn over. (49 stitches)

ROW 47: As Row 3. (49 stitches)

ROW 48: As Row 2.

Repeat Rows 17–48 for the pattern.

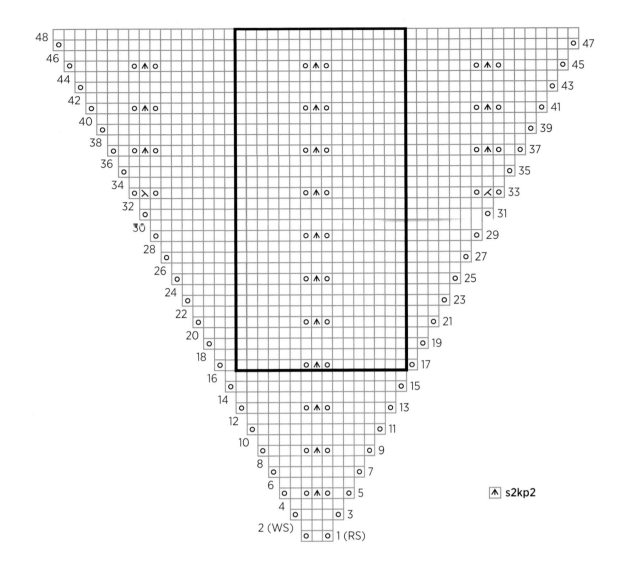

▲ s2kp2

115

ROW 1 (RS): Yarn over, k1, yarn over. (3 stitches)

ROWS 2, 4, 8, 10, 12, 14, 16, 18, 20, 22, 24, 28, 30, 32, 34, 36, 40, 42, 44, AND 46: Knit the knit stitches and purl the purl stitches and yarn overs.

ROW 3: Yarn over, k3, yarn over. (5 stitches)

ROW 5: Yarn over, p1, k3, p1, yarn over. (7 stitches)

ROWS 6 AND 38: K1, knit the knit stitches and purl the purl stitches and the yarn overs until the last stitch before the marker, k1.

ROW 7: Yarn over, p3, k1, p3, yarn over. (9 stitches)

ROW 9: Yarn over, p2tog, p2, yarn over, k1, yarn over, p2, ssp, yarn over. (11 stitches)

ROW 11: Yarn over, p2tog, p2, (k1, yarn over) twice, k1, p2, ssp, yarn over. (13 stitches)

ROW 13: Yarn over, p2tog, p2, k2, yarn over, k1, yarn over, k2, p2, ssp, yarn over. (15 stitches)

ROW 15: Yarn over, p2tog, p2, k3, yarn over, k1, yarn over, k3, p2, ssp, yarn over. (17 stitches)

ROW 17: Yarn over, *k1, yarn over, p3, k2tog, k5, ssk, p3, yarn over; repeat from the * to 1 stitch before the marker, ending this section with k1, yarn over. (19 stitches)

ROW 19: Yarn over, k1, *k1, yarn over, k1, p3, k2tog, k3, ssk, p3, k1, yarn over; repeat from the * to 2 stitches before the marker, ending this section with k2, yarn over. (21 stitches)

ROW 21: Yarn over, k2, *k1, yarn over, k2, p3, k2tog, k1, ssk, p3, k2, yarn over; repeat from the * to 3 stitches before the marker, ending this repeat with k3, yarn over. (23 stitches)

ROW 23: Yarn over, k3, *k1, yarn over, k3, p3, s2kp2 (page 282), p3, k3, yarn over; repeat from the * to 4 stitches before the marker, ending this section with k4, yarn over. (25 stitches)

ROW 25: Yarn over, p1, k3, *k3, ssk, p3, yarn over, k1, yarn over, p3, k2tog, k2; repeat from the * to 5 stitches before the marker, ending this section with k4, p1, yarn over. (27 stitches)

ROW 26: K2, p4, *(p3, k3) twice, p4; repeat from the * to 5 stitches before the marker, ending this section with p3, k2.

ROW 27: Yarn over, p3, k2, *k2, ssk, p3, (k1, yarn over) twice, k1, p3, k2tog, k1; repeat from the * to 6 stitches before the marker, ending this section with k3, p3, yarn over. (29 stitches)

ROW 29: Yarn over, k1, yarn over, p3, k2tog, *k1, ssk, p3, k2, yarn over, k1, yarn over, k2, p3, k2tog; repeat from the * to 7 stitches before the marker, ending this section with k1, ssk, p3, yarn over, k1, yarn over. (31 stitches)

ROW 31: Yarn over, k3, yarn over, p3, *s2kp2, p3, k3, yarn over, k1, yarn over, k3, p3; repeat from the * to 9 stitches before the marker, ending this section with s2kp2, p3, yarn over, k3, yarn over. (33 stitches)

ROW 33: Yarn over, k3, ssk, p3, yarn over, *k1, yarn over, p3, k2tog, k5, ssk, p3, yarn over; repeat from the * to 9 stitches before the marker, ending this section with k1, yarn over, p3, k2tog, k3, yarn over. (35 stitches)

ROW 35: Yarn over, k3, ssk, p3, k1, yarn over, *k1, yarn over, k1, p3, k2tog, k3, ssk, p3, k1, yarn over; repeat from the * to 10 stitches before the marker, ending this section with k1, yarn over, k1, p3, k2tog, k3, yarn over. (37 stitches)

ROW 37: Yarn over, p1, k2, ssk, p3, k2, yarn over, *k1, yarn over, k2, p3, k2tog, k1, ssk, p3, k2, yarn over; repeat from the * to 11 stitches before the marker, ending this section with k1, yarn over, k2, p3, k2tog, k2, p1, yarn over. (39 stitches)

ROW 38: K2, p3, k3, p4,* (p3, k3) twice, p4; repeat from the * to 11 stitches before the marker, ending this section with p3, k3, p3, k2.

ROW 39: Yarn over, p3, ssk, p3, k3, over, *k1, yarn over, k3, p3, s2kp2, p3, k3, yarn over; repeat from the * to 12 stitches before the marker, ending this section with k1, yarn over, k3, p3, k2tog, p3, yarn over. (41 stitches)

ROW 41: Yarn over, p2tog, p2, yarn over, k1, yarn over, p3, k2tog, k2, *k3, ssk, p3, yarn over, k1, yarn over, p3, k2tog, k2; repeat from the * to 13 stitches before the marker, ending this section with k3, ssk, p3, yarn over, k1, yarn over, p2, ssp, yarn over. (43 stitches)

ROW 43: Yarn over, p2tog, p2, (k1, yarn over) twice, k1, p3, k2tog, k1, *k2, ssk, p3, (k1, yarn over) twice, k1, p3, k2tog, k1; repeat from the * to 14 stitches before the marker, ending this section with k2, ssk, p3, (k1, yarn over) twice, k1, p2, ssp, yarn over. (45 stitches)

ROW 45: Yarn over, p2tog, p2, k2, yarn over, k1, yarn over, k2, p3, k2tog, *k1, ssk, p3, k2, yarn over, k1, yarn over, k2, p3, k2tog; repeat from the * to 15 stitches before the marker, ending this section with k1, ssk, p3, k2, yarn over, k1, yarn over, k2, p2, ssp, yarn over. (47 stitches)

ROW 47: Yarn over, p2tog, p2, k3, yarn over, k1, yarn over, k3, p3, *s2kp2, p3, k3, yarn over, k1, yarn over, k3, p3; repeat from the * to 17 stitches before the marker, ending this section with s2kp2, p3, k3, yarn over, k1, yarn over, k3, p2, ssp, yarn over. (49 stitches)

ROW 48: P1, k3, p9, k3, p1, *k3, p9, k3, p1; repeat from the * to 16 stitches before the marker, ending this section with k3, p9, k3, p1.

Repeat Rows 17–48 for the pattern.

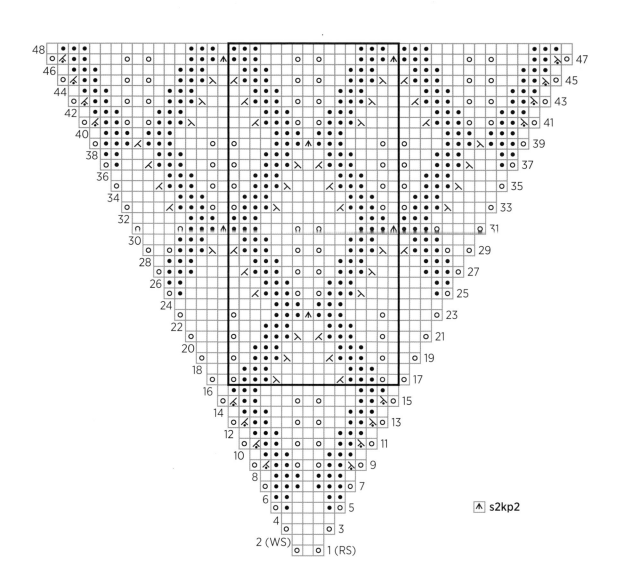

⊼ s2kp2

116

ROW 1 (RS): Yarn over, k1, yarn over. (3 stitches)

ROWS 2, 4, 6, 8, 10, 12, 14, 18, 20, 22, 24, 26, 28, AND 30: Purl across.

ROW 3: Yarn over, k3, yarn over. (5 stitches)

ROW 5: Yarn over, k5, yarn over. (7 stitches)

ROW 7: Yarn over, k7, yarn over. (9 stitches)

ROW 9: Yarn over, k1, yarn over, k2, s2kp2 (page 282), k2, yarn over, k1, yarn over. (11 stitches)

ROW 11: Yarn over, k3, yarn over, k1, s2kp2, k1, yarn over, k3, yarn over. (13 stitches)

ROW 13: Yarn over, k5, yarn over, s2kp2, yarn over, k5, yarn over. (15 stitches)

ROW 15: Yarn over, purl across to the marker, ending this section with yarn over. (17 stitches)

ROW 16: Knit across.

ROW 17: Yarn over, *k1, yarn over, k6, s2kp2, k6, yarn over; repeat from the * to 1 stitch before the marker, ending this section with k1, yarn over. (19 stitches)

ROW 19: Yarn over, k1, *k2, yarn over, k5, s2kp2, k5, yarn over, k1; repeat from the * to 2 stitches before the marker, ending this section with k2, yarn over. (21 stitches)

ROW 21: Yarn over, k2, *k3, yarn over, k4, s2kp2, k4, yarn over, k2; repeat from the * to 3 stitches before the marker, ending this section with k3, yarn over. (23 stitches)

ROW 23: Yarn over, k3, *k4, yarn over, k3, s2kp2, k3, yarn over, k3; repeat from the * to 4 stitches before the marker, ending this section with k4, yarn over. (25 stitches)

ROW 25: Yarn over, k4, *k5, yarn over, k2, s2kp2, k2, yarn over, k4; repeat from the * to 5 stitches before the marker, ending this section with k5, yarn over. (27 stitches)

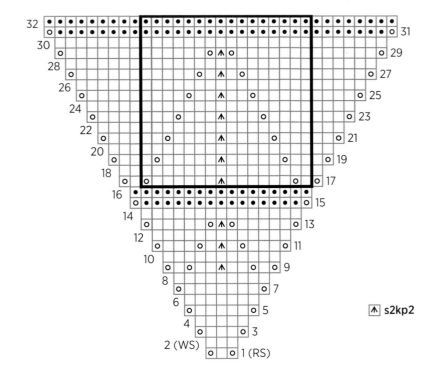

⊼ s2kp2

ROW 27: Yarn over, k5, *k6, yarn over, k1, s2kp2, k1, yarn over, k5; repeat from the * to 6 stitches before the marker, ending this section with k6, yarn over. (29 stitches)

ROW 29: Yarn over, k6, *k7, yarn over, s2kp2, yarn over, k6; repeat from the * to 7 stitches before the marker, ending this section with k7, yarn over. (31 stitches)

ROW 31: Yarn over, purl across to the marker, yarn over. (33 stitches)

ROW 32: Knit across.

Repeat Rows 17–32 for the pattern.

SHAWL #6
Adding colored stripes makes any shawl more playful. See page 273 for instructions.

117

ROW 1 (RS): Yarn over, k1, yarn over. (3 stitches)

ROW 2 AND ALL WS ROWS: Purl across.

ROW 3: Yarn over, k3, yarn over. (5 stitches)

ROW 5: Yarn over, k2tog, yarn over, k1, yarn over, ssk, yarn over. (7 stitches)

ROW 7: Yarn over, k2tog, (k1, yarn over) twice, k1, ssk, yarn over. (9 stitches)

ROW 9: Yarn over, k2tog, k2, yarn over, k1, yarn over, k2, ssk, yarn over. (11 stitches)

ROW 11: Yarn over, k2tog, k3, yarn over, k1, yarn over, k3, ssk, yarn over. (13 stitches)

ROW 13: Yarn over, k2tog, k4, yarn over, k1, yarn over, k4, ssk, yarn over. (15 stitches)

ROW 15: Yarn over, k2tog, k5, yarn over, k1, yarn over, k5, ssk, yarn over. (17 stitches)

ROW 17: Yarn over, *k1, yarn over, k6, s2kp2 (page 282), k6, yarn over; repeat from the * to 1 stitch before the marker, ending this section with k1, yarn over. (19 stitches)

ROW 19: Yarn over, k1, *k1, yarn over, k6, s2kp2, k6, yarn over; repeat from the * to 2 stitches before the marker, ending this section with k2, yarn over. (21 stitches)

ROW 21: Yarn over, k2, *k1, yarn over, k6, s2kp2, k6, yarn over; repeat from the * to 3 stitches before the marker, ending this section with k3, yarn over. (23 stitches)

ROW 23: Yarn over, k3, *k1, yarn over, k6, s2kp2, k6, yarn over; repeat from the * to 4 stitches before the marker, ending this section with k4, yarn over. (25 stitches)

ROW 25: Yarn over, k4, *k2tog, k6, yarn over, k1, yarn over, k6; repeat from the * to 6 stitches before the marker, ending this section with ssk, k4, yarn over. (27 stitches)

ROW 27: Yarn over, k5, *k2tog, k6, yarn over, k1, yarn over, k6; repeat from the * to 7 stitches before the marker, ending this section with ssk, k5, yarn over. (29 stitches)

ROW 29: Yarn over, k6, *k2tog, k6, yarn over, k1, yarn over, k6; repeat from the * to 8 stitches before the marker, ending this section with ssk, k6, yarn over. (31 stitches)

ROW 31: Yarn over, k7, *k2tog, k6, yarn over, k1, yarn over, k6; repeat from the * to 9 stitches before the marker, ending this section with ssk, k7, yarn over. (33 stitches)

ROW 33: Yarn over, k2tog, k6, yarn over, *k1, yarn over, k6, s2kp2, k6, yarn over; repeat from the * to 9 stitches before the marker, ending this section with k1, yarn over, k6, ssk, yarn over. (35 stitches)

ROW 35: Yarn over, k1, k2tog, k6, yarn over, *k1, yarn over, k6, s2kp2, k6, yarn over; repeat from the * to 10 stitches before the marker, ending this section with k1, yarn over, k6, ssk, k1, yarn over. (37 stitches)

ROW 37: Yarn over, k2, k2tog, k6, yarn over, *k1, yarn over, k6, s2kp2, k6, yarn over; repeat from the * to 11 stitches before the marker, ending this section with k1, yarn over, k6, ssk, k2, yarn over. (39 stitches)

ROW 39: Yarn over, k3, k2tog, k6, yarn over, *k1, yarn over, k6, s2kp2, k6, yarn over; repeat from the * to 12 stitches before the marker, ending this section with k1, yarn over, k6, ssk, k3, yarn over. (41 stitches)

ROW 41: Yarn over, k5, yarn over, k6, *s2kp2, k6, yarn over, k1, yarn over, k6; repeat from the * to 14 stitches before the marker, ending this section with s2kp2, k6, yarn over, k5, yarn over. (43 stitches)

ROW 43: Yarn over, k6, yarn over, k6, *s2kp2, k6, yarn over, k1, yarn over, k6; repeat from the * to 15 stitches before the marker, ending this section with s2kp2, k6, yarn over, k6, yarn over. (45 stitches)

ROW 45: Yarn over, k7, yarn over, k6, *s2kp2, k6, yarn over, k1, yarn over, k6; repeat from the * to 16 stitches before the marker, ending this section with s2kp2, k6, yarn over, k7, yarn over. (47 stitches)

ROW 47: Yarn over, k8, yarn over, k6, *s2kp2, k6, yarn over, k1, yarn over, k6; repeat from the * to 17 stitches before the marker, ending this section with s2kp2, k6, yarn over, k8, yarn over. (49 stitches)

ROW 48: As Row 2.

Repeat Rows 17–48 for the pattern.

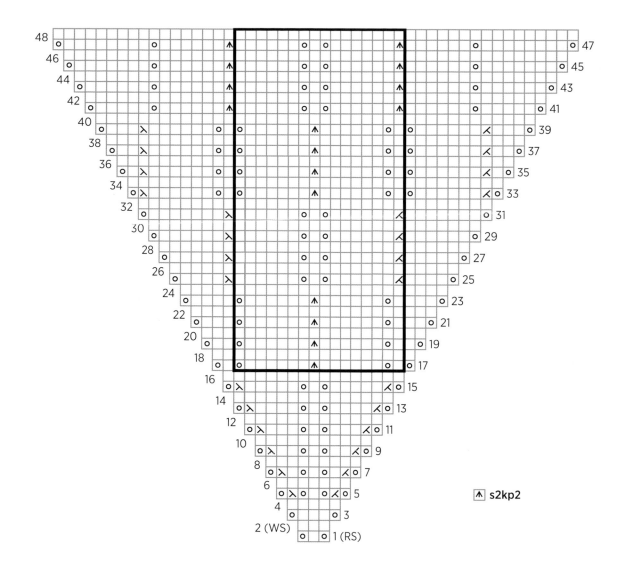

⩓ s2kp2

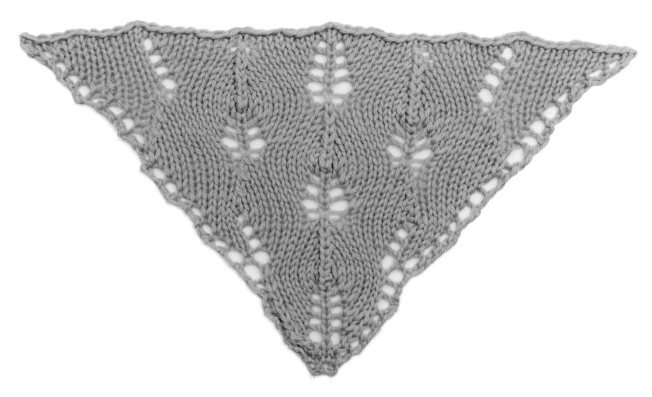

118

ROW 1 (RS): Yarn over, k1, yarn over. (3 stitches)

ROWS 2, 4, AND 6: Purl across.

ROW 3: Yarn over, k3, yarn over. (5 stitches)

ROW 5: Yarn over, k5, yarn over. (7 stitches)

ROW 7: Yarn over, k2, yarn over, s2kp2 (page 282), yarn over, k2, yarn over. (9 stitches)

ROW 8: K1, p7, k1.

ROW 9: Yarn over, p1, k7, p1, yarn over. (11 stitches)

ROW 10: K2, p7, k2.

ROW 11: Yarn over, p2, yarn over, ssk, k3, k2tog, yarn over, p2, yarn over. (13 stitches)

ROW 12: K3, p7, k3.

ROW 13: Yarn over, p3, k1, yarn over, ssk, k1, k2tog, yarn over, k1, p3, yarn over. (15 stitches)

ROWS 14, 16, 18, 26, 28, 30, 32, 34, 36, 38, 46, 48, 50, 58, 60, AND 62: Knit the knit stitches and purl the purl stitches and yarn overs.

ROW 15: Yarn over, k1, p3, k2, yarn over, s2kp2, yarn over, k2, p3, k1, yarn over. (17 stitches)

ROW 17: Yarn over, k2, p3, k7, p3, k2, yarn over. (19 stitches)

ROW 19: Yarn over, k3, p3, yarn over, ssk, k3, k2tog, yarn over, p3, k3, yarn over. (21 stitches)

ROW 20: K1, p3, k3, p7, k3, p3, k1.

ROW 21: Yarn over, p1, yarn over, s2kp2, yarn over, p3, k1, yarn over, ssk, k1, k2tog, yarn over, k1, p3, yarn over, s2kp2, yarn over, p1, yarn over. (23 stitches)

ROW 22: K2, p3, k3, p7, k3, p3, k2.

ROW 23: Yarn over, p2, yarn over, s2kp2, yarn over, p3, k2, yarn over, s2kp2, yarn over, k2, p3, yarn over, s2kp2, yarn over, p2, yarn over. (25 stitches)

ROW 24: K3, p3, k3, p7, k3, p3, k3.

ROW 25: Yarn over, p3, yarn over, s2kp2, yarn over, p3, k7, p3, yarn over, s2kp2, yarn over, p3, yarn over. (27 stitches)

ROW 27: Yarn over, k1, p3, yarn over, s2kp2, yarn over, p3, yarn over, ssk, k3, k2tog, yarn over, p3, yarn over, s2kp2, yarn over, p3, k1, yarn over. (29 sts)

ROW 29: Yarn over, k2, p3, yarn over, s2kp2, yarn over, p3, k1, yarn over, ssk, k1, k2tog, yarn over, k1, p3, yarn over, s2kp2, yarn over, p3, k2, yarn over. (31 stitches)

ROW 31: Yarn over, k3, p3, yarn over, s2kp2, yarn over, p3, k2, yarn over, s2kp2, yarn over, k2, p3, yarn over, s2kp2, yarn over, p3, k3, yarn over. (33 stitches)

ROW 33: Yarn over, k4, p3, yarn over, *s2kp2, yarn over, p3, k7, p3, yarn over; repeat from the * to 10 stitches before the marker, ending this section with s2kp2, yarn over, p3, k4, yarn over. (35 stitches)

ROW 35: Yarn over, k3, k2tog, yarn over, p3, yarn over, *s2kp2, yarn over, p3, yarn over, ssk, k3, k2tog, yarn over, p3, yarn over; repeat from the * to 11 stitches before the marker, ending this section with s2kp2, yarn over, p3, yarn over, ssk, k3, yarn over. (37 stitches)

ROW 37: Yarn over, k3, k2tog, yarn over, k1, p3, yarn over, *s2kp2, yarn over, p3, k1, yarn over, ssk, k1, k2tog, yarn over, k1, p3, yarn over; repeat from the * to 12 stitches before the marker, ending this section with s2kp2, yarn over, p3, k1, yarn over, ssk, k3, yarn over. (39 stitches)

ROW 39: Yarn over, k2, yarn over, s2kp2, yarn over, k2, p3, yarn over, *s2kp2, yarn over, p3, k2, yarn over, s2kp2, yarn over, k2, p3, yarn over; repeat from the * to 13 stitches before the marker, ending this section with s2kp2, yarn over, p3, k2, yarn over, s2kp2, yarn over, k2, yarn over. (41 stitches)

ROW 40: K1, p7, k3, p2, *p1, k3, p7, k3, p2; repeat from the * to 12 stitches before the marker, ending this section with p1, k3, p7, k1.

(continued on page 209)

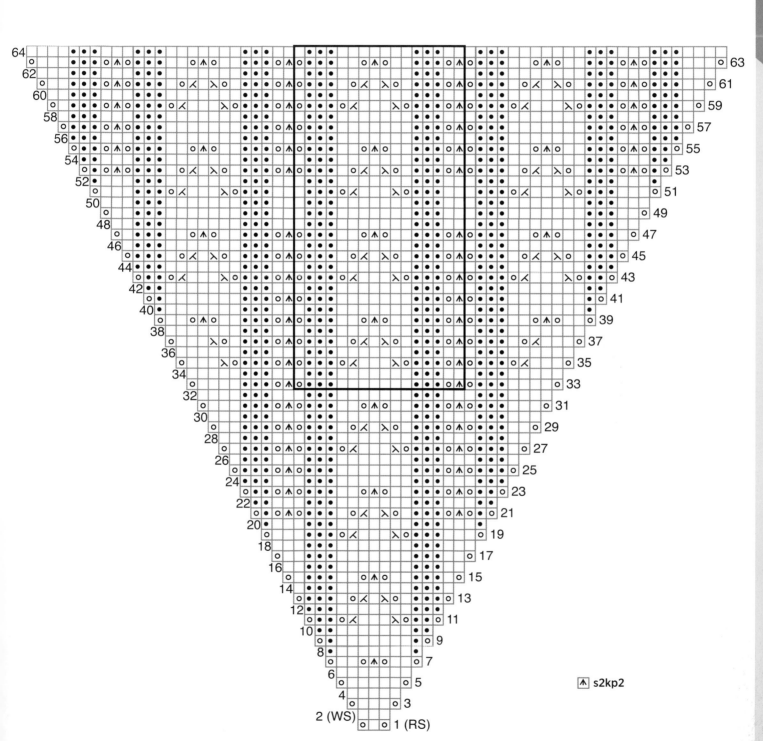

⊼ s2kp2

SHAWL #5

In this shawl, it's easy to see how the pattern orientation is reversed when worn. See page 272 for instructions.

ROW 41: Yarn over, p1, k7, p3, yarn over, *s2kp2, yarn over, p3, k7, p3, yarn over; repeat from the * to 14 stitches before the marker, ending this section with s2kp2, yarn over, p3, k7, p1, yarn over. (43 stitches)

ROW 42: K2, p7, k3, p2, *p1, k3, p7, k3, p2; repeat from the * to 13 stitches before the marker, ending this section with p1, k3, p7, k2.

ROW 43: Yarn over, p2, yarn over, ssk, k3, k2tog, yarn over, p3, yarn over, *s2kp2, yarn over, p3, yarn over, ssk, k3, k2tog, yarn over, p3, yarn over; repeat from the * to 15 stitches before the marker, ending this section with s2kp2, yarn over, p3, yarn over, ssk, k3, k2tog, yarn over, p2, yarn over. (45 stitches)

ROW 44: K3, p7, k3, p2, *p1, k3, p7, k3, p2; repeat from the * to 14 stitches before the marker, ending this section with p1, k3, p7, k3.

ROW 45: Yarn over, p3, k1, yarn over, ssk, k1, k2tog, yarn over, k1, p3, yarn over, *s2kp2, yarn over, p3, k1, yarn over, ssk, k1, k2tog, yarn over, k1, p3, yarn over; repeat from the * to 16 stitches before the marker, ending this section with s2kp2, yarn over, p3, k1, yarn over, ssk, k1, k2tog, yarn over, k1, p3, yarn over. (47 stitches)

ROW 47: Yarn over, k1, p3, k2, yarn over, s2kp2, yarn over, k2, p3, yarn over, *s2kp2, yarn over, p3, k2, yarn over, s2kp2, yarn over, k2, p3, yarn over; repeat from the * to 17 stitches before the marker, ending this section with s2kp2, yarn over, p3, k2, yarn over, s2kp2, yarn over, k2, p3, k1, yarn over. (49 stitches)

ROW 49: Yarn over, k2, p3, k7, p3, yarn over, *s2kp2, yarn over, p3, k7, p3, yarn over; repeat from the * to 18 stitches before the marker, ending this section with s2kp2, yarn over, p3, k7, p3, k2, yarn over. (51 stitches)

ROW 51: Yarn over, k3, p3, yarn over, ssk, k3, k2tog, yarn over, p3, yarn over, *s2kp2, yarn over, p3, yarn over, ssk, k3, k2tog, yarn over, p3, yarn over; repeat from the * to 19 stitches before the marker, ending this section with s2kp2, yarn over, p3, yarn over, ssk, k3, k2tog, yarn over, p3, k3, yarn over. (53 stitches)

ROW 52: K1, p3, k3, p7, k3, p2, *p1, k3, p7, k3, p2; repeat from the * to 18 stitches before the marker, ending this section with p1, k3, p7, k3, p3, k1.

ROW 53: Yarn over, p1, yarn over, s2kp2, yarn over, p3, k1, yarn over, ssk, k1, k2tog, yarn over, k1, p3, yarn over, *s2kp2, yarn over, p3, k1, yarn over, ssk, k1, k2tog, yarn over, k1, p3, yarn over; repeat from the * to 20 stitches before the marker, ending this section with s2kp2, yarn over, p3, k1, yarn over, ssk, k1, k2tog, yarn over, k1, p3, yarn over, s2kp2, yarn over, p1, yarn over. (55 stitches)

ROW 54: K2, p3, k3, p7, k3, p2, *p1, k3, p7, k3, p2; repeat from the * to 19 stitches before the marker, ending this section with p1, k3, p7, k3, p3, k2.

ROW 55: Yarn over, p2, yarn over, s2kp2, yarn over, p3, k2, yarn over, s2kp2, yarn over, k2, p3, yarn over, *s2kp2, yarn over, p3, k2, yarn over, s2kp2, yarn over, k2, p3, yarn over; repeat from the * to 21 stitches before the marker, ending this section with s2kp2, yarn over, p3, k2, yarn over, s2kp2, yarn over, k2, p3, yarn over, s2kp2, yarn over, p2, yarn over. (57 stitches)

ROW 56: K3, p3, k3, p7, k3, p2, *p1, k3, p7, k3, p2; repeat from the * to 20 stitches before the marker, ending this section with p1, k3, p7, k3, p3, k3.

ROW 57: Yarn over, p3, yarn over, s2kp2, yarn over, p3, k7, p3, yarn over, *s2kp2, yarn over, p3, k7, p3, yarn over; repeat from the * to 22 stitches before the marker, ending this section with s2kp2, yarn over, p3, k7, p3, yarn over, s2kp2, yarn over, p3, yarn over. (59 stitches)

ROW 59: Yarn over, k1, p3, yarn over, s2kp2, yarn over, p3, yarn over, ssk, k3, k2tog, yarn over, p3, yarn over, *s2kp2, yarn over, p3, yarn over, ssk, k3, k2tog, yarn over, p3, yarn over; repeat from the * to 23 stitches before the marker, ending this section with s2kp2, yarn over, p3, yarn over, ssk, k3, k2tog, yarn over, p3, yarn over, s2kp2, yarn over, p3, k1, yarn over. (61 stitches)

ROW 61: Yarn over, k2, p3, yarn over, s2kp2, yarn over, p3, k1, yarn over, ssk, k1, k2tog, yarn over, k1, p3, yarn over, *s2kp2, yarn over, p3, k1, yarn over, ssk, k1, k2tog, yarn over, k1, p3, yarn over; repeat from the * to 24 stitches before the marker, ending this section with s2kp2, yarn over, p3, k1, yarn over, ssk, k1, k2tog, yarn over, k1, p3, yarn over, s2kp2, yarn over, p3, k2, yarn over. (63 stitches)

ROW 63: Yarn over, k3, p3, yarn over, s2kp2, yarn over, p3, k2, yarn over, s2kp2, yarn over, k2, p3, yarn over, *s2kp2, yarn over, p3, k2, yarn over, s2kp2, yarn over, k2, p3, yarn over; repeat from the * to 25 stitches before the marker, ending this section with s2kp2, yarn over, p3, k2, yarn over, s2kp2, yarn over, k2, p3, yarn over, s2kp2, yarn over, p3, k3, yarn over. (65 stitches)

ROW 64: As Row 14.

Repeat Rows 33–64 for the pattern.

HORIZONTAL INSERTIONS

Use these patterns as a single repeat to set off other simple and lace patterns. No stitch counts are given at the end of the rows because the number of stitches you incorporate into any horizontal insertion depends on your custom shawl design. As always, though, be sure to start with the correct multiple of stitches per section plus 1 (see Accounting for Multiples, page 8).

NOTE: The swatch photographs in this section show the horizontal insertions how you'll knit them. On the finished shawl, the orientation of the insertion will be reversed. (To understand why, see page 15.) In the photos, each horizontal insertion pattern is shown on a stockinette background.

119

ROWS 1, 3, 9, AND 11 (RS): Yarn over, knit across to the marker, ending this section with yarn over.

ROWS 2, 4, 8, AND 10: Knit across.

ROW 5: Yarn over, ssk, yarn over, *ssk, yarn over; repeat from the * to 3 stitches before the marker, ending this section with ssk, yarn over, k1, yarn over.

ROWS 6: Purl across.

ROW 7: (Yarn over, ssk) twice, *yarn over, ssk; repeat from the * to 3 stitches before the marker, ending this section with yarn over, ssk, yarn over, k1, yarn over.

ROW 12: As Row 6.

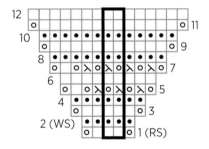

120

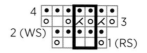

ROW 1 (RS): Yarn over, knit across to the marker, ending this section with yarn over.

ROW 2: Knit across.

ROW 3: Yarn over, k2tog, *yarn over, k2tog; repeat from the * to 1 stitch before the marker, ending this section with k1, yarn over.

ROW 4: As Row 2.

121

ROW 1 (RS): Yarn over, knit across to the marker, ending this section with k1, yarn over.

ROW 2: Knit across.

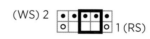

ROW 1 (RS): Yarn over, *(k2tog, yarn over) twice; repeat from the * to 1 stitch before the marker, ending this section with k1, yarn over.

ROW 2 AND ALL WS ROWS: Purl across.

ROWS 3 AND 17: Yarn over, knit across to the marker, ending this section with yarn over.

ROW 5: Yarn over, k2, *k1, k2tog, yarn over, k1; repeat from the * to 3 stitches before the marker, ending this section with k3, yarn over.

ROW 7: Yarn over, k3, *k2tog, yarn over, k2; repeat from the * to 4 stitches before the marker, ending this section with k2tog, yarn over, k2, yarn over.

ROW 9: Yarn over, k3, k2tog, *yarn over, k2, k2tog; repeat from the * to 4 stitches before the marker, ending this section with yarn over, k4, yarn over.

ROW 11: Yarn over, k4, yarn over, *ssk, k2, yarn over; repeat from the * to 7 stitches before the marker, ending this section with ssk, k2, yarn over, ssk, k1, yarn over.

ROW 13: Yarn over, k2, yarn over, ssk, k2, *yarn over, ssk, k2; repeat from the * to 7 stitches before the marker, ending this section with yarn over, ssk, k2, yarn over, ssk, k1, yarn over.

ROW 15: Yarn over, k4, yarn over, ssk, k1, *k1, yarn over, ssk, k1; repeat from the * to 8 stitches before the marker, ending this section with k1, yarn over, ssk, k2, yarn over, ssk, k1, yarn over.

ROW 19: (Yarn over, k2tog) 5 times, *(yarn over, k2tog) twice; repeat from the * to 9 stitches before the marker, ending this section with (yarn over, k2tog) 4 times, yarn over, k1, yarn over.

ROW 20: As Row 2.

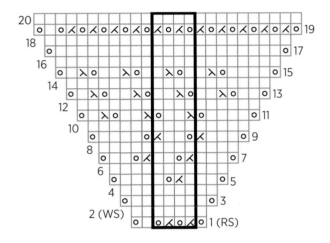

SHAWL #13
Bold color choices
make this piece
stand out from
the crowd. See
page 275 for
instructions.

123

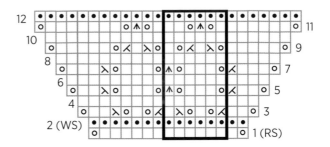

ROW 1 (RS): Yarn over, knit across to the marker, yarn over.

ROW 2: Knit across.

ROW 3: Yarn over, k2, *k2tog, yarn over, k1, yarn over, ssk, k1; repeat from the * to 7 stitches before the marker, ending this section with k2tog, yarn over, k1, yarn over, ssk, k2, yarn over.

ROWS 4, 6, 8, AND 10: Purl across.

ROW 5: Yarn over, k2, k2tog, *yarn over, k3, yarn over, s2kp2 (page 282); repeat from the * to 7 stitches before the marker, ending this section with yarn over, k3, yarn over, ssk, k2, yarn over.

ROW 7: Yarn over, k3, k2tog, *yarn over, k3, yarn over, s2kp2; repeat from the * to 8 stitches before the marker, ending this section with yarn over, k3, yarn over, ssk, k3, yarn over.

ROW 9: Yarn over, k5, *yarn over, ssk, k1, k2tog, yarn over, k1; repeat from the * to 10 stitches before the marker, ending this section with yarn over, ssk, k1, k2tog, yarn over, k5, yarn over.

ROW 11: Yarn over, k6, *k1, yarn over, s2kp2, yarn over, k2; repeat from the * to 11 stitches before the marker, ending this section with k1, yarn over, s2kp2, yarn over, k7, yarn over.

ROW 12: As Row 2.

⋀ s2kp2

214

124

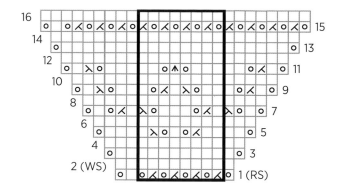

ROW 1 (RS): Yarn over, *(k2tog, yarn over) 4 times; repeat from the * to 1 stitch before the marker, ending this section with k1, yarn over.

ROW 2 AND ALL WS ROWS: Purl across.

ROWS 3 AND 13: Yarn over, knit across to the marker, ending this section with yarn over.

ROW 5: Yarn over, k2, *k2, k2tog, yarn over, k1, yarn over, ssk, k1; repeat from the * to 3 stitches before the marker, ending this section with k3, yarn over.

ROW 7: Yarn over, k1, yarn over, ssk, *k1, k2tog, yarn over, k3, yarn over, ssk; repeat from the * to 4 stitches before the marker, ending this section with k1, k2tog, yarn over, k1, yarn over.

ROW 9: Yarn over, k1, k2tog, yarn over, k1, *k2, yarn over, ssk, k1, k2tog, yarn over, k1; repeat from the * to 5 stitches before the marker, ending this section with k2, yarn over, ssk, k1, yarn over.

ROW 11: Yarn over, k1, k2tog, yarn over, k2, *k3, yarn over, s2kp2 (page 282), yarn over, k2; repeat from the * to 6 stitches before the marker, ending this section with k3, yarn over, ssk, k1, yarn over. (13 stitches)

ROW 15: Yarn over, *k2tog, yarn over; repeat from the * to 1 stitch before the marker, ending this section with k1, yarn over.

ROW 16: As Row 2.

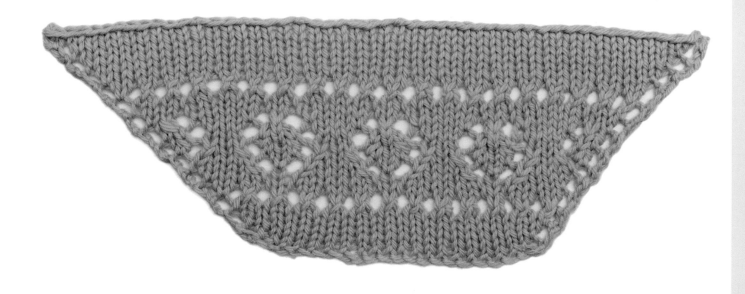

⊼ s2kp2

125

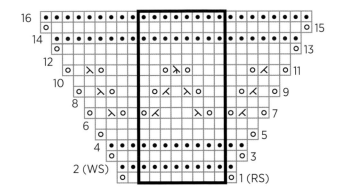

ROWS 1, 3, 5, 13, AND 15 (RS): Yarn over, knit across to the marker, ending this section with yarn over.

ROWS 2, 4, AND 14: Knit across.

ROWS 6, 8, 10, AND 12: Purl across.

ROW 7: Yarn over, k1, k2tog, yarn over, *k1, yarn over, ssk, k3, k2tog, yarn over; repeat from the * to 4 stitches before the marker, ending this section with k1, yarn over, ssk, k1, yarn over.

ROW 9: Yarn over, k1, k2tog, yarn over, k1, *k2, yarn over, ssk, k1, k2tog, yarn over, k1; repeat from the * to 5 stitches before the marker, ending this section with k2, yarn over, ssk, k1, yarn over.

ROW 11: Yarn over, k1, k2tog, yarn over, k2, *k3, yarn over, sssk (page 285), yarn over, k2; repeat from the * to 6 stitches before the marker, ending this section with k3, yarn over, ssk, k1, yarn over.

ROW 16: As Row 2.

⅄ sssk

216

126

ROWS 1, 5, AND 13 (RS): Yarn over, knit across to the marker, ending this section with yarn over.

ROWS 2, 4, AND 14: Knit across.

ROW 3: Yarn over, k2tog, *(yarn over, k2tog) 4 times; repeat from the * to 1 stitch before the marker, ending this section with yarn over, k1, yarn over.

ROWS 6, 8, 10, AND 12: Purl across.

ROW 7: Yarn over, k3, *k2, ssk, yarn over, k1, yarn over, k2tog, k1; repeat from the * to 4 stitches before the marker, ending this section with k4, yarn over.

ROW 9: Yarn over, k4, *k1, ssk, yarn over, k3, yarn over, k2tog; repeat from the * to 5 stitches before the marker, ending this section with k5, yarn over.

ROW 11: Yarn over, k5, *k3, yarn over, s2kp2 (page 282), yarn over, k2; repeat from the * to 6 stitches, ending this section with k6, yarn over.

ROW 15: (Yarn over, k2tog) 4 times, *(yarn over, k2tog) 4 times; repeat from the * to 7 stitches before the marker, ending this section with (yarn over, k2tog) 3 times, yarn over, k1, yarn over.

ROW 16: As Row 2.

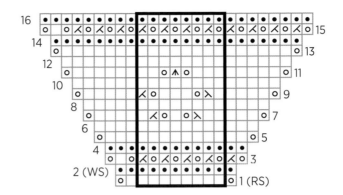

⬆ s2kp2

127

ROW 1 (RS): Yarn over, *k3, k2tog, yarn over, k3; repeat from the * to 1 stitch before the marker, ending this section with k1, yarn over.

ROW 2 AND ALL WS ROWS: Purl across.

ROW 3: Yarn over, k1, *k2, k2tog, yarn over, k1, yarn over, ssk, k1; repeat from the * to 2 stitches before the marker, ending this section with k2, yarn over.

ROW 5: Yarn over, k2, *k1, k2tog, yarn over, k3, yarn over, ssk; repeat from the * to 3 stitches before the marker, ending this section with k3, yarn over.

ROW 7: Yarn over, k2, yarn over, *s2kp2 (page 282), yarn over, k5, yarn over; repeat from the * to 5 stitches before the marker, ending this section with s2kp2, yarn over, k2, yarn over.

ROW 9: Yarn over, k3, k2tog, *yarn over, k6, k2tog; repeat from the * to 4 stitches before the marker, ending this section with yarn over, k4, yarn over.

ROW 11: Yarn over, k5, *k1, yarn over, ssk, k3, k2tog, yarn over; repeat from the * to 6 stitches before the marker, ending this section with k6, yarn over.

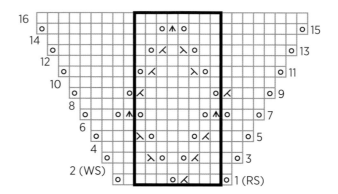

⤒ s2kp2

ROW 13: Yarn over, k6, *k2, yarn over, ssk, k1, k2tog, yarn over, k1; repeat from the * to 7 stitches before the marker, ending this section with k7, yarn over.

ROW 15: Yarn over, k7, *k3, yarn over, s2kp2, yarn over, k2; repeat from the * to 8 stitches before the marker, ending this section with k8, yarn over.

ROW 16: As Row 2.

128

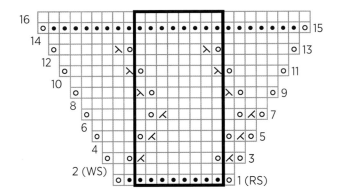

ROWS 1 AND 15 (RS): Yarn over, purl across to the marker, yarn over.

ROW 2 AND ALL WS ROWS: Purl across.

ROW 3: Yarn over, k2tog, *yarn over, k6, k2tog; repeat from the * to 1 stitch before the marker, ending this section with yarn over, k1, yarn over.

ROW 5: Yarn over, k2tog, yarn over, *k6, k2tog, yarn over; repeat from the * to 3 stitches before the marker, ending this section with k3, yarn over.

ROW 7: Yarn over, k2tog, yarn over, k1, *k5, k2tog, yarn over, k1; repeat from the * to 4 stitches before the marker, ending this section with k4, yarn over.

ROW 9: Yarn over, k2, yarn over, ssk, *k6, yarn over, ssk; repeat from the * to 5 stitches before the marker, ending this section with k5, yarn over.

ROW 11: Yarn over, k4, yarn over, *ssk, k6, yarn over; repeat from the * to 7 stitches before the marker, ending this section with ssk, k5, yarn over.

ROW 13: Yarn over, k6, *yarn over, ssk, k6; repeat from the * to 7 stitches before the marker, ending this section with yarn over, ssk, k5, yarn over.

ROW 16: As Row 2.

129

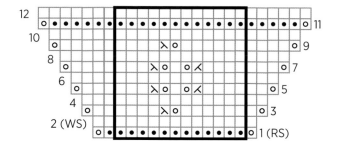

ROWS 1 AND 11 (RS): Yarn over, purl across to the marker, ending this section with yarn over.

ROW 2 AND ALL WS ROWS: Purl across.

ROW 3: Yarn over, k1, *k6, yarn over, ssk, k4; repeat from the * to 2 stitches before the marker, ending this section with k2, yarn over.

ROW 5: Yarn over, k2, *k4, k2tog, yarn over, k1, yarn over, ssk, k3; repeat from the * to 3 stitches before the marker, ending this section with k3, yarn over.

ROW 7: Yarn over, k3, *k4, k2tog, yarn over, k1, yarn over, ssk, k3; repeat from the * to 4 stitches before the marker, ending this section with k4, yarn over.

ROW 9: Yarn over, k4, *k6, yarn over, ssk, k4; repeat from the * to 5 stitches before the marker, ending this section with k5, yarn over.

ROW 12: As Row 2.

130

ROW 1 (RS): Yarn over, *k1, yarn over, ssk, k7, k2tog, yarn over; repeat from the * to 1 stitch before the marker, ending this section with k1, yarn over.

ROW 2 AND ALL WS ROWS: Purl across.

ROW 3: Yarn over, k1, *k2, yarn over, ssk, k5, k2tog, yarn over, k1; repeat from the * to 2 stitches before the marker, ending this section with k2, yarn over.

ROW 5: Yarn over, k2, *k3, yarn over, ssk, k3, k2tog, yarn over, k2; repeat from the * to 3 stitches before the marker, ending this section with k3, yarn over.

ROW 7: Yarn over, k3, *k4, yarn over, ssk, k1, k2tog, yarn over, k3; repeat from the * to 4 stitches before the marker, ending this section with k4, yarn over.

ROW 9: Yarn over, k4, *k5, yarn over, s2kp2 (page 282), yarn over, k4; repeat from the * to 5 stitches before the marker, ending this section with k5, yarn over.

ROW 11: Yarn over, k5, *k6, yarn over, ssk, k4; repeat from the * to 6 stitches before the marker, ending this section with k6, yarn over.

ROW 12: As Row 2.

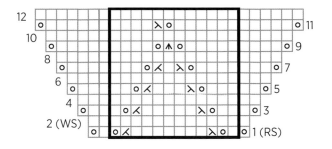

⩗ s2kp2

131

ROWS 1 AND 13 (RS): Yarn over, purl across to the marker, yarn over.

ROW 2: Knit across.

ROW 3: Yarn over, k1, *k2, (yarn over, ssk) twice, yarn over, s2kp2 (page 282), (yarn over, k2tog) twice, yarn over, k1; repeat from the * to 2 stitches before the marker, ending this section with k2, yarn over.

ROWS 4, 6, 8, 10, AND 12: Purl across.

ROW 5: Yarn over, k2tog, yarn over, *k1, (yarn over, ssk) twice, k1, yarn over, s2kp2, yarn over, k1, (k2tog, yarn over) twice; repeat from the * to 3 stitches before the marker, ending this section with k1, yarn over, ssk, yarn over.

ROW 7: Yarn over, k2tog, yarn over, k1, *k2, (yarn over, ssk) twice, yarn over, s2kp2, (yarn over, k2tog) twice, yarn over, k1; repeat from the * to 4 stitches before the marker, ending this section with k2, yarn over, ssk, yarn over.

ROW 9: Yarn over, (k2tog, yarn over) twice, *k1, (yarn over, ssk) twice, k1, yarn over, s2kp2, yarn over, k1, (k2tog, yarn over) twice; repeat from the * to 5 stitches before the marker, ending this section with k1, (yarn over, ssk) twice, yarn over.

ROW 11: Yarn over, (k2tog, yarn over) twice, k1, *k2, (yarn over, ssk) twice, yarn over, s2kp2, (yarn over, k2tog) twice, yarn over, k1; repeat from the * to 6 stitches before the marker, ending this section with k2, (yarn over, ssk) twice, yarn over.

ROW 14: As Row 2.

⚠ s2kp2

VERTICAL INSERTIONS

Highlight simple fabrics or even other lace patterns with these lacy panels.
A vertical insertion may be used in place of a spine stitch between two wedges.

132

ROW 1 (RS): K2tog, yarn over, k1, yarn over, ssk.

ROW 2 AND ALL WS ROWS: Purl across.

ROW 3: K1, yarn over, s2kp2 (page 282), yarn over, k1.

ROW 4: As Row 2.

Repeat Rows 1–4 for the pattern.

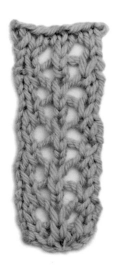

133

ROW 1 (RS): K1, yarn over, k2, s2kp2 (page 282), k2, yarn over, k1.

ROW 2 AND ALL WS ROWS: Purl across.

ROW 3: K2, yarn over, k1, s2kp2, k1, yarn over, k2.

ROW 5: K3, yarn over, s2kp2, yarn over, k3.

ROW 6: As Row 2.

Repeat Rows 1–6 for the pattern.

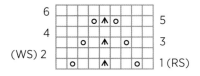

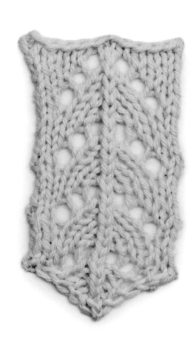

△ s2kp2
(applies to both patterns on this page)

134

ROWS 1, 3, AND 5 (RS): P1, ssk, k2, yarn over, k1, yarn over, k2, k2tog, p1.

ROW 2 AND ALL WS ROWS: Knit the knit stitches and purl the purl stitches and yarn overs.

ROW 7: P1, yarn over, ssk, k5, k2tog, yarn over, p1.

ROW 9: P1, k1, yarn over, ssk, k3, k2tog, yarn over, k1, p1.

ROW 11: P1, k2, yarn over, ssk, k1, k2tog, yarn over, k2, p1.

ROW 13: P1, k3, yarn over, sssk (page 285), yarn over, k3, p1.

ROW 14: As Row 2.

Repeat Rows 1–14 for the pattern.

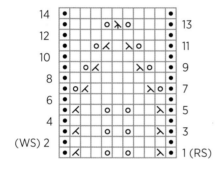

ᐅ **sssk**

135

ROW 1 (RS): K3, k2tog, yarn over, k1, yarn over, ssk, k3.

ROW 2 AND ALL WS ROWS: Knit the knit stitches and purl the purl stitches and yarn overs.

ROW 3: K2, k2tog, yarn over, k3, yarn over, ssk, k2.

ROW 5: K1, k2tog, yarn over, k5, yarn over, ssk, k1.

ROW 7: K2, yarn over, ssk, k3, k2tog, yarn over, k2.

ROW 9: K3, yarn over, ssk, k1, k2tog, yarn over, k3.

ROW 11: K4, yarn over, s2kp2 (page 282), yarn over, k4.

ROW 12: As Row 2.

Repeat Rows 1–12 for the pattern.

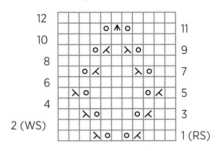

ᐱ **s2kp2**

136

ROW 1 (RS): (K1, yarn over, ssk) twice, k1, (k2tog, yarn over, k1) twice.

ROW 2 AND ALL WS ROWS: Purl across.

ROW 3: K2, yarn over, ssk, k1, yarn over, s2kp2 (page 282), yarn over, k1, k2tog, yarn over, k2.

ROW 5: K3, yarn over, ssk, k3, k2tog, yarn over, k3.

ROW 7: K4, yarn over, ssk, k1, k2tog, yarn over, k4.

ROW 9: K5, yarn over, s2kp2, yarn over, k5.

ROW 10: As Row 2.

Repeat Rows 1–10 for the pattern.

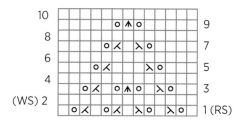

⟑ **s2kp2**

137

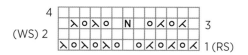

ROW 1 (RS): (K2tog, yarn over) 3 times, k1, (yarn over, ssk) 3 times.

ROW 2: Purl across.

ROW 3: K1, (k2tog, yarn over) twice, k1, nupp (page 279), k1, (yarn over, ssk) twice, k1.

ROW 4: As Row 2.

Repeat Rows 1–4 for the pattern.

N Nupp

138

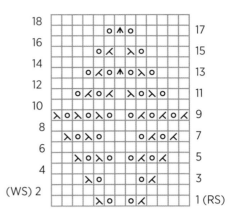

ROW 1 (RS): K4, k2tog, yarn over, k1, yarn over, ssk, k4.

ROW 2 AND ALL WS ROWS: Purl across.

ROW 3: K3, k2tog, yarn over, k3, yarn over, ssk, k3.

ROW 5: K2, (k2tog, yarn over) twice, k1, (yarn over, ssk) twice, k2.

ROW 7: K1, (k2tog, yarn over) twice, k3, (yarn over, ssk) twice, k1.

ROW 9: (K2tog, yarn over) 3 times, k1, (yarn over, ssk) 3 times.

ROW 11: K2, (yarn over, ssk) twice, k1, (k2tog, yarn over) twice, k2.

ROW 13: K3, yarn over, ssk, yarn over, s2kp2 (page 282), yarn over, k2tog, yarn over, k3.

ROW 15: K4, yarn over, ssk, k1, k2tog, yarn over, k4.

ROW 17: K5, yarn over, s2kp2, yarn over, k5.

ROW 18: As Row 2.

Repeat Rows 1–18 for the pattern.

ⴿ **s2kp2**

139

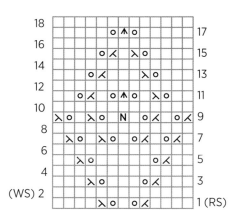

ROW 1 (RS): K4, k2tog, yarn over, k1, yarn over, ssk, k4.

ROW 2 AND ALL WS ROWS: Purl across.

ROW 3: K3, k2tog, yarn over, k3, yarn over, ssk, k3.

ROW 5: K2, k2tog, yarn over, k5, yarn over, ssk, k2.

ROW 7: (K1, k2tog, yarn over) twice, k1, (yarn over, ssk, k1) twice.

ROW 9: (K2tog, yarn over, k1) twice, nupp (page 279), (k1, yarn over, ssk) twice.

ROW 11: K2, yarn over, ssk, k1, yarn over, s2kp2 (page 282), yarn over, k1, k2tog, yarn over, k2.

ROW 13: K3, yarn over, ssk, k3, k2tog, yarn over, k3.

ROW 15: K4, yarn over, ssk, k1, k2tog, yarn over, k4.

ROW 17: K5, yarn over, s2kp2, yarn over, k5.

ROW 18: As Row 2.

Repeat Rows 1–18 for the pattern.

N Nupp

⋀ s2kp2

140

ROW 1 (RS): P1, k3, yarn over, k2, ssk, k1, k2tog, k2, yarn over, p1.

ROW 2 AND ALL WS ROWS: Knit the knit stitches and purl the purl stitches and yarn overs.

ROW 3: P1, k4, yarn over, k2, k3tog, k2, yarn over, k1, p1.

ROW 5: P1, k6, k2tog, k2, yarn over, k2, p1.

ROW 7: P1, yarn over, k2, ssk, k1, k2tog, k2, yarn over, k3, p1.

ROW 9: P1, k1, yarn over, k2, sssk (page 285), k2, yarn over, k4, p1.

ROW 11: P1, k2, yarn over, k2, ssk, k6, p1.

ROW 12: As Row 2.

Repeat Rows 1–12 for the pattern.

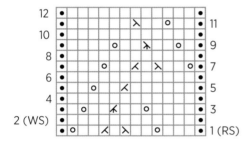

☒ k3tog

☒ sssk

141

NOTE: Two cable needles are used in this pattern.

ROW 1 (RS): K1, yarn over, k2, ssk, k5, k2tog, k2, yarn over, k1.

ROW 2 AND ALL WS ROWS: Purl across.

ROW 3: K2, yarn over, k2, ssk, k3, k2tog, k2, yarn over, k2.

ROW 5: K3, yarn over, k2, ssk, k1, k2tog, k2, yarn over, k3.

ROW 7: K4, yarn over, k2, s2kp2 (page 282), k2, yarn over, k4.

ROW 9: K5, Knitted RC Axis (page 285), k5.

ROW 10: As Row 2.

Repeat Rows 1–10 for the pattern.

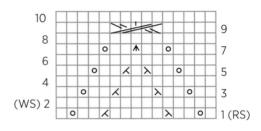

Knitted RC Axis

☒ s2kp2

142

ROW 1 (RS): P1, Right Twist (page 279), p1, yarn over, ssk, k3, k2tog, yarn over, p1, Right Twist, p1.

ROW 2 AND ALL WS ROWS: Knit the knit stitches and purl the purl stitches and yarn overs.

ROW 3: P1, Right Twist, p1, k1, yarn over, ssk, k1, k2tog, yarn over, k1, p1, Right Twist, p1.

ROW 5: P1, Right Twist, p1, k2, yarn over, sssk (page 285), yarn over, k2, p1, Right Twist, p1.

ROW 6: As Row 2.

Repeat Rows 1–6 for the pattern.

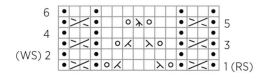

⋏ sssk

⟩⟨ Right Twist

143

ROW 1 (RS): K1, k2tog, yarn over, k1, yarn over, ssk, k5, k2tog, yarn over, k1, yarn over, ssk, k1.

ROW 2 AND ALL WS ROWS: Purl across.

ROW 3: K2tog, yarn over, k1, nupp (page 279), k1, yarn over, ssk, k3, k2tog, yarn over, k1, nupp, k1, yarn over, ssk.

ROW 5: K2, yarn over, s2kp2 (page 282), yarn over, k7, yarn over, s2kp2, yarn over, k2.

ROW 7: K6, k2tog, yarn over, k1, yarn over, ssk, k6.

ROW 9: K5, k2tog, yarn over, k1, nupp, k1, yarn over, ssk, k5.

ROW 11: K7, yarn over, s2kp2, yarn over, k7.

ROW 12: As Row 2.

Repeat Rows 1–12 for the pattern.

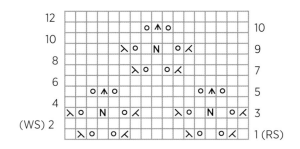

Ⓝ Nupp

⋀ s2kp2

144

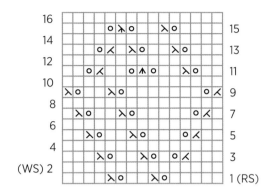

ROW 1 (RS): K5, yarn over, ssk, k2, yarn over, ssk, k4.

ROW 2 AND ALL WS ROWS: Purl across.

ROW 3: K3, k2tog, yarn over, k1, yarn over, ssk, k2, yarn over, ssk, k3.

ROW 5: K2, k2tog, yarn over, k3, yarn over, ssk, k2, yarn over, ssk, k2.

ROW 7: K1, k2tog, yarn over, k5, yarn over, ssk, k2, yarn over, ssk, k1.

ROW 9: K2tog, yarn over, k7, yarn over, ssk, k2, yarn over, ssk.

ROW 11: K2, yarn over, ssk, k2, yarn over, s2kp2 (page 282), yarn over, k2, k2tog, yarn over, k2.

ROW 13: K3, yarn over, ssk, k2, yarn over, ssk, k1, k2tog, yarn over, k3.

ROW 15: K4, yarn over, ssk, k2, yarn over, sssk (page 285), yarn over, k4.

ROW 16: As Row 2.

Repeat Rows 1–16 for the pattern.

↑ s2kp2

⅄ sssk

145

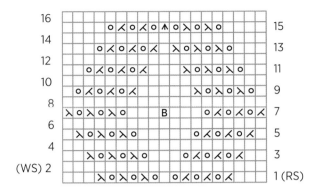

ROW 1 (RS): K3, (k2tog, yarn over) 3 times, k1, (yarn over, ssk) 3 times, k3.

ROW 2 AND ALL WS ROWS: Purl across.

ROW 3: K2, (k2tog, yarn over) 3 times, k3, (yarn over, ssk) 3 times, k2.

ROW 5: K1, (k2tog, yarn over) 3 times, k5, (yarn over, ssk) 3 times, k1.

ROW 7: (K2tog, yarn over) 3 times, k3, bobble (page 279), k3, (yarn over, ssk) 3 times.

ROW 9: K1, (yarn over, ssk) 3 times, k5, (k2tog, yarn over) 3 times, k1.

ROW 11: K2, (yarn over, ssk) 3 times, k3, (k2tog, yarn over) 3 times, k2.

ROW 13: K3, (yarn over, ssk) 3 times, k1, (k2tog, yarn over) 3 times, k3.

ROW 15: K4, (yarn over, ssk) twice, yarn over, s2kp2 (page 282), (yarn over, k2tog) twice, yarn over, k4.

ROW 16: As Row 2.

Repeat Rows 1–16 for the pattern.

B Bobble

↑ s2kp2

146

ROW 1 (RS): K2tog, yarn over, k4, k2tog, yarn over, k1, yarn over, ssk, k2, k2tog, yarn over, k2.

ROW 2 AND ALL WS ROWS: Ssp (page 281), yarn over, p11, ssp, yarn over, p2.

ROW 3: K2tog, yarn over, k3, k2tog, yarn over, k3, yarn over, ssk, k1, k2tog, yarn over, k2.

ROW 5: K2tog, yarn over, k2, k2tog, yarn over, k5, yarn over, ssk, k2tog, yarn over, k2.

ROW 7: K2tog, yarn over, k4, yarn over, ssk, k1, k2tog, yarn over, k2, k2tog, yarn over, k2.

ROW 9: K2tog, yarn over, k5, yarn over, s2kp2 (page 282), yarn over, k3, k2tog, yarn over, k2.

ROW 10: As Row 2.

Repeat Rows 1–10 for the pattern.

⊼ s2kp2

147

ROW 1 (RS): K1, k2tog, yarn over, k2, k2tog, yarn over, k1, yarn over, sssk (page 285), yarn over, k1, yarn over, ssk, k2, yarn over, ssk, k1.

ROW 2 AND ALL WS ROWS: Purl across.

ROW 3: K1, k2tog, k3, yarn over, k2tog, yarn over, k3, yarn over, ssk, yarn over, k3, ssk, k1.

ROW 5: K1, k2tog, k2, yarn over, k2, yarn over, ssk, k1, k2tog, yarn over, k2, yarn over, ssk, k1.

ROW 7: K1, k2tog, k1, yarn over, k3, yarn over, ssk, k1, k2tog, yarn over, k3, yarn over, ssk, k1.

ROW 8: As Row 2.

Repeat Rows 1–8 for the pattern.

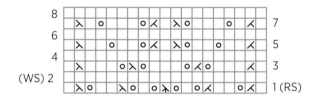

⅄ sssk

148

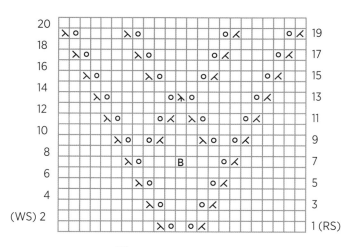

B Bobble   Х sssk

ROW 1 (RS): K9, k2tog, yarn over, k1, yarn over, ssk, k9.

ROW 2 AND ALL WS ROWS: Purl across.

ROW 3: K8, k2tog, yarn over, k3, yarn over, ssk, k8.

ROW 5: K7, k2tog, yarn over, k5, yarn over, ssk, k7.

ROW 7: K6, k2tog, yarn over, k3, bobble (page 279), k3, yarn over, ssk, k6.

ROW 9: K5, k2tog, yarn over, k1, yarn over, ssk, k3, k2tog, yarn over, k1, ssk, k5.

ROW 11: K4, k2tog, yarn over, k3, yarn over, ssk, k1, k2tog, yarn over, k3, yarn over, ssk, k4.

ROW 13: K3, k2tog, yarn over, k5, yarn over, sssk (page 285), yarn over, k5, yarn over, ssk, k3.

ROW 15: K2, k2tog, yarn over, k4, k2tog, yarn over, k3, yarn over, ssk, k4, yarn over, ssk, k2.

ROW 17: K1, k2tog, yarn over, k4, k2tog, yarn over, k5, yarn over, ssk, k4, yarn over, ssk, k1.

ROW 19: K2tog, yarn over, k4, k2tog, yarn over, k7, yarn over, ssk, k4, yarn over, ssk.

ROW 20: As Row 2.

Repeat Rows 1–20 for the pattern.

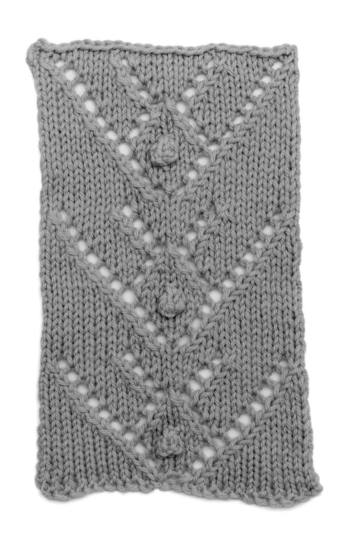

LOWER BORDERS

Decorate your beautiful shawl with one of the following lace borders. You will knit all of the following lower borders in the same direction as the main part of the shawl. Before you begin, don't forget to count the stitches in each section to make sure you have the correct multiple plus one!

NOTE: The swatch photographs in this section show the lower borders how you'll knit them. On the finished shawl, though, the orientation of the border will be reversed. (To understand why, see page 15.)

149

ROW 1 (RS): Yarn over, *k1, yarn over, s2kp2 (page 282), yarn over; repeat from the * to 1 stitch before the marker, ending this section with k1, yarn over.

ROW 2 AND ALL WS ROWS: Purl across.

ROW 3: Yarn over, k1, *k1, yarn over, s2kp2, yarn over; repeat from the * to 2 stitches before the marker, ending this section with k2, yarn over.

ROW 5: Yarn over, k2tog, yarn over, *k1, yarn over, s2kp2, yarn over; repeat from the * to 3 stitches before the marker, ending this section with k1, yarn over, ssk, yarn over.

ROW 7: Yarn over, k1, k2tog, yarn over, *k1, yarn over, s2kp2, yarn over; repeat from the * to 4 stitches before the marker, ending this section with k1, yarn over, ssk, k1, yarn over.

ROW 9: Yarn over, k1, yarn over, s2kp2, yarn over; *k1, yarn over, s2kp2, yarn over; repeat from the * to 5 stitches before the marker, ending this section with k1, yarn over, s2kp2, yarn over, k1, yarn over.

ROW 11: Yarn over, k2, yarn over, s2kp2, yarn over, *k1, yarn over, s2kp2, yarn over; repeat from the * to 6 stitches before the marker, ending this section with k1, yarn over, s2kp2, yarn over, k2, yarn over.

ROW 12: As Row 2.

Repeat Rows 1–12 for pattern.

⚠ s2kp2

150

ROW 1 (RS): Yarn over, *k1, yarn over, s2kp2 (page 282), yarn over; repeat from the * to 1 stitch before the marker, ending this section with k1, yarn over.

ROW 2 AND ALL WS ROWS: Purl across.

ROW 3: Yarn over, k1, *(yarn over, ssk) twice; repeat from the * to 2 stitches before the marker, ending this section with yarn over, ssk, yarn over.

ROW 5: Yarn over, k2tog, yarn over, *k1, yarn over, s2kp2, yarn over; repeat from the * to 3 stitches before the marker, ending this section with k1, yarn over, ssk, yarn over.

ROW 7: Yarn over, k1, yarn over, ssk, *(yarn over, ssk) twice; repeat from the * to 4 stitches before the marker, ending this section with (yarn over, ssk) twice, yarn over.

ROW 9: Yarn over, k1, yarn over, s2kp2, yarn over, *k1, yarn over, s2kp2, yarn over; repeat from the * to 5 stitches before the marker, ending this section with k1, yarn over, s2kp2, yarn over, k1, yarn over.

ROW 11: Yarn over, k1, (yarn over, ssk) twice, *(yarn over, ssk) twice; repeat from the * to 6 stitches before the marker, ending this section with (yarn over, ssk) 3 times, yarn over.

ROW 13: Yarn over, k2tog, yarn over, k1, yarn over, s2kp2, yarn over, *k1, yarn over, s2kp2, yarn over; repeat from the * to 7 stitches before the marker, ending this section with k1, yarn over, s2kp2, yarn over, k1, yarn over, ssk, yarn over.

ROW 15: Yarn over, k1, (yarn over, ssk) 3 times, *(yarn over, ssk) twice; repeat from the * to 8 stitches before the marker, ending this section with (yarn over, ssk) 4 times, yarn over.

ROW 16: As Row 2.

Repeat Rows 1–16 for pattern.

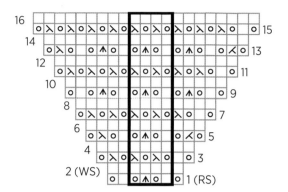

⊼ s2kp2

151

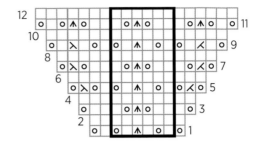

ROW 1 (RS): Yarn over, *k1, yarn over, k1, s2kp2 (page 282), k1, yarn over; repeat from the * to 1 stitch before the marker, ending this section with k1, yarn over.

ROW 2 AND ALL WS ROWS: Purl across.

ROW 3: Yarn over, k1, *k2, yarn over, s2kp2, yarn over, k1; repeat from the * to 2 stitches before the marker, ending this section with k2, yarn over.

ROW 5: Yarn over, k2tog, yarn over, *k1, yarn over, k1, s2kp2, k1, yarn over; repeat from the * to 3 stitches before the marker, ending this section with k1, yarn over, ssk, yarn over.

ROW 7: Yarn over, k2tog, yarn over, k1, *k2, yarn over, s2kp2, yarn over, k1; repeat from the * to 4 stitches before the marker, ending this section with k2, yarn over, ssk, yarn over.

ROW 9: Yarn over, k1, k2tog, k1, yarn over, *k1, yarn over, k1, s2kp2, k1, yarn over; repeat from the * to 5 stitches before the marker, ending this section with k1, yarn over, k1, ssk, k1, yarn over.

ROW 11: Yarn over, k1, yarn over, s2kp2, yarn over, k1, *k2, yarn over, s2kp2, yarn over, k1; repeat from the * to 6 stitches before the marker, ending this section with k2, yarn over, s2kp2, yarn over, k1, yarn over.

ROW 12: As Row 2.

Repeat Rows 1–12 for the pattern.

⋏ **s2kp2**

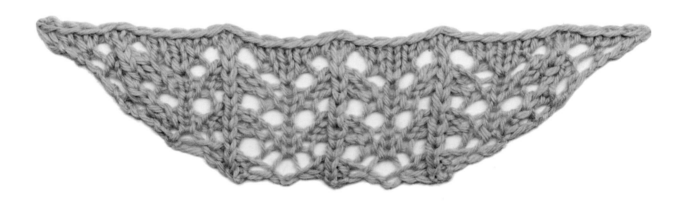

152

ROW 1 (RS): Yarn over, *k1, yarn over, k1, s2kp2 (page 282), k1, yarn over; repeat from the * to 1 stitch before the marker, ending this section with k1, yarn over.

ROW 2 AND ALL WS ROWS: Purl across.

ROW 3: Yarn over, k1, *k1, yarn over, k1, s2kp2, k1, yarn over; repeat from the * to 2 stitches before the marker, ending this section with k2, yarn over.

ROW 5: Yarn over, k2, *k1, yarn over, k1, s2kp2, k1, yarn over; repeat from the * to 3 stitches before the marker, ending this section with k3, yarn over.

ROW 7: Yarn over, k2tog, k1, yarn over, *k1, yarn over, k1, s2kp2, k1, yarn over; repeat from the * to 4 stitches before the marker, ending this section with k1, yarn over, k1, ssk, yarn over.

ROW 9: Yarn over, k1, k2tog, k1, yarn over, *k1, yarn over, k1, s2kp2, k1, yarn over; repeat from the * to 5 stitches before the marker, ending this section with k1, yarn over, k1, ssk, k1, yarn over.

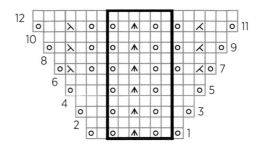

∧ s2kp2

ROW 11: Yarn over, k2, k2tog, k1, yarn over, *k1, yarn over, k1, s2kp2, k1, yarn over; repeat from the * to 4 stitches before the marker, ending this section with k1, yarn over, k1, ssk, k2, yarn over.

ROW 12: As Row 2.

Repeat Rows 1–12 for the pattern.

153

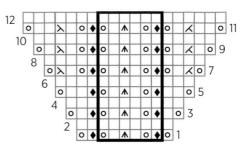

Place bead

s2kp2

ROW 1 (RS): Yarn over, *place bead and knit the stitch (page 280), yarn over, k1, s2kp2 (page 282), k1, yarn over; repeat from the * to 1 stitch before the marker, ending this section with place bead and knit the stitch, yarn over.

ROW 2 AND ALL WS ROWS: Purl across.

ROW 3: Yarn over, k1, *place bead and knit the stitch, yarn over, k1, s2kp2, k1, yarn over; repeat from the * to 2 stitches before the marker, ending this section with place bead and knit the stitch, k1, yarn over.

ROW 5: Yarn over, k2, *place bead and knit the stitch, yarn over, k1, s2kp2, k1, yarn over; repeat from the * to 3 stitches before the marker, ending this section with place bead and knit the stitch, k2, yarn over.

ROW 7: Yarn over, k2tog, k1, yarn over, *place bead and knit the stitch, yarn over, k1, s2kp2, k1, yarn over; repeat from the * to 4 stitches before the marker, ending this section with place bead and knit the stitch, yarn over, k1, ssk, yarn over.

ROW 9: Yarn over, k1, k2tog, k1, yarn over, *place bead and knit the stitch, yarn over, k1, s2kp2, k1, yarn over; repeat from the * to 5 stitches before the marker, ending this section with place bead and knit the stitch, yarn over, k1, ssk, k1, yarn over.

ROW 11: Yarn over, k2, k2tog, k1, yarn over, *place bead and knit the stitch, yarn over, k1, s2kp2, k1, yarn over; repeat from the * to 4 stitches before the marker, ending this section with place bead and knit the stitch, yarn over, k1, ssk, k2, yarn over.

ROW 12: As Row 2.

Repeat Rows 1–12 for the pattern.

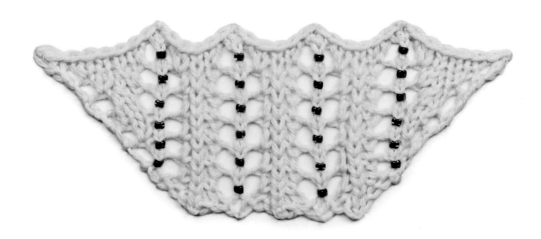

154

ROW 1 (RS): Yarn over, *k2, yarn over, ssk, k1, k2tog, yarn over, k1; repeat from the * to 1 stitch before the marker, ending this section with k1, yarn over.

ROW 2 AND ALL WS ROWS: Purl across.

ROW 3: Yarn over, k1, *k1, yarn over, ssk, yarn over, s2kp2 (page 282), yarn over, k2tog, yarn over; repeat from the * to 2 stitches before the marker, ending this section with k2, yarn over.

ROW 5: Yarn over, k2, *k2, yarn over, ssk, k1, k2tog, yarn over, k1; repeat from the * to 3 stitches before the marker, ending this section with k3, yarn over.

ROW 7: Yarn over, k1, k2tog, yarn over, *k1, yarn over, ssk, yarn over, s2kp2, yarn over, k2tog, yarn over; repeat from the * to 4 stitches before the marker, ending this section with k1, yarn over, ssk, k1, yarn over.

ROW 9: Yarn over, k1, k2tog, yarn over, k1, *k2, yarn over, ssk, k1, k2tog, yarn over, k1; repeat from the * to 5 stitches before the marker, ending this section with k2, yarn over, ssk, k1, yarn over.

ROW 11: Yarn over, k1, ssk, yarn over, k2tog, yarn over, *k1, yarn over, ssk, yarn over, s2kp2, yarn over, k2tog, yarn over; repeat from the * to 6 stitches before the marker, ending this section with k1, yarn over, ssk, yarn over, k2tog, k1, yarn over.

ROW 13: Yarn over, k3, k2tog, yarn over, k1, *k2, yarn over, ssk, k1, k2tog, yarn over, k1; repeat from the * to 7 stitches before the marker, ending this section with k2, yarn over, ssk, k3, yarn over.

ROW 15: Yarn over, k2, yarn over, s2kp2, yarn over, k2tog, yarn over, *k1, yarn over, ssk, yarn over, s2kp2, yarn over, k2tog, yarn over; repeat from the * to 8 stitches before the marker, ending this section with k1, yarn over, ssk, yarn over, s2kp2, yarn over, k2, yarn over.

ROW 16: As Row 2.

Repeat Rows 1–16 for pattern.

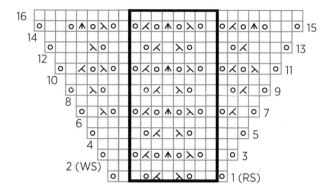

⊼ **s2kp2**

155

ROW 1 (RS): Yarn over, *k1, yarn over, k2, s2kp2 (page 282), k2, yarn over; repeat from the * to 1 stitch before the marker, ending this section with k1, yarn over.

ROW 2 AND ALL WS ROWS: Purl across.

ROW 3: Yarn over, k1, *k1, yarn over, k2, s2kp2, k2, yarn over; repeat from the * to 2 stitches before the marker, ending this section with k2, yarn over.

ROW 5: Yarn over, k2tog, yarn over, *k1, yarn over, k2, s2kp2, k2, yarn over; repeat from the * to 3 stitches before the marker, ending this section with k1, yarn over, ssk, yarn over.

ROW 7: Yarn over, k1, k2tog, yarn over, *k1, yarn over, k2, s2kp2, k2, yarn over; repeat from the * to 4 stitches before the marker, ending this section with k1, yarn over, ssk, k1, yarn over.

ROW 8: As Row 2.

Repeat Rows 1–8 for pattern.

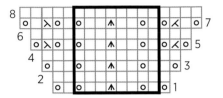

⟰ s2kp2

156

ROW 1 (RS): Yarn over, *k1, yarn over, ssk, k3, k2tog, yarn over; repeat from the * to 1 stitch before the marker, ending this section with k1, yarn over.

ROW 2 AND ALL WS ROWS: Purl across.

ROW 3: Yarn over, k1, *k1, yarn over, k1, ssk, k1, k2tog, k1, yarn over; repeat from the * to 2 stitches before the marker, ending this section with k2, yarn over.

ROW 5: Yarn over, k2, *k1, yarn over, k2, s2kp2 (page 282), k2, yarn over; repeat from the * to 3 stitches before the marker, ending this section with k3, yarn over.

ROW 7: Yarn over, k3, *k1, yarn over, k2, s2kp2, k2, yarn over; repeat from the * to 4 stitches before the marker, ending this section with k4, yarn over.

ROW 8: As Row 2.

Repeat Rows 1–8 for pattern.

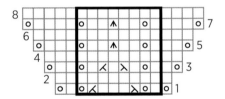

⟰ s2kp2

157

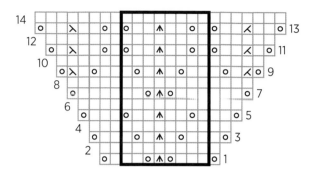

ROW 1 (RS): Yarn over, *k3, yarn over, s2kp2 (page 282), yarn over, k2; repeat from the * to 1 stitch before the marker, ending this section with k1, yarn over.

ROW 2 AND ALL WS ROWS: Purl across.

ROW 3: Yarn over, k1, *k2, yarn over, k1, s2kp2, k1, yarn over, k1; repeat from the * to 2 stitches before the marker, ending this section with k2, yarn over.

ROW 5: Yarn over, k2, *k1, yarn over, k2, s2kp2, k2, yarn over; repeat from the * to 3 stitches before the marker, ending this section with k3, yarn over.

ROW 7: Yarn over, k3, *k3, yarn over, s2kp2, yarn over, k2; repeat from the * to 4 stitches before the marker, ending this section with k4, yarn over.

ROW 9: Yarn over, k2tog, k1, yarn over, k1, *k2, yarn over, k1, s2kp2, k1, yarn over, k1; repeat from the * to 5 stitches before the marker, ending this section with k2, yarn over, k1, ssk, yarn over.

⊼ s2kp2

ROW 11: Yarn over, k1, k2tog, k2, yarn over, *k1, yarn over, k2, s2kp2, k2, yarn over; repeat from the * to 6 stitches before the marker, ending this section with k1, yarn over, k2, ssk, k1, yarn over.

ROW 13: Yarn over, k2, k2tog, k2, yarn over, *k1, yarn over, k2, s2kp2, k2, yarn over; repeat from the * to 7 stitches before the marker, ending this section with k1, yarn over, k2, ssk, k2, yarn over.

ROW 14: As Row 2.

Repeat Rows 1–14 for pattern.

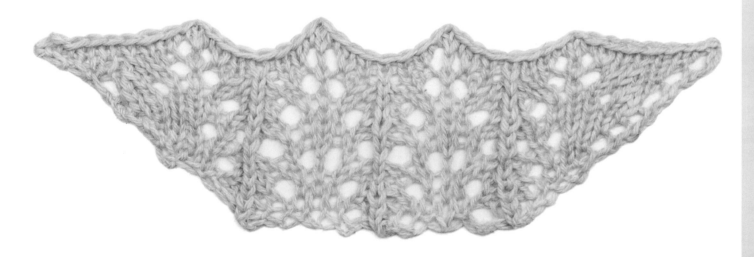

158

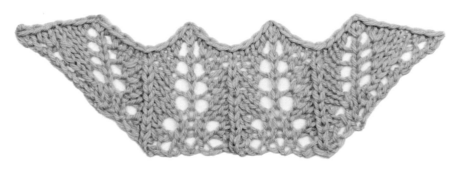

ROW 1 (RS): Yarn over, *k3, yarn over, s2kp2 (page 282), yarn over, k2; repeat from the * to 1 stitch before the marker, ending this section with k1, yarn over.

ROW 2 AND ALL WS ROWS: Purl across.

ROW 3: Yarn over, k1, *k2, yarn over, k1, s2kp2, k1, yarn over, k1; repeat from the * to 2 stitches before the marker, ending this section with k2, yarn over.

ROW 5: Yarn over, k2tog, yarn over, *k1, yarn over, k2, s2kp2, k2, yarn over; repeat from the * to 3 stitches before the marker, ending this section with k1, yarn over, ssk, yarn over.

ROW 7: Yarn over, k2tog, k1, yarn over, *k1, yarn over, k2, s2kp2, k2, yarn over; repeat from the * to 4 stitches before the marker, ending this section with k1, yarn over, k1, ssk, yarn over.

ROW 9: Yarn over, k2tog, k2, yarn over, *k1, yarn over, k2, s2kp2, k2, yarn over; repeat from the * to 5 stitches before the marker, ending this section with k1, yarn over, k2, ssk, yarn over.

ROW 11: Yarn over, k1, k2tog, k2, yarn over, *k1, yarn over, k2, s2kp2, k2, yarn over; repeat from the * to 6 stitches before the marker, ending this section with k1, yarn over, k2, ssk, k1, yarn over.

ROW 12: As Row 2.

Repeat Rows 1–12 for the pattern.

⋀ s2kp2

159

ROW 1 (RS): Yarn over, *place bead and knit the stitch (page 280), yarn over, k2, s2kp2 (page 282), k2, yarn over; repeat from the * to 1 stitch before the marker, ending this section with place bead and knit the stitch, yarn over.

ROW 2 AND ALL WS ROWS: Purl across.

ROW 3: Yarn over, k1, *place bead and knit the stitch, yarn over, k2, s2kp2, k2, yarn over; repeat from the * to 2 stitches before the marker, ending this section with place bead and knit the stitch, k1, yarn over.

ROW 5: Yarn over, k2tog, yarn over, *place bead and knit the stitch, yarn over, k2, s2kp2, k2, yarn over; repeat from the * to 3 stitches before the marker, ending this section with place bead and knit the stitch, yarn over, ssk, yarn over.

ROW 7: Yarn over, k1, k2tog, yarn over, *place bead and knit the stitch, yarn over, k2, s2kp2, k2, yarn over; repeat from the * to 4 stitches before the marker, ending this section with place bead and knit the stitch, yarn over, ssk, k1, yarn over.

ROW 8: As Row 2.

Repeat Rows 1–8 for the pattern.

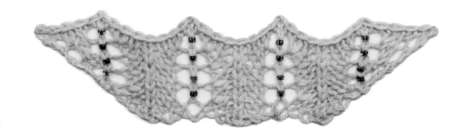

◆ Place bead

⋀ s2kp2

SHAWL #16

Choose patterns
with complementary
elements such as
the diamond motifs
here. See page 276
for instructions.

160

ROW 1 (RS): Yarn over, *k5, yarn over, ssk, k3; repeat from the * to 1 stitch before the marker, ending this section with k1, yarn over.

ROW 2 AND ALL WS ROWS: Purl across.

ROW 3: Yarn over, k1, *k3, k2tog, yarn over, k1, yarn over, ssk, k2; repeat from the * to 2 stitches before the marker, ending this section with k2, yarn over.

ROW 5: Yarn over, k2, *k2, k2tog, yarn over, k3, yarn over, ssk, k1; repeat from the * to 3 stitches before the marker, ending this section with k3, yarn over.

ROW 7: Yarn over, k3, *k3, yarn over, k2tog, k1, ssk, yarn over, k2; repeat from the * to 4 stitches before the marker, ending this section with k4, yarn over.

ROW 9: Yarn over, ssk, yarn over, k2, *k3, yarn over, k2tog, k1, ssk, k2; repeat from the * to 5 stitches before the marker, ending this section with k3, yarn over, k2tog, yarn over.

ROW 11: Yarn over, k1, ssk, yarn over, k2, *k3, yarn over, k2tog, k1, ssk, k2; repeat from the * to 6 stitches before the marker, ending this section with k3, yarn over, k2tog, k1, yarn over.

ROW 13: Yarn over, k2, ssk, yarn over, k2, *k3, yarn over, k2tog, k1, ssk, k2; repeat from the * to 7 stitches before the marker, ending this section with k3, yarn over, k2tog, k2, yarn over.

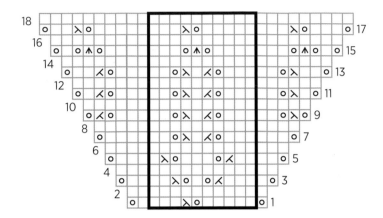

△ s2kp2

ROW 15: Yarn over, k1, yarn over, s2kp2 (page 282), yarn over, k3, *k4, yarn over, s2kp2, yarn over, k3; repeat from the * to 8 stitches before the marker, ending this section with k4, yarn over, s2kp2, yarn over, k1, yarn over.

ROW 17: Yarn over, k3, yarn over, ssk, k3, *k5, yarn over, ssk, k3; repeat from the * to 9 stitches before the marker, ending this section with k5, yarn over, ssk, k2, yarn over,

ROW 18: As Row 2.

Repeat Rows 1–18 for pattern.

161

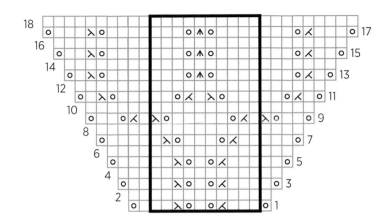

ROW 1 (RS): Yarn over, *k3, k2tog, yarn over, k1, yarn over, ssk, k2; repeat from the * to 1 stitch before the marker, ending this section with k1, yarn over.

ROW 2 AND ALL WS ROWS: Purl across.

ROW 3: Yarn over, k1, *k3, k2tog, yarn over, k1, yarn over, ssk, k2; repeat from the * to 2 stitches before the marker, ending this section with k2, yarn over.

ROW 5: Yarn over, k2, *k3, k2tog, yarn over, k1, yarn over, ssk, k2; repeat from the * to 3 stitches before the marker, ending this section with k3, yarn over.

ROW 7: Yarn over, k3, *k2, k2tog, yarn over, k3, yarn over, ssk, k1; repeat from the * to 4 stitches before the marker, ending this section with k4, yarn over.

ROW 9: Yarn over, k2, yarn over, ssk, *k1, k2tog, yarn over, k5, yarn over, ssk; repeat from the * to 5 stitches before the marker, ending this section with k1, k2tog, yarn over, k2, yarn over.

ROW 11: Yarn over, k1, k2tog, yarn over, k2, *k3, yarn over, ssk, k1, k2tog, yarn over, k2; repeat from the * to 6 stitches before the marker, ending this section with k3, yarn over, ssk, k1, yarn over.

ROW 13: Yarn over, k1, k2tog, yarn over, k3, *k4, yarn over, s2kp2 (page 282), yarn over, k3; repeat from the * to 7 stitches before the marker, ending this section with k4, yarn over, ssk, k1, yarn over.

⊼ **s2kp2**

ROW 15: Yarn over, k2, k2tog, yarn over, k3, *k4, yarn over, s2kp2, yarn over, k3; repeat from the * to 8 stitches before the marker, ending this section with k4, yarn over, ssk, k2, yarn over.

ROW 17: Yarn over, k3, k2tog, yarn over, k3, *k4, yarn over, s2kp2, yarn over, k3; repeat from the * to 9 stitches before the marker, ending this section with k4, yarn over, ssk, k3, yarn over.

ROW 18: As Row 2.

Repeat Rows 1–18 for pattern.

162

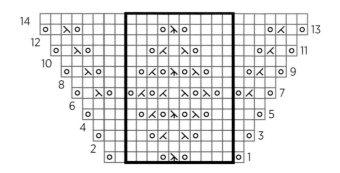

ROW 1 (RS): Yarn over, *k4, yarn over, sssk (page 285), yarn over, k3; repeat from the * to 1 stitch before the marker, ending this section with k1, yarn over.

ROW 2 AND ALL WS ROWS: Purl across.

ROW 3: Yarn over, k1, *k3, yarn over, ssk, k1, k2tog, yarn over, k2; repeat from the * to 2 stitches before the marker, ending this section with k2, yarn over.

ROW 5: Yarn over, k2, *k2, yarn over, ssk, yarn over, sssk, yarn over, k2tog, yarn over, k1; repeat from the * to 3 stitches before the marker, ending this section with k3, yarn over.

ROW 7: Yarn over, k1, k2tog, yarn over, *k1, (yarn over, ssk) twice, k1, (k2tog, yarn over) twice; repeat from the * to 4 stitches before the marker, ending this section with k1, yarn over, ssk, k1, yarn over.

ROW 9: Yarn over, k1, k2tog, yarn over, k1, *k2, yarn over, ssk, yarn over, sssk, yarn over, k2tog, yarn over, k1; repeat from the * to 5 stitches before the marker, ending this section with k2, yarn over, ssk, k1, yarn over.

ROW 11: Yarn over, k1, k2tog, yarn over, k2, *k3, yarn over, ssk, k1, k2tog, yarn over, k2; repeat from the * to 6 stitches before the marker, ending this section with k3, yarn over, ssk, k1, yarn over.

ROW 13: Yarn over, k1, k2tog, yarn over, k3, *k4, yarn over, sssk, yarn over, k3; repeat from the * to 7 stitches before the marker, ending this section with k4, yarn over, ssk, k1, yarn over.

ROW 14: As Row 2.

Repeat Rows 1–14 for pattern.

163

ROW 1 (RS): Yarn over, *k4, yarn over, s2kp2 (page 282), yarn over, k3; repeat from the * to 1 stitch before the marker, ending this section with k1, yarn over.

ROW 2 AND ALL WS ROWS: Purl across.

ROW 3: Yarn over, k1, *k3, yarn over, k1, s2kp2, k1, yarn over, k2; repeat from the * to 2 stitches before the marker, ending this section with k2, yarn over.

ROW 5: Yarn over, k2, *k2, yarn over, k2, s2kp2, k2, yarn over, k1; repeat from the * to 3 stitches before the marker, ending this section with k3, yarn over.

ROW 7: Yarn over, k2tog, k1, yarn over, *k1, yarn over, k3, s2kp2, k3, yarn over; repeat from the * to 4 stitches before the marker, ending this section with k1, yarn over, k1, ssk, yarn over.

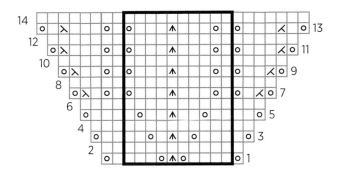

⊼ s2kp2

ROW 9: Yarn over, k2tog, k2, yarn over, *k1, yarn over, k3, s2kp2, k3, yarn over; repeat from the * to 5 stitches before the marker, ending this section with k1, yarn over, k2, ssk, yarn over.

ROW 11: Yarn over, k2tog, k3, yarn over, *k1, yarn over, k3, s2kp2, k3, yarn over; repeat from the * to 6 stitches before the marker, ending this section with k1, yarn over, k3, ssk, yarn over.

ROW 13: Yarn over, k1, k2tog, k3, yarn over, *k1, yarn over, k3, s2kp2, k3, yarn over; repeat from the * to 7 stitches before the marker, ending this section with k1, yarn over, k3, ssk, k1, yarn over.

ROW 14: As Row 2.

Repeat Rows 1–14 for pattern.

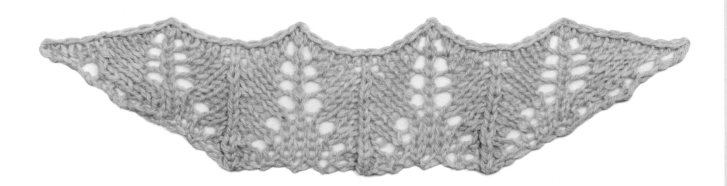

164

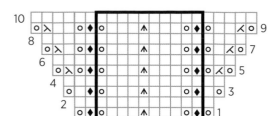

♦ Place bead

⋏ s2kp2

ROW 1 (RS): Yarn over, *place bead and knit the stitch (page 280), yarn over, k3, s2kp2 (page 282), k3, yarn over; repeat from the * to 1 stitch before the marker, ending this section with place bead and knit the stitch, yarn over.

ROW 2 AND ALL WS ROWS: Purl across.

ROW 3: Yarn over, k1, *place bead and knit the stitch, yarn over, k3, s2kp2, k3, yarn over; repeat from the * to 2 stitches before the marker, ending this section with place bead and knit the stitch, k1, yarn over.

ROW 5: Yarn over, k2tog, yarn over, *place bead and knit the stitch, yarn over, k3, s2kp2, k3, yarn over; repeat from the * to 3 stitches before the marker, ending this section with place bead and knit the stitch, yarn over, ssk, yarn over.

ROW 7: Yarn over, k2tog, k1, yarn over, *place bead and knit the stitch, yarn over, k3, s2kp2, k3, yarn over; repeat from the * to 4 stitches before the marker, ending this section with place bead and knit the stitch, yarn over, k1, ssk, yarn over.

ROW 9: Yarn over, k2tog, k2, yarn over, *place bead and knit the stitch, yarn over, k3, s2kp2, k3, yarn over; repeat from the * to 5 stitches before the marker, ending this section with place bead and knit the stitch, yarn over, k2, ssk, yarn over.

ROW 10: As Row 2.

Repeat Rows 1–10 for pattern.

165

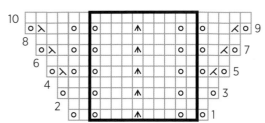

⋏ s2kp2

ROW 1 (RS): Yarn over, *k1, yarn over, k3, s2kp2 (page 282), k3, yarn over; repeat from the * to 1 stitch before the marker, ending this section with k1, yarn over.

ROW 2 AND ALL WS ROWS: Purl across.

ROW 3: Yarn over, k1, *k1, yarn over, k3, s2kp2, k3, yarn over; repeat from the * to 2 stitches before the marker, ending this section with k2, yarn over.

ROW 5: Yarn over, k2tog, yarn over, *k1, yarn over, k3, s2kp2, k3, yarn over; repeat from the * to 3 stitches before the marker, ending this section with k1, yarn over, ssk, yarn over.

ROW 7: Yarn over, k2tog, k1, yarn over, *k1, yarn over, k3, s2kp2, k3, yarn over; repeat from the * to 4 stitches before the marker, ending this section with k1, yarn over, k1, ssk, yarn over.

ROW 9: Yarn over, k2tog, k2, yarn over, *k1, yarn over, k3, s2kp2, k3, yarn over; repeat from the * to 5 stitches before the marker, ending this section with k1, yarn over, k2, ssk, yarn over.

ROW 10: As Row 2.

Repeat Rows 1–10 for pattern.

166

ROW 1 (RS): Yarn over, *k5, yarn over, k3tog, yarn over, k4; repeat from the * to 1 stitch before the marker, ending this section with k1, yarn over.

ROW 2 AND ALL WS ROWS: Purl across.

ROW 3: Yarn over, k1, *k4, yarn over, k1, k3tog, k1, yarn over, k3; repeat from the * to 2 stitches before the marker, ending this section with k2, yarn over.

ROW 5: Yarn over, k2, *k3, yarn over, k2tog, yarn over, k3tog, yarn over, ssk, yarn over, k2; repeat from the * to 3 stitches before the marker, ending this section with k3, yarn over.

ROW 7: Yarn over, k2tog, yarn over, k1, *k2, yarn over, k2tog, yarn over, k1, k3tog, k1, yarn over, ssk, yarn over, k1; repeat from the * to 4 stitches before the marker, ending this section with k2, yarn over, ssk, yarn over.

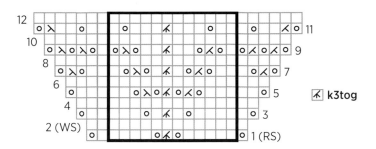

⟰ k3tog

ROW 9: (Yarn over, k2tog) twice, yarn over, *k1, yarn over, k2tog, yarn over, k2, k3tog, k2, yarn over, ssk, yarn over; repeat from the * to 6 stitches before the marker, ending this section with k1, (yarn over, ssk) twice, yarn over.

ROW 11: Yarn over, k2tog, k2, yarn over, k1, *k2, yarn over, k3, k3tog, k3, yarn over, k1; repeat from the * to 6 stitches before the marker, ending this section with k2, yarn over, k2, ssk, yarn over.

ROW 12: As Row 2.

Repeat Rows 1–12 for pattern.

167

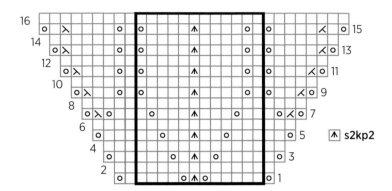

ROW 1 (RS): Yarn over, *k5, yarn over, s2kp2 (page 282), yarn over, k4; repeat from the * to 1 stitch before the marker, ending this section with k1, yarn over.

ROW 2 AND ALL WS ROWS: Purl across.

ROW 3: Yarn over, k1, *k4, yarn over, k1, s2kp2, k1, yarn over, k3; repeat from the * to 2 stitches before the marker, ending this section with k2, yarn over.

ROW 5: Yarn over, k2, *k3, yarn over, k2, s2kp2, k2, yarn over, k2; repeat from the * to 3 stitches before the marker, ending this section with k3, yarn over.

ROW 7: Yarn over, k2tog, yarn over, k1, *k2, yarn over, k3, s2kp2, k3, yarn over, k1; repeat from the * to 4 stitches before the marker, ending this section with k2, yarn over, ssk, yarn over.

ROW 9: Yarn over, k2tog, k2, yarn over, *k1, yarn over, k4, s2kp2, k4, yarn over; repeat from the * to 5 stitches before the marker, ending this section with k1, yarn over, k2, ssk, yarn over.

ROW 11: Yarn over, k2tog, k3, yarn over, *k1, yarn over, k4, s2kp2, k4, yarn over; repeat from the * to 6 stitches before the marker, ending this section with k1, yarn over, k3, ssk, yarn over.

⚭ s2kp2

ROW 13: Yarn over, k2tog, k4, yarn over, *k1, yarn over, k4, s2kp2, k4, yarn over; repeat from the * to 7 stitches before the marker, ending this section with k1, yarn over, k4, ssk, yarn over.

ROW 15: Yarn over, k2tog, k5, yarn over, *k1, yarn over, k4, s2kp2, k4, yarn over; repeat from the * to 8 stitches before the marker, ending this section with k1, yarn over, k5, ssk, yarn over.

ROW 16: As Row 2.

Repeat Rows 1–16 for pattern.

168

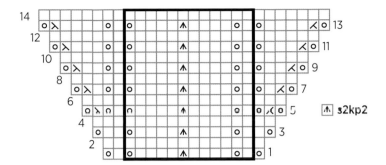

ROW 1 (RS): Yarn over, *k1, yarn over, k4, s2kp2 (page 282), k4, yarn over; repeat from the * to 1 stitch before the marker, ending this section with k1, yarn over.

ROW 2 AND ALL WS ROWS: Purl across.

ROW 3: Yarn over, k1, *k1, yarn over, k4, s2kp2, k4, yarn over; repeat from the * to 2 stitches before the marker, ending this section with k2, yarn over.

ROW 5: Yarn over, k2tog, yarn over, *k1, yarn over, k4, s2kp2, k4, yarn over; repeat from the * to 3 stitches before the marker, ending this section with k1, yarn over, ssk, yarn over.

ROW 7: Yarn over, k2tog, k1, yarn over, *k1, yarn over, k4, s2kp2, k4, yarn over; repeat from the * to 4 stitches before the marker, ending this section with k1, yarn over, k1, ssk, yarn over.

ROW 9: Yarn over, k2tog, k2, yarn over, *k1, yarn over, k4, s2kp2, k4, yarn over; repeat from the * to 5 stitches before the marker, ending this section with k1, yarn over, k2, ssk, yarn over.

ROW 11: Yarn over, k2tog, k3, yarn over, *k1, yarn over, k4, s2kp2, k4, yarn over; repeat from the * to 6 stitches before the marker, ending this section with k1, yarn over, k3, ssk, yarn over.

ROW 13: Yarn over, k2tog, k4, yarn over, *k1, yarn over, k4, s2kp2, k4, yarn over; repeat from the * to 7 stitches before the marker, ending this section with k1, yarn over, k4, ssk, yarn over.

ROW 14: As Row 2.

Repeat Rows 1–14 for pattern.

⋀ s2kp2

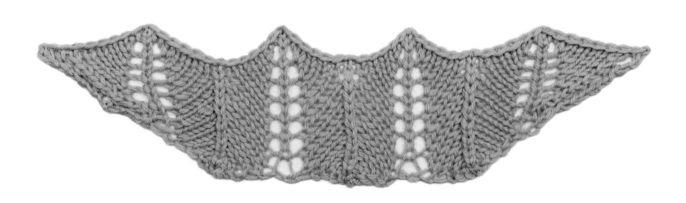

169

ROW 1 (RS): Yarn over, *k5, yarn over, s2kp2 (page 285), yarn over, k4; repeat from the * to 1 stitch before the marker, ending this section with k1, yarn over.

ROW 2 AND ALL WS ROWS: Purl across.

ROW 3: Yarn over, k1, *k4, yarn over, ssk, k1, k2tog, yarn over, k3; repeat from the * to 2 stitches before the marker, ending this section with k2, yarn over.

ROW 5: Yarn over, k2, *k3, yarn over, ssk, yarn over, s2kp2 (page 282), yarn over, k2tog, yarn over, k2; repeat from the * to 3 stitches before the marker, ending this section with k3, yarn over.

ROW 7: Yarn over, k2tog, yarn over, k1, *k2, (yarn over, ssk) twice, k1, (k2tog, yarn over) twice, k1; repeat from the * to 4 stitches before the marker, ending this section with k2, yarn over, ssk, yarn over.

ROW 9: Yarn over, (k2tog, yarn over) twice, *k1, (yarn over, ssk) twice, yarn over, s2kp2, yarn over, (k2tog, yarn over) twice; repeat from the * to 5 stitches before the marker, ending this section with k1, (yarn over, ssk) twice, yarn over.

ROW 11: Yarn over, (k2tog, yarn over) twice, k1, *k2, (yarn over, ssk) twice, k1, (k2tog, yarn over) twice, k1; repeat from the * to 6 stitches before the marker, ending this section with k2, (yarn over, ssk) twice, yarn over.

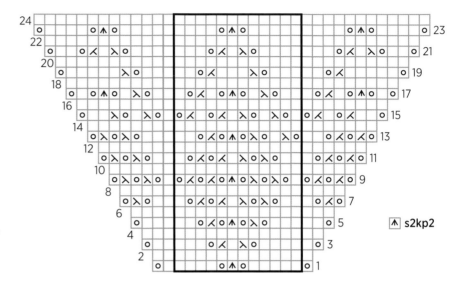

△ s2kp2

ROW 13: Yarn over, (k2tog, yarn over) twice, k2, *yarn over, ssk, k1, yarn over, ssk, yarn over, s2kp2, yarn over, k2tog, yarn over, k2; repeat from the * to 7 stitches before the marker, ending this section with k3, (yarn over, ssk) twice, yarn over.

ROW 15: Yarn over, k2, k2tog, yarn over, k1, k2tog, yarn over, *(k1, yarn over, ssk) twice, (k1, k2tog, yarn over) twice; repeat from the * to 8 stitches before the marker, ending this section with (k1, yarn over, ssk) twice, k2, yarn over.

ROW 17: Yarn over, k1, yarn over, s2kp2, yarn over, k1, k2tog, yarn over, k1, *k2, yarn over, ssk, k1, yarn over, s2kp2, yarn over, k1, k2tog, yarn over, k1; repeat from the * to 9 stitches before the marker, ending this section with k2, yarn over, ssk, k1, yarn over, s2kp2, yarn over, k1, yarn over.

ROW 19: Yarn over, k5, k2tog, yarn over, k2, *k3, yarn over, ssk, k3, k2tog, yarn over, k2; repeat from the * to 10 stitches before the marker, ending this section with k3, yarn over, ssk, k5, yarn over.

ROW 21: Yarn over, k2, yarn over, ssk, k1, k2tog, yarn over, k3, *k4, yarn over, ssk, k1, k2tog, yarn over, k3; repeat from the * to 11 stitches before the marker, ending this section with k4, yarn over, ssk, k1, k2tog, yarn over, k2, yarn over.

ROW 23: Yarn over, k4, yarn over, s2kp2, yarn over, k4, *k5, yarn over, s2kp2, yarn over, k4; repeat from the * to 12 stitches before the marker, ending this section with k5, yarn over, s2kp2, yarn over, k4, yarn over.

ROW 24: As Row 2.

Repeat Rows 1–24 for pattern.

SHAWL #9

Vertically stacked decreases can be blocked (page 283) to create the scalloped edge on this shawl. See page 274 for instructions.

170

ROW 1 (RS): Yarn over, *place bead and knit the stitch (page 280), yarn over, k4, s2kp2 (page 282), k4, yarn over; repeat from the * to 1 stitch before the marker, ending this section with place bead and knit the stitch, yarn over.

ROW 2 AND ALL WS ROWS: Purl across.

ROW 3: Yarn over, k1, *place bead and knit the stitch, yarn over, k4, s2kp2, k4, yarn over; repeat from the * to 2 stitches before the marker, ending this section with place bead and knit the stitch, k1, yarn over.

ROW 5: Yarn over, k2tog, yarn over, *place bead and knit the stitch, yarn over, k4, s2kp2, k4, yarn over; repeat from the * to 3 stitches before the marker, ending this section with place bead and knit the stitch, yarn over, ssk, yarn over.

ROW 7: Yarn over, k2tog, k1, yarn over, *place bead and knit the stitch, yarn over, k4, s2kp2, k4, yarn over; repeat from the * to 4 stitches before the marker, ending this section with place bead and knit the stitch, yarn over, k1, ssk, yarn over.

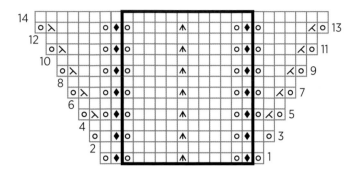

♦ **Place bead**

⋏ **s2kp2**

ROW 9: Yarn over, k2tog, k2, yarn over, *place bead and knit the stitch, yarn over, k4, s2kp2, k4, yarn over; repeat from the * to 5 stitches before the marker, ending this section with place bead and knit the stitch, yarn over, k2, ssk, yarn over.

ROW 11: Yarn over, k2tog, k3, yarn over, *place bead and knit the stitch, yarn over, k4, s2kp2, k4, yarn over; repeat from the * to 6 stitches before the marker, ending this section with place bead and knit the stitch, yarn over, k3, ssk, yarn over.

ROW 13: Yarn over, k2tog, k4, yarn over, *place bead and knit the stitch, yarn over, k4, s2kp2, k4, yarn over; repeat from the * to 7 stitches before the marker, ending this section with place bead and knit the stitch, yarn over, k4, ssk, yarn over.

ROW 14: As Row 2.

Repeat Rows 1–14 for pattern.

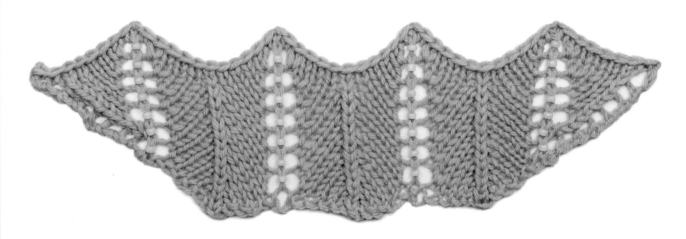

171

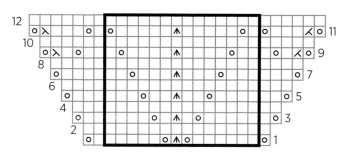

ROW 1 (RS): Yarn over, *k6, yarn over, s2kp2 (page 282), yarn over, k5; repeat from the * to 1 stitch before the marker, ending this section with k1, yarn over.

ROW 2 AND ALL WS ROWS: Purl across.

ROW 3: Yarn over, k1, *k5, yarn over, k1, s2kp2, k1, yarn over, k4; repeat from the * to 2 stitches before the marker, ending this section with k2, yarn over.

ROW 5: Yarn over, k2, *k4, yarn over, k2, s2kp2, k2, yarn over, k3; repeat from the * to 3 stitches before the marker, ending this section with k3, yarn over.

ROW 7: Yarn over, k3, *k3, yarn over, k3, s2kp2, k3, yarn over, k2; repeat from the * to 4 stitches before the marker, ending this section with k4, yarn over.

ROW 9: Yarn over, k2tog, k1, yarn over, k1, *k2, yarn over, k4, s2kp2, k4, yarn over, k1; repeat from the * to 5 stitches before the marker, ending this section with k2, yarn over, k1, ssk, yarn over.

ROW 11: Yarn over, k2tog, k3, yarn over, *k1, yarn over, k5, s2kp2, k5, yarn over; repeat from the * to 6 stitches before marker, ending this section with k1, yarn over, k3, ssk, yarn over.

ROW 12: As Row 2.

Repeat Rows 1–12 for pattern.

⊼ **s2kp2**

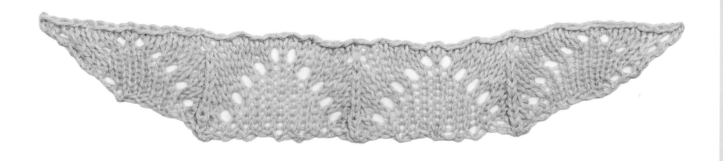

172

ROW 1 (RS): Yarn over, *k1, yarn over, k5, s2kp2 (page 282), k5, yarn over; repeat from the * to 1 stitch before the marker, ending this section with k1, yarn over.

ROW 2 AND ALL WS ROWS: Purl across.

ROW 3: Yarn over, k1, *k1, yarn over, k5, s2kp2, k5, yarn over; repeat from the * to 2 stitches before the marker, ending this section with k2, yarn over.

ROW 5: Yarn over, k2tog, yarn over, *k1, yarn over, k5, s2kp2, k5, yarn over; repeat from the * to 3 stitches before the marker, ending this section with k1, yarn over, ssk, yarn over.

ROW 7: Yarn over, k2tog, k1, yarn over, *k1, yarn over, k5, s2kp2, k5, yarn over; repeat from the * to 4 stitches before the marker, ending this section with k1, yarn over, k1, ssk, yarn over.

ROW 9: Yarn over, k2tog, k2, yarn over, *k1, yarn over, k5, s2kp2, k5, yarn over; repeat from the * to 5 stitches before the marker, ending this section with k1, yarn over, k2, ssk, yarn over.

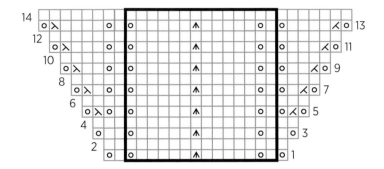

⊼ s2kp2

ROW 11: Yarn over, k2tog, k3, yarn over, *k1, yarn over, k5, s2kp2, k5, yarn over; repeat from the * to 6 stitches before the marker, ending this section with k1, yarn over, k3, ssk, yarn over.

ROW 13: Yarn over, k2tog, k4, yarn over, *k1, yarn over, k5, s2kp2, k5, yarn over; repeat from the * to 7 stitches before the marker, ending this section with k1, yarn over, k4, ssk, yarn over.

ROW 14: As Row 2.

Repeat Rows 1–14 for pattern.

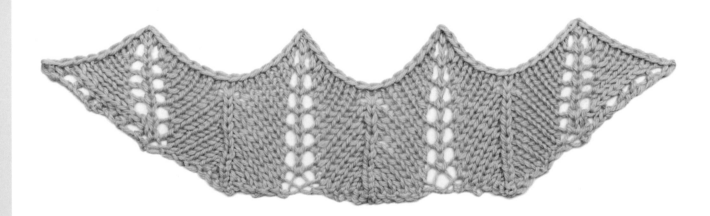

173

ROW 1 (RS): Yarn over, *k1, yarn over, ssk, k3, yarn over, s2kp2 (page 282), yarn over, k3, k2tog, yarn over; repeat from the * to 1 stitch before the marker, ending this section with k1, yarn over.

ROW 2 AND ALL WS ROWS: Purl across.

ROW 3: Yarn over, k1, *k2, yarn over, ssk, k2, yarn over, s2kp2, yarn over, k2, k2tog, yarn over, k1; repeat from the * to 2 stitches before the marker, ending this section with k2, yarn over.

ROW 5: Yarn over, k1, yarn over, *s2kp2, yarn over, k4, yarn over, s2kp2, yarn over, k4, yarn over; repeat from the * to 4 stitches before the marker, ending this section with s2kp2, yarn over, k1, yarn over.

ROW 7: Yarn over, k3, *k6, yarn over, s2kp2, yarn over, k5; repeat from the * to 4 stitches before the marker, ending this section with k4, yarn over.

ROW 9: Yarn over, k2, k2tog, yarn over, *k1, yarn over, ssk, k3, yarn over, s2kp2, yarn over, k3, k2tog, yarn over; repeat from the * to 5 stitches before the marker, ending this section with k1, yarn over, ssk, k2, yarn over.

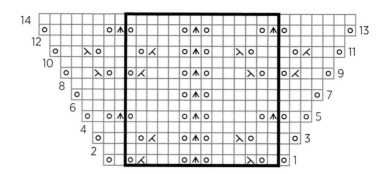

 s2kp2

ROW 11: Yarn over, k2, k2tog, yarn over, k1, *k2, yarn over, ssk, k2, yarn over, s2kp2, yarn over, k2, k2tog, yarn over, k1; repeat from the * to 6 stitches before the marker, ending this section with k2, yarn over, ssk, k2, yarn over.

ROW 13: Yarn over, k5, yarn over, *s2kp2, yarn over, k4, yarn over, s2kp2, yarn over, k4, yarn over; repeat from the * to 8 stitches before the marker, ending this section with s2kp2, yarn over, k5, yarn over.

ROW 14: As Row 2.

Repeat Rows 1–14 for pattern.

174

ROW 1 (RS): Yarn over, *place bead and knit the stitch (page 280), yarn over, k5, s2kp2 (page 282), k5, yarn over; repeat from the * to 1 stitch before the marker, ending this section with place bead and knit the stitch, yarn over.

ROW 2 AND ALL WS ROWS: Purl across.

ROW 3: Yarn over, k1, *place bead and knit the stitch, yarn over, k5, s2kp2, k5, yarn over; repeat from the * to 2 stitches before the marker, ending this section with place bead and knit the stitch, k1, yarn over.

ROW 5: Yarn over, k2tog, yarn over, *place bead and knit the stitch, yarn over, k5, s2kp2, k5, yarn over; repeat from the * to 3 stitches before the marker, ending this section with place bead and knit the stitch, yarn over, ssk, yarn over.

ROW 7: Yarn over, k2tog, k1, yarn over, *place bead and knit the stitch, yarn over, k5, s2kp2, k5, yarn over; repeat from the * to 4 stitches before the marker, ending this section with place bead and knit the stitch, yarn over, k1, ssk, yarn over.

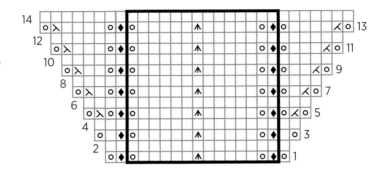

♦ Place bead

⋏ s2kp2

ROW 9: Yarn over, k2tog, k2, yarn over, *place bead and knit the stitch, yarn over, k5, s2kp2, k5, yarn over; repeat from the * to 5 stitches before the marker, ending this section with place bead and knit the stitch, yarn over, k2, ssk, yarn over.

ROW 11: Yarn over, k2tog, k3, yarn over, *place bead and knit the stitch, yarn over, k5, s2kp2, k5, yarn over; repeat from the * to 6 stitches before the marker, ending this section with place bead and knit the stitch, yarn over, k3, ssk, yarn over.

ROW 13: Yarn over, k2tog, k4, yarn over, *place bead and knit the stitch, yarn over, k5, s2kp2, k5, yarn over; repeat from the * to 7 stitches before the marker, ending this section with place bead and knit the stitch, yarn over, k4, ssk, yarn over.

ROW 14: As Row 2.

Repeat Rows 1–14 for pattern.

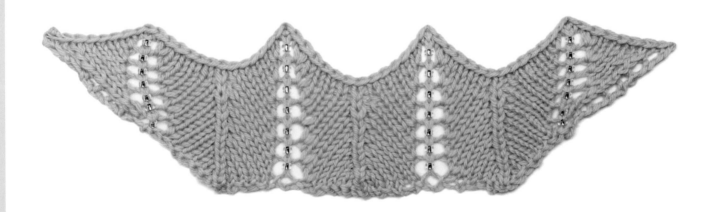

175

ROW 1 (RS): Yarn over, *k1, yarn over, k6, s2kp2 (page 280), k6, yarn over; repeat from the * to 1 stitch before the marker, ending this section with k1, yarn over.

ROW 2 AND ALL WS ROWS: Purl across.

ROW 3: Yarn over, k1, *k1, yarn over, k6, s2kp2, k6, yarn over; repeat from the * to 2 stitches before the marker, ending this section with k2, yarn over.

ROW 5: Yarn over, k2tog, yarn over, *k1, yarn over, k6, s2kp2, k6, yarn over; repeat from the * to 3 stitches before the marker, ending this section with k1, yarn over, ssk, yarn over.

ROW 7: Yarn over, k2tog, k1, yarn over, *k1, yarn over, k6, s2kp2, k6, yarn over; repeat from the * to 4 stitches before the marker, ending this section with k1, yarn over, k1, ssk, yarn over.

ROW 9: Yarn over, k2tog, k2, yarn over, *k1, yarn over, k6, s2kp2, k6, yarn over; repeat from the * to 5 stitches before the marker, ending this section with k1, yarn over, k2, ssk, yarn over.

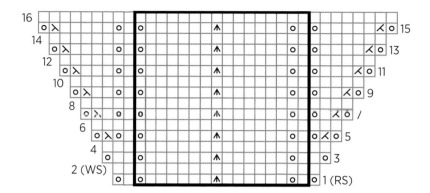

⚠ s2kp2

ROW 11: Yarn over, k2tog, k3, yarn over, *k1, yarn over, k6, s2kp2, k6, yarn over; repeat from the * to 6 stitches before the marker, ending this section with k1, yarn over, k3, ssk, yarn over.

ROW 13: Yarn over, k2tog, k4, yarn over, *k1, yarn over, k6, s2kp2, k6, yarn over; repeat from the * to 7 stitches before the marker, ending this section with k1, yarn over, k4, ssk, yarn over.

ROW 15: Yarn over, k2tog, k5, yarn over, *k1, yarn over, k6, s2kp2, k6, yarn over; repeat from the * to 8 stitches before the marker, ending this section with k1, yarn over, k5, ssk, yarn over.

ROW 16: As Row 2.

Repeat Rows 1–16 for pattern.

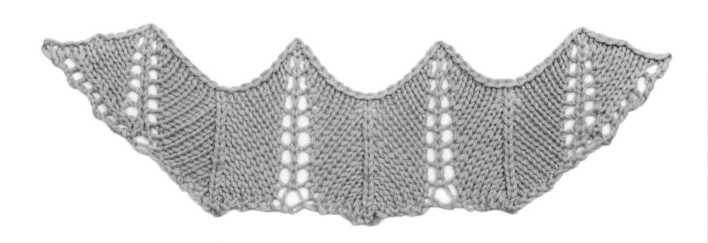

PERPENDICULAR BORDERS

Any of the following traditional lace borders can be added to a piece with any multiple of stitches, since they're knitted perpendicular to the edge of the shawl. See pages 11–12 to learn how. **NOTE:** When going around the point of a triangle (or any irregular shape), use "double joins" to gather the border and prevent it from puckering (see page 12).

- S Slip stitch knitwise
- V Kf&b on right side; pf&b on wrong side
- → Slip last border stitch, knit next stitch from body of shawl, pass slipped stitch over
- ⊖ Bind off 1 stitch
- ★ Stitch remaining after binding off

176

Cast on 9 stitches.

ROW 1 (RS): Slip the first stitch knitwise (page 285), k1, yarn over, k2tog, k2, yarn over, k1, yarn over, k2. (11 stitches)

ROW 2: P6, pf&b (page 282), p3, slip the last border stitch knitwise with the yarn in back, knit the next live stitch from the shawl body, then psso (page 285).

ROW 3: Slip the first stitch knitwise, k1, yarn over, k2tog, k1, p1, k2, yarn over, k1, yarn over, k3. (14 stitches)

ROW 4: P8, pf&b, p4, slip the last border stitch knitwise with the yarn in back, knit the next live stitch from the shawl body, then psso.

ROW 5: Slip the first stitch knitwise, k1, yarn over, k2tog, k1, p2, k3, yarn over, k1, yarn over, k4. (17 stitches)

ROW 6: P10, pf&b, p5, slip the last border stitch knitwise with the yarn in back, knit the next live stitch from the shawl body, then psso.

ROW 7: Slip the first stitch knitwise, k1, yarn over, k2tog, K1, p3, ssk, k5, k2tog, k1. (16 stitches)

ROW 8: P8, pf&b, p6, slip the last border stitch knitwise with the yarn in back, knit the next live stitch from the shawl body, then psso.

ROW 9: Slip the first stitch knitwise, k1, yarn over, k2tog, (k1, p1) twice, p1, ssk, k3, k2tog, k1. (15 stitches)

ROW 10: P6, pf&b, p7, slip the last border stitch knitwise with the yarn in back, knit the next live stitch from the shawl body, then psso.

ROW 11: Slip the first stitch knitwise, k1, yarn over, k2tog, (k1, p1) twice, p2, ssk, k1, k2tog, k1. (14 stitches)

ROW 12: P4, pf&b, p2, k1, p5, slip the last border stitch knitwise with the yarn in back, knit the next live stitch from the shawl body, then psso.

ROW 13: Slip the first stitch knitwise, k1, yarn over, k2tog, (k1, p1) twice, p3, s2kp2 (page 288), k1. (13 stitches)

ROW 14: P2tog, bind off the next 3 stitches in pattern, p1, k1, p5, slip the last border stitch knitwise with the yarn in back, knit the next live stitch from the shawl body, then psso.

Repeat Rows 1–14 for the pattern, attaching one live shawl stitch to the edging every 2 rows.

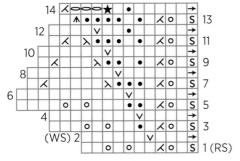

Cast on 9 stitches.

177

Cast on 7 stitches.

ROW 1 (RS): Slip the first stitch knitwise (page 285), k1, yarn over, k2tog, yarn over, k3. (8 stitches)

ROW 2: K3, p4, slip the last border stitch knitwise with the yarn in back, knit the next live stitch from the shawl body, then psso (page 285).

ROW 3: Slip the first stitch knitwise, k1, yarn over, k2tog, k4.

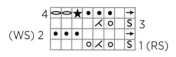

Cast on 7 stitches.

ROW 4: Bind off 2 stitches in pattern, k3, p1, slip the last border stitch knitwise with the yarn in back, knit the next live stitch from the shawl body, then psso.

Repeat Rows 1–4 for the pattern, attaching one live shawl stitch to the edging every 2 rows.

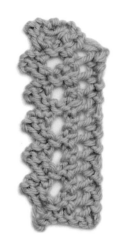

178

Cast on 8 stitches.

ROW 1 (RS): Slip the first stitch knitwise (page 285), k3, yarn over, ssk, yarn over, k2. (9 stitches)

ROW 2: P5, yarn over, p2tog, p1, slip the last border stitch knitwise with the yarn in back, knit the next live stitch from the shawl body, then psso (page 285).

ROW 3: Slip the first stitch knitwise, k3, yarn over, ssk, k1, yarn over, k2. (10 stitches)

ROW 4: P6, yarn over, p2tog, p1, slip the last border stitch knitwise with the yarn in back, knit the next live stitch from the shawl body, then psso.

ROW 5: Slip the first stitch knitwise, k3, yarn over, ssk, k2, yarn over, k2. (11 stitches)

ROW 6: P7, yarn over, p2tog, p1, slip the last border stitch knitwise with the yarn in back, knit the next live stitch from the shawl body, then psso.

ROW 7: Slip the first stitch knitwise, k3, yarn over, ssk, k3, yarn over, k2. (12 stitches)

Cast on 8 stitches.

ROW 8: P8, yarn over, p2tog, p1, slip the last border stitch knitwise with the yarn in back, knit the next live stitch from the shawl body, then psso.

ROW 9: Slip the first stitch knitwise, k3, yarn over, ssk, k4, yarn over, k2. (13 stitches)

ROW 10: P9, yarn over, p2tog, p1, slip the last border stitch knitwise with the yarn in back, knit the next live stitch from the shawl body, then psso.

ROW 11: Slip the first stitch knitwise, k3, yarn over, ssk, k5, yarn over, k2. (14 stitches)

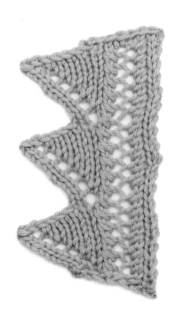

ROW 12: Bind off 6 stitches in pattern, p3, yarn over, p2tog, p1, slip the last border stitch knitwise with the yarn in back, knit the next live stitch from the shawl body, then psso.

Repeat Rows 1–12 for the pattern, attaching one live shawl stitch to the edging every 2 rows.

179

Cast on 8 stitches.

ROW 1 (RS): Slip the first stitch knitwise (page 285), k1, yarn over, k2tog, k1, yarn over, k2tog, yarn over, k1. (9 stitches)

ROW 2: K5, p3, slip the last border stitch knitwise with the yarn in back, knit the next live stitch from the shawl body, then psso (page 285).

ROW 3: Slip the first stitch knitwise, k1, (yarn over, k2tog) 3 times, yarn over, k1. (10 stitches)

ROW 4: K6, p3, slip the last border stitch knitwise with the yarn in back, knit the next live stitch from the shawl body, then psso.

ROW 5: Slip the first stitch knitwise, k1, yarn over, k2tog, k1, (yarn over, k2tog) twice, yarn over, k1. (11 stitches)

ROW 6: K7, p3, slip the last border stitch knitwise with the yarn in back, knit the next live stitch from the shawl body, then psso.

ROW 7: Slip the first stitch knitwise, k1, (yarn over, k2tog) 4 times, yarn over, k1. (12 stitches)

ROW 8: K8, p3, slip the last border stitch knitwise with the yarn in back, knit the next live stitch from the shawl body, then psso.

ROW 9: Slip the first stitch knitwise, k1, yarn over, k2tog, k1, (yarn over, k2tog) 3 times, yarn over, k1. (13 stitches)

ROW 10: K9, p3, slip the last border stitch knitwise with the yarn in back, knit the next live stitch from the shawl body, then psso.

ROW 11: Slip the first stitch knitwise, k1, (yarn over, k2tog) 5 times, yarn over, k1. (14 stitches)

ROW 12: K10, p3, slip the last border stitch knitwise with the yarn in back, knit the next live stitch from the shawl body, then psso.

ROW 13: Slip the first stitch knitwise, k1, yarn over, k2tog, k1, (yarn over, k2tog) 4 times, yarn over, k1. (15 stitches)

ROW 14: Bind off 7 stitches in pattern, p6, slip the last border stitch knitwise with the yarn in back, knit the next live stitch from the shawl body, then psso.

Repeat Rows 1–14 for the pattern, attaching one live shawl stitch to the edging every 2 rows.

Cast on 8 stitches.

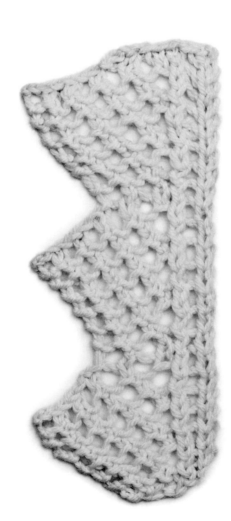

180

Cast on 11 stitches.

ROW 1 (RS): Slip the first stitch knitwise (page 285), k3, yarn over, ssk, k1, yarn over, k2tog, yarn over, k2. (12 stitches)

ROWS 2, 4, 6, AND 8: Purl across until 4 stitches remain in the row, ending with yarn over, p2tog, p1, slip the last border stitch knitwise with the yarn in back, knit the next live stitch from the shawl body, then psso (page 285).

ROW 3: Slip the first stitch knitwise, k3, yarn over, ssk, k2, yarn over, k2tog, yarn over, k2. (13 stitches)

ROW 5: Slip the first stitch knitwise, k3, yarn over, ssk, k3, yarn over, k2tog, yarn over, k2. (14 stitches)

ROW 7: Slip the first stitch knitwise, k3, yarn over, ssk, k4, yarn over, k2tog, yarn over, k2. (15 stitches)

Cast on 11 stitches.

ROW 9: Slip the first stitch knitwise, k3, yarn over, ssk, k2, yarn over, k2tog, k5.

ROW 10: Bind off the first 4 stitches in pattern, p6, yarn over, p2tog, p1, slip the last border stitch knitwise with the yarn in back, knit the next live stitch from the shawl body, then psso. (11 stitches)

Repeat Rows 1–10 for the pattern, attaching one live shawl stitch to the edging every 2 rows.

181

Cast on 12 stitches.

ROW 1 (RS): Slip the first stitch knitwise (page 285), k1, yarn over, k2tog, K3, k2tog, yarn over, k3tog. (10 stitches)

ROWS 2 AND ALL WS ROWS: Yarn over, purl across until 1 stitch remains in the row, ending with slip the last border stitch knitwise with the yarn in back, knit the next live stitch from the shawl body, then psso (page 285).

ROW 3: Slip the first stitch knitwise, k1, yarn over, k2tog, k2, k2tog, yarn over, k1, yarn over, k2tog. (11 stitches)

ROW 5: Slip the first stitch knitwise, k1, yarn over, k2tog, k1, k2tog, yarn over, k3, yarn over, k2tog. (12 stitches)

ROW 7: Slip the first stitch knitwise, k1, yarn over, (k2tog) twice, yarn over, k2, yarn over, ssk, k1, yarn over, k2tog. (13 stitches)

Cast on 12 stitches.

☒ **k3tog**

ROW 9: Slip the first stitch knitwise, k1, yarn over, k2tog, k2, yarn over, ssk, k1, k2tog, yarn over, k3tog. (12 stitches)

ROW 11: Slip the first stitch knitwise, k1, yarn over, k2tog, k3, (yarn over, k3tog) twice. (11 stitches)

ROW 12: As Row 2.

Repeat Rows 1–12 for the pattern, attaching one live shawl stitch to the edging every 2 rows.

182

Cast on 14 stitches.

ROW 1 (RS): Slip the first stitch knitwise (page 285), k3, yarn over, ssk, C2R (page 280), k2, yarn over twice, k2. (16 stitches)

ROW 2: K3, p9, yarn over, p2tog, p1, slip the last border stitch knitwise with the yarn in back, knit the next live stitch from the shawl body, then psso (page 285).

ROW 3: Slip the first stitch knitwise, k3, yarn over, ssk, k2, C2L (page 280), k4.

ROW 4: Bind off 2 stitches in pattern, p9, yarn over, p2tog, p1, slip the last border stitch knitwise with the yarn in back, knit the next live stitch from the shawl body, then psso.

Repeat Rows 1–4 for the pattern, attaching one live shawl stitch to the edging every 2 rows.

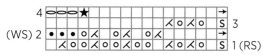

Cast on 14 stitches.

C2R

C2L

Double Yarn Overs

The double yarn over used in Row 1 of this pattern, as well as in several others, is easy to do. Just wrap the yarn twice instead of once to create the yarn over. On the subsequent row, you'll work 2 stitches into the exaggerated hole.

183

Cast on 14 stitches.

ROW 1 (RS): Slip the first stitch knitwise (page 285), k1, (yarn over, k2tog) twice, k1, (yarn over twice, k2tog) 3 times (see Double Yarn Overs, above), k1. (17 stitches)

ROW 2: K3, yarn over, p2tog, p1, yarn over, p2tog, p1, yarn over, p2tog, p5, slip the last border stitch knitwise with the yarn in back, knit the next live stitch from the shawl body, then psso (page 285).

ROW 3: Slip the first stitch knitwise, k1, (yarn over, k2tog) twice, k11.

ROW 4: Bind off 3 stitches in pattern, p12. (13 stitches)

Repeat Rows 1–4 for the pattern, attaching one live shawl stitch to the edging every 2 rows.

Cast on 14 stitches.

SHAWL #17
Bobbles add textural interest. If you don't like knitting bobbles, consider placing large beads instead (page 280). See page 276 for shawl instructions.

265

184

Cast on 13 stitches.

ROW 1 (RS): Slip the first stitch knitwise (page 285), k3, yarn over, ssk, (k2tog, yarn over) twice, k2tog, k1. (12 stitches)

ROW 2: P8, yarn over, p2tog, p1, slip the last border stitch knitwise with the yarn in back, knit the next live stitch from the shawl body, then psso (page 285).

ROW 3: Slip the first stitch knitwise, k3, yarn over, ssk, k2, yarn over, k2tog, yarn over, k2. (13 stitches)

ROW 4: P9, yarn over, p2tog, p1, slip the last border stitch knitwise with the yarn in back, knit the next live stitch from the shawl body, then psso.

ROW 5: Slip the first stitch knitwise, k3, yarn over, ssk, k3, yarn over, k2tog, yarn over, k2. (14 stitches)

ROW 6: P10, yarn over, p2tog, p1, slip the last border stitch knitwise with the yarn in back, knit the next live stitch from the shawl body, then psso.

ROW 7: Slip the first stitch knitwise, k3, yarn over, ssk, k4, yarn over, k2tog, yarn over, k2. (15 stitches)

ROW 8: P11, yarn over, p2tog, p1, slip the last border stitch knitwise with the yarn in back, knit the next live stitch from the shawl body, then psso.

ROW 9: Slip the first stitch knitwise, k3, yarn over, ssk, k5, yarn over, k2tog, yarn over, k2. (16 stitches)

ROW 10: P12, yarn over, p2tog, p1, slip the last border stitch knitwise with the yarn in back, knit the next live stitch from the shawl body, then psso.

ROW 11: Slip the first stitch knitwise, k3, yarn over, ssk, k3, (k2tog, yarn over) twice, k2tog, K1. (15 stitches)

ROW 12: P11, yarn over, p2tog, p1, slip the last border stitch knitwise with the yarn in back, knit the next live stitch from the shawl body, then psso.

ROW 13: Slip the first stitch knitwise, k3, yarn over, ssk, k2, (k2tog, yarn over) twice, k2tog, k1. (14 stitches)

ROW 14: P10, yarn over, ssp (page 281), p1, slip the last border stitch knitwise with the yarn in back, knit the next live stitch from the shawl body, then psso.

ROW 15: Slip the first stitch knitwise, k3, yarn over, ssk, k1, (k2tog, yarn over) twice, K2tog, k1. (13 stitches)

ROW 16: P9, yarn over, ssp, p1, slip the last border stitch knitwise with the yarn in back, knit the next live stitch from the shawl body, then psso.

Repeat Rows 1–16 for the pattern, attaching one live shawl stitch to the edging every 2 rows.

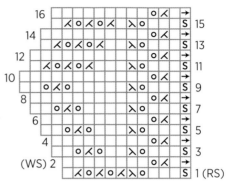

Cast on 13 stitches.

185

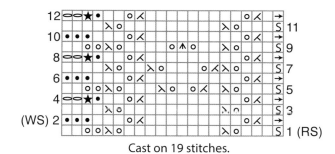

Cast on 19 stitches.

ROW 1 (RS): Slip the first stitch knitwise (page 285), k3, yarn over, ssk, k9, yarn over, ssk, (yarn over) twice, k2. (21 stitches)

ROWS 2, 6, AND 10: K3, p3, yarn over, p2tog, p9, yarn over, p2tog, p1, slip the last border stitch knitwise with the yarn in back, knit the next live stitch from the shawl body, then psso (page 285).

ROW 3: Slip the first stitch knitwise, k3, yarn over, ssk, k9, yarn over, ssk, k4.

ROWS 4 AND 8: Bind off the first 2 stitches in pattern, k1, p2, yarn over, p2tog, p9, yarn over, p2tog, p1, slip the last border stitch knitwise with the yarn in back, knit the next live stitch from the shawl body, then psso. (19 stitches)

ROW 5: Slip the first stitch knitwise, k3, yarn over, ssk, k1, k2tog, yarn over, k1, yarn over, ssk, k3, yarn over, ssk, (yarn over) twice, k2.

ROW 7: Slip the first stitch knitwise, k3, yarn over, ssk, k2tog, yarn over, k3, yarn over, ssk, k2, yarn over, ssk, k4.

ROW 9: Slip the first stitch knitwise, k3, yarn over, ssk, k2, yarn over, s2kp2 (page 282), yarn over, k4, yarn over, ssk, (yarn over) twice, k2.

ROW 11: Slip the first stitch knitwise, k3, yarn over, ssk, k9, yarn over, ssk, k4.

ROW 12: As Row 4.

Repeat Rows 1–12 for the pattern, attaching one live shawl stitch to the edging every 2 rows.

Cast on 19 stitches.

⬆ s2kp2

THE GALLERY OF SHAWLS IN 7 EASY STEPS

It always helps to see a few examples when first starting out, so I've created 20 sample shawls to show you exactly how easy and fun it is to create your own beautiful shawl patterns. I've written out full instructions for two of the shawls to walk you through the process, along with the "recipe" that the pattern is based on. (If you prefer to work from charts rather than written-out instructions, refer to the stitch patterns referenced in the recipes.) Each recipe consists of seven steps showing which components were combined to create the shawl. For the remaining 18 shawls, I've provided just the recipe I used for each. Have fun with these, and then create your own gorgeous shawls by coming up with your own recipes!

SHAWL #1

This shawl is worked from the top down, beginning with a stockinette tab; the shape is formed by increasing 4 stitches every 2 rows: 2 stitches just inside the outside borders, plus 2 stitches on either side of the center "spine" stitch. Although both right-side and wrong-side rows are shown on the charts, if you'd like to think of the wrong-side rows as "rest rows," imagine them like this: "Purl across."

FINISHED SIZE
Approximately 52" wide Q 23" deep, blocked

MATERIALS
- Malabrigo's Mora, 100% mulberry silk, 225 yds/50 g, 900 yds of Indiecita (#416)

- US size 4 (3.5 mm) circular needle, 29" long, or size needed to obtain gauge

- US size H/8 (5 mm) crochet hook (used only for the provisional cast on)

- Smooth waste yarn (used only for the provisional cast on)

- Stitch markers

GAUGE
- 24 stitches and 34 rows = 4", in stockinette stitch, unblocked

- 19 stitches and 33 rows = 4", in stockinette stitch, blocked

SETUP

Begin with a garter tab as follows:

Use a provisional cast on, waste yarn, and crochet hook to chain 7 stitches (page 10). Cut the yarn and pull the end through the last chain made to secure it. Tie a loose knot on this tail to mark it as the end you'll use later to unravel the chain.

Turn the crocheted chain over and use a knitting needle to pick up and knit 1 stitch through the back loop of each crocheted chain until you have cast on 3 stitches.

Begin by knitting 7 rows of garter stitch.

Rotate the piece 90°, and pick up 3 stitches along the side edge, picking up 1 stitch for each ridge; rotate the piece 90° again, unzip your provisional cast on, and pick up the 3 live stitches along the provisional cast-on edge with your free needle and knit them. (9 stitches) Turn.

SETUP ROW: Purl one row. (9 stitches)

KNITTING THE SHAWL

ROW 1 (RS): K3, place a marker, k1, place a marker, k1, place a marker, k1, place a marker, k3.

ROW 2 AND ALL WS ROWS FOR MAIN BODY OF THE SHAWL: K3, purl across until 3 stitches remain, end with k3. This creates a basic stockinette stitch fabric (Simple **4**) with Side Edging **1**.

ROW 3: K3, slip the marker, yarn over, knit across to the next marker, yarn over, slip the marker, k1, slip the marker, yarn over, knit across to the next marker, yarn over, slip the marker, k3. (13 stitches)

ROWS 4–121: Repeat Rows 2 and 3. (249 stitches)

ROW 122: As Row 2.

ROWS 123–146: Work Rows 13–36 of Wedge **82** (page 134) once. (297 stitches)

ROWS 147–158: Work Rows 1–12 of Lower Border **166** (page 249) once. (321 stitches)

Work the Super-Stretchy Bind Off (page 279).

FINISHING

Block the piece to measurements (page 283).

SHAWL #1 RECIPE

For more photos of this shawl, see page 135.

Step 1 (Silhouette): Two triangles

Step 2 (Stitch Patterns)

Simple **4** (page 18)

Wedge **82** (page 134)

Step 3 (Background Texture): Stockinette Stitch

Step 4 (Edging): Side Edging **1** (page 17)

Step 5 (Cast On): Provisional with Garter Tab

Step 6 (Border): Lower Border **166** (page 249)

Step 7 (Bind Off): Super-Stretchy Bind Off (page 279)

Yarn: Malabrigo's Mora in Indiecita (#416)

Needle Size: US 4 (3.5 mm)

SHAWL #2

The shape of this shawl is formed by increasing 4 stitches every 2 rows: 2 stitches just inside the outer vertical insertions, plus 2 stitches on each side of the center vertical insertion.

FINISHED SIZE

Approximately 68" wide
x 31" deep, blocked

MATERIALS

- Louet's Euroflax Lace, 100% wet-spun linen, 630 yds/110 g, 930 yds of Limestone (#2502)

- One US size 4 (3.5 mm) circular needle, 29" long, or size needed to obtain gauge

- One US size 4 (3.5 mm) double-pointed needle (used only for knitted-on border)

- One US size H/8 (5 mm) crochet hook (used only for the provisional cast on)

- Smooth waste yarn (used only for the provisional cast on)

- Stitch markers

GAUGE

- 23 stitches and 38 rows = 4", in stockinette stitch, unblocked

- 23 stitches and 39 rows = 4", in stockinette stitch, blocked

SETUP

Begin with a garter tab as follows:

Use a provisional cast on to chain 7 stitches (page 10).

Cut the yarn, and pull the end through the last chain made to secure it. Tie a loose knot on this tail to mark it as the end you'll use later to unravel the chain.

Turn the crocheted chain over, and use a knitting needle to pick up and knit 1 stitch through the back loop of each crocheted chain until you have cast on 3 stitches.

Begin by knitting 106 rows.

Rotate the piece 90°, and pick up 53 stitches along the side edge, picking up 1 stitch for each ridge; rotate the piece 90° again, unzip your provisional cast on, and pick up and knit 3 stitches along the cast-on edge. (59 stitches) Turn.

You have just formed the edging that will lie flat across the back of the neck.

SHAWL

ROW 1 (RS): K3, place a marker, work Row 1 of Vertical Insertion **146** (page 232), place a marker, work Row 1 of Wedge **66** (page 110), place a marker, work Row 1 of Vertical Insertion **146**, place a marker, work Row 1 of Wedge **66**, place a marker, work Row 1 of Vertical Insertion **146**, place a marker, k3. (63 stitches)

ROW 2 AND ALL WS ROWS: K3, slip the marker, work the next row of Vertical Insertion **146**, slip the marker, purl across to the next marker, slip the marker, work the next row of Vertical Insertion **146**, slip the marker, purl across to the next marker, slip the marker, work the next row of Vertical Insertion **146**, slip the marker, k3.

ROW 3 (RS): K3, slip the marker, work the next row of Vertical Insertion **146**, slip the marker, work the next row of Wedge **66**, slip the marker, work the next row of Vertical Insertion **146**, slip the marker, work the next row of Wedge **66**, slip the marker, work the next row of Vertical Insertion **146**, slip the marker, k3. (67 stitches)

ROWS 4–169: Repeat Rows 2 and 3 eighty-three times. Each 10-row repeat will add two more 10-stitch repeats of Wedge **66** between their sets of markers. After Row 50 of Wedge **66**, begin at Row 11. Repeat Rows 11–50 three more times. (399 stitches)

ROW 170 (WS): K3, purl across to the last 3 stitches, k3. Cut yarn.

FINISHING

Work a perpendicular border (page 261) onto the live stitches as follows:

Cast on 8 stitches onto the double-pointed needle.

With the right-side of the shawl facing you, begin Perpendicular Border **178** (page 261) on the left-hand side.

Repeat Rows 1–16 along the two sides of the shawl, attaching one live shawl stitch to the edging every 2 rows, and one double join (page 12) at the 2nd stitch marker, two double joins at the 3rd and 4th stitch markers, and one double join at the 5th stitch marker.

Block piece to measurements (page 283).

SHAWL #2 RECIPE

For more photos of this shawl, see page 111.

Step 1 (Silhouette): Two triangles with three vertical insertions

Step 2 (Stitch Patterns):

Wedge **66** (page 110)

Vertical Insertion **146** (page 232)

Step 3 (Background Texture): Stockinette Stitch

Step 4 (Edging): Side Edging **1** (page 17)

Step 5 (Cast On): Provisional with Garter Tab

Step 6 (Border): Perpendicular Border **178** (page 261)

Step 7 (Bind Off): Not applicable

Yarn: Louet's Euroflax Lace in Limestone (#2502)

Needle Size: US 4 (3.5 mm)

SHAWL #3

For more photos of this shawl, see page 65.

Step 1 (Silhouette): Two triangles

Step 2 (Stitch Patterns):

Wedge **43** (page 64)

Horizontal Insertion **124** (page 215)

Wedge **15** (page 28)

Step 3 (Background Texture): Stockinette Stitch

Step 4 (Edging): Side Edging **2** (page 17)

Step 5 (Cast On): Provisional with Stockinette Tab

Step 6 (Border): Lower Border **149** (page 234), garter version (knit all wrong-side rows)

Step 7 (Bind Off): Super-Stretchy Bind Off (page 279)

Yarn: Universal Yarn's Bamboo Pop in Silken (#115)

Needle Size: US 5 (3.75 mm)

SHAWL #4

For more photos of this shawl, see page 101.

Step 1 (Silhouette): Four triangles knit in the round to create a square

Step 2 (Stitch Patterns):

Wedge **59** (page 96)

Wedge **61** (page 100)

Horizontal Insertion **119** (page 210)

Step 3 (Background Texture): Garter Stitch (knit all wrong-side rows in each pattern)

Step 4 (Edging): Not applicable

Step 5 (Cast On): Magic Loop

Step 6 (Border): Lower Border **175** (page 259)

Step 7 (Bind Off): Super-Stretchy Bind Off (page 279)

Yarn: Knit One Crochet Too's Cozette in Midnight (#682)

Needle Size: US 5 (3.75 mm)

SHAWL #5

For more photos of this shawl, see pages 14 and 208.

Step 1 (Silhouette): Six triangles

Step 2 (Stitch Patterns):

Wedge **118** (page 206)

Horizontal Insertion **128** (page 219)

Step 3 (Background Texture): Stockinette Stitch

Step 4 (Edging): Side Edging **2** (page 17)

Step 5 (Cast On): Provisional with Stockinette Tab

Step 6 (Border): Lower Border **155** (page 240)

Step 7 (Bind Off): Picot Bind Off (page 279)

Yarn: Lion Brand Collection's Silk in Meteor (#151)

Needle Size: US 7 (4.5 mm)

SHAWL #6

For more photos of this shawl, see page 203.

Step 1 (Silhouette): Two triangles

Step 2 (Stitch Patterns):

Wedge `116` (page 202)

Step 3 (Background Texture): Stockinette Stitch

Step 4 (Edging): Side Edging `2` (page 17)

Step 5 (Cast On): Provisional with Stockinette Tab

Step 6 (Border): Lower Border `175` (page 259)

Step 7 (Bind Off): Picot Bind Off (page 279)

Yarn: Anzula's It Could Be Worsted in Seaside and Boysenberry

Needle Size: US 9 (5.5 mm)

SHAWL #7

For more photos of this shawl, see page 47.

Step 1 (Silhouette): Four triangles

Step 2 (Stitch Patterns):

Wedge `31` (page 46)

Wedge `13` (page 25)

Step 3 (Background Texture): Stockinette Stitch

Step 4 (Edging): Side Edging `1` (page 17)

Step 5 (Cast On): Provisional with Garter Tab

Step 6 (Border): Lower Border `154` (page 239)

Step 7 (Bind Off): Picot Bind Off (page 279)

Yarn: Universal Yarn's Revolutions in Harmony (#107)

Needle Size: US 10 (6 mm)

SHAWL #8

For more photos of this shawl, see pages 11 and 167.

Step 1 (Silhouette): Two triangles

Step 2 (Stitch Patterns):

Wedge `100` (page 166)

Wedge `101` (page 168)

Horizontal Insertion `129` (page 220)

Step 3 (Background Texture): As charted

Step 4 (Edging): Side Edging `1` (page 17)

Step 5 (Cast On): Provisional with Garter Tab

Step 6 (Border): Perpendicular Border `179` (page 262)

Step 7 (Bind Off): Not applicable

Yarn: Baah Yarn's Sonoma in Obsidian and Glacier

Needle Size: US 6 (4 mm)

SHAWL #9

For more photos of this shawl, see page 253.

Step 1 (Silhouette): Two triangles

Step 2 (Stitch Patterns):

Simple **5** (page 18)

Horizontal Insertion **123** (page 214)

Step 3 (Background Texture): Garter Stitch

Step 4 (Edging): Side Edging **3** (page 17)

Step 5 (Cast On): Provisional with Fagoted Tab

Step 6 (Border): Lower Border **169** (page 252)

Step 7 (Bind Off): Super-Stretchy Bind Off (page 279)

Yarn: Ancient Arts' Meow Sportweight in Russian (Silver) Blue

Needle Size: 5 (3.75 mm)

SHAWL #10

For more photos of this shawl, see page 27.

Step 1 (Silhouette): Four triangles

Step 2 (Stitch Patterns):

Simple **8** (page 21)

Wedge **14** (page 26)

Step 3 (Background Texture): As charted

Step 4 (Edging): Side Edging **1** (page 17)

Step 5 (Cast On): Provisional with Garter Tab

Step 6 (Border): Perpendicular Border **185** (page 267)

Step 7 (Bind Off): Not applicable

Yarn: Koigu Yarns' KPM in #2423

Needle Size: 5 (3.75 mm)

SHAWL #11

For more photos of this shawl, see page 197.

Step 1 (Silhouette): Two triangles

Step 2 (Stitch Patterns):

Wedge **113** (page 195)

Horizontal Insertion **120** (page 211)

Wedge **15** (page 28)

Horizontal Insertion **120** (page 211)

Step 3 (Background Texture): Garter Stitch (knit all wrong-side rows in each pattern)

Step 4 (Edging): Side Edging **1** (page 17)

Step 5 (Cast On): Provisional with Garter Tab

Step 6 (Border): Lower Border **150** (page 235)

Step 7 (Bind Off): Super-Stretchy Bind Off (page 279)

Yarn: Space Cadet's Maia in Plume

Needle Size: US 3 (3.25 mm)

SHAWL #12

For more photos of this shawl, see pages 6 and 151.

Step 1 (Silhouette): Three triangles sewn together to create a trapezoid

Step 2 (Stitch Patterns):

Wedge **83** (page 136)

Wedge **92** (page 150)

Step 3 (Background Texture): Stockinette Stitch

Step 4 (Edging): Side Edging **2** (page 17)

Step 5 (Cast On): Provisional with Stockinette Tab

Step 6 (Border): Not applicable

Step 7 (Bind Off): Super-Stretchy Bind Off (page 279)

Yarn: Classic Elite's Fresco in Saxony Blue (#5348)

Needle Size: US 5 (3.75 mm)

SHAWL #13

For more photos of this shawl, see page 213.

Step 1 (Silhouette): Two triangles

Step 2 (Stitch Patterns):

Simple **5** (page 18)

Horizontal Insertion **122** (page 212)

Step 3 (Background Texture): Garter Stitch

Step 4 (Edging): Side Edging **1** (page 17)

Step 5 (Cast On): Provisional with Garter Tab

Step 6 (Border): Perpendicular Border **184** (page 266)

Step 7 (Bind Off): Not applicable

Yarn: Cascade Yarns' Ultra Pima in Brick (#3792), Natural (#3718), and Zen Green (#3757)

Needle Size: US 6 (4 mm)

SHAWL #14

For more photos of this shawl, see page 19.

Step 1 (Silhouette): Four triangles sewn together to create a parallelogram

Step 2 (Stitch Patterns):

Simple **5** (page 18)

Step 3 (Background Texture): Garter Stitch

Step 4 (Edging): Side Edging **1** (page 17)

Step 5 (Cast On): Provisional with Garter Tab

Step 6 (Border): Not applicable

Step 7 (Bind Off): Super-Stretchy Bind Off (page 279)

Yarn: Zealana's Air in Slate Blue (#A03) and Gray (#A15)

Needle Size: US 4 (3.5 mm)

SHAWL #15

For more photos of this shawl, see page 76.

Step 1 (Silhouette): Two triangles

Step 2 (Stitch Patterns):

Wedge **49** Right (page 74)

Wedge **49** Left (page 74)

Horizontal Insertion **126** (page 217)

Step 3 (Background Texture): Stockinette Stitch

Step 4 (Edging): Side Edging **2** (page 17)

Step 5 (Cast On): Provisional with Stockinette Tab

Step 6 (Border): Not applicable

Step 7 (Bind Off): Crochet Bind Off (page 278)

Yarn: Manos del Uruguay's Fino in Mother of Pearl (#437)

Needle Size: US 5 (3.75 mm)

SHAWL #16

For more photos of this shawl, see pages 70 and 243.

Step 1 (Silhouette): Three triangles

Step 2 (Stitch Patterns):

Simple **7** (page 20)

Wedge **47** (page 71)

Horizontal Insertion **127** (page 218)

Step 3 (Background Texture): As charted

Step 4 (Edging): Side Edging **2** (page 17)

Step 5 (Cast On): Provisional with Stockinette Tab

Step 6 (Border): Lower Border **158** (page 242)

Step 7 (Bind Off): Super-Stretchy Bind Off (page 279)

Yarn: Miss Babs's Kaweah in Blackwatch

Needle Size: US 8 (5 mm)

SHAWL #17

For more photos of this shawl, see page 265.

Step 1 (Silhouette): Two triangles with a vertical insertion

Step 2 (Stitch Patterns):

Simple **5** (page 18)

Vertical Insertion **145** (page 231)

Horizontal Insertion **120** (page 211)

Step 3 (Background Texture): Garter Stitch

Step 4 (Edging): Side Edging **3** (page 17)

Step 5 (Cast On): Provisional with Fagoted Tab

Step 6 (Border): Perpendicular Border **182** (page 264)

Step 7 (Bind Off): Not applicable

Yarn: Cascade Yarns' Ultra Pima Fine in Tourmaline (#3817)

Needle Size: US 5 (3.75 mm)

SHAWL #18

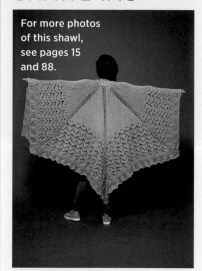

For more photos of this shawl, see pages 15 and 88.

Step 1 (Silhouette): Six triangles

Step 2 (Stitch Patterns):

Simple **4** (page 18)

Wedge **54** (page 86)

Horizontal Insertion **121** (page 211)

Step 3 (Background Texture): Stockinette Stitch

Step 4 (Edging): Side Edging **1** (page 17)

Step 5 (Cast On): Provisional with Garter Tab

Step 6 (Border): Lower Border **155** (page 240)

Step 7 (Bind Off): Super-Stretchy Bind Off (page 279)

Yarn: Plymouth Yarn's Baby Alpaca Grande in Sea Green (#2548)

Needle Size: US 10½ (6.5 mm)

SHAWL #19

For more photos of this shawl, see page 129.

Step 1 (Silhouette): Three triangles

Step 2 (Stitch Patterns):

Wedge **77** (page 127)

Wedge **76** (page 126)

Step 3 (Background Texture): Stockinette Stitch

Step 4 (Edging): Side Edging **2** (page 17)

Step 5 (Cast On): Provisional with Stockinette Tab

Step 6 (Border): Lower Border **164** (page 248)

Step 7 (Bind Off): Super-Stretchy Bind Off (page 279)

Yarn: Freia Fine Handpaints' Ombré Lace in Vintage

Needle Size: US 4 (3.5 mm)

SHAWL #20

For more photos of this shawl, see page 185.

Step 1 (Silhouette): Four triangles

Step 2 (Stitch Patterns):

Wedge **109** Right (page 182)

Wedge **109** Left (page 182)

Horizontal Insertion **131** (page 222)

Wedge **108** (page 180)

Step 3 (Background Texture): Stockinette Stitch

Step 4 (Edging): Side Edging **1** (page 17)

Step 5 (Cast On): Provisional with Garter Tab

Step 6 (Border): Lower Border **173** (page 257)

Step 7 (Bind Off): Super-Stretchy Bind Off (page 279)

Yarn: Lorna's Laces' Honor in Ogden

Needle Size: US 5 (3.75 mm)

RESOURCES

Glossary of Knitting Techniques

CASTING ON

Cable Cast On

1. Make a slip knot on your knitting needle. Pull the ends of the yarn so that the knot is snug on the needle.

2. Insert the tip of your right needle knitwise into the loop that's sitting on the left needle and knit up a stitch, but don't remove the original stitch from the left needle. Rather, transfer the new stitch from the right needle back to the left one so it is not twisted: 1 new stitch has been cast on.

3. For each successive stitch to be cast on, insert the tip of the right needle *between the first 2 stitches* on the left needle to knit up a stitch (a). As before, do not remove the old stitch, but instead slip the new one back onto the left needle (b); repeat until you have cast on the required number of stitches.

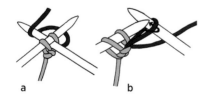

Magic Loop Cast On. Use this when you will work on your shawl in the round.

1. Leaving a 6″ tail, make a double loop in the yarn.

2. Insert an appropriately sized crochet hook into the center of the loop, then reach up and grab the working yarn with the hook.

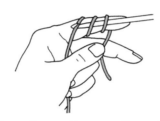

3. Draw the working yarn through the center loop (a), then yarn over the hook and draw it through the loop that is on the hook (b).

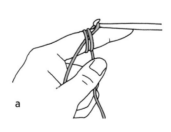

a

b

4. Reinsert the hook into the center of the loop, and repeat steps 2 and 3 as many times as necessary (single crochet stitches) until all stitches are cast onto the hook. Pull the yarn tail to tighten the loop, and transfer the stitches onto the double-pointed needles or a long circular needle to begin working in the round.

Provisional Cast On

See page 10.

BINDING OFF

Crochet Bind Off. *Insert an appropriately sized crochet hook into the back of 3 stitches at once and single crochet 3 together (a), slide the 3 stitches off the left needle (b), ch 7 (c); repeat from the * until all stitches have been bound off (d).

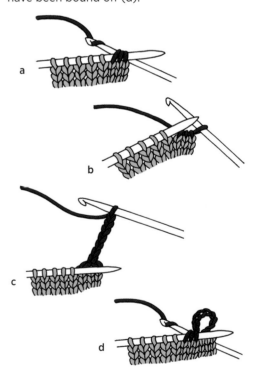

Picot Bind Off. *Use the cable cast on to cast on 2 stitches, then bind off 4 stitches and return the last stitch back to the left needle; repeat from the * across until all stitches have been bound off. This will place a picot between 2 knit stitches. To center a picot over a stitch, bind off that stitch, pick up the stitch you just bound off and place it back on the left-hand needle. Slip the working stitch purlwise, then work the picot, ending with the previously bound-off stitch.

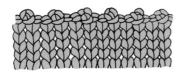

Super-Stretchy Bind Off. Use this bind off when you're working a scalloped border or any time you require an elastic edge. Here's how it's done: K2, *return the 2 stitches to the left needle without twisting, k2tog through their back loops, k1; repeat from the * across until all stitches have been bound off.

DIRECTION OF STITCHES

Knitwise. Enter the stitch with the tip of your right needle as if you were about to knit that stitch; in other words, *from left to right and from front to back.*

Purlwise. Insert the tip of the right needle into the stitch as if you were about to purl that stitch; in other words, *from right to left* and *from back to front.*

TEXTURED STITCHES

Bobbles. Bobbles add unexpected texture to knitted fabric. Knitters have several methods to make bobbles, but here is my favorite one:

1. Knit into the (front, back, front) of the next stitch, turn. (3 stitches formed from 1 stitch)

2. P1, (p1, yarn over, p1) *all into the next stitch*, p1, turn. (5 stitches)

3. K5, turn.

4. P2tog, p1, p2tog, turn. (3 stitches)

5. Slip the next 2 stitches at once knitwise, k1, pass the 2 slipped stitches over the stitch you just knitted. (1 stitch)

Nupp. A nupp is a tidy, puffy bobble that is worked over 2 rows.

1. Knit into the stitch, leaving it on the left needle, *yarn over, knit into the original stitch again; repeat from the * twice more: 7 stitches have been made out of 1 stitch.

2. On the subsequent row, purl all 7 stitches together to return to the original stitch count.

Tip: If you find it difficult to insert the needle into all 7 stitches, use a small crochet hook.

Left Twist. A miniature cable, the left twist crosses 2 stitches to the left.

1. Skip the first stitch, and knit the next stitch through its back loop.

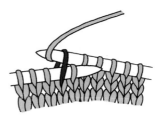

2. Knit the skipped stitch, and slip both stitches off the left needle together.

Right Twist. The right twist is a miniature cable that crosses 2 stitches to the right.

1. K2tog, leaving the stitches on the left needle.

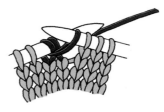

2. Insert the point of the right needle between these 2 stitches and knit the first one again.

Cable 2 Stitches Left (C2L). This simple cable crosses 2 stitches over 2 stitches to the left.

1. Slip 2 stitches onto a cable needle and hold in front (a); k2 (b).

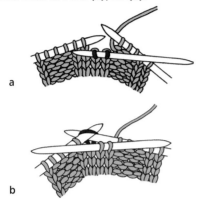

a

b

2. K2 from cable needle.

Cable 2 Stitches Right (C2R). This cable crosses 2 stitches over 2 stitches to the right.

1. Slip 2 stitches onto a cable needle and hold in back (a); k2 (b).

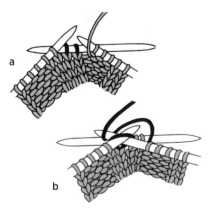

a

b

2. K2 from cable needle.

Placing Beads

1. Choose a crochet hook that will accommodate your selected bead. (See Yarn Weight and Appropriate Bead Size table below.)

2. With the bead already placed on the crochet hook, insert the hook purl-wise into the stitch to be beaded, and slip it off the needle.

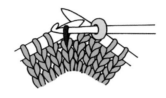

3. Slip the bead over the stitch.

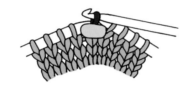

4. Slip the beaded stitch back onto the left needle, taking care not to twist the stitch.

5. Knit (or purl) the stitch as indicated by the pattern.

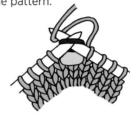

6. Completed.

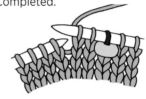

YARN WEIGHT AND APPROPRIATE BEAD SIZE

Be sure to choose the best bead size for your working yarn. When using yarns thicker than worsted weight, beads may make the finished fabric too heavy. Refer to the table below. NOTE: Some beads have rough inside edges that could shred the threaded yarn. Look for beads with smooth holes. For example, Japanese seed beads tend to have very uniform and smooth holes, making them perfect for use in knitting.

YARN WEIGHT	BEAD SIZE
Lace	6/0 or 8/0
Fingering	6/0
Sport	5/0 or 6/0
DK	3/0 or 5/0
Worsted	3/0 or 5/0

DECREASES

Knit 2 Together Decrease (k2tog).
This is a right-leaning decrease.

With the working yarn toward the back, insert the right needle from front to back, knitwise, into the first 2 stitches on the left needle as if they were a single stitch, and wrap the yarn around the right needle as you would for a knit stitch (a). Pull the yarn through both stitches, and slip both stitches off the left needle at once (b): 1 stitch has been decreased, and the resulting stitch slants to the right.

a

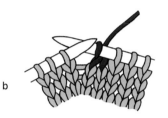

b

Slip, Slip, Knit Decrease (ssk). This left-leaning decrease requires an extra step, but it creates a mirror image of the k2tog decrease described at left.

1. With the working yarn toward the back, insert the right needle from the left to the right, knitwise, into the first and second stitches on the left needle, *one at a time*, and slip them onto the right needle.

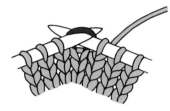

2. Insert the tip of the left needle into the fronts of both slipped stitches, and knit them together from this position, through their back loops: 1 stitch has been decreased, and the resulting stitch slants to the left.

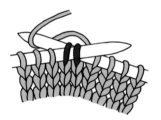

Slip, Slip, Purl (ssp). This technique is often used on wrong-side rows to mimic the left-slanting look of the ssk decrease on the knit side of the fabric.

With the working yarn toward the front, slip the first 2 stitches knitwise, one at a time, from the left needle to the right needle (a). Then, slip these 2 stitches back to the left needle in their twisted position (b). Finally, insert the tip of the right needle into the back loops of these 2 stitches, going into the second stitch first, and then the first stitch, and purl them together through their back loops as if they were a single stitch (c): 1 stitch has been decreased, and the resulting stitch leans toward the left on the knit side of the fabric (d).

a

b

c

d

New and Improved ssk and sssk Decreases

For many knitters, the ssk decrease worked the typical way appears "wobbly" and doesn't mirror the k2tog decrease perfectly. If you would like to make your left-leaning decrease look smoother and less like stairsteps, try this method:

1. Slip the first stitch *knitwise* and the second stitch *purlwise* from the left needle to the right needle. Slipping the first stitch knitwise keeps it from twisting at the bottom, producing a smoother and neater stitch.

2. Then, insert the left needle into the fronts of both slipped stitches and knit them together from this position, through their back loops.

For an improved sssk decrease (a double decrease that slants to the left), slip 3 stitches (knitwise, purlwise, and purlwise) instead of 2 stitches in the first step, and k3tog in the second step. Easy!

Slip 1, Knit 2 Together, Pass (sk2p). A left-leaning double decrease, the sk2p stitch is easy to do.

1. Slip the next stitch knitwise, k2tog.

2. Pass the slipped stitch over the k2tog.

Central Double Decrease (s2kp2). This double decrease takes 3 stitches down to 1 stitch without slanting in any direction.

1. Slip 2 stitches at once knitwise.

2. Knit the next stitch.

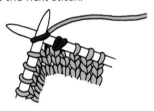

3. Pass the 2 slipped stitches over the stitch you just knit.

4. Central double decrease, completed.

To Execute Central Double Decrease on the Purl Side (s2pp2)

Insert the needle into the second and then the first stitch (in that order) as if to p2tog-tbl, slip both stitches at once onto the right needle from this position, purl the next stitch, and then pass the 2 slipped stitches over the purled stitch.

INCREASES

Knit into the Front and Back of a Stitch (kf&b)

1. Insert the right needle into the stitch knitwise, wrap the working yarn around the needle the regular way to knit up a stitch, *but don't remove the original stitch off the left needle.*

2. Reinsert your right needle knitwise, right to left, into the back of the same stitch, wrap the yarn around the needle to knit up a stitch, then slip the original stitch off: 2 stitches are made out of 1 stitch.

Purl into the Front and Back of a Stitch (pf&b). Insert the right needle into the indicated stitch purlwise, wrap the working yarn around the regular way to purl a stitch *but don't remove the original stitch off the left needle;* then, purl *through the back* loop of the same stitch; finally, slip the original stitch off the left needle: 2 stitches are made out of 1 stitch.

Make One Increase (M1)

1. Insert the left needle from front to back under the horizontal strand between 2 stitches.

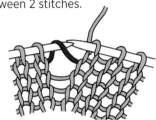

2. Knit it through its back loop.

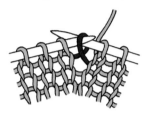

Yarn-Over Increase. Lace fabrics are built with open increases, called yarn overs. The method of making a yarn over differs depending on whether the stitch following the yarn over is a knit or a purl stitch.

- **For a yarn over before a knit stitch:** Bring the yarn to the front of the work, then wrap the yarn around the right needle and bring it to the back. As you knit the next stitch, the yarn-over stitch will be created.

- **For a yarn over before a purl stitch:** Make sure the yarn is in front of the work. Wrap it completely around the right needle, from front to back to front to create the yarn over, then purl the next stitch the regular way.

SEAMING

Invisible Weaving. Use this technique for garter and fagoted lace edgings. Thread a blunt-tip yarn needle, and with the pieces of fabric next to each other on a flat surface, insert the needle into the top loop of the edge stitch (the ridge) of one piece of fabric and then into the bottom loop of the corresponding stitch (or ridge) on the other side. Continue this way to sew the seam.

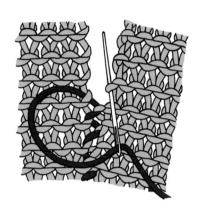

Mattress Stitch. Use this technique for stockinette edgings.

1. With the right side facing you, lay the fabric pieces flat, matching stripes, if applicable.

2. Thread a blunt-end yarn needle with a strong sewing yarn that matches the color of the project, and bring the needle up *from back to front* through the left-hand piece of fabric, going one stitch in from the side edge, leaving a 6" tail.

3. Bring the yarn up *from back to front* through the corresponding spot on the right-hand piece, securing the lower edges.

4. Insert the needle down *from front to back into the same spot on the left-hand piece where the needle emerged last time*, and bring it up through the corresponding place in the next row of fabric, grabbing the horizontal bar that's between the stitches.

5. Insert the needle down *from front to back into the same spot on the right-hand piece where the needle emerged last time*, and bring it up through the corresponding place in the next row, grabbing the horizontal bar that's between the stitches.

Repeat the last two steps, grabbing those horizontal bars between stitches, until you've sewn a couple of inches, and then pull firmly on the sewing yarn, bringing the pieces of knitting together. The edge stitch of each piece of fabric will roll to the wrong side and the seaming yarn will disappear. Continue this way until the seam is complete.

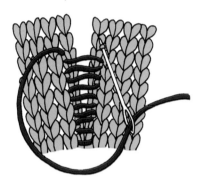

Finishing Your Shawl

Blocking. Blocking is a finishing process that helps "set" your project to your desired size. It serves to even out stitches, almost magically making the overall fabric look as if it's perfectly knit. For lace projects, blocking opens up the fabric, making it airy and beautiful. Knitters have several methods of blocking, but wet-blocking is usually best for shawls.

Begin by laundering the knitted piece, being sure to follow the manufacturer's instructions on the yarn label. While it is still damp, lay the shawl flat on a padded surface out of direct sunlight, patting it gently to your desired measurements. Using rust-proof pins, pin the damp fabric down and allow it to dry. In some cases, it's necessary to manipulate the knitted fabric more vigorously to make sure the pattern "pops" or that certain shapes (like points) are distinct.

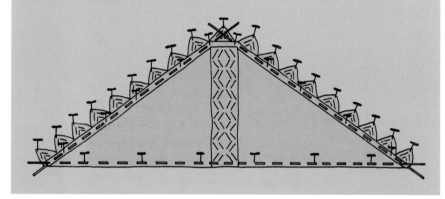

The Best and Easiest Way to Block a Shawl

Blocking wires will make pinning your triangular lace shawl a breeze. They keep the lines straight and minimize the number of pins required.

Dealing with Yarn Tails. Shawls tend to be seen on both the right and wrong sides, so it is important to deal with yarn tails carefully. Use a pointed-end yarn needle to make short running stitches on the wrong side of your fabric in a diagonal line for about 1" or so, piercing the yarn strands that make up the stitches of your fabric. Then stitch back again to where you began, working alongside your previous running stitches. Finally, to secure the tail, work a stitch or two and actually pierce the stitches you just created. Be sure to work each tail individually, in opposite diagonal directions, and you will secure your yarn ends while keeping the public side of your fabric beautiful.

Tassels. Tassels are the perfect accent for shawls. Attach one to the corners for a boho look.

1. Wrap the yarn around your hand 25 to 35 times, depending on the thickness you want, and cut on one side to create even lengths. Tie a 6" strand around the center of the bundle.

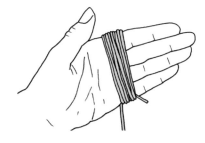

2. Use another 6" strand of yarn to create the head of the tassel by wrapping it several times around the complete bundle approximately ½" to 1" from the top. Secure with a knot. Trim the ends evenly.

How to Read Knitting Charts

At first, knitting charts and their symbols might seem like a foreign language or cryptic code, but they are actually a visual representation of knitted fabric, where each square of the grid corresponds to 1 stitch and each row of squares corresponds to 1 row of stitches. It's worth taking the time to learn — and to practice — knitting from charts. You might even find yourself translating long, wordy patterns into symbols before you want to knit them! I'll bet that with some practice — and yes, a little bit of patience — you'll find knitting from charts easy, fast, and probably even fun! Here's how to use them.

- Read the charts from the lower edge up, with the first row at the bottom of the chart and the last row at the top.

- Read right-side rows from right to left, in the same order that stitches present themselves to you on the left needle. Of course, at the end of this first row, you flip your knitting before starting the next row, and the wrong side of the fabric faces you. Physically, the first stitch of this wrong-side row is the same stitch as the last stitch of the right-side row you just completed. Therefore, wrong-side rows on charts are read in the opposite direction, from left to right.

- Charts make it easy to see how many stitches are involved in a pattern. Charts in this book use a bold box to indicate the stitch and row repeat, and when extra stitches are required on each side to center the pattern, they are shown to the left and right of the repeat.

- Each symbol on a chart indicates the way a stitch or group of stitches is worked, and the arrangement of symbols on the chart determines the stitch pattern.

- Typically, charts for stitch patterns use symbols that visually resemble the way the resulting stitches will appear once knitted. The symbol for a knit stitch, for example, is a blank box, mimicking the flat appearance of the knit stitch itself; the dot symbol for a purl stitch depicts the bumpy appearance of a purled stitch. Just by quickly scanning the chart, you can visualize the knitted fabric!

- All rows in charts are shown *as they appear on the right side of the fabric*. Consequently, the same symbol means different things on right-side and wrong-side rows. The blank box, for instance, represents a knit stitch on a right-side row, but if you're on a wrong-side row and want the stitch to appear as a knit stitch on the reverse side of the fabric, you must purl it. If a symbol is used on both right- and wrong-side rows of the chart, the stitch key will tell you which knitting maneuver to use where. There's no need to memorize anything!

Keeping Track of Your Place

To keep track of where you are on the chart, use sticky notes or a metal board with magnetic strips. Place them above the row you're on so you can see how that row relates to the rows you've already completed. Once you finish a row, just move the marker up and you'll never lose your place!

LIST OF SYMBOLS AND ABBREVIATIONS

GENERAL

K	Knit.
☐	On right-side rows, knit; on wrong-side rows, purl.
P	Purl.
⊡	On right-side rows, purl; on wrong-side rows, knit.
ch	Chain.
cn	Cable needle.
psso	Pass the stitch over.
rnd(s)	Round(s).
RS	Right side (of work).
st(s)	Stitch(es).
WS	Wrong side (of work).
k1-tbl	Knit the next stitch through its back loop. On wrong-side rows, k1 through back loop, twisting the stitch.
S	Slip stitch knitwise with the yarn in back.
→	Slip last border stitch knitwise with yarn in back, knit next stitch from body of the shawl, pass slipped stitch over.
⊖	Bind off 1 stitch.
★	Stitch remaining after binding off.
◆	Place bead, then knit or purl as per instructions (see page 280).
*	Repeat instructions after asterisk or between asterisks across row or for as many times as instructed.
( )	Repeat instructions within parentheses for as many times as instructed.
☐	Stitch and row repeat.

INCREASES

V kf&b	Knit into the front and back of a stitch (1 stitch increased; see page 282).
pf&b	Purl into the front and back of a stitch (1 stitch increased; see page 282).
M1	Make 1 (1 stitch increased; see page 282).
O	Yarn over.

DECREASES

k2tog	On right-side rows, knit the next 2 stitches together (see page 281); on wrong-side rows, p2tog.
p2tog	On right-side rows, purl the next 2 stitches together; on wrong-side rows, k2tog.
k3tog	On right-side rows, knit the next 3 stitches together; on wrong-side rows, p3tog.

DECREASES (CONTINUED)

p3tog	On right-side rows, p3tog; on wrong-side rows, k3tog.
ssk	On right-side rows, slip, slip, knit (page 281); on wrong-side rows, ssp (page 281).
ssp	Slip, slip, purl (see page 281).
sssk	Slip, slip, slip, knit: On right-side rows, slip the next 3 stitches, one at a time, knitwise; knit the 3 stitches together through their back loops. On wrong-side rows, sssp.
sssp	Slip 3 stitches, one at a time, knitwise, then slip all 3 stitches together back to the left needle; purl together through their back loops.
sk2p	Slip 1, knit 2 together, pass (see page 282).
s2kp2	Slip, slip, knit, pass 2 stitches over: On right-side rows, slip 2, knit 1, pass 2 stitches over (page 282).
s2pp2	Slip, slip, purl, pass 2 stitches over: On wrong-side rows, insert the needle into the second and then the first stitch (in that order) as if to p2tog-tbl, slip both stitches at once onto the right needle from this position, purl the next stitch, then pass the 2 slipped stitches over the purled stitch (a centered double decrease).

TEXTURED STITCHES

B	Bobble (see page 279).
N	Nupp (see page 279).
⊠	Left Twist (see page 279).
⊠	Right Twist (see page 279).
C1L	Cable 1 left: Slip the next stitch onto cable needle and hold in front, k2, k1 from cable needle.
C1R	Cable 1 right: Slip the next 2 stitches onto cable needle and hold in back, k1, k2 from cable needle.
C2L	Cable 2 stitches left (see page 280).
C2R	Cable 2 stitches right (see page 280).
LC Axis	Slip the next 2 stitches onto cable needle 1 and hold in front, slip next stitch onto cable needle 2 and hold in back, k2 from left-hand needle, p1 from cable needle 2, k2 from cable needle 1.
RC Axis	Slip the next 2 stitches onto cable needle 1 and hold in back, slip next stitch onto cable needle 2 and hold in front, k2 from left-hand needle, p1 from cable needle 2, k2 from cable needle 1.
Knitted RC Axis	Slip the next 2 stitches onto cable needle 1 and hold in back, slip next stitch onto cable needle 2 and hold in back, k2 from the left-hand needle, k1 from cable needle 2, k2 from cable needle 1.

STITCH MULTIPLE CROSS-REFERENCE CHART

WEDGES (pages 22-206) **Wedges from this column . . .**	SIDE EDGES (page 17)	SIMPLE FABRICS (pages 18-21)	*HORIZONTAL INSERTIONS (pages 210-222)	**VERTICAL INSERTIONS (pages 223-233)	LOWER BORDERS (pages 234-259)	PERPENDICULAR BORDERS (pages 260-267)
2-stitch multiple (patterns 10-14, pages 22-26)	all	all	all	all	all	all
4-stitch multiple (patterns 15-17, pages 28-30)	all	all	2-stitch (patterns 119-121) 4-stitch (pattern 122) 8-stitch (patterns 124-128) 12-stitch (patterns 129-130)	all	4-stitch (patterns 149-150) 8-stitch (patterns 154-159) 12-stitch (patterns 166-170) 16-stitch (pattern 175)	all
6-stitch multiple (patterns 18-28, pages 31-42)	all	all	2-stitch (patterns 119-121) 6-stitch (pattern 123) 12-stitch (patterns 129-130)	all	6-stitch (patterns 151-153) 12-stitch (patterns 166-170)	all
8-stitch multiple (patterns 29-55, pages 44-90)	all	all	2-stitch (patterns 119-121) 4-stitch (pattern 122) 8-stitch (patterns 124-128)	all	4-stitch (patterns 149-150) 8-stitch (patterns 154-159) 12-stitch (patterns 166-170)	all
10-stitch multiple (patterns 56-78, pages 93-130)	all	all	2-stitch (patterns 119-121)	all	10-stitch (patterns 160-165)	all
12-stitch multiple (patterns 79-105, pages 131-177)	all	all	2-stitch (patterns 119-121) 4-stitch (pattern 122) 6-stitch (pattern 123) 12-stitch (patterns 129-130)	all	4-stitch (patterns 149-150) 6-stitch (patterns 151-153) 12-stitch (patterns 166-170)	all
14-stitch multiple (patterns 106-112, pages 178-192)	all	all	2-stitch (patterns 119-121) 14-stitch (pattern 131)	all	14-stitch (patterns 171-174)	all
16-stitch multiple (patterns 113-118, pages 195-206)	all	all	2-stitch (patterns 119-121) 4-stitch (pattern 122) 8-stitch (patterns 124-128)	all	4-stitch (patterns 149-150) 8-stitch (patterns 154-159) 16-stitch (pattern 175)	all

* Total number of stitches in each wedge must be a multiple of the Horizontal Insertion multiple.
  For example, if there are 104 stitches, you can use a 4 or 8 stitch Horizontal Insertion, but not a 12 or 16 stitch pattern.
** If you use a Vertical Insertion, this will add an odd number of stitches, with the exception of pattern 140.
  You will need to use a Perpendicular Border instead of a Lower Border, since the total number of stitches will not be
  a multiple of any of the available options.

METRIC CONVERSION CHART

TO CONVERT	TO	MULTIPLY
inches	millimeters	inches by 25.4
inches	centimeters	inches by 2.54
inches	meters	inches by 0.0254
yards	centimeters	yards by 91.44
yards	meters	yards by 0.9144